Asian American Religions

Asian American Religions

The Making and Remaking of
Borders and Boundaries

EDITED BY

Tony Carnes and Fenggang Yang

New York University Press

NEW YORK AND LONDON

NEW YORK UNIVERSITY PRESS
New York and London

Library of Congress Cataloging-in-Publication Data

Asian American religions :
the making and remaking of borders and boundaries /
edited by Tony Carnes and Fenggang Yang.
p. cm.
Includes bibliographical references and index.
ISBN 0-8147-1629-6 (cloth : alk. paper) —
ISBN 0-8147-1630-X (pbk. : alk. paper)
1. Asian Americans—Religion.
2. United States—Religion.
I. Carnes, Tony.   II. Yang, Fenggang.
BL2525.A84   2004
200'.89'95073—dc22   2003023815

New York University Press books are printed on acid-free paper,
and their binding materials are chosen for strength and durability.

Manufactured in the United States of America

c 10 9 8 7 6 5 4 3 2 1
p 10 9 8 7 6 5 4 3 2 1

Contents

Acknowledgments

We thank the scholars who went before us, friends, and family for building the foundation of knowledge and lives. We thank the religious leaders and congregants who helped us for their generosity. We remember Stanford M. Lyman's pioneer work and Ashakant Nimbark's heroic completion of his chapter shortly before he passed away. We particularly thank Darilyn Carnes, Ruth J. Carnes, Jose Casanova, Karen Chai, Carolyn Chen, members of the Columbia University Seminar on Contents and Methods in the Social Sciences, Bob Fu, Despina Papazoglou Gimbel, Melissa Gorton, Jennifer Hammer, Weishan Huang, Anatoliy Khotsyn, Samuel Kliger, Andrew Lee, Samuel Ling, Man-Wai Lun, Tim Morgan, the Annie E. Casey Foundation, Gary Y. Okihiro, David Shek, Doug Shin, Bella Tsai, Carmen Tsui, R. Stephen Warner, Henry Woo, Kenneth F. Wong, Lai Fan Wong, Joanne Yang, and Cecilia Yau.

Asian American Religions

Introduction

Tony Carnes and Fenggang Yang

The border between heaven and earth swings low when Asian immigrants cross national borders to America. Most Asian immigrants come with distinct religious beliefs and practices, and some gain them here. Asian Americans who have been here for five generations have also built a plethora of religious sites and organizations. Consequently, religion and related Faith-Based Organizations (FBOs) are one of the most significant cultural and social features of Asian American life. Stereotypes of the heathen Oriental, inscrutable Asian, model minority, and ethnic political activist are deeply flawed, not least because they don't recognize the deepness of the Asian American soul. What anthropologist Ulf Hannerz (1969) said of African Americans might very well be said about Asian Americans, "Their social life cannot be understood apart from their understanding of soul, its struggles and its hopes."

The new and old Asian American religionists of America have brought redemptive energies to the neglected, worn-out churches and street corners of our metropolitan areas. The process is vivid: vast Hindu dioramas of Himalayan mountains in formerly abandoned warehouses, Christian music wafting into the streets from the fruit stands, neat storefront churches, and new towering steeples among Koreans, faith-based community groups, and street dances celebrating religious values. Even the litter is different, with religious posters depicting spiritual struggles in the subways and bus stops. The Asian American religionists have a genius for transforming dead urban spaces into convivial social places.

In the 1990s, Thirty-Sixth Avenue, the Main Street of Dutch Kills in Queens, New York, was bedraggled, shuttered, and grim. Today, Indian

Asian American Hindus from the computer service industry in the neighborhood are gathering for a fund-raising dinner for the building of a new Ganesh temple. Next door, Asian American Muslims prepare for their Friday Jumah services at the two mosques on Thirty-Sixth Avenue and book tables hawk videos of a debate between a Muslim cleric and Baptist Rev. Jimmy Swaggart. Tonight, a Pentecostal church will throw open its doors to the many Asian immigrants in the area. Two Chinese restaurants rimmed with shrines and religious posters bookend the E—W poles of Thirty-Sixth Avenue, with the East end restaurant displaying offerings to Fujianese Chinese gods while the West end leaps into action with Hong Kong–styled religion.

Did you know that:

almost two-thirds of Asian Americans say that religion has a very important role in their lives?

many more Asian Americans actively identify with a religion than a political party or work in the computer field?

Filipino and Korean Americans are the most religious people in America?

the largest pan-Asian American movement is religious?

over 60 percent of Asian Americans who have a religious identification are Christian?

one-third of Muslims in the United States are Asian Americans?

Indian Asian Americans are more religious than Indians in India?

the largest Asian American college and university student organizations are religious?

tens of thousands of Asian Americans are refugees from torture on account of their faith?

Earthly *and* heavenly borders and boundaries are an integral ingredient of Asian Americans' identities and lives. Upon crossing the U.S. border, Asian immigrants confront boundary issues. Legally, they have a new status both in their countries of origin and in the United States. Immersion into a dynamic new culture produces intensely felt and conflicting emotions. Emotionally and socially, the new Asian immigrant is at first a stranger (cp. Simmel 1950; Stonequist 1937; Hurh 1977; Kerokhuff and McCormick 1977).

In this sense immigration is a catastrophe for the Asian immigrant and the receptor society. Immigration significantly disrupts immigrants' lives so that their habits and customs are at least temporarily unsettled (Mahler 1995; Handlin 1951). Further, migrants are intruders in a relatively settled U.S. society and its neighborhoods. One common response among immigrants is to practice religious incorporation and difference (on the concept of intrusions across borders as key loci of social change, see Teggart 1972/1941; Nisbet 1969; Carnes 1999).[1] Asian Americans use religious conversations in religious spaces to face questions about their relation to their country of origin, personal and collective identities, and the organization of American society and culture (Smith 1971; Smith 1978). Religious imperatives powerfully intersect self, family, and society and prescribe certain relationships among them (Becker 2002; Booth, Crouter, and Landale 1997). Asian Americans may be using religion as a way of maintaining or renegotiating these relationships.

Yet, until recently, there was very little writing on Asian American religions or their effects on the boundaries of social life. A widely used anthology of Chinese American and Japanese American literature by Jeffery Paul Chan and others (Chan et al. 1991; see comments by Yoo 1996, xiii–xxii) barely mentions religion. The conceptualization of Asian Americans didn't include the religious factor. Standard social science had created a soulless stereotype that is far from the actual lives of Asian Americans. Current research, however, has begun to fill the yawning gap in Asian American studies. This volume summarizes some of this empirical research on Asian American religions and how it advances our conceptualization of immigrant religions, borders, and boundaries.

In particular this book focuses on the role of Asian American religions in negotiating, accepting, redefining, changing, and creating boundaries in the metropolitan areas of New York City, Houston, Los Angeles, and the Silicon Valley/Bay Area. These localities have some of the largest number of Asians and Asian Americans and the best research completed so far. From the many Asian American nationality groups, we have selected large and small groups from every area of Asia: Chinese, Filipinos, Indians, Koreans, Pakistanis and Bangladeshis, and Thais.

Religion

The boundary between religion and nonreligion is an intellectually and politically contentious issue. Every major sociologist has a different definition. In a circular manner, Max Weber (1963, 1) suggested leaving the definition of religion to the end of studying religion. "To define 'religion,' to say what it is, is not possible at the start of a presentation. . . . Definition can be attempted, if at all, only at the conclusion of the study," Weber warned. Roland Robertson (1972, 35) concluded, "Weber did not arrive at a conclusive definition of the religious phenomenon." The debate still goes on.

The adherents of Asian American religions are themselves not agreed, except perhaps in the legal arena, about what religion is. In the first place at least some adherents of every religion say that their beliefs and practices are the Truth or highest way of life, while other beliefs are man-made or lesser religions. Buddhists sometimes claim that their faith is not a religion at all. Although classified as one of the three orthodox religions (*jiao*) in the Ch'ing Dynasty (Yang 1961), Confucianists usually say that their convictions amount to ethics and philosophy. Muslims claim that Islam is a whole way of life that is true to reality and not localized in something called religion. Asian American Calvinists make a similar wide-ranging claim. This holistic view clashes with American religious notions of pluralism and church-state separation.

This book uses commonly accepted definitions and typologies of religion and religiosity. This means that for this study we are not using W. C. Smith's definition of religion as what we bind ourselves to or Paul Tillich's "ultimate ground of being." By these definitions humanism, selfishness, communitarianism, and the like would be religions. Nor do we accept the self-definition of some groups like Buddhists who say that they don't practice a religion.[2]

Further, Robert Wuthnow observes in *After Heaven* (1998) that "growing numbers of Americans say they are spiritual but not religious." However, we have mostly opted to narrow our scope to religion as organizations or movements which self-consciously identify themselves as "religious." In other words, we are reporting on what is commonly called the "institutionalized religion" of new immigrants. Even at that, we have no hope of covering all institutionalized religions or every important facet of the ones we do cover.

Anthropologist Robert Redfield contrasted the big religious tradition formalized by the elite in capital cities with the little religious traditions of common people. In this volume, Guest, Nimbark, and Carnes note that Asian Americans often have business and home shrines to folk, personal, or regional gods and spirits. Guest (2003) has traced how this folkish style has been transferred from China to the United States, while Nimbark indicates that local folk Hinduism is growing among Indian Americans.

Social scientists have frequently noted that religious life doesn't stop at the exit doors of churches and temples. In the first place some religion is not even located in a formal organization. Bender and Smith explore the "lived religion" of Muslim taxi drivers who have informally created worship spaces at restaurants, on the roadsides, and in the trunks of their cars.

Most Asian religious organizations bring a formalized, traditional, hierarchical, group-orientated culture with them. The emphasis is on religion as a doing—rather than a believing—of ritual, worship attendance, charity, and age hierarchy—and an especially strong patriarchy. The children of Asian immigrants, however, are influenced by the American religious culture of individualism, equality, and informality. As a result, the 1.5 and second generations are inclined to define religion as authentic self-expression and religious community as a democratic fraternity. They often label their parents' religion as inauthentic. Park in her chapter on Korean American evangelical college students quotes one student as saying that her parents' worship is formal and hypocritical while the second generation's more spontaneous worship is "spiritual" and "true." Kim and Kurien report similar generational conflicts over the definition of what religion is.

Politically and legally, the definition of religion in the United States has immense importance in creating constitutionally appropriate boundaries between religion and the state (Vaino 1980). From conversations around the United States it appears that Asian American religionists have been particularly concerned over

either preserving or changing the privileged position of Christianity in the United States;

meeting legal definitions of religious organization to receive immigration status for religious members, zoning approvals, tax exemptions, and other legally defined advantages that religious organizations have in the United States;

access to religious education by their children at public schools either through state-approved courses, release-time for religiously taught courses or after-school programs;

the accreditation for religiously based schools;

the enforcement of laws against antireligious prejudice and discrimination;

the promotion of religious freedom and prevention of persecution overseas;

the resettlement of persecuted and tortured religious believers from overseas; and

the institutionalization of moral convictions like profamily policies in state programs.

Overseas, political definitions of religion are sometimes aimed at maintaining state or religious hegemony. For example, nondemocratic Chinese governments have viewed religion warily as another competitor for power. Up until recently, the Chinese government did not view religion as a vital part of an autonomous civil society. Consequently, Chinese governments have distinguished between orthodox religion which is incorporated as part of the government and heterodox religion which is viewed as "evil religion" (Spiegel 2002) or "heresy" that needs to be suppressed for the good of society (also see Guest 2003, 91–100). States whose official religion is Islam often clamp down on other religions as paths to social disharmony and degradation. Malaysia and Indonesia remain notable partial exceptions.

Faith-Based Organizations (FBOs)

Currently, social scientists are rediscovering that worship centers offer a great variety of social services. Harvard's Robert Putnam (2000) summarized a massive study of social capital in the United States, "Houses of worship build and sustain more social capital—and social capital of more varied forms—than any other type of institution in America. . . . Roughly speaking, nearly half of America's stock of social capital is religious or religiously affiliated." Further, many primarily social service organizations are religiously based. Consequently, the concept of "faith-based organization" has gained popularity in order to encompass not just the worship practices of religion but also its social service practices. Indeed, such a larger definition of religion redefines worship as social relations between self, other worshipers, and, in most cases, invisible beings or forces.

According to Gonzalez and Maison, Filipinos in the San Francisco Bay Area practice a holistic religion so that bowling, eating, playing, job hunting, and worshiping are all tied together within religious networks. Nimbark found a similar knitting together of Indian Asian Americans through their burgeoning newspapers, magazines, television, video, and websites.

Guest describes how Fujianese Chinese youth get connected to jobs and temporary help through their churches.

Asian Americans and Conservative Religion

For most Asian American religious adherents, religion means conservative religion. Almost every scholar in this book has found this phenomenon. Conservative religions like Charismatic Catholicism, evangelical Protestantism, and fundamentalist Islam have found ways to thrive among new Asian immigrants. Nimbark points out that highly educated Hindu immigrants swing not toward secularization and liberalism but toward Hindu fundamentalism and ethnic particularity. In India the highly educated were complaisantly religious, if not secular. However, here in the United States they adopt religioethnic fundamentalism. The growth of conservative religion among Asian Americans parallels its growth in America as a whole (Hout, Greeley, and Wilde 2001). A survey of 14,301 religious congregations found strong evidence that congregations that "uphold high standards of personal morality were the most alive and had the most support and growth" (Dudley and Roozen 2001).

Conservative religion grows in part because crossing national boundaries generates a need for order or a move toward freedom. On the one hand, immigration is disruptive and immigrants seek new order in their lives. This seems to be the case for the Asian immigrants that Park, Guest, and others report on. Indian American Hindus adopt fundamentalism to sustain their ancestral identity and, particularly, that of their children. This ethnoreligious fundamentalism, which has displaced pan-Hinduism, seems likely to continue its ascendancy as the new immigrant generation climbs ladders of economic and social success. This will undoubtedly lead to clashes with the larger society, but even more so with their own children.

For the Korean American first generation, continued connection to Korea means conservative religion. Their ethnic Bible institutes and seminaries sustain for now a Korean church denominational orientation often that harks back to a more conservative theology of Korea. Consequently, many Korean churches are much more conservative than their American denominational partners.

On the other hand, Asian American religionists are divided on what "conservative" really means. Kurien, Park, and Yang note that some younger female religionists want to redefine their role in conservative religion. Kurien and Park find that redefinition involves rejecting the traditionalism of their parents' home countries. However, Yang says that highly educated young immigrants from China come with gender definitions that are more egalitarian than those of other Chinese American religionists. Their move into Chinese American churches is a move away from equality for females. He identifies American evangelical seminaries as the main source of the more conservative Christianity found in Chinese American churches.

Sometimes, the conservative religious move is accompanied by the creation of a counterorder to society. For example, Korean American immigrant males compensate for their loss of status by gaining status in churches. Asian American Indians become more religious here in the United States as a way of fitting into American society outside a racial hierarchy that might relegate them to the low status of "nonwhites."

Many immigrants find that entering into a conservative religion is actually a move toward freedom from the oppression of kin rules and tradition. Kurien, Kim, and Park detail how second-generation Asian American college students find a freedom in evangelicalism compared to their parents' churches' traditionalism and strict hierarchies.

Conservative religion doesn't necessarily mean conservative politics. Nimbark details how Hindu Indian Americans are tending toward religious fundamentalism and Indian nationalism, while Lien and Klineberg show that Hindu Indian Americans are politically liberal in U.S. politics. Although born-again college freshmen are much more conservative than non-born-agains, many have liberal values. Thirty-nine percent are in favor of or neutral on legalization of homosexual relations. Thirty-nine percent say that abortion should be legalized (see Boggess and Bradner 2000, 118–123).[3] Forty percent favor abolishing the death penalty.[4] For Asian American student evangelicals, college is also "a place where there is freedom to explore and decide for yourself."

Boundaries

Drawing boundaries is a universal act. "*Every* person, for example, distinguishes that which is edible ('food') from that which is inedible. By the same token . . . *all* humans distinguish that which is dangerous from that which is safe" (Zerubavel 1991, 53). Each person and group needs to distinguish itself in order to survive and flourish. As Durkheim noted, religion has always been centrally involved in how humans make, sustain, cross, and create their personal and social boundaries.[5]

From early times the paradigm for all boundaries has been the division of the divine from the not divine. Even a monistic religion like Hinduism emphasizes that the all-encompassing divinity has special sites of manifestation. Often, the divine-nondivine division was tied to geography: sacred versus secular or profane places.

Every worldview and, consequently, every social theory has an explanation for the origins, functions, and changes of mental and social boundaries (cf. the overview of "boundary control" issues in modern social theory by Loomis and Loomis 1987).[6] For some social theories like functionalism and symbolic interactionism, boundaries play a central role. Further, the changing of social boundaries is a major theme in social science discoveries about Asian American life. Fundamentally, the creation and operation of social boundaries has to do with the rejection of what some people dislike and the acceptance of alternative cosmological and social patterns. Consequently, the question of social boundaries lies close to the religious questions of order, meaning, and reality. Humans use heaven to justify and reorder earth in pleasing ways (see Douglas 1966).

We can liken the patterns of our cognition, feeling, and actions to grids by which we associate and divide concepts, feelings, and actions. Thus, for example, we cognitively distinguish our parents from ourselves and reserve certain feelings and actions toward them that we may not associate with other people in our lives. Sociality is rightly discerning the social divisions and acting toward them with appropriate emotions and actions. Socialization is training to more or less unselfconsciously recognize, feel, and act within the boundaries of society. Since the boundaries are charged with rationalizations, and with moral and emotional force, their violation provokes confusion, moral qualms, uneasiness, fear, and rage.

Of course, actors may value the violation of boundaries and even derive purpose, moral clarity, and exaltation in crossing, breaking, or changing habits of mind, prejudices, and customs. Actors may also prefer to skirt along boundaries or take advantage of their ambiguities because they are ambivalent between different choices or may want to hide their indiscretions.

Douglas (1996/1973) has documented how some societies have rather rigid, tightly organized boundaries while others do not. Asian societies today place a higher emphasis on order and hierarchies than the United

States does. Consequently, immigration is not only a crossing of national boundaries but also a mixing of the way boundaries are organized and implemented.

When Asian American immigrants arrive in the United States, their homegrown and American ways of thinking, feeling, and acting may clash. The situation is analogous to placing a grid on top of another grid; if they are distinctly different you get gridlock—confused cognitions, ambivalent feelings, and uncertain actions. One comfortable accommodation that Asian immigrants make is to adjust to American ways of thinking, feeling, and action in the public sphere while bounding off the religious sphere where one can "let one's hair down," "speak one's piece," and interact in an old country sociality. This pleasant dualism, however, gets upset by the arrival of an Americanized second generation. Then the ordering of cognition, emotion, and action becomes a contest.

Asian immigrants often come with a group-enforced morality and are shocked by American individualism. They tend to see American individualism as antimoral, selfish, narcissistic, and untrustworthy. Carnes found that Chinatown seniors recast their own desires and fears into terms of care for their families rather than for themselves. So first-generation immigrants are disturbed when their children start to act morally as individuals. The parents see public obedience to social norms as moral; their children see it as hypocrisy. The parents insist that what one feels about an action is irrelevant. The children believe that one's heart should be consistent with one's rules. The parents emphasize more community; the children emphasize conscience. Thus, moral orders, moral reasoning, and esteemed character (Hunter 2000; Taylor 1989) are not the same, a fact that sets up numerous religiomoral conflicts.

Fundamental to every Asian American religious and social boundary are also their revealing and concealing capacities. Religion claims to offer the most mystery and greatest understanding of the depths of existence. It does this by simultaneously concealing and revealing the divine, salvation or damnation, morality, persons, groups, time, and space. The concealing is accomplished by establishing boundaries like sacred-secular and mystery-reason, while the revealing is done by making the boundaries permeable in some ways through evangelism, conversion, prophecy, preaching, and methods of insight.

Social invisibilities also underlie religious and social divisions. First, a group or society places its outcasts and outsiders in social darkness. The social world is tidied up by putting nonconformists and criminals into hidden seclusion. Religion may play a large role in this process. Second, certain roles, knowledge, and sensibilities are systematically denied to outsiders. Some things become too sacred for anyone, particularly outsiders, to closely examine and criticize. Indeed, the fact that some things are hidden from outsiders is a marker of social boundaries.

Religious groups also provide rewards through sets of secrets and revelations. Fame and ceremonial awards may be quite visibly displayed. Honor is also bestowed by admission to personal confidences and leadership groups. Further, religions bestow the benefits of hiding social crimes through pardons, forgiveness, and forgetfulness.

Religion, of course, is only one of several causes of boundary change. It competes with the powerful impact of demography, economy, society, and culture. National and local demographic and cultural changes are creating disruptions and opportunities for new religious, cultural, and social forms.

The Boundary Resources Provided by Asian American Religions

Asian American religions offer vast spiritual, symbolic-cultural, therapeutic, and socioeconomic resources for maintaining, changing, and crossing existential and social boundaries. These resources can affect the members of religious organizations, groups, or even the ecology of a whole neighborhood (DiIulio 2002).

1. Spiritual Resources—Socialization with Invisible Others

Religions usually emphasize that their boundary resources include providing relationships with invisible spiritual beings or realities (Pollner 1989). In a practical sense religions provide significant Others (divinities, spirits, and so on) that Asian Americans say they need to have in order to feel "at home," safe, comforted, empowered, healed, saved, socially connected, and purposeful. Park reports that second-generation Korean American Christians typically talk about how "God came down and met me where I was at." Carnes reports that the Chinese elderly gain comfort, purpose, freedom from fear by doing spiritual exercises in "the morning wind from Heaven." For some Asian Americans their relationships to invisible beings are mostly located in the private sphere, except for specified times like prayer and services. For others, there can be no social interaction without the presence of invisible partners. So, among many Southeast Asian Americans occasions of healing, making agreements, and decision making need to take place in the presence of divine beings or power and their appointed human agents like shamans, healers, priests, and the like (see Fadiman 1997; Numrich 2000a).

Southeast Asian Buddhism includes a belief in a wide variety of spirits, souls, deities, and ghosts. Additionally, Southeast Asians may believe in fortune-telling, charms, and the like. For example, some Southeast Asians won't start projects on days of bad luck or those which their fortune-teller tells them to avoid. Likewise, certain streets or areas may be avoided because of rumors that malevolent ghosts inhabit them. The ills of the body may not be cured without the presence and permission of a ritual specialist and his special healing methods (Numrich 2000b). Laotians in Seattle, Washington, experienced a Cannibal Ghost scare in the summer of 1989. Laotians claimed that the ghost had cost several people their lives in Sudden Adult Nocturnal Death Syndrome (Muecke 1998).

2. Symbolic-Cultural Resources for Centering, Organization, Continuity, and Control of Boundaries

Every Asian American religious organization also offers symbolic centers, a moral organization of life patterns (Lamont and Fournier 1992), cultural continuity, and boundary control. Of course, this is particularly accomplished at worship sites. But all Faith-Based Organizations play a part in the symbolic-cultural integration and differentiation of Asian Americans. The rhetoric of Asian American religions testifies to their identity, social lives, exemplary leaders, ritual centers, and how to avoid dangers. The services may include cultural centers, publications, culture and language classes, and the like.

3. Asian American Religion as Therapeutic—Emotions

The therapeutic role of Asian American religions is their most commonly recognized resource. It ranges from job advice to marital counseling.

Asian Americans find new or renewed individual and social identities in strong religious worldviews that are offered in counseling, worship, and other venues. Therapy for these Asian American religionists is a process of hiddenness and revelation. In a program called Victory Outreach of Los Angeles Koreatown, Korean Americans have discovered that Christianity can help them throw off the label "thug," "criminal," or even "convict" in favor of "child of God"—an eternal return, so to speak, to the everyday outside world. Asian Indian Hindus throw off their anger about racial slights onto the temple altar and return empowered and dignified human beings. Leaving their scarlet letters behind through various techniques of "neutralization" at the temple (Sykes and Matza 1957; Lyman and Scott 1970, 111–143), they walk with a more chipper clip down the street. In such ways, religious activities have become essential locations for affirming and making visible self-reflection and new identities for Asian American immigrants (cf. Orsi 1999, 55).

Further, at their best religious organizations offer a network of mentors and friends that simultaneously envelope new Asian Americans with emotional support while empowering them to independence. Religious therapeutics also helps to establish boundaries of inclusion and exclusion for these religionists. Some Buddhist temples use their teaching to persuade their adherents that the United States is not outside the boundaries of the Buddhist life (cf. Zerubavel 1991, 6–9).

4. Socioeconomic Services

Asian American religious organizations offer five types of socioeconomic resources for boundary actions: economic; political and legal; educational; recreational; and health related. Asian American religionists wrestle with whether these services are too "worldly," outside the proper boundary for their religions.

Asian American adherents to religions like Islam, Buddhism, and Hinduism don't have a well-developed tradition in their home countries of their religious organizations providing social services. Buddhist monks are supposed to be otherworldly as part of their duty as spiritual exemplars. Christianity, Islam, and Buddhism celebrate great preachers and teachers, not social workers. Pentecostals-charismatic Korean Americans and Hmong American shamans prize social service through miracles, not organizational canniness. We can call this the "heritage" argument against providing social services. Yet this doesn't mean that these religions have a theological argument against the provision of social services.

Also, many churches, temples, mosques, and synagogues don't have the personnel to do much social service and neighborhood building. Many Korean immigrant churches have part-time pastors, and mosques are often lay-run. Most Asian American FBOs have modest budgets. This is the argument from lack of resources, even poverty.

Yet, regardless of the religions' worldviews, various surveys reveal that most religious organizations provide a number of informal and formal social services, and the previously skeptical religionists are now mostly in favor of providing them. In one recent survey of fifty thousand FBOs in California, 71 percent favored social service activities.

Korean American Protestant churches probably have the most well-developed commitment to socioeconomic services of all Asian American religious groups (Hurh and Kim 1990; Kim 1981; Min 1992). Other Asian American religions are increasing their commitment to social services in competition with Christians and to meet immigrant demands. For example, Korean Buddhist groups are quite aware that evangelical Protestant churches have outstripped them in a number of ways and they are devising ways to compete. The head priest at Korean Buddhist Bul Kwang Zen Meditation Center in Upstate New York observes, "For social services we can learn a lot from Christians. In order to compete successfully with Christian churches, Korean Buddhist denominations began to develop social service programs from the 1980s on" (Min and Kim 2002, 16, 28–29; also see Suh 2000; Kwon, Kim, and Warner 2001, 211–226).

Muslims are generally required to give about 2.5 percent of their wealth to the mosque alms fund. This is called *zakat* (alms giving), the fourth pillar of Islam. In the United States South Asian American Muslim mosques have often come to resemble Protestant congregations as centers for community life.

Economic services from Asian American religious organizations are mainly resources for successfully crossing national boundaries (immigration) or dangerous periods of life. They include loans and gifts, job training and referrals, shelter, food, and clothing. Guest details how important religious institutions are for young Fujianese Americans in locating jobs and temporary help (also see Guest 2003).

Political-legal services include resources for inclusion into the United States like citizenship classes, voter registration, immigrant rights advocacy, immigration legal advice and filling out forms, and various types of legal representation. For example, Guest details how illegal Fujianese immigrants gain legal help through their churches.

Educational services often support the other types of services like offering job training and citizenship classes. The most common services are ESL, cultural, and native language classes. Carnes found that even elderly Chinese Americans highly value educational classes at their religious sites. Most first-generation religionists also see their youth educational programs as reinforcing their national heritage and protection against negative trends in American society.

Some Asian Americans are very quickly creating schools: cultural and home country language schools; after-school programs to make up for poor public schools; precollege cram programs; elementary and secondary schools; religious leadership training schools; and even universities.

Recreational services offer social integration for insiders, escape from the normal rigors of life, and a way to open religious organizations to outsiders. The activities include everything from bingo, choral singing, and soccer to overnight trips to Las Vegas or Washington, D.C. Second-generation Korean and Chinese American Protestants go on summer and winter retreats that promote unity, act as existential turning points, and are symbolic recreational highlights for the year. Korean Americans have created an extensive collegiate network of a capella singing groups. Kim mentions how these groups have become a hallmark on campus, along with evangelistic skits and film.

Health services offer help in persisting through rough times, social integration, and a bridge to outsiders. They range from preventive health information campaigns to hospitals (Numrich 2000a).

Asian American Immigrant Crossings

Immigrants to the United States come from every Asian country and people-group.[7] Asian Americans and mixed-race Asian Americans make up 4.2 percent of the U.S. population (11.9 million people)[8] and is growing very quickly (over 5 percent per year). Chinese, Filipinos, Indians, Koreans, Vietnamese, and Japanese have come by the millions. The really large arrival of new Asian American immigrants began with the relaxation of immigration laws in 1965. Sometimes, what is a tiny number of nationals to us here in America looms as a major event in the countries of origin. One quarter of the entire population of the South Pacific island kingdom of Tonga now lives here, and the rest are immersed in American culture (Small 1998).

Old and New Asian American Immigrants

Old Asian American immigrants are those who came to the United States prior to 1965. Chinese and Japanese Americans make up most of this immigrant wave from Asia. Consequently, many of their religious organizations are older than fifty years old. New Asian American immigrants are those who came to the United States since 1965, and particularly those who came since 1990. We include immigrants of all immigration statuses (recent overviews include Foner, Rumbaut, and Gold 2000; Hirschman, Kasinitz, and DeWind 1999).

The results of the 1965 Immigration Act brought unexpected increases in immigration and new civic religions like Islam, Hinduism, Buddhism, and Sikhism. Clergy and seminary students also were able to come here more easily. As a result, the demography of religious groups and their educational institutions have changed. In the cities the new immigration has led to the revitalization of Christianity.

Illegal Immigrants

The material in this book includes the new illegal Asian American immigrants. One recent estimate concluded that 3.08 million illegal immigrants arrived within the last nine years and 4 million arrived ten years ago or earlier (Lowell and Fry 2002). Others put the number of illegal immigrants between 6 and 13 million, that is between 2 to 5 percent of the U.S. population (Zittner 2001). Indeed, many Asian American immigrant religious organizations provide extensive help to illegal immigrants, though the subject is sometimes characterized by internal debate. A number of Asian American FBOs are almost totally staffed by illegal immigrants.

TABLE INTRO.1
Asian Americans in the U.S., 2000

		1990–2000 Change
Total U.S. Population	281,421,906	+13 percent
Total Asian in U.S.	10,242,998	+48 percent

Figures based on single-race plus multiracial Asians. Single-race Asians increased 48 percent. U.S. Census Bureau 2000.

Mixed Asian respondents (like Chinese-Japanese) are classified solely as "Asian." An additional 1.7 million people, or 0.6 percent, reported themselves as Asians as well as one or more other races (U.S. Census Bureau 2002 February. *The Asian Population: 2000.* Washington, DC: U.S. Census Bureau).

The number of Asians alone and Asians in combination with other races went up by 72 percent from 1990 to 2000.

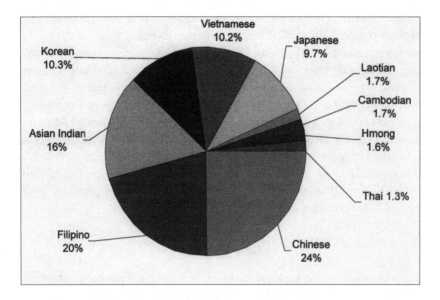

Asian Population of U.S., 2000 Census (Single- and Mixed-Race Asians)

Refugees

Immigrants who are refugees are caught in a different dynamic social process from that of the normal immigrant (Stein 1986; Zolberg 1994; UNHCR 2001). Typically, they were violently abused and uprooted from their homeland and arrive in the United States with fragmented personalities and social networks. They may arrive with a tragic sense of loss and be highly traumatized (Pipher 2002).

The United States has made political commitments to receive large numbers of refugees from Asian Communist lands: China, North Korea, Southeast Asia, and the southern tier states of the former Soviet Union. The United States has also legally received people persecuted for their politics or faith in South Asia and Indonesia. Additionally, a good number of people fleeing persecution, chaos, and famine have come to the United States as illegal refugees.

Refugees have two advantages: the United States has provided a good deal of aid to legal refugees: and refugees are relieved to be here to start healing and are focused on putting down their roots. Many of these refugees fled religious or ethnoreligious persecution and torture. The U.S.

Refugee Act of 1980 incorporates the definition of a refugee or asylum seeker contained in the 1951 UN Convention Related to the Status of Refugees and its 1967 Protocol (see Martin 2000, 1995). A refugee or asylum seeker is a person who is unable or unwilling to return to his or her home country because of persecution or a well-founded fear of persecution on account of religion, race, nationality, membership in a particular social group, or political opinion. A refugee applies from abroad while an asylum seeker is already legally or illegally in the United States. In recent years the U.S. government has granted about one hundred thousand petitions for refugee or asylum status per year. In some years, like after the end of the Vietnam War the United States admitted by special provision over one million Southeast Asians.

Torture Victims

Experts estimate that as many as 12 million people have been subject to torture worldwide. Some estimate that more than two hundred thousand torture victims have fled to the United States (UNHCR 2001; Zolberg, Suhrke, and Aguayo 1989). After examining the problem in 1998, Congress passed the Torture Victims Relief Act and allocated $31 million for 1999. Today there are fourteen torture-victim treatment centers in the United States and at least one hundred and fifty around the world (Chester 1990; Keller, Saul, and Eisenman 1998; Jacobsen and Vesti 1992).

Two of the largest populations of refugee torture victims are Southeast Asians and Chinese. However, there are significant populations from around the world (Padilla 1989; Kinzie, Fredrickson, and Ben 1984; Lee and Lu 1989); Mollica, Wyshak, and Lavelle 1987; Mollica et al. 1990; Carlson 1991; Kinzie 1993; Mollica 1990).

Asian American Religious Semiotics

Asian American boundaries are established, maintained, crossed, and changed through the use of religious signs, symbols, and rhetoric. Testimonies of lives changed, religious media, and the rituals and symbolism of worship centers are some of the most important vehicles of Asian American religious signification. Through them, selves, peoples, and religions are narrated into being, time and place marked, dangers circumscribed, and hopes expressed (Peacock and Hollis 1999).

Testimony: The Semiotics of Crossing Spiritual Boundaries

Because it is a movement of faiths, the Asian American immigrant communities in the United States have become places of testimony. Congregants are eager to recount their "but-for-the-grace-of-God-go-I" stories (cf. Booth 1991; Burke 1970; Caldwell 1983; Harding 1987; Hawkins 1985; Holte 1992; James 1902; Johnson 1945; Keane 1997; Lawless 1991; Morrison 1992; Payne 1998; Stromberg 1993). Further, testimonies often reveal what the new immigrant fears or values. Testimony is the existential platform of Asian American immigrant life.

One can hardly overestimate the importance of such stories of the heart for the country's soul—testimonies of release from addictive "isms" like egoism, alcoholism, workaholism, and materialism. On the other end of the social scale, often the only thing left unsold in a poor addict's apartment is the lifeline of religious literature from family and friends.

Asian American religionists testify about conversions, enlightenment, salvation histories, persecution, torture, discrimination, and migrations. The stories, often accompanied by ritual acts like baptism, speak of leaving the world of lost identities, chaos, meaninglessness, and evil and crossing a boundary or a turning point toward a renewed self, peace, meaning, and goodness. Implicitly, the testimonies are history, morals, and worldview rolled into one. Jones has likened conversions to paradigm shifts; Snow and Machalek (1983, 265) have likened them to changing to a new universe of discourse; Tipton (1982) to a new ethos; and Lofland and Stark (1965) to a new worldview. In fact all types of testimonies share these features with conversion stories.

Guest describes the Fujianese teenage youth at the Church of Grace to the Fujianese who have been thrust out of adolescence and into the intensely liminal state of illegality and into adult life, often without parents to guide them. Liminality, the state of being on the border between different ways of life, is a time of heightened vulnerability, a search for direction, and an openness to "turning points" in one's life. Similar groups of isolated Asian American youth like those among the Vietnamese boat people have entered a drift into delinquency. These young undocumented workers find purpose and meaning through ritual and a conversion narrative that tells where they are going and who they are. Guest suggests that the youth see conversion and baptism as a metanarrative for their life journey from China to the United States. During baptisms, the congregants recount and reflect on their life journeys, how they searched for a meaningful framework for understanding their lives, and how conversion made all their upheavals understandable.

The narrative and its high publicity at ritual baptism illuminates a different counterreality, unknown to outsiders, where dignity is assured and hope not disappointed. Later, the youth fashion official legal narratives for the INS out of these informal insider testimonies. Likewise, for millions of Asian Americans the door to America was unlocked by affidavits of religious (or political) persecution. Southeast Asian Christians, Muslims, and Buddhists, Chinese Christians and Falungong exercisers, Indonesian, Burmese, and North Korean Christians, Tamil Hindus, and scores of other religious groups tell of their lives pivoting around discrimination, arrests, torture, and executions.

Yang's analysis of over one hundred conversion stories of Chinese in a Washington, D.C., church indicates that conversion narratives pivot around different aspects of the immigrants' lives (1999a). The stories recount three types of experiences: preimmigration experiences; postimmigration experiences; and childhood socialization in Christian families. Overseas political catastrophes and social turmoil unhinged settled identities, beliefs, and destinies. Immigrants from such intrusive situations say that the stage of their drama of conversion was set there. Other immigrants experienced their sojourn in the United States as homelessness and consequently tell of their trip to permanence and hope in faith in Christ. Children born into religious homes often testify of faith as crossing over into a new level of maturity.

Testimonies are not peculiar to Asian American Christians. Buddhists also recount conversion or enlightenment stories (Park 1983). Nichiren Shoshu Buddhists learn how to testify in such a way that their religious role is bounded off from any comparison with other things and beliefs in the world (Snow 1976; Snow and Machalek 1983). Preston (1981) observes that Zen practitioners learn to recount their spiritual development in a stereotyped fashion. Korean Buddhists in Los Angeles talk about "finding their minds" and recentering lives that had fallen apart (Suh 2000, 108). Some Hindus speak about how a mixture of signs and acts can transport one into another plane of existence (Combs 1985). Muslim converts reject certain aspects of secular modernity.

Not all Asian American religionists locate the center of their testimonies in conversion or enlightenment experiences. Montagnard-Dega Christians show little interest in their conversions. Thomas Pearson (2001, 99) says that "very few Dega in North Carolina have ever told me stories about how and why they became Christians." Instead, the Dega have elaborate, historically well-ordered personal narratives of how God saved them and their people at certain moments in time. Dega "*are* very much intent on telling a different kind of story about the experience of God in their lives," Pearson says (ibid., 101). "They tell me war stories that pivot on God's miraculous intervention to save them from certain death" and how their culture was revitalized (Wallace 1956).

For many Asian American immigrants the founding of their religion or worship site is their mythic testimony. This is particularly true for Hindus who invite their gods to live here in a temple based on the promise of a twenty-four-hour presence of worshipers. Other types of testimonies include stories of migration (Kim, A. 1996), overcoming discrimination and prejudice (Kim, J. H. 1996; Kim, E. 1997), prophecies (cp. Bennetta 1986; Berger 1963; Buss 1979, 1981; Carroll 1979; Gager 1975; Lewis 1971; Overholt 1981; Wilson 1977), certain types of prayers (Griffith 1998), and the elite religious systemizations of sermons and theologies (Ng 1996; Lee 1997; Palinkas 1989; Yoo 1993).

Asian American Religious Media

The study of the burgeoning Asian American religious media has hardly even started. At most South Asian American mosques, audio and video tapes, CD-ROMS, and website advertisements are laid out on tables or in the bookstores after the services. Chinese American Christians and Buddhists have their own national newspapers, television programs, and websites. And the media is one of the main tools for creating transnational religions.

Is the media secularizing or religiously homogenizing, as McLuhan seemed to imply? Nimbark offers a counterexample. He looks at the desecularization of the Asian Indian American Hindu media and how it has created an increasingly seamless semiotic world with Hindu temples in which many first-generation Asian Indian Americans mentally reside. The result, Nimbark fears, is the growth of an increasingly self-referential Indian Hindu nationalism.

The Semiotics of Asian American Worship Sites

Asian American worship is surrounded by systems of practices and symbols that simultaneously divide the worshiper off from the world while

joining the worshiper with a transnational community of fellow religionists. Smith and Bender describe South Asian American Muslim taxi cab
drivers in New York who are so mobile that at prayer times they can't depend on finding a mosque which has the appropriately pure worship
space. Stopping at the side of the road provides spaces of dubious unknown histories, while worshiping in the back seat or the trunk seems
contorted. So, the taxi cab drivers have innovated non-mosque but pure
spaces in South Asian American restaurants in which to practice their
faith. Their worship sites also bring together Pakistanis and Bangladeshis,
which cannot be done easily at the multiethnic mosques.

Hawley illuminates the transnational symbolism of an Asian American
religion. Hindu temple environments encode a transnational vision of
global coherence and historical connection. Hawley notes that the diasporic condition of Indian Hindus is provoking a rethinking of how Hinduism and India are linked. Is Hinduism merely an ethnoreligion of Indians? Or does it somehow go beyond ethnonational symbolics?

Hawley suggests that instead of dropping the ethnic and national, Indian Hindus are reconfiguring "India" as a cosmological idea that honors
ethnonational Indian consciousness but reaches beyond to symbolize a
mythic existence. The Hindu temples encode this realization of the cosmological India in the purely and seemingly ethnic local. Could this encoded universality become the basis for a great world civilizational movement of Hinduism claiming to find symbolic manifestations of ideal India
growing like flowers everywhere?

South Asian American Muslims also do visible performances like the
Moslem World Day Parades down Fifth Avenue (Slyomovics 1995,
157–177) to make the claim that Muslims are part of America's civic life
and that pluralist America is a part of Muslim religious life. To be American is to be visibly religious and ethnic and to be Muslim is to be visibly
American and religious (Schneider 1990, 41; Slyomovics 1995, 159–160;
Metcalf 1996; on performative spectacles, see McNamara and Kirshenblatt-Gimblett 1985). These spatial spectacles also socially unify South
Asian American Muslims and assert an ethnic identity.

Asian American Religions and the Boundaries of Time:
Events, Generation, and Age

Events, generation, and age are some of the most important temporal boundaries of Asian Americans and their religions.

"I saw the plane go right into the floor that our son was on," a Chinese American senior recounted to Carnes about September 11, 2001. "It was an event that I will never get over." This story of an elderly Chinese American has affected all aspects of her religious life. It also vividly and sadly illustrates how secular and religious events loom large in Asian American souls and their religious organizations. Some of the events are claimed by a generation, others transcend generations, forming "rembrance environments" for social life (Zerubavel 1997, 81).

For the "old immigrant wave" of Asian Americans the events of discrimination and the cutting off of Asian immigration meant that their religious organizations remained relatively small, insular, and home country–oriented. Today, sacred memories of older Chinese and Japanese Americans are informed by a sense that their churches were havens in a hostile American world that they had to ignore. In interviews with Chinese elders in New York City's Chinatown, one is struck by the way the memory of bad discriminatory conditions is suppressed in favor of nostalgia for those "better" days for family and community.

For all first-generation immigrants, religiously significant events in the old country shape their attitudes here in the United States. Chinese Americans remember their conversions and the coming of pastors and missionaries. Their vivid memories of Communist persecution also deeply inform their religious dynamics here. On the one hand, it made Chinese American religionists more accepting of difficult conditions in the United States. On the other hand, the memory of persecutions pushed them toward supporting the Guomindang Party (which founded the Republic of China in Taiwan) and the Republican Party in the United States. It also made them disinclined to think about the old country or of going back. The memory of religious adherents under persecution, the society-shattering Cultural Revolution (1966–76) or the 1989 suppression of the democracy movement also motivates religious exploration here in the United States (Yang 1999a).

First-generation Korean American religionists carry memories of Japanese colonial rule, World War II, and the Communist invasion of

South Korea. A majority of Southeast Asian Americans are religious refugees. Older Filipino immigrants come with memories of the United States liberating their country from Japan, and some are resentful of American colonialism.

Indian, Pakistani, and Bangladeshi American religionists often recall significant events of conflict between Hindus and Muslims. Leaders are using these memories to drive Hindu and Muslim fundamentalism. September 11, 2001, seems to be a decisive temporal boundary line for Asian American Muslims, much like World Wars I and II were for German Americans. The most important religious effect is that President Bush has made Islam one of the standard religions of the United States. To the standard refrain of "Protestant-Catholic-Jew" describing U.S. religion has been added "Muslim."

Generations

The presence of a large second-plus generation has provided a majority of the population growth among Asian Americans and has acutely raised issues of generational identity, assimilation, and conflict. Almost in every case the religions of Asian Americans differ in their content according to generation. Further, second-plus generations of Asian Americans are notable for their religious switching.

Effects of Generational Demography

Some of the dynamics of Asian American religions arise out of generational demography. The religious organizations of the old immigration from China play a significant role today. They are more traditional, Cantonese, and are an established part of the Chinatown establishment.

For Japanese Americans the second generation of the 1920s–40s (the Nisei) created most of the religious organizations that continue today. Moreover, because the majority of Japanese Americans are at least three generations from their immigrant forebears and are highly intermarried, their Christian churches have become leaders in supporting pan-Asian churches. On the other hand, because three-quarters of Vietnamese Americans are part of the post-1965 immigrant wave, their churches are monoethnic and somewhat insular compared to other religious organizations. Even though Vietnamese Catholics are usually organized within a multiethnic parish, Catholic leaders say that the Vietnamese "keep mostly to themselves."

Asian Indian religious organizations are sharply divided between the first generation and the third-plus generation. First-generation religious organizations are trending toward fundamentalist and regional Hinduism while the third-plus-generation organizations are either ecumenical pan-Hindus or Punjabi Sikhs.

Parents and Children

Once immigrants have children, there is a first- and second-generation divide, which often affects religious dynamics. The second generation's social and cultural mobility may also create class and cultural divisions within immigrant churches (cp. Perlmann and Waldinger 1997; Rumbaut 1994).

Some come to the United States as children—collectively they are commonly called the 1.5 generation. The 1.5 generation is made up of kids who were born abroad but came to the United States when they were less than fifteen years old. This generation likely lives within first-generation ethnic neighborhoods and worships there. Conflicts with the older generation do occur and this places them with the second generation. They conflict with the older generation over authority systems (age and gendered autocracy versus egalitarian democracy), careers and intermarriage, and the handling of money. Their social psychological goal is to succeed at work within mainstream society while remaining largely within the immigrant community for their private lives. They plan on marrying within the

TABLE INTRO.2
Nativity and Recency of Immigration, 1990 and 1998–2000

	1990 Foreign-born	1998–2000 Foreign-born	Second Generation	3rd + Later Generation
Asian total	66.8%	49.2%	23.7%	27.1%
Chinese	70.4%	47.1%	19.5%	33.4%
Filipinos	68.5%	49.5%	29.1%	21.4%
Japanese	35.2%	22.7%	22.2%	55.2%
Asian Indians	77.0%	41.1%	13.1%	45.9%
Koreans	82.2%	52.4%	21.9%	25.7%
Vietnamese	81.8%	75.9%	23.5%	0.6%
Other Asians	70.0%	41.8%	57.8%	0.4%

Source: John Logan with the assistance of Jacob Stowell and Elena Vesselinov, October 6, 2001, *From Many Shores: Asians in Census 2000* (Albany, NY: Lewis Mumford Center for Comparative Urban and Regional Research, SUNY at Albany).

ethnic community, so they don't go to college for its social life. Rather, they locate their social life within their religious home.

Generation 2.A is similar to the 1.5 generation. This variant of the second generation also stays within the ethnic community as far as religion is concerned. They feel comfortable with the immigrant religion's authoritarian structures, moralism, and culture. They speak English quite well and usually prefer English religious services. They plan on marrying within the ethnic group. However, they like to think that they are not old-fashioned like their parents and not heartless and homeless like 2.B. Some accept patriarchal authority but try to gradually soften it while staying in the first generation's churches. Others form English fellowships, usually after some conflict with the first generation.

A good number of Asians leave their parents' authority and religion behind (Mullins 1987). Generation 2.B is made up of home-leavers. They feel uncomfortable with ethnic religious culture and its authoritarianism. If they are Christians, a few form purely second-generation churches, a phenomenon more common in California than in New York City at present. Or they may prefer going to a white church like Redeemer Presbyterian Church in New York City (which is over one-third Asian) or to no church at all. They will more often intermarry than not. Generation 2.B often wants to join Anglo-related institutions that emphasize prestige, quality, and social and racial concerns.

Second-Generation Asian Americans on Campus

The battle of Asian American generations plays itself out in the parents' religious homes and on college and university campuses across the United States. As Park explains in her chapter on Korean American evangelicals, the second generation is struggling to draw boundaries between the demands of their parents' ethnic religious organizations, college religious organizations, and American society. The question that they are attempting to answer is: how can they limit the demands of each of the social structures so that they have space for their own unique identity? Kurien looks at how the second generation divides itself off within the first-generation Indian American church. Kim looks at how Korean American evangelicals justify their racial-ethnic separation at a U.S. university.

The story of Asian American religions on college and university campuses is particularly important, given that record numbers of Asian Americans are attending colleges and universities. In 1997 Asian Americans made up 3 percent of the U.S. population, 4 percent of enrollment in all public school districts (National Center for Education Statistics), and 5.3 percent of college and university freshmen students in the United States. By fall 2001 Asian Americans/Asians had increased their proportion by 30 percent to 6.9 percent of all entering freshmen.

The main religious groups of Asian Americans on college campuses are evangelical Christians, Muslims, and, increasingly, Hindus. Only a few studies have been done on the impact of religion on students in college, but most have found that the religious factor along with ethnicity and gender continues to have a major impact. Often, collegiate Asian American religionists say they face prejudice and discrimination on account of their faith. For example, in his study of two Asian American congregations made up of mainly college students and recent graduates, Alumkal (2000, 48–49) found that most members shared the view that "they are treated as second-class citizens by the surrounding society." Sociologist Christian Smith says that despite a widening openness toward and interest in things religious in the academy, "just below the surface . . . there abides a tenacious anti-religious sensibility" (Smith 2003).

On the East and West Coasts a hefty proportion of the enlarged presence of religious groups on campus are the Asian American evangelical Christians. Indeed, at New York City colleges and universities Asian Americans account for one in four evangelical college students, about equal numbers being born-again Chinese American/Chinese and Korean American/Korean students. Their numbers were equal to the numbers of

TABLE INTRO.3
Denominations of Freshmen Students

	Born-again NYC Asian Freshmen	Born-again NYC Freshmen	Non-born-again NYC Freshmen	Freshmen, USA, 1997
Other Christian	37%	37%	4%	11%
Presbyterian	26%	10%	2%	4%
Baptist	9%	15%	2%	17%
Roman Catholic	9%	18%	42%	30%
Methodist	5%	5%	1%	9%
None	4%	3%	20%	12%
Other Religion	3%	4%	5%	4%
Buddhist	3%	.6%	2%	.6%
United Church of Christ	2%	2%	1%	2%
Lutheran	1%	1%	0%	6%
Jewish	1%	1%	13%	2%
Episcopal	1%	2%	2%	2%
7th Day Adventist	0%	2%	1%	.3%
Islamic	0%	0%	2%	.5%

whites/Caucasians. These figures are an extrapolation from a 1997 survey of entering freshmen at U.S. colleges and universities. The survey, conducted by UCLA's Higher Education Research Institute, is the most recent nationwide survey of the number of "born-again" or evangelical Christians among college students (Sax et al. 1997).

The increased presence of Asian American evangelicals on college campuses is also part of the increasing visibility of evangelicals on the campus scene. Twenty-nine and a half percent of entering freshmen identified themselves as born-agains, making them the single largest religious group on campus. Their religious organizations on campus have been growing for some time. Cherry, Deberg, and Porterfield (2001) noted that the largest religious organizations on the campuses that they studied were evangelical student groups.[9]

Gender Tensions

Gender issues can also play a significant part in the tensions between generations. The prevalence of American egalitarianism is a tremendous force among immigrant religionists. As a result, traditional gender conceptions are frequently contested within religions. For example, Muslim women are exiting from strong patriarchal mosques (cf. Abusharaf 1998), and immigrant congregations are also currently engaged in numerous second-generation disputes over gender roles.

Generally speaking, new Asian immigrants have conservative patriarchal definitions of gender. They institutionalize these gender definitions within their religious organizations. Kwon, Kim, and Warner (2001, 14) claim, "The immigrant [Korean] church seems designed to serve the needs of men." In this book Yang points out a similar situation in Chinese churches. Other studies have documented patriarchy in South and Southeast Asian American religious organizations. Yang asks why patriarchy is the rule among Asian American religionists. Kwon, Hurh, and Kim emphasize that for Korean men patriarchy acts as a means of compensating for lost status incurred by coming to the United States (Kwon, Kim, and Warner 2001, Hurh and Kim 1990). Other observers trace the origins of patriarchy to traditional culture, class, homeland religious institutions, or theology.

Yang notes that highly educated Chinese immigrants in the United States experience something quite unique for first-generation immigrants:

being less patriarchal than the young people of the second generation. His explanation for the rise of patriarchy is organizational: conservative American seminaries socialize the American-born Chinese toward patriarchy. His chapter reminds us that religious patriarchies differ and that we still have very few typologies about them. Another example is that middle-class South Asian American Muslims have more relaxed patriarchal rules than lower-class Muslims from the Middle East (cf. Husain and Vogelaar 1994, 231–258). Indeed, the fastest growing type of South Asian American Islamic organization seems to be social services for abused or abandoned Muslim women.

Hindu women have also set up programs for abused women, though often with tepid encouragement from the male leaders of their temples. At Sri Meenakshi, a southern Indian Tamil Hindu temple in Houston, a number of women have formed a Mercy Group to help women in abusive relationships. Temple leaders didn't actively encourage the group but say that the temple should address such problems.

Religion of the Elderly Asian Americans

One group almost entirely overlooked by recent research is the religion of elderly Asian Americans. It seems to be assumed that elderly Asian American religion is merely an extension of the religion of the first generation as it ages. Nor have social scientists fully comprehended that the post-1965 immigrants are now getting old and retiring. Additionally, many elderly Asian Americans are very recent immigrants, usually joining their families. Carnes's study of these three elderly groups in New York City's Chinatown shows how important and varied their religion is.

Asian American Religions and Political Boundaries

The politics of Asian American religionists mainly focuses on the issues in their country of origin and religious refugees, tensions within their religious organizations, relations to other religious groups, ethnicity and race, or American electoral politics.

Religious conflicts in their country of origin often define the politics of first-generation Asian Americans. Many Chinese, Tibetan, and Southeast Asian Americans experienced religious persecution in their homelands from Communists. Consequently, in the United States they became strong supporters of the Republican Party, which is noted for its strong opposition to Communist governments. Moreover, their experiences of persecution can carry over into their religious life here.

After their arrival in the United States, Southeast Asians often have a hard time establishing trust with each other. Their experiences of betrayal during persecution and war have left them bruised and wary. In the Vietnamese community Catholics, Buddhists, and Cao Dai (a syncretistic indigenous Vietnamese religion) are distrustful and sometimes hostile toward each other. There have also been numerous conflicts in Cambodian temples over rumors about monks who were said to be former murderous Khmer Rouge (Communist) soldiers.

Nimbark and Kurien have noted that South Asian American Hindus become more religious and nationalistic in the United States. Their organizations have become one of the primary sources of funds for the BJP, the nationalistic Hindu political party in India. After the Hindu destruction of a sixteenth-century Muslim shrine in December 1992, some Hindu immigrant elites became radicalized. In 2002 these elites were further radicalized by the burning of a train near the site in India and the nationwide clashes between Hindus and Muslims that followed.

Asian American Muslim mosques tend to be divided between the relatively nonpolitical and political ones. The mosques are sometimes also internally divided according to home country politics. Arab American mosques are more likely to be radical in their theology and politics than South Asian American mosques. For example, the Islamic Center of Greater Houston is the center of South Asian Muslim activity in the Houston area. However, the Center's leaders are engaged in a power struggle with those Muslims, mainly Arabs, who want imam leadership, "pure Islam," the teaching of the Arabic language, and women wearing the *hijab* (face or head covering). Other South Asian American mosques report similar struggles (Husain and Vogelaar 1994; Livezey 2000, 187–212). Often the conflicts also intertwine with issues of immigrants' time of arrival, class, and ethnicity.

Before September 11, 2001, 77 percent of mosque leaders of all ethnicities said that they "strongly agreed" that Muslims should participate in American institutions (Zogby 2001). After the attacks, Muslims expressed almost unanimous interest in becoming involved in American civic life (Bagby, Perl, and Froehle 2001; Zogby 2001). September 11 appears to have been a watershed for Muslims in America.

Religion and Asian American Electoral Politics

The presence of Asian American religions and religionists has also challenged the boundaries of action and discourse of the major American political parties. The challenges range over discussions about local church building and traffic controversies, racial and ethnic conflict and cooperation, and national and international politics. The significance of religion has also determined everyday bargaining for a new covenant of pluralism and freedom between native Americans and Asian Americans.

U.S. politicians would be wise to pay attention to religion among Asian Americans. According to Lien, about three-quarters of Asian Americans identify with a religion and about half regularly participate in religious services. Most Muslims, Protestants, and Catholics are quite serious about their religion as indicated by their attendance at weekly services. Lien's general rule of thumb is that if an Asian American goes to a religious service every week, that person is much more likely to be politically active.

Further, Lien notes that between 85 and 95 percent of Asian Americans are citizens or planning to get citizenship. Once they gain citizenship most Asian Americans register to vote, and almost one half of Asian Americans have deepened their political participation beyond just voting.

Religion also divides Asian Americans according to political ideology. According to Lien and Klineberg, Hindus are the biggest Asian American supporters of liberalism (61 percent), closely followed by Muslims. Some political analysts argue that the political liberalism of South Asian Hindus and Muslims reflects the institutionalization of British socialism in the universities and government in South Asia. Further, when South Asians move to the United States, they usually move into politically liberal areas, which reinforces their political heritage.

More Protestant (29 percent) and Catholic (28 percent) Asian Americans lean to the conservative side than Asians as a whole (22 percent). Only 4 percent of the Protestant Asian Americans would say that they were very "liberal." Although Asian American Muslims tend to be liberal, one in four say that they have conservative political views. Buddhists (41 percent) and the nonreligious (36 percent) are more likely to say that their political ideology is "middle of the road." Both groups are also much more likely to say that they don't think in political partisan terms or are unsure where they fit on the political party spectrum.

Hindu and Muslim Asian Americans appear to be much more politically minded than other Asian American religionists. Compared to other

Asian Americans, far fewer Hindus and Muslims think in nonpartisan terms. They are relatively sure that they are Republicans, Democrats, or Independents. Hindus and Muslims are the bulwark of the Democratic Party among Asian Americans. There are more Republican identifiers among the Protestants and Buddhists but fewer Independents.

Politics within Asian American Religious Organizations

In addition to internal divisions caused by country of origin politics, Asian American religionists have struggled politically over creating new congregations and determining the proper boundaries between the first and second generations. Kim and Kwon have observed that Korean American Christian pastors join other congregations in order to learn the ropes of the local area and to pull away enough members to start their own church. This phenomenon probably exists within other Asian American religious groups but doesn't seem as pronounced as among Korean Americans.

The tension between the first and second generations has elicited the most research, though most of it is through the lens of identity rather than politics. The second generation's struggle to become autonomous is mainly conditioned by the resources it can mobilize and the ideals of family unity. When religious organizations split they also divide families and such splits are therefore emotionally intense. Consequently, Asian American religious organizations try to avoid splits by offering various compromises over second-generation autonomy. Moreover, the second generation doesn't at first have the monetary resources, organizational experience, or political savvy to win its conflicts. However, as it matures it gradually creates greater autonomy for itself either within immigrant religious organizations or in second-generation ones.

Asian American Religions and the Transcendence of Borders and Boundaries

Transcending important boundaries is one of the most courageous and difficult of all acts. It is fraught with both peril and promise. Asian Americans have used religion as a vehicle for a new sensibility among previously separate Asian American groups, as a meeting ground for racial and religious intermarriage, as a transnational link for transporting social and cultural capital, and as a bridge between the East and West.

The Pan-Asian American Sensibility

Sensibility is a set of emotional and cognitive cues that seem to be appropriate to one's situation. Sensibility is not gathered together all at once, but is an accretion of continuous experiences of social and cultural transcendence. Such large processes as globalization, transnationalism, fraternization, universalization, and rationalization of the way life is organized convey the experience that life is about boundaries being crossed. These experiences give rise to a transcendent sensibility, a sense that being a boundary crosser is a fitting way of being human.

This sensibility starts overseas when Asians contemplate immigration to the United States. This is a huge step but one that germinates with the idea that America is like a golden land which if actually touched will transform and fulfill one's life. But America is not only an idea to prospective Asian immigrants, it is a reality in its geopolitical and cultural presence. Because the United States has defended the freedoms of Asian peoples and invested in their development, most Asians have a positive attitude toward the United States before immigrating. Indeed, after gaining citizenship a majority of Asian immigrants identify with the Republican Party, which they perceive as the more patriotic party that defended Korea, Taiwan, Southeast Asia, and Japan during the second half of the twentieth century.

On the downside, U.S. involvement in Asia has sometimes made enemies. During the Cold War, the Chinese Communist government was relentlessly hostile until 1972. Also, in the scramble to prevent the greater tyranny of Communism, the United States supported authoritarian governments in South Korea, Taiwan, the Philippines, and elsewhere. Furthermore, neutralist socialist India was politically and philosophically critical of the United States. Finally, discrimination and prejudice in the United States against nonwhites has belied U.S. democratic values. The history of anti-Asian legislation, the internment of Japanese Americans during World War II, unflattering popular stereotypes, and persistent discrimination have created much ill will among Asians.

Resisting fatalism, immigrants are actively involved in transcending their own fate and everyone else's too, to some extent. They are forming a new social world for themselves to inhabit (Fucks 1990), something which sociologists call a habitus, and a new social world for the receptor society. To use a musical metaphor, new immigrants create a new major chord for themselves and minor chords for the receptor society. For some, particularly second-plus generations, their new sensibility feels more at home within a religious context that transcends country of ancestry boundaries.

Russell Jeung examines how religious claims to universal brotherhood are interpreted by Asian Americans. Jeung looks at a universalizing movement toward pan-Asian ethnicity among Asian Americans in Silicon Valley. Here, amidst the globalization and scientific technical rationalization of the northern California computer industry, Asian Americans say that they are breaking old ethnic boundaries but stopping short of total deethnicization. Pan-Asian congregationalism balances universal fraternization with the strong impetus to ethnic solidarity given by political competition and racial politics in the American system.

After studying Grace Community Covenant Church and over twenty other churches in the San Francisco Bay Area, Jeung concluded that their pan-Asian American character didn't derive from any one source like a sense of common primordial racial identity or multicultural politics. Rather, a variety of social trends vectored upon Californian Asian Americans, producing experiences which crossed ethnic boundaries. A new boundary crossing sensibility arose which was felt to cognitively and emotionally fit the situation.

A New Cosmopolitan Religion?

The increasing presence of interracial interfaith families in a Thai Buddhist temple at Silicon Valley could be devastating. However, Perreira found that ethnic and religious intermarriage and the dynamic boundary-blurring Silicon Valley is creating a new type of boundary crossing in Thai Buddhism. The result is a cosmopolitan Thai American Buddhism that encourages intermarriage and a multivalent religion that is simultaneously two religious options at once, much like a body has two hands without conflict. The non-Thai husbands of the Thai American women have neither rejected nor fully converted to Thai Buddhism. Instead, they practice their inherited religion while participating in Buddhism. Their children are part of both religions as if they were one. Perreira foresees the rise of a new indigenously American cosmopolitan Thai Buddhism built upon this transcending experience.

Transnational Religion

Just a few miles away from the Thai Buddhist temple Perreira studied, Gonzalez and Maison found that Filipinos use their truly transnational Protestant and Catholic religions to transport social and cultural capital to rebuild the dead zones of San Francisco, connect to the non-Filipino community in Daly City, and provide a national and international network of "families" for traveling Filipinos.

Recent studies reaffirm and expand Herberg's insight that new immigrants became Americans precisely by maintaining transnational religious spheres (Levitt 2002). The immigrant is expected to be religious. His religion is a source of homely solace and strength, allowing him to assume an American national identity. At the same time technological changes like cheap air travel, phone service, and the Internet make transnational life easier to create and maintain.

This book is a call for more creative theoretical thinking about Asian Americans and their religions. It is obvious that crossing earthly borders and heavenly boundaries defines much of the Asian American experience. From the creation of spiritual narratives by young Chinese workers to the transnational religious networks of Filipinos, the chapters in this book speak to the ways in which religion matters. We hope through these contributions to show how the systematic exploration of the conceptual framework of borders and boundaries reveals more than the obvious, while deeply informing, exciting, and propelling the imagination.

NOTES

1. Closely related are theories and studies of frontiers, starting with Frederick Jackson Turner's 1895 essay, "The Frontier in American History," Alfred T. Mahan's *The Influence of Seapower in History,* and Halford Mackinder's "Geography as Statecraft." Robert Park's famous conceptualization of Zone 2 of cities as the urban frontier where conflict, creativity, ethnicities, and religions arise owes its origins largely to Teggart (cf. Lyman 1994, 43–59; Hughes and Hughes 1952).

The recent surge in borderland studies and border theory is summarized by Scott Michaelson and David E. Johnson (Michaelson and Johnson 1997). They point out that boundaries and borders cannot just be assumed as features of the immigrant situation but are themselves dynamically changing.

2. Important but inconclusive discussions of the definition of religion include Banton 1966; Berger 1967, 175–178; Goody 1961; Horton 1960.

3. Still, being born again is strongly associated with a decrease in proabortion attitudes among youth.

4. Statistics taken from 1997 survey of entering college freshmen in New York City by UCLA/HERI.

5. Current theoretical interest in boundaries and ethnicity was kicked off in 1969 by Frederik Barth's *Ethnic Groups and Boundaries* (see Barth 1994, 9–32); on the borders created to preserve the small village way of life, also see Cohen 1985, 1986, 1987; cp. Goffman 1959.

6. According to Loomis and Loomis (1987), boundary maintenance is one of the comprehensive master processes of social life (ibid., 16) covered by such theorists as Howard Becker, Kingsley Davis, George C. Homans, Robert K. Merton, Talcott Parsons, Pitirim Sorokin, Robin M. Williams, Jr., and Alvin Gouldner. In a later work Carnes adds coverage of Frederick J. Teggart, Herbert Blumer, and Harold Garfinkel (Carnes 2004).

7. The United States is a country where "doing it by the numbers" is a statement about life. In a nation where the number One looms like a god, claims about the number of immigrants and religious adherents are fraught with contest. At present there is fierce debate about how many people make up the United States, their ethnicities and religions. These debates can be quite technical but have large outcomes in terms of visibility, power, prestige, money, and practical action to help the needy.

We have sorted through the debates as best we can. Every number is not the last word in this highly contested terrain. In practice different numbers may be relevant for different intellectual projects.

Classifications in use by immigrants and immigrant researches are a result of several sociopolitical imperatives:

Politics/Law + Race + Nationality + Class + Prestige + Ideologies such as Americanism, Multiculturalism, and Religion

"Asian" could mean anybody born as a citizen of an Asian country. However, because the U.S. Census uses an aboriginal definition of Asians, most statistics on Asians omit Australians, New Zealanders, and Central Asians of the former Soviet Union. For the U.S. Census (U.S. Census Bureau 2000, 1) "the term 'Asian' refers to people having origins in any of the original peoples of the Far East, Southeast Asia, or the Indian subcontinent." The Census definition also includes some Pacific Islanders like Filipinos. Although most Asian countries practice rigid racial exclusions to immigration, Australia, Central Asian countries, and Singapore are multiethnic societies.

For a review of evolving definitions of "Asian Americans" in the U.S. Census, see Lien 2003.

8. Southeast Asians can also turn up in unlikely places. Nearly four thousand Vietnamese live in South New Jersey, particularly in Camden, Pennsauken, and Woodlynne. A large concentration of Christian Montagnards, Vietnamese hill

people, have recreated a village centered around their church in the mountains of North Carolina (Pearson 2001).

In 2000 the U.S. Census made extensive efforts to obtain accurate counts of illegal immigrants from Asia. However, some claim that the Census still undercounted the Asian illegal immigrant population.

9. An influential Danforth report described the decline and weaknesses of liberal Christian campus ministries (see Underwood 1969). On the history and impact of one parachurch campus ministry, see Hunt and Hunt (1991).

The Religious Demography of
Asian American Boundary Crossing

Pei-te Lien and Tony Carnes

Charting the religious demography of Asian Americans is not an easy task because of the scarcity of statistical information. The lack of demographic research may be attributed to a lack of interest among academics and the absence of questions on religion in survey data collected by U.S. government and other agencies (Warner 1998). Another major reason, which also contributes to the absence of survey research on Asian Americans in general, is that their population in the United States is small, extremely dispersed, and heterogeneous (Lien 2001).

A large step toward improving our portrait of the religious demography of Asian Americans was taken by a recent survey, the Pilot National Asian American Political Survey (PNAAPS). Along with the Asian sample in the Houston Area Survey, we now have the best religious portrait of Asian Americans that we have ever had (see chapters 10 and 11 by Klineberg and Lien, respectively, for further information about the surveys). Recent comprehensive surveys of Muslim Americans also fill in additional details on South Asian Americans.

How Many Asian Americans Identify with a Religion?

The vast majority (72 percent) of Asian Americans have a religious identity. Asian Americans are much more likely to have a religious identity than identification with a major political party (50 percent). Indeed, by every measure Asian Americans are more active in their religion than in any other voluntary organization.

Nevertheless, in comparison to the general public, 86 percent of whom had a religious identity in 2001 (Pew and Pew 2002, 55), Asian Americans are less likely to have one. However, the fact that Houston Asian Americans—84 percent of whom affirm a religious identity—appear to be as religious as the general public, indicates that there may be significant regional variations in the religiosity of Asian Americans. In Houston, religion commands much more popular support and visibility than in California or Hawaii, the states toward which the Pilot National Asian American Political Survey is weighted. The West Coast general population also has the lowest religious identification rates in the United States.

The majority of Asian Americans who have no religious identification are Chinese and Japanese Americans. All other major groups of Asian Americans are higher in religious identification than the American public as a whole. Further, some nonreligious Chinese Americans may actually engage in various types of folk religious practices that they see as part of Chinese culture rather than of religion. The social context also affects Japanese and Chinese American nonreligiosity. Japanese Americans are more concentrated in the West Coast than any other Asian American group. The more secular context depresses nominal religious identification rates as well as making it harder to sustain religious programs and public impact. Also, Japanese American religious identity may be lower because while interned during World War II they were banned from practicing some forms of religion. Chinese Americans are also concentrated in more secular areas of the country like the West and East Coasts. Chinese Americans in Houston, Texas, however, have a higher religious identification rate than Chinese Americans as a whole.[1] Possibly reflecting the restraint of religion by Confucianism and by Chinese Communism, Chinese respondents not only report the highest share of nonidentification, but they also have the largest percentage of refusals (18 percent).

Filipino Americans are the most religious Asian American group. Almost all (94 percent) offer a religious identification, and almost three-quarters (71 percent) go to religious services at least once a month. Korean Americans are a close second in religious identification (87 percent), with even more practicing their faith by going to church or temple (77 percent). Between 69 and 82 percent of Vietnamese, South Asian, and Japanese Americans claim religious identifications.

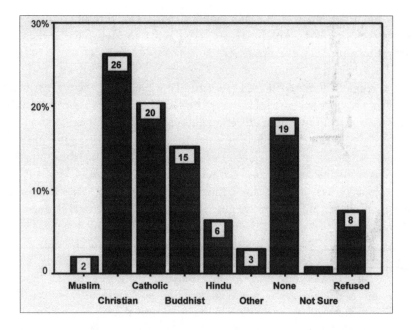

What Is Your Religious Preference?
Source: Pilot National Asian American Political Survey 2000–1. (N = 1,218)

Types of Asian American Religious Identification

Asian Americans in the PNAAPS survey had five major religious identifications: Christian (likely Protestant); Catholic; Buddhist; Hindu; and Muslim.

Christians (46 percent) make up the largest Asian American religious group. This percentage is made up of the self-identifiers of "Christian," "Protestant," and "Catholic." We have combined "Christian" and "Protestant" into one category, "Christian (likely Protestant)," because some scholars believe that Chinese and Koreans, and probably also Japanese and Vietnamese, Protestants usually identify themselves just as "Christian" as distinguished from "Catholics." For example, the 68 percent of Koreans who identify themselves as "Christian" certainly are mostly Protestants. Although the numbers of Asian American Christians is large, their proportion is much smaller than among the general public (82 percent). Almost nine out of ten (86 percent) Filipino Americans say that they are Christian, as do three-quarters of Korean Americans. South Asian Americans are the least likely to be Christian (3 percent). The majority of Christians among Asians are likely to be Protestant. Korean Americans are by far the most Protestant group, followed by Japanese Americans.

One out of five Asian Americans are Catholic, with Filipino Americans being two-thirds Catholic. There are also significant numbers (20 percent) of Vietnamese American Catholics.

It is likely that evangelical Catholics and Protestants make up around 25 percent of Asian Americans. Most of the Asian American Protestants are probably evangelical Christians. Liberals are found in large numbers only among the Japanese American Protestants. Further, religious surveys indicate that 20 percent of Catholics have a "born-again" identity similar to evangelical Protestants.

Because of the high visibility of new immigrants and some stark contrasts in their public religious presence, many people have overestimated how much the United States has changed in its religious makeup. Diana Eck has famously proclaimed that the nation has moved from being a religiously Christian nation to "a new multi-religious America" (Eck 2001; also see the claims in Linder 2001; Smith 2001a). Yet Muslims, Buddhists, and Hindus make up at most only 4 percent of the U.S. population.

Because Christianity is the dominant religious framework in the United States, Asian Americans may largely define their religious identity in terms of dealing with a predominantly Christian nation. For one, Asian Christians like Koreans are more likely to seek affirmation of their religious identity by immigrating to the United States. Second, non-Christian Asian American religions may continue to adopt Christian, particularly Protestant, forms like congregationalism, lay leadership, sermons, hymns, and social services (see Yang and Ebaugh 2001a). Third, the fast growth of American-style Christianity in Asia has already sparked competitive adaptations of its forms by other religions in Asia (see Min 2000; Kwon 2000).

Furthermore, a large proportion of the new Asian immigrants are Christian, and their presence is fostering a renaissance of urban Christianity, particularly evangelical Protestant and Roman Catholic Christianity. Some Asian American Christians are proclaiming a new urbanism, "a Glorious Urbanism" (Carnes 2002). This new vision will tone down the "Sodom and Gomorrah" image of cities, while bolstering faith-based social initiatives.

Finally, migration to the United States is also freeing people to experiment with new religious identities. As a result, there is a distinct increase in the number of evangelical Protestant congregations made up of immigrants from countries that have had few evangelicals because of persecution (see Yang and Ebaugh 2001b). At the same time Asian immigrants with a secular preference sometimes find it easier to be open about their religious disaffection here. Migration of religions relatively new to the United States has also opened up new avenues of faith for native-born Americans.

About one-fourth of Asians identify themselves with a religion other than Christianity. Buddhists (15 percent) make up the third largest religious group among Asian Americans, with Vietnamese Americans (49 percent) more likely to be Buddhist than the members of any other Asian American group surveyed. Buddhism is the second largest religion indicated by Chinese (19 percent) and Japanese (24 percent) Americans. Hindus (6 percent) are mostly from South Asia. However, small numbers of Hindus are also somewhat surprisingly found among Filipino (2 percent) and Japanese (1 percent) Americans.

Muslims make up only 2 percent of Asian Americans, though this includes most of the 17 percent of South Asian Americans. Further, nonsurveyed Asian American groups also have significant numbers of Muslims. Thus, some Malaysians and a majority of Indonesians are Muslim.

The other Asian American religious identifications are much smaller (3 percent), as they are in the general population. However, there is much regional variation in the distribution of Asian American groups and consequently of the numerical predominance of various religions. For example, Sikhs are very concentrated in Northern California near Sacramento, as are Hmong Buddhists and Christians who are also concentrated in the Minneapolis–St. Paul, Minnesota area. Cambodian Buddhists predominate in Springfield, Massachusetts.

Conversion, Religious Switching, and Disaffiliation

Asian American religious groups differ widely in the number of people that they convert and bring into church attendance. The highest conversion rate seems to be found among Christian churches that reach out to youth and new immigrants, particularly those reaching Chinese intellectuals and the new Fujian churches like the Church of Grace to the Fujianese.

First-generation Asian American parents have differing attitudes toward their youth leaving their religious organizations. Indeed, the proportion of the Asian American second generation leaving their parents' religions varies by ethnicity and religion. In a much-cited journalistic article, Korean American Helen Lee (1996) proclaimed that there was a "silent exit" of second-generation Asian Americans from Christian churches. Subsequent studies have found that this exit is true to some extent for Korean Americans but not as noticeable among Chinese Americans.

Still, according to a 1997 survey of college freshmen in New York City, there appears to be a great deal of reshuffling of religious identification going on among Asian Americans/Asians. There are two general trends: a falling away from the Christian faith by second-generation Korean Americans/Koreans; and a move of Asian Americans/Asians away from Buddhism and "no religion" into evangelical, Pentecostal, and Charismatic groups designated as "Other Christian" in the survey.[2]

Although 60 to 70 percent of Korean Americans/Koreans in New York City belong to evangelical churches, only 33 percent of Korean American college students in the city say that they are born-again Christians. A "silent exit" of Asian American youth from faith and churches seems to be true for Korean Americans. The largest proportion of religious switchers to evangelical Christianity appears to be Asian Americans from Buddhist families. A large number of born-again Asian American/Asian freshmen (12 percent) have Buddhist mothers. Most of the freshmen born-agains have dropped this Buddhist identification, though a number still retain some Buddhist identity. It also appears that conversions of the born-again Asian Americans/Asians are coming from kids who grew up with no particular religious identity.

In general, freshmen from Buddhist families are leaving their parents' religion. Nationally, according to the UCLA/HERI survey of college freshmen in 1997, about 33 percent indicate that they no longer identify with their mothers' Buddhism. Nationally, the only religion that is losing a higher percentage of its youth is the Episcopal Church (Korn and Asburg 1994).

Worship Attendance

As gauged by religious service attendance, Asians are split in half. About half of Asians (49 percent) attend religious services at least once a month. Thirty-seven percent attend almost every week. About half (43 percent) seldom or never attend religious services. In an area like Houston, Texas, where church attendance is the norm, Asian American attendance at religious worship services is about 5 percentage points higher, but they are still largely divided between the religious attenders and the complete nonattenders.

However, religious service attendance may mean different things to different religious groups. Almost two-thirds of Muslims and about half of "Christians (Protestant)" and Catholics report attending services every week. On the other hand, very few Buddhists (4 percent) attend weekly services. The weekly attendance of Hindus and people of "other" religions is between the high Muslim and low Buddhist rates. The low Buddhist rate of attendance at weekly services may be the result of religious nominalism or of a different way of practicing religion through home and workplace rituals, health exercises, or other practices. Other researchers have also noted the inclination of many Hindus to practice their religion at home or to be only nominally committed.

Religiosity as indicated by religious attendance also varies by ethnicity. Koreans, Filipinos, and South Asians report relatively strong levels of weekly attendance, with Koreans the highest (51 percent), followed by Filipinos (44 percent) and South Asians (32 percent). In contrast, Chinese, Vietnamese, and Japanese Americans report high rates of minimal or no attendance at religious services. About half (51 percent) of Chinese indicate that they never attend a religious service, likewise for 41 percent of Vietnamese and 34 percent of Japanese.

Religious Demography of Asian American Nationality Groups

Chinese Americans appear to be the most secular of Asian Americans. Thirty-nine percent say that they have no religious identification. However, many folk religious practices have seeped into Chinese culture to the

TABLE 1
*Chinese American
Religious Demography*

Christian (likely Protestant)	20%
Buddhist	19%
Catholic	3%
Other	1%
None	39%
Refused to Answer	18%
Not sure	1%

extent that many Chinese Americans don't consider them religious. Further, an astounding one out of five (18 percent) Chinese Americans refused to answer the question about their religion. A plausible guess is that the refusals were offered by religionists who still live in fear of persecution inspired by the mainland Chinese government.

Nonetheless, the relatively high percentage of ostensibly nonreligious Chinese Americans has meant that a visible role for religion is less accepted and, sometimes, more controversial in the Chinese community. Sympathizers with the PRC government have adamantly opposed the participation of Falungong devotees in Chinatown parades.

Still, if we assume that the refusals are mostly shy religionists, then up to 61 percent of Chinese Americans have a religious identification. At present there are six major religious demographic trends among Chinese American religionists:

> replacement of the "old immigrants," mainly Cantonese, as the numerically predominant congregants by mainland and Taiwanese immigrants;
>> fast growth of Fujianese, Taiwanese, and college-educated mainland Chinese religious groups;
>> transnational religious contacts;
>> relatively large numbers of refugees from religious persecution;
>> particularly fast growth of Protestant churches; and
>> a renewed vigor for Chinese folk or popular religion.

A similar result (32 percent Christian) was obtained by a *Los Angeles Times* survey of Chinese in Southern California, also in 1997. Forty-five percent indicated that they had no religion, 20 percent Buddhism, and 1 percent other. The survey also found that about 80 percent of Chinese Christians are evangelical Protestants, and 20 percent Catholics. Many Chinese follow popular Buddhism through home and personal rituals. However, very few attend Buddhist temples.

Filipino American Religious Demography

Filipino Americans are the most religious Asian American group. Almost all (94 percent) offer a religious identification and most regularly attend worship services.

TABLE 2
Filipino Americans

Catholic	68%
Christian (likely Protestant)	18%
Hindu	4%
Buddhist	1%
None	3%
Other	2%
Refused to Answer	3%

Filipino Americans are also a Catholic group, with 68 percent affirming a Catholic identification. There is also a fast-growing evangelical Protestant presence (18 percent). In urban areas Filipino Americans have revitalized many Catholic institutions.

South Asian American Religious Demography

South Asian American religionists are mostly Hindu or Muslim. There are also significant numbers of Sikhs.[3]

Most South Asian American Hindus are from India. Although earlier immigrants subscribed to a Hinduism universal to all regional and denominational groups in India, recent immigration and Hindu nationalism have revived regional and denominational differences.

South Asian Americans constitute 33 percent of all Muslims in the United States. Southeast Asian Americans make up 1 percent. South Asian American Muslims are found all over the urban United States. Increasingly, Muslims are engaged in secondary migration from the largest U.S. cities to suburbs and smaller cities.

There is great controversy over the figures for Muslims. A National Opinion Research Center (NORC) study concluded that there are between 1.5 and 3.4 million Muslims in the United States (Smith 2001b). The Mosque Study Project found that mosques report 2 million Muslims associating with their mosques (350,000 weekly attenders) and estimated that 6–7 million people identify as Muslims (Bagby, Perl, and Froehle 2001).[4] Whichever total population figure one uses, the numbers of Muslims in the United States have been growing rapidly since the 1970s.

Religion and Islam are important to South Asian American Muslims. Two-thirds do at least some of their five daily prayers (Zogby 2001). Immigrants at several mosques say that since they began living in the United

States, religion has become more important to them and that it helps them to exist within a society from which they sometimes feel disconnected. Mosques here thus often play a different role than in Muslim countries, where most mosques are essentially places for prayer services. However, Indonesian American Muslims report that their homeland mosques do act as community centers with many social services. Still, in Muslim countries the state provides the framework for an Islamic way of life, while in the United States the mosque is the social, cultural, and educational center encompassing the Muslim's whole life.

South Asian American Muslims seem to divide into three groups in terms of religious observance:

about half are very devout, attending the mosque at least once a week and say that they are involved with the activities of the mosque;

about one-fifth are nominal Muslims, attending mosque prayers only once or twice a month at most and only occasionally doing daily prayers; and

one in ten have little or no interest in Islam, never attending mosque for services and never doing daily prayers. (Zogby 2001)

TABLE 3
South Asian Americans

Hindu	46%
Muslim	17%
Christian (likely Protestant)	2%
Catholic	1%
Buddhist	1%
Other	13%
None	12%
Not Sure	1%
Refused to Answer	7%

Southeast Asian Religious Demography

The religious institutions of the Vietnamese, Laotians, and Thai have been most effective in helping their adherents to incorporate into the United States. They act as cultural centers to re-create a sense of identity, providing a social network for information, jobs, and homes, giving lay people leadership positions and status and offering counseling. Cambodian and

TABLE 4
Vietnamese Americans

Buddhist	49%
Catholic	20%
Christian (likely Protestant)	13%
None	14%
Other	1%
Not Sure	3%
Refused to Answer	1%

Hmong Buddhist temples have provided mainly cultural continuity and counseling. However, the churches have offered quite a few social services.

Buddhist temples in the United States have lost the communal role that they had in Cambodia and Laos (Van Esterik 1992, 46). In pre–Vietnam War Cambodia, the Buddhist temple (*wat*) was a central fixture in their villages. In addition to being a spiritual center, the temple provided education, refuge, and social help (Smith-Hefner 1999, 21–25). Now, although most Cambodians are at least nominal Buddhists, few are regularly active in their local temples.

Religious Demography of Korean Americans

Any consideration of Korean Americans must start with their faith and churches. In Los Angeles's Koreatown the founding of churches began within months of the founding of the first Korean grocery, the Olympic Market at the corner of Olympic Boulevard and Hobart Street in 1969 (Yu 1985). Koreans come to America as Christians or become Christians soon after they arrive. Sixty-eight percent identify themselves as Protestant and 11 percent as Catholic. In a 1997–98 survey 79 percent of Korean immigrants in New York City reported that they were Christians (Min 2002). Korean Americans are also very active in their religion. In a 1986 survey 67 percent of Koreans said that they attended a Korean church at least every two weeks. In the 1997–98 New York City survey an astounding 89 percent reported that they attended church at least once or twice a month, most reporting church attendance once or more a week.

The *2001 Korean Church Directory of America* lists 3,402 Korean Protestant churches in the United States. About half of Korean churches are Presbyterian. There are also substantial numbers of Methodist, Baptist, nondenominational, Catholic, and Charismatic churches. An Internet website, *Korean Catholic,* lists 154 Korean Catholic communities in the United States. *Modern Buddhism* (2001), a monthly Korean Buddhist journal, lists 100 Korean Buddhist temples in the United States. Very few immigrants attend a non-Korean church.

At the corner of Third and Oxford Streets in the heart of Los Angeles's Koreatown, four religious centers are across from each other. There are three churches—two Korean churches, one recently established Latino church, and a Buddhist temple. They tell us much about the religious story of Koreans today. First, the Christian church is overwhelmingly predominant in the Korean community. In fact, the ratio of churches to Buddhist temples is much greater than the 3 to 1 that we find at this intersection; the real ratio is perhaps ten to one. Moreover, the membership ratio is probably 40 to 1, and the active membership ratio is 50 to 1. Protestant churches provide most of the FBO social services for the Korean community and the range of services for their size probably dwarfs that of any other religious group in the United States.

A second way this corner is symbolic of Koreans today is that one church has become a Pentecostal Latino storefront church. Korean Americans are moving out of American city centers at a quick clip and are being replaced by Latinos in Los Angeles and Chicago, and by Chinese in New York City.

TABLE 5
Korean Americans

Christian (likely Protestant)	68%
Catholic	11%
Buddhist	5%
None	6%
Other	3%
Not Sure	1%
Refused to Answer	6%

TABLE 6
Religions of Koreans in New York City:
Congregation Attendance
Once a Week or More

Protestants	84%
Catholics	72%
Buddhists	0%

Source: Results of 1997–1998 Survey of Korean, Chinese, and Indian Immigrants in Queens, New York, cited in Min 2002.

Religious Demography of Japanese Americans

Although a majority of Japanese immigrants claimed a Buddhist identity in the early stages of their immigration, today only 24 percent do so. Second-generation (Nisei) Japanese Americans became Christians in large numbers and established most of the Japanese American churches that exist. Presently, 43 percent of Japanese Americans claim a Christian identity.

Religious Demography of Asian "New Age" Adherents

One of the most visible effects of Asian religion has been the rise of "alternative," "new age," or "Eastern" religions among white professionals. "In all its forms, Hinduism has influenced tens of millions of people in America. By itself Maharishi Mahesh Yogi's Transcendental Meditation, a form of Advaita Vedanta Hinduism, has over three million graduates. The New Age movement, with a collective following in the millions, has been powerfully influenced by Hinduism. . . . In addition, literally tens of millions of Americans have taken up Hindu practices, such as yoga, meditation, developing altered states of consciousness, seeking Hindu 'enlightenment,' and various other occultic practices" (Ankerberg and Weldon 1991). Celebrity Hinduism and Buddhism, visits by the Dalai Lama, gurus from India, Zen teachers from Japan, and the like have created a practice of Asian religions among non-Asian Americans. Consequently, even Asian American temples and mosque leaders have often created parallel congregations for non-Asians in their worship places.

TABLE 7
Japanese Americans

Christian (likely Protestant)	37%
Buddhist	24%
Catholic	6%
Hindu	1%
None	26%
Other	2%
Not Sure	1%
Refused to Answer	4%

Source: Pilot National Asian American Political Survey 2000–1.

NOTES

1. However, part of the difference in Houston may be explained by the relatively high concentration of Taiwanese immigrants who have higher religious identification rates than Chinese immigrants from Mainland China. However, the demographic difference is still not enough to explain the differing regional rates in Chinese American religiosity.

2. Unless otherwise specified, statistics for the 1997 and 2001 U.S. freshmen group come from Sax et al., 1997, 2001.

3. Pei's survey indicates a much lower percentage of Christians among Indian Americans than was offered by previous estimates. Hofrenning and Chiswick (1999) have estimated that Hindus made up 45–50 percent of immigrants from India.

4. Besides the NORC and Mosque Study Project estimates, others who have contributed their own figures are: Kosmin and Lachman 1993; Kosmin, Mayer, and Keysar 2001; Ba-Yanus 1997; Linder 2001; Gallup 2000, 2001; Zogby 2001; Numan 1992; Stone 1991; Barna Research Group 1999; Davis, Smith, and Marsden 2001.

Part I

Symbols and Rituals

1

Liminal Youth among Fuzhou Chinese Undocumented Workers

Kenneth J. Guest

A Liminal Space

Entering the Church of Grace is strikingly reminiscent of walking into a church anywhere in rural China, particularly the churches around Fuzhou. The language and narratives change. The clothing changes. Personal kinship and village networks become revitalized. The food changes. Even the smells change. The foyer of the Church of Grace is a liminal space for young Fuzhounese Christian immigrants, a place of transition between one reality and another, a place that removes them, even if temporarily, from their day-to-day reality and affords them a glimpse of something different (Turner 1969). Young immigrants who outside these churches are foreigners in a very strange land are transformed into insiders. Outside the youth cannot speak the dominant U.S. language, English, or even the dominant Chinese dialects of Cantonese and Mandarin spoken in Chinatown. They have little contact with non-Fujianese youth. Inside, their language, Fuzhounese, is predominant. Outside they are seen by earlier Chinese immigrants as "country bumpkins" (*tubaozi*) and derided as uncultured and uncouth youth. Inside, they celebrate a common cultural story of an exploring people.

In subtle ways the Church of Grace and other Fuzhounese religious communities in New York City provide sites for counterhegemonic discourse and community building that are central to young immigrants' ability to create narratives and identities for survival. Outside, the youth are considered poor; inside, they are considered adventurous wage earners supporting a church in New York City and family and community at home in China. Outside, they are itinerant workers moving from city to city, job to job. Inside, they find a central meeting place—a location for connection and reconnection with fellow Fuzhounese and with home. Outside, they may be young illegal immigrants, undocumented workers, invisible to the U.S. state or even targets of INS raids and crackdowns. Inside, they are children of God who through the death of Jesus have had their sins. God's grace is available to all, regardless of age, home village, kin group, debt burden, social position, or legal status.

This religious self-understanding distinguishes the Church of Grace and other emerging Fuzhounese religious communities from other Chinatown social institutions. It demarcates the religious institution from the village or surname association, from the union or political party. People participate and contribute not only because of the familiarity of friendship and village, but also because of the church's ability to convey meaning and religious significance to immigrants whose lives are more regularly filled with disorientation and dislocation. Outside, the unsophisticated youth can hardly articulate their story in a way that will be understood. Inside the church, they have a rich narrative of wandering and salvation.

Liminal Youth and a Rite of Passage

The Church of Grace is jam-packed, even more than usual. It is Easter Sunday and family, friends, and the congregation fill every inch of space with their curiosity. The sanctuary has standing room only. The foyer, the upstairs social hall, the downstairs classrooms are all full. Closed circuit televisions beam the service into each room. The crowds spill out of the front doors and into Allen Street where Chinatown's northern border meets the Lower East Side.

Fifty mostly young Fuzhounese, including the recently immigrated Chen Qiang, fill the front rows of the sanctuary at the Church of Grace waiting their turn for immersion into the faith. One by one they file into especially constructed dressing rooms beside the altar where they shed their street clothes and don long white robes. Assisted by members of the Board of Deacons they step into the pool, socks and all.

"I baptize you in the name of the Father, and of the Son, and of the Holy Spirit, Amen!" says Rev. Chen and plunges a young man under the water. He arises gasping, startled, crying from the experience. He steps out of the pool drenched and, braced by church members, staggers back to the dressing room, the water cascading from his soaked robes and hair onto the marble floor of the old bathhouse-turned-church in Manhattan's Chinatown, cleansed spiritually as generations before have been cleansed physically in that space.

This moment marks a dramatic transition in the lives of these young people. Stepping out of the Chinatown street, they leave behind a U.S. society by which they are exploited and from which they are totally marginalized. Through this rite of passage they are invited to join their stories to a rich narrative of a sojourning people seeking freedom and salvation. In a process carefully orchestrated by church volunteers, within forty-five minutes each person will receive an official certificate of baptism, complete with name, date, location, pastor's signature, and color photograph commemorating and documenting the occasion. Some may have very practical uses for these documents, perhaps needing them to support applications for political asylum. But for most they serve a much more metaphoric role, marking a dramatic spiritual, physical, and emotional transition and a reconceptualization of their lives and their system of meaning in the harsh reality of New York City's Chinese immigrant community.

This baptism signifies a ritual welcoming to a safe place between a distant Chinese homeland and the harsh sweatshop conditions of New York City. For the young Fuzhounese the ritual opens a doorway for examining the intersection of changing ideas of community, identity, and meaning.

The Church of Grace is full of young people who have recently emigrated from Fuzhou, the capital of Fujian Province on China's southeast coast. Survey responses show 38 percent of the congregation under thirty years old and 63 percent under age forty. Since the late 1980s tens of thousands of mostly rural young Fuzhounese have flooded into the United States, with New York City's Chinatown serving as their main point of entry. Their numbers have increased so rapidly that today Fuzhounese have supplanted the Cantonese as Chinatown's largest ethnic Chinese community and they are vying for leadership in the area's economics, politics, social life, and even language use. Fueled by this massive migration, the Church of Grace is now one of the two largest Chinese churches in New York City.

Leaving China

Over a bowl of noodles after church a few months later, Chen Qiang talked about his journey to America and the Church of Grace.

> To tell you the truth, I never really thought much about coming to America. I had been going to high school. Then all of a sudden my parents said I was going to America. They said there wasn't much of a future for me in China. No way of making a living. In the beginning I really didn't want to come. I didn't have a very good impression of America, only what I had seen on TV. Lots of bad things. Lots of violence. How many people were killed each month. That's the kind of news we got from the TV. But I was being sent to make money.
>
> I didn't know anything about Christians in China. There is a church in my town, but I never went in. My only memory is that my little sister got into a fight with another little girl who was a Christian. But they were just kids. There are a lot of temples in my hometown. My parents visit them to light incense and make offerings to the gods. They don't go regularly, but on holidays—New Years, Autumn Festival. They make offerings for my grandparents. And they visit their graves. But they don't talk about it very much.

Since the early 1980s whole segments of Fuzhounese communities have been uprooted. Most young people between the ages of eighteen and forty have gone abroad, spurred by economic restructuring in both China and the United States, and enabled by a vast and highly organized human smuggling syndicate. Younger teenagers await their opportunity to go. This massive international migration has dislocated people economically, culturally, and legally, and placed them in a receiving country for which they are unprepared and which is unprepared to incorporate them. The undocumented status of many of the new immigrants further complicates the picture.

Their primary destination is Chinatown, New York City, a densely populated Chinese community on Manhattan's Lower East Side where they hope to utilize kinship, village, and faith connections to survive in an unfamiliar environment. New York City is the primary entry point for these highly transient workers who move constantly to fill jobs across the United States in "all-you-can-eat" Chinese buffets, garment sweatshops, or construction sites. And New York City's Chinatown is their home base, the place to which they return to recuperate, reconnect with family and friends, and find their next job.

Fuzhounese Youth and Family Economic Strategy

The towns and villages around Fuzhou, previously reliant on farming and fishing, are not wealthy. Nor are they poverty stricken. The steady inflow of remittances from workers already in the United States stabilized the standard of living during the 1990s. Despite recent industrial growth fueled by foreign investment, local opportunities for economic development remain limited. Many Fuzhounese have turned to outmigration as an economic strategy.

Few immigrants make this momentous decision on their own. The journey is too dangerous and too expensive. Most, like Chen Qiang, are sent by their families in the hope of beginning a chain migration—or continuing one already begun—that eventually will extend to the whole kin group. Outmigration is a form of family economic diversification and leaving Fuzhou is usually a family decision.

Chen Qiang's story follows this pattern. To launch his journey, he did not borrow the money himself. Rather, his family made the arrangements, securing a $48,000 loan to pay his smuggling fees to the United States, a relative bargain compared to the standard $60,000–70,000. He recounts,

> My family made all the arrangements. My uncle's friend knew someone who knew a snakehead [smuggler] and they set everything up.

While his elder brother had previously attempted to migrate to Japan, Chen Qiang would be the first in his family to go to the United States. So, Chen Qiang began his long elaborate journey, alone in the hands of a vast human smuggling network with the hopes of his family resting heavily on his shoulders.

> We flew from Changle [Fuzhou] airport to Hong Kong, then to Cambodia, Hong Kong again, Holland, then Brazil. From Brazil we were put on a fishing boat, which put us ashore on the U.S. Virgin Islands. We were all detained there and claimed political asylum.

Six Waves of Fuzhounese Immigrants

The vast majority of Fuzhounese immigrants to the United States have come since the 1980s. The Church of Grace, for instance, is comprised primarily of immigrants who have arrived since 1980, 82 percent since 1990. Interviews and surveys reveal that among this group there are several compressed waves or generations, which comprise recent Fuzhounese immigration history.

The first contemporary wave of Fuzhounese began to arrive in the late 1970s and continued through the early 1980s. A second wave arrived in the mid-1980s through 1989. This group, whose passage was provided largely by smugglers, began to empty the smaller towns and villages outside Fuzhou. These immigrants were largely rural poor willing to take a risk to improve a difficult life. Fortuitously for these immigrants, most were able to regularize their immigration status as a result of the amnesties granted in 1986 and 1990. In turn they were able to bring immediate family members to the United States as well, initiating a continuous chain of legal migration.

Chen Qiang represents a third wave of Fujianese immigrants to arrive in America. This wave began in the 1990s and continues today. Increasingly, this is comprised of young immigrants who come to the United States without legal documentation and by means of human smugglers. They arrive significantly indebted to the snakeheads or to family members who advanced payment. Many remain indebted for years. A limited number successfully apply for political asylum. The rest remain undocumented, working in the informal economy and easily exploited.

A fourth wave of immigrants also spans the 1990s. These legal immigrants include children and siblings of earlier immigrants. This fourth wave is not monolithic but is comprised of two distinct segments. One segment includes relatives from Hong Kong, Macao, or Singapore reuniting with their families. These immigrants, particularly the young people, are urbanized and often well educated by the public school systems in those countries. They often arrive with the added advantages of English and Cantonese language skills, advanced education or expectations of such, and a basic introduction to the skills needed in the urban economy. Most of these immigrants enter directly into the U.S. educational system, particularly the City University and State University of New York systems.

The other segment of the fourth wave is from the rural areas outside Fuzhou. They are also legal immigrants arriving by virtue of family reunification provisions of the immigration law. These immigrants come with little preparation for success in the mainstream U.S. economy. They have completed junior high school at most and speak only a little English and imprecise Mandarin. Despite their legal status, the older immigrants in this group, mostly parents of earlier immigrants, remain largely isolated in their family groupings. And despite their legal status, the young immigrants are often relegated to the ethnic enclave economy in Chinatown or its extension through the network of Chinese restaurants that crisscrosses the country.

A fifth wave of the Fuzhounese immigrant community is comprised of children born in the United States who are growing up here. Among the Fuzhounese, this group is small but growing, mostly under ten years of age. A sixth wave, largely invisible to the public, is made up of children born in the United States but sent back to China as infants. These children are often born to struggling Fuzhounese workers who came here illegally and remain without status. By virtue of their U.S. birth, they are automatically citizens; although raised in China by grandparents or other family members, they carry U.S. passports. Because of their parents' poverty and lack of U.S.-based support networks, however, they cannot be maintained in the United States.

Lost in the United States: Social and Legal Limbo

Nineteen-year-old Chen Qiang sat quietly in his little room in the old tenement building on Catherine Street, a tenement where countless generations of immigrant workers—Irish, German, Italians, Jews, Chinese—had lived before him. He leaned over a little table, head in his hands. Every once in a while his fingers would run back through his hair, as if trying to squeeze the pressure out of his skull. His room was no more than eight feet by twelve feet. A toilet was packed into one closet, a bathtub in another. There was a small sink in one corner. Most of the room was taken up by a bunkbed that he shared with another Chinese worker. He was fighting back the tears as he told his story.

It was a Monday night in November 2002. For three days I had futilely scoured the Chinese employment agencies at the corner of Division and

Eldridge under the Manhattan Bridge looking for work in the New York area. The tension was building.

With interest accumulating daily, it was essential that he keep working to pay off the debt. Failure to keep up would mean threats of violence against his family back home. To compound the pressure, Chen Qiang had learned the week before that his older brother, who had been smuggled to Japan, had been arrested and would soon be deported to China. This was the third time he had been caught and sent back. Each time he faced higher fines and longer imprisonment in China. Now, these debts too would fall on Chen Qiang.

For the past eight weeks he had been working as a busboy in a Chinese restaurant in New Hampshire, arranged through a Chinatown employment agency. He lived and ate in the restaurant, working seven days a week, fourteen to sixteen hours a day. He made $1,300 a month. It was a long way from New York City, but it was a job, an increasingly scarce commodity in a rapidly shrinking economy.

The previous week he had returned to New York City to attend an immigration court hearing of his application for political asylum. After months of waiting and several postponements, he and his lawyer would argue that his family had been persecuted in China based on the government's one child per family policy and that he feared reprisals from the government if he were sent home. Despite waiting all day, Chen Qiang's case was never heard. The judge's docket was full. The hearing was postponed again for six months. In Chen Qiang's room three days later, his disappointment was palpable and his sense of being in limbo was debilitating. What would he do next? Where could he turn for help? His options were extremely limited.

Catching the Christian Network Lifeline

One place Chen Qiang had successfully sought support was the network of Christian churches and agencies assisting recent immigrants. His first encounter with Christianity came at the Children's Home where he was sent after he came ashore on the United States. He explained, "Since I wasn't eighteen yet they sent me to a children's home in Georgia until we could find a sponsor." Members of local churches would visit each Sunday and take the detainees out to worship services in the nearby city. They provided Chen Qiang's first entry into a Christian network that would play a significant role in his survival of the immigrant experience.

> I didn't know anything about Christianity until after my detention by the INS. I spent a year in the children's home. People came on Sundays to take us to different churches. It was nice to get out. And the services were very interesting. That's the first time I had ever been in a church. It's the first time I had heard about God or Jesus.

The social worker at the children's home in Georgia also contacted a representative of Lutheran Family and Community Services in New York City to enlist her help. After Chen Qiang's arrival in New York City, the Lutheran caseworker followed his progress carefully, visiting his apartment and inquiring about employment. She linked him with a Lutheran-sponsored lawyer who would manage his application for political asylum. She also introduced him to the Church of Grace where the Lutherans were conducting some activities for other Fuzhounese juvenile detainees.

> I wasn't really that worried when I was in the children's home. Life there was pretty good. When I got to New York the social worker at the children's home put me in touch with a social worker from Lutheran Family and Community Services. She checked on me to make sure I had a job and a place to stay. She took me to the Church of Grace the first time. I went to church when I was in town. They kept asking me to be baptized. I really didn't want to.

Aid and Obligations: Chinese Kinship Networks

Although Chen Qiang was the first from his family to arrive in the United States, his family in China was still able to assist him by mobilizing a network of friends and fellow villagers in New York City. The network came into play at a crucial early juncture as Chen Qiang sought someone to sponsor his release from custody while his application for political asylum was being processed.

> Finding a sponsor to get me out of detention in the children's home was a big problem. I don't have any relatives or friends in the United States. So I needed to find someone I could pay to be my sponsor. I was looking. My

family was looking. Even the INS was looking for us. Finally a worker in a garment shop run by the daughter of my uncle's friend agreed to sponsor me. I gave her $3,000.

Despite his family's early success in mobilizing their social network, Chen Qiang's release from the children's home revealed his relative isolation in the United States.

It was only after I was released that I got worried. Find a place to stay. Find a job. Food to eat. How to get through the day. I had to rely on myself. I didn't have any friends. It was very hard. When I first got to New York, my uncle's friend helped me find a place to stay for a while. I had to find my own work. I went to the employment agencies. I've been working in restaurants, mostly doing deliveries on a bicycle.

The pressure to find work quickly and to work as hard as possible is driven by the severe debt burden carried by these new immigrants. Many earlier Fuzhounese arrivals borrowed the smuggling fees directly from the snakeheads. But in recent years the snakeheads have turned the lending over to relatives, local gangs, local loan sharks, or village associations.

When I got out of the children's home my family had to pay the snakeheads $48,000. We've paid them, but now we owe our relatives and we're paying them back with very high interest. So it's a lot of pressure on me now to make money and send it back. I send back as much as I can and they pay off the debts. Most months I can send at least $1,000. But that's a disaster! Definitely not enough. Other people who are waiters can make $2,000 a month. If you speak English, you can take phone orders and make more. At best I can only work as a busboy right now. I only use a little bit of money to live on. I eat in the restaurant and live in the restaurant if I can. Otherwise, I stay wherever I can find a place to lie down. At a friend's. At the church.

The financial and emotional pressure on young people like Chen Qiang is intense. In the post September 11 economy, jobs are hard to find. Failure to keep up with debt payments leads to threats and violence against them and their families in China. When family networks prove inadequate, these marginalized yet resourceful immigrants seek to mobilize alternative sources of support. Religious communities like the Church of Grace are primary locations for Fuzhounese youth to supplement both their social capital and their emotional support. In fact religious communities may provide family-like acceptance without the harsh financial obligations and allow youth to subtly transform their family connections with a religious framework. Chen's turn to the religious community is not unusual among Fuzhounese immigrant youth.

Building an Alternative Community: Supplementing and Transforming Chinese Kinship Networks

For many young immigrants, religious communities like the Church of Grace are an initial point of entry into the U.S. reality. They are a place for reconnection with family and fellow villagers, for sharing news of home, for exchanging ideas about how to survive in this alien and exploitative environment, to give thanks to their particular deity for safe passage, and to make petitions for a successful continuation of the journey. As testimony to this role, fourteen independent Fuzhounese religious communities were established in Chinatown by 2002. These include Protestant and Catholic churches as well as Buddhist, Daoist, and Chinese popular religion temples.

The Church of Grace is the largest and most successful of these communities, serving as a ritual and community center for thousands of Fuzhounese as they navigate the complexities of the U.S. economic, social, and legal systems and seek to make sense of the hardships they are experiencing. In the complex economic, political, and social environment of Chinatown's ethnic enclave, many of these religious organizations have become central locations for a transient Fuzhounese population to build a community, activate networks of support built on kinship, region, and faith, and establish links to their home churches, temples, and communities in China.

Key to the Church of Grace's allure among recent young immigrants has been its use of the Fuzhou dialect in its worship and programs. Prior to the arrival of the Fuzhounese, Cantonese had been the predominant Chinese dialect in Chinatown. But with the dramatic increase of immigrants from Fuzhou, use of their local dialect increased and in many cases Mandarin became a lingua franca in the community. From the beginning the congregation conducted worship services in Fuzhou dialect with simultaneous translation into Mandarin. Board meetings were conducted in Fuzhou dialect and Fuzhounese was the dialect of most informal conversations. Among the older members it is often the only language they speak, though they may understand some spoken Mandarin. For the mostly rural immigrants from the Fuzhou area the use of Fuzhou dialect proved a significant unifying factor for the young and old in the midst of an ethnic enclave dominated by Cantonese and Mandarin speakers. Within the congregation, the use of Fuzhou dialect is still predominant and in the wider Chinatown community the church has established a distinct identity as the "Fuzhounese church."

After worship on Sunday the renovated bathhouse that holds the Church of Grace changes from ritual center to community center. Over bowls of noodles served after worship the conversations roar. News of home from new arrivals. News of jobs and places to live. Discussions of recent events in China or in the U.S. media. A member of the Board of Deacons passes along a videotape from his home church outside Fuzhou that describes their building project and solicits funds from overseas compatriots. The president of the Women's Fellowship collects money from members for an emergency relief gift for a middle-aged garment shop seamstress whose husband just died of cancer in a Lower East Side hospital. She collects over $2,000 by the end of the day. A bulletin board lists job openings and beds for rent. The evangelists gather together first-time visitors for a discussion of basic principles of the Christian faith and invite them to join the baptism and membership class that will be starting in a few weeks. A group of college students meets in a corner to discuss their upcoming exams. The decentralized interactions are wide-ranging and have their own style and order.

A bulletin board for job postings and apartment listings has been revived after succumbing several years earlier to complaints that "a church should not be an employment agency." Representatives of a neighborhood women's health program set up a table in the lobby after church to sign up more than thirty women for consultations about services ranging from birth control and AIDS testing to nutrition and prenatal care.

While these developments are not a radical comprehensive organizational response, they do reflect an attempt to supplement the informal networking that has emerged spontaneously among the congregants. The developments suggest a movement from an island of nurturing personal piety toward a civic evangelicalism encompassing the worldly needs of Fuzhounese immigrants as well. The church is gradually establishing itself as a bridge between its largely young membership and the structures of American society.

Marginalization and Meaning: Fuzhounese Youth Convert

Twice a year, at Easter and again in the fall before the weather turns too cold, the Church of Grace conducts a baptism ritual during Sunday worship. Congregation leaders place a tremendous emphasis on this event and persistently recruit potential converts. Over the past few years as many as fifty people have been baptized on each occasion.

Although Chen Qiang had grown quite familiar with the Church of Grace in his early days in New York City, he was not exactly sure what baptism entailed or what it would mean for his life. His family in China was Buddhist. He had never been to a church before coming to the United States. He would be the family's first Christian.

> I haven't told my parents [about possibly converting to Christianity]. I'm too scared to tell them! They wouldn't understand. They don't think very highly of Christianity. My uncle said that I could go to the church to meet nice young girls or to get some help. But I shouldn't get too involved there. No, my family wouldn't understand.

Interaction with clergy and lay members of the Church of Grace launched Chen Qiang on a quest to understand his immigrant journey. In the midst of his turmoil and marginalization, what does his life mean? Chen Qiang recalls wrestling with these questions one particular Sunday.

> I heard a sermon by the minister. He said, "Be careful. Life can be very short. You don't know when your time may come. You don't know when the end of the world will come. You may be walking down the street and be struck by a car. You may only have a few minutes left. Don't delay. Don't wait to accept Jesus. Don't miss your chance to turn your life around. Don't miss your chance for salvation." That really scared me! I was really afraid. What if I die crossing the street? I finally decided to get baptized.

By choosing to be baptized, Chen Qiang joined the 26 percent of the Church of Grace congregation who have been baptized since their arrival in the United States.

This Fuzhounese congregation also draws upon a strong base of Protestants born into Chinese Christian families or converted in China prior to migration. Surveys show that 60 percent of those in attendance at the

TABLE 1.1
The Church of Grace: Location of Conversion of Its Members

Gender	China	% China	U.S.	% U.S.	No Response	% No Response	Other Location
Men	46	57	29	35.8	4	4.9	2 = 2.5%
Women	75	62.5	24	20	21	17.5	0
Totals	121	60	53	26.4	25	12.4	2 = 1%

Church of Grace had become Christians in China. Twelve percent made no response, suggesting they may still be uncommitted seekers.

One of the Church of Grace evangelists categorizes conversions of Fuzhounese in New York City into four categories. The first includes long-time members of churches in China who because of extenuating circumstances never received baptism. Clergy may not have been available to conduct the ritual or, in the case of underground churches, no opportunity was available. The second category of converts includes those who attended church irregularly or were familiar with Christianity in China but never made the commitment to "believe in the Lord" until they arrived in the United States. The third category includes Fuzhounese who heard about Christianity only after arriving in New York City. The fourth is comprised of people who are not Christians and do not believe in the fundamentals of Christian teaching, but are using the conversion process to bolster their claims for political asylum based on religious persecution. This, believes the evangelist, is not a small number, but one that is very difficult to be specific about. "It is hard to be sure who is insincere. We ask them basic questions about their faith and provide basic teachings about the church. But ultimately it is between them and God."

The Ritual Transition

The ritual emphasis placed on baptisms reflects their symbolic importance for this religious community. They are at their core outward and visible signs of inner conversion, a transformation of these individuals in both body and spirit. And they are for many a personal yet public identification of their life journeys with a larger metanarrative, that of the Christian faith and of the United States, which many Chinese immigrants consider to be inextricably linked with Christianity. This is no small shift for Chinese born and raised in an environment infused with non-Christian reli-

gious practices, a culture deeply tied to popular religious traditions en-
twining the individual with family, lineage, and village, and a political discourse which has disparaged and at times harshly repressed all religious
belief.

The baptism ritual also has tremendous importance for the congregants observing or administering this sacrament as they recall their own
conversion and reflect on their own life journey. At the Church of Grace,
the baptism—the washing away of sins, the purification of body and soul,
the acceptance of Jesus Christ as personal Lord and Savior, as guiding light
and source of life—represents for many of these immigrants a claim to a
new life narrative and a search for new frameworks of meaning for their
radically changed reality.

Building the Church of Grace

The Church of Grace originated in 1978 as a small group of Fuzhounese
immigrant women gathered for prayer and Bible study, eventually establishing the first Fuzhou dialect Christian group in Chinatown. Among its
early members were many undocumented young people. Some had over-
stayed tourist visas. A few came with the help of a fledgling human smuggling network. All worked in garment shops and restaurants in lower
Manhattan. The garment shops were beginning to rebuild after the off-
shoring of the 1970s. Restaurants serving the growing tourist trade and
the American taste for Chinese cuisine continued to expand. Owners readily welcomed young low-wage laborers to fuel this growth.

In 1993 the Church of Grace moved into an old public bathhouse built
in 1904 on Allen Street that had served Jewish and Italian immigrants who
lived in tenements without hot water or bathing facilities. Today the
Church of Grace is experiencing explosive growth. By the summer of 2002
average attendance exceeded five hundred people for its main service—
nearly doubling in two years—plus another fifty for a year-old English-
language service. At 11:00 A.M. as the ninety-minute service begins the
sanctuary is packed with three hundred and fifty people. In addition sixty
people sit on folding chairs in the foyer watching the service on closed-cir-
cuit television. The scene is replicated with seventy attendees upstairs in
the church's social hall. In the basement three Sunday school classes total-
ing nearly fifty children squeeze into tiny spaces.

The mailing list for the Church of Grace newsletter is well over two thousand with addresses across the United States, including some Immigration and Naturalization detention centers. The Fuzhounese population is highly transient and attendance at these churches reflects this. The pews may be consistently filled, but the participants change from week to week. On Christmas Day, one of the few days of the year that all Chinese workers are likely to have off and a time when Fuzhounese employed across the United States return to New York City to visit friends and relatives, the Church of Grace rents a local high school auditorium to hold the crowd of more than a thousand that gathers for worship.

Recently the Church of Grace has moved toward a more formal engagement with the social concerns of the Fuzhounese community as well as a closer integration into local, national, and international networks of Chinese evangelical Christians. An early Sunday English-language worship service—distinctly lacking in Fuzhou flavor—has been started, ostensibly for the congregation's 1.5 and second generation but attended primarily by recent immigrants wishing to hear and learn English. Weekly ESL (English as a Second Language) classes have been launched. A cooperative program with Lutheran Family and Community Services provides activities for Fuzhounese minors, like Chen Qiang, detained by the United States.

The Youth Fellowship

The preponderance of young people is visibly evident in the Church of Grace congregation. Three children's Sunday school classes run concurrently with the main worship service. The choir, with over twenty members each Sunday, is virtually an extension of the youth group. Young people provide the simultaneous translation during worship, run the sound system, play the piano, and staff the library and bookstore. On Sunday afternoons and evenings the church building belongs almost exclusively to the youth fellowship, which spans older teenagers to young adults in their midthirties. After worship they have choir rehearsal, youth fellowship meetings, Bible study, informal dinners and recreation, including setting up a ping-pong table in the main foyer. The youth group is comprised of generations three and four. Members are both documented and undocumented, rural and urban, college oriented and work oriented.

The youth fellowship's members include undocumented restaurant, construction, and garment shop workers who work grueling hours, speak no English, have little or no contact with mainstream U.S. society, and little hope of advancement beyond the Chinatown ethnic enclave economy. Like Chen Qiang, they often come to the United States alone, first-generation immigrants in their own right, hoping to initiate a migration chain that will extend to include their whole family. They usually carry heavy debts, constantly struggling to make the next payment. They are extremely isolated, marginalized both in their own community and in the larger U.S. society. They are transient and fragile, in and out of hospitals. The physical strain shows on their faces and in their bodies. In the Youth Fellowship they take no leadership roles and attend as they are able, rarely lingering for informal conversation and activities. Their lives are too full of pressure and anxiety.

At the core of the group's leadership are college students and recent graduates, quite a few having grown up in Hong Kong, who easily cross from their parents' Chinese culture to the broader U.S. culture. Switching easily between languages, they clearly imagine themselves succeeding in the mainstream U.S. economy. This portion of the group serves as a bridge between the congregation and U.S. culture: they are well represented on the Board of Deacons; they lead the English-language children's Sunday School classes; they handle the congregation's financial accounting; they manage the computer database, library, and bookstore. Once a year the youth fellowship organizes a weekend trip for the entire congregation. Buses are rented, a retreat center visited and booked, sightseeing side trips arranged, and money is collected. The youth handle all the arrangements, primarily because they are the ones in the congregation with the cultural skills to negotiate a foray of more than one hundred Fuzhounese immigrants beyond New York City's Chinatown.

With such a complex mix of participants, tensions sometimes run high within the fellowship. In one recent incident, some of the young people from rural areas in Fuzhou had advocated for more Bible study and prayer in the youth fellowship meetings. From their perspective, the group's inclination toward fun, games, food, and outside activities detracted from the main reason to have a church group—namely to know God better and develop a deeper spiritual life. The church staff proposed splitting the youth fellowship into two groups to address what they saw as competing programmatic and spiritual desires. Leaders of the youth group, drawn exclusively from the college educated, urbanized immigrant group resisted a permanent split, fearing it would ultimately diminish their cohesiveness and power within the congregation. As an interim step to address the tension, church staff initially formed a separate youth Bible study and prayer group that met on Sunday afternoons following the full youth fellowship meeting. A later reorganization has the full group meeting together, then splitting into three small groups, one for students, one for workers, and one for beginners. While serving as a successful compromise for the time being, this also leaves open the possibility of furthering congregational stratification along lines of education, employment, and legal status.

Tensions also arise between the youth fellowship and the rest of the congregation. With its aggregate set of skills, the youth fellowship holds significant power in the congregation, second only to the Board of Deacons. They are well organized with a full slate of officers elected annually by the youth fellowship members. But this base of power also has considerable potential for creating tension and conflict. For instance, the youth group has advocated strongly for programs it supports and personnel assignments it views as helpful. It has also pushed the congregation to modernize its worship and structure, proceeding more rapidly than older members and rural young members are comfortable with.

A Fuzhounese second generation—children born in the United States to immigrant parents—is only now emerging. Its development is complicated by the large number of children whose parents are too busy working and lack an adequate family support network in the United States and so immediately send their children home to China to be raised by grandparents. In the pattern now emerging, most of these children are being brought back to the United States at age five or six to attend school. But leaving behind their surrogate parents in China, being reintroduced to parents in the United States they don't remember, and attending school in

TABLE 1.2
The Church of Grace: Age of Members

Age	Men	Men (Percentage of Total Membership)	Women	Women (Percentage of Total Membership)	Total	Percentage of Total Membership
1–9	2	2.5	3	2.5	5	2.5
10–19	9	11.1	15	12.5	24	11.9
20–29	19	23.5	28	23.33	47	23.4
30–39	24	29.6	26	21.67	50	24.9
40–49	13	16	23	19.2	36	17.9
50–59	5	6.2	12	10.0	17	8.5
60–69	3	3.7	6	5	9	4.5
70–79	1	1.2	5	4.2	6	3
80–89	1	1.2	2	1.6	3	1.5
No Response	4	5.0	0	0	4	2

a language and culture with which they are not familiar is proving to be a very difficult transition for many of these children and their parents. The Church of Grace Sunday School classes for children ten and under are filled with these children. Some speak little English. Others who were raised in New York City speak little Chinese. The ability of the church's volunteer teachers to cope with this complexity is severely limited and the future engagement of these children with the larger congregation is not yet clear, though it appears to be terribly problematic.

The Dream

Even as a nineteen-year-old undocumented worker, burdened by crushing debt and locked into an exploitative ethnic economic network by virtue of his lack of English language skills, Chen Qiang, like other young Fuzhounese, struggles to keep alive a dream of success here in America.

> Someday I hope I can move up from delivery boy to busboy, then waiter, then to reception and then finally to open my own restaurant. Fuzhounese in America all have this hope. They don't speak any English. They have a huge problem with their legal status. So they dream of working their way up and someday owning their own restaurant.

> Someday I would really like to fully enter American society. This is an American place. There are not a lot of Chinese in America. But being in this Chinese environment in Chinatown is like being in jail. If you go out you can't speak English. If you want to travel, you don't know where to go. Life here is so much worse than in most of America. Being in Chinatown is just like being in China! So I would like to be able to get out into American society. I need to learn English. If only I had the opportunity! I'd like to go to school. But that's probably unrealistic considering how much money I have to pay back.

But Chen Qiang's dream is not only a dream of economic success. It is also a dream to understand the significance of his immigrant journey.

After his baptism, I asked Chen Qiang what it felt like and why he had decided to become a Christian. He took down from his bunkbed the baptism certificate from the Church of Grace and gently handed it to me to see. It was clear that this simple piece of paper marked a significant transition in his life.

> After my baptism I realize that I have something important that they [the rest of his family] don't have—the most important thing. One of the evangelists said that baptism in your life is like the coming of Jesus in the history of the world. Before Jesus, the world didn't know him and strayed from God. Then Jesus came and the world was different. He showed the world a different way. That's the way my life is too. Now I have a way of understanding what's going on in my life, the big changes from my life before to my life now. That's something my parents don't have. That's the most important thing.

Baptism, the outward and visible sign of conversion to Christianity, marked a liminal moment when he could step back from the normative activities of his life and attempt to gain perspective on the larger questions of meaning and existence.

One evening about a year after his baptism Chen Qiang and I took a walk. He hadn't found a job in a few days. His father had just called to ask how much he could pay toward the debt that month. He said he wanted to take his mind off things. We walked around Chinatown for a while, visiting a nighttime fruit vendor, lingering under the statue of the Fujianese patriot Lin Zexu in Chatham Square, and gazing north along the Bowery toward the lights of midtown. I suggested we head downtown, perhaps to a part of the city he hadn't seen. We walked past the courthouses of Foley Square, the African slave memorial, the Brooklyn Bridge, the brightly lit City Hall. Our feet kept leading us south along Broadway, first to the makeshift memorial along the cemetery fence of St. Paul's Church, then to the glaring brilliance of the World Trade Center site itself. The size of the crater spoke of the magnitude of the devastation. The new construction of subway and train lines spoke of New York City's will to move on, making sense of its difficulties by continuing to live. After a long while looking at the pictures on display and gazing down into the construction site we walked slowly back toward the East River and Chinatown. "What are you thinking about?" I asked. "What do you think God is really like?" he asked. After a few moments he continued, "I still don't really know. Sometimes it is very confusing. I better go home now, though. Tomorrow I have to get up early and try to find another job."

Fuzhounese youth in New York, like Chen Qiang, are among the most vulnerable and marginalized members of American society. They lack the language skills to enter the mainstream economy. They lack the background to pursue further education. They are deeply indebted and obligated either to smugglers, their family networks, or both. And many are undocumented, leaving them cut off from the right to fully participate in this society and constantly concerned about being caught and deported.

In the midst of this harsh reality, Fuzhounese youth consistently prove to be resilient, persistent, and sometimes ingenious innovators who sustain themselves and their dependent families against great odds. Over the past fifteen years they have sought out—and at times helped create—religious networks and communities to mobilize the resources needed for surviving their immigrant experience. These religious communities, like the Church of Grace described in this chapter, serve as locations to access social, financial, and emotional support. They serve as bridges between these isolated youth and the social structures of the Chinese enclave and the broader U.S. society. And they serve as ritual locations where Fuzhounese young people are offered the opportunity to reflect on the meaning of their immigrant journey and the radical transformations that have occurred in their lives between China and the Lower East Side of Manhattan.

2

The Creation of Urban Niche Religion
South Asian Taxi Drivers in New York City

Elta Smith and Courtney Bender

Numerous studies have confirmed that "new" immigrants forming religious communities in the American context effectively fashion mosques, temples, and gurdwaras into structures that exhibit cultural and structural elements similar to those constituting Christian and Jewish congregations (Warner 1994; Warner and Wittner 1998; Ebaugh and Chafetz 2000a; Yang and Ebaugh 2001a). The emerging "structural adaptation" model, as it is sometimes called, focuses attention on the ways in which immigrant religious groups change their organizational structures to resemble American congregations. However, this focus does not adequately address the immigrants' religious experience outside the congregation and the way it alters the immigrants' expectations of congregations.

The limitations of the structural adaptation model came to our attention while interviewing Muslim taxi drivers in New York City in 2000. The taxi drivers we spoke with wish to fulfill the religious injunction to pray five times daily and pursue a number of strategies in order to do so. They pray in a number of mosques, both in Manhattan and in the outer boroughs. They also pray in prayer spaces located in airports, garages, and "ethnic" restaurants. These prayer spaces represent an organizational innovation within the existing field of American mosques and complicate the analysis of immigrant religious life that focuses solely on congregational participation. Such prayer spaces take on additional import when we see how taxi drivers use them in conjunction with mosques.

The existence and uses of freestanding prayer spaces—especially those located in restaurants—demonstrates the importance of incorporating a view toward "lived religion" within the broader study of new immigrant religions. We argue that the daily religious practices of "new immigrants" are central keys to understanding the development of immigrant religiosity as a whole. Daily practices are not an "additional" or "subsequent" element in the study of immigrant religious communities but are part and parcel of immigrants' ideas and choices in developing any kind of religious organization. By extending the conceptual boundaries of organized religion in our investigations of immigrant life, we provide a more complete view of immigrant religious experience. This view, in turn, lends itself to a better understanding of the roles that immigrants' activities play in reconstructing the boundaries of public and private, ethnic and religious identities.

"De Facto Congregationalism" as a Form of Structural Adaptation

The structural adaptation model has extended R. Stephen Warner's overview of recent changes in the American religious organizational landscape and the growing importance of the congregation itself within it (1994). Warner states that the modern American religious realm is characterized by "de facto congregationalism" by which local religious bodies have become increasingly central and powerful in helping individuals form religious identities and meaning. Protestant denominations and denominational authorities have, for a number of reasons, become less powerful than they were a generation earlier (Wuthnow 1998; Marty 1994). Warner argues that congregationalism, with deep roots in American voluntarism, likewise extends beyond the borders of American Protestantism. It also characterizes Jewish synagogues and even Catholic parish life, to some degree. Warner also argues that when new immigrant groups form religious organizations, they adopt this dominant congregational model as well (1994; Warner and Wittner 1998).

Warner observes that the reasons why immigrant groups adopt the congregational form have "less to do with their assimilation to American culture than their discovery that congregationalism suit[s] their circumstances" (1998, 22). Adopting a congregational model is, in other words, a "pragmatic" decision made possible because local and state laws, regulations, and cultural expectations make it so. Assimilation happens via structural adaptation to the dominant organizational model, which compels actors to adopt many of the cultural or social expectations embedded within it.

The structural adaptation model resonates with a "neoinstitutional" perspective wherein groups "solve" practical problems of organizing and decision making by observing and adapting the habits and strategies of other similar groups (DiMaggio and Powell 1983). By associating with a field or set of similar organizations, groups will find that they are also subject to the same laws, regulations, and normative constraints placed on other groups within their class. Taking on a congregational form thus justifies and legitimates new religions within the context of American religious pluralism, providing room for new religious groups to practice and teach as they wish. A number of congregational and community studies establish that structural adaptation has indeed occurred and continues to occur (Warner and Wittner 1998; Ebaugh and Chafetz 2000a, 2000b; Yang and Ebaugh 2001a). New immigrant religious groups, be they Muslim, Buddhist, Hindu, Sikh, or Zoroastrian, adapt their communal religious lives and expectations to the congregational model dominant in the United States. A structural adaptation may promote cultural adaptations. Yang and Ebaugh (2001a) identify two primary forms of cultural change: a "return to theological foundations" for legitimacy; and a move toward tolerance and openness toward other religious groups.

Focusing directly on congregational developments has, nevertheless, obscured other aspects of immigrants' religious lives. The structural adaptation model tells us little about immigrants' religious pursuits outside congregational or community participation. These pursuits, including devotional, dietary, or hygienic practices, and observing rites of passage and rituals that do not easily "fit" the de facto Christian character of sacred time in America, pose issues and questions for immigrants about how they can, and how they should, practice their faiths. Although congregations and their leaders have many practical examples and ideas for helping negotiate these aspects of religious life, immigrants also use practices developed outside the congregation.

Learning how immigrants make choices about religious practice and negotiate these perceived necessities is certainly important in its own right. In addition, however, understanding such activities in light of participation in local congregational mosques and temples and other places of worship broadens our understanding of immigrant adaptations. We do not, therefore, argue that the structural adaptation model is incorrect. To the contrary: if historical studies and previous immigrant adaptations are any guide, such trends are to be expected (Dolan 1985; Kane 1994). Nevertheless, religious historians remind us that while previous immigrant religious groups drew upon dominant American organizational forms, they also developed (or imported) religious meaning, practices, and perspectives that altered the American religious landscape in both subtle and profound ways (Schmidt 1989; Joselit 1994; Orsi 1985). We have no reason to suspect that the introduction of "new" immigrant groups' religious expressions, daily experiences, and deeply rooted habits will have less of an impact on American culture or American religious organization in this current period than they did in the past.

The Complicating Perspective of Lived Religious Practice

Our perspective of immigrant religious experience couples structural adaptation and lived religion models. We take as a fact that the analytic boundary drawn between congregational religious life and daily religious practice has no clear analogue in the lives of most religious persons and can unnecessarily limit our analysis of influences between them.

"Lived religious practice" means more than the "private" and domestic religious practices of immigrants. While these are important sites of study as well, particularly for understanding the transmissions of culture and religion within families, our interest here is in aspects of religious devotion that occur in the public or semipublic regions of American life. These are the "regions" where immigrants think about how, or whether, to present their religious differences through choices in dress (for instance, wearing a veil, growing a beard, or wearing a turban) and choices regarding public devotion. These decisions should be construed as religious ones, as, for example, when a Pakistani cab driver considers whether or not to grow a beard. One such driver told us that growing a beard is one way to follow the Prophet's example, and is thus highly recommended. Yet he notes that not all Muslim taxi drivers do so, because as he tells us, wearing a beard draws passengers' attention to the driver's Muslim identity, and such attention often leads to unwanted verbal attacks on Islam. "Simple" issues of whether to wear a beard are, thus, wrapped in issues about what it means to be a good Muslim, and what it means to protect one's own self and integrity.

"Lived religion" does more than bring attention to daily practice. It emphasizes both the connections and fissures between "daily" decisions, such as whether to wear a beard, and congregational or community orthodox positions on such matters. "Lived religion" developed in response to the limitations of models that counterposed "popular" and "official" religion (Hall 1997; Bourdieu 1990). Such dualistic oppositions were difficult to sustain in empirical research as scholars rarely encountered individuals who exclusively practiced either popular or orthodox religion. Developing a model that took the variety of understood and habitual "lived" practices into account does more than surmount this false opposition between the "real" religion that happens in church and the "folk" religion that happens elsewhere. It also allowed scholars to express and analyze power dynamics with more complex models than either "resistance" or "acquiescence." Scholars thus pay more attention to the variety of cultural tools and practices developed by actors to make their way in the world (McNally 1997). Lived religion emphasizes ongoing negotiations between various orthodoxies and daily contingencies, beliefs and practices, and power groupings that make religion "lived" as such. This phenomenological position is interested in what people do with religious practice, "what they make with it of themselves and their worlds" (Orsi 1997, 7).

As we can see, this framework provides several additions to the structural adaptation model. Because it focuses on religious practices both inside and outside the congregational structure, an understanding of lived religion can incorporate a broader portrait of religion that includes how it is practiced and interpreted in daily life outside congregational structures (Bender 2003). Second, lived religion emphasizes understanding how groups "make sense" of the transformations and structures that they adopt, that is, how congregational life and structuring is also lived religious experience (Griffith 1998). In short, then, lived religion models allow researchers to interpret responses to change like acculturation and adaptation in ways that extend beyond dominant stories of "accommodation" and "resistance."

Muslim Taxi Drivers in New York City

Our study of "lived religion" focuses on the daily religious practices of Muslim taxi drivers in New York City. Currently, almost half of the twenty-three thousand active taxi drivers in New York City are from South Asia (Pakistan, Bangladesh, India). A majority of these drivers, according to Bhairavi Desai, director of the New York City Taxi Worker's Alliance

(NYCTWA), are from Pakistan and Bangladesh and are predominantly Muslim. Other Muslim drivers hail from West Africa, Eastern Europe, Turkey, and Afghanistan. We estimate that roughly half of New York City's yellow cab drivers are Muslim. We hasten to note, however, that as far as anyone can estimate, only a small percentage of New York City's Muslim population are taxi drivers (roughly 5 percent of an estimated population of 600,000).

We contacted observant Muslim drivers through the NYCTWA and interviewed seven men during October–November 2000. (Our plans to conduct further interviews in fall 2001 were put on hold by events in New York City.) All the cab drivers were immigrants: four have lived in New York City for three to five years; the others have each been in New York for almost fifteen years. Four of our respondents are Pakistani, two Bangladeshi, and one West African. Three drivers work the day shift and four work at night. Five drivers are married and two are single. Three of the married Pakistani drivers live apart from their wives and children, who have not emigrated. A significant number of each driver's extended family continues to live in their native country; drivers send a large portion of their earnings overseas. Excepting our West African respondent who lives in upper Manhattan, all the drivers live in Queens or Brooklyn.

According to the Muslim taxi drivers we spoke with, driving a cab provides an honest, though far from easy, means to make money. Taxi driving in New York City is a strenuous, low-paying occupation. Drivers are typically immigrants who have exhausted other options for earning a living in the city (Schaller 1994). A full-time driver working six or seven days a week makes an annual income of roughly $20,000. Drivers receive no Social Security or unemployment, health care, or other benefits (Kolsky 1998; Schaller 2001). The number of taxi cab medallions in New York City (authorizing a vehicle to pick up fares as a "yellow cab") is strictly limited by city government. The short supply (12,178 to be exact) places their market value at over $200,000. These high costs, coupled with the limited economic capital of most immigrant drivers, forces the majority to lease their cabs from a "fleet" owner, either by the day or on a long-term lease. Most taxi drivers lease a cab for a twelve-hour shift (typically from 5:00 A.M. to 5:00 P.M., or a night shift from 5:00 P.M. to 5:00 A.M.): drivers make an income only after their fares and tips have covered the lease fee and fuel costs. On a good day, a cab driver will pick up thirty to forty fares by cruising Manhattan's streets or at taxi stands at airports and in midtown. Drivers are required by law to take passengers anywhere they wish within city limits and cannot choose their passengers. This introduces chronic uncertainty into a cab driver's daily routine.

The uncertainty is heightened for Muslim drivers who profess an obligation to fulfill the command to pray five times each day. Muslim prayers are prescribed at particular times of the day, based on the position of the sun: at daybreak, just after high noon, in the midafternoon, at sundown, and once after dark. In Muslim countries, this temporal structure is part of the daily atmosphere like the weather. Prayer times are announced from minarets. The conditions in the United States are quite different. Most Muslims receive no such audible reminders. Also, though prayers may be said anywhere, Islam requires that the Friday afternoon prayer be performed in a mosque with other Muslims and an imam.[1]

Prayer must be performed in a clean space like a mosque, or in a place where activities counter to Muslim doctrine do not occur. A Muslim may also pray on ritually clean ground. As one driver observed, "The ground is clean because Allah made it." The ground, which includes its sidewalks, must have on it no visible signs of feces, spilled alcoholic beverages, or recent sexual acts.

A worshiper must be clean. Ritual cleanliness is usually achieved by washing with water; mosques provide space in which to wash. Third, prayers are composed of between two and four repetitions of a *rak'ah*, a liturgical module that includes oral recitations from the Qur'an in Arabic as the supplicant stands, bows, kneels, and prostrates twice. Finding a mosque at which to perform prayers is becoming easier, but the demands of driving a cab and the limited number of mosques in Manhattan make it extremely difficult for drivers to attend a mosque for each required prayer.

Muslim taxi drivers who wish to fulfill this last obligation and its ritual components must strategize how to perform these duties. In theory, cab driving allows Muslim men to set their schedules, so that they can make time for prayer in the middle of their workday. Religiously speaking, this gives Muslim cab drivers a distinct advantage over other Muslim immigrants who are day or manual laborers and who do not have so much control over their work hours or shifts (see Goldwasser 1998). Yet structuring time for prayer often comes at the expense of making a living. All the drivers we spoke with discussed this tension. They think deeply about where they will conduct their prayers, and how they will juggle their search for a suitable place to pray with the vicissitudes of fares' destinations. A Bangladeshi driver told us,

Taxi driving is very stressful, and the commission is tough on the drivers. It's hard to be as devoted as possible with so much stress. It can be hard for regular prayer. But there is also more freedom to take the time. Prayer is not just five times a day but all the time. It is a way of life. When we drive we always think about God. Everything we do. We start every day saying, "I do this in the name of God."

Without exception, the drivers we spoke with took seriously the injunction to pray. This did not mean that they all prayed with equal attention to ritual perfection, however. Although prayers may be performed in virtually any "clean" space, the drivers we spoke with, like most Muslims, thought it optimal to pray in mosques. As drivers told us, the question of whether to pray in a mosque is not one that arises much when they are in Pakistan or Bangladesh. It only becomes an issue in the United States, where mosques are few and far between and where the non-Muslim majority does not understand, or make ready accommodation for, those who wish to pray in the Muslim fashion. Some drivers managed to pray in mosques by limiting their work shifts (and income) so that they could pray the evening and morning prayers at home or in a mosque in their neighborhood. Day drivers admitted that they sometimes "double up" their prayers. One promises to God that he will "say [his] prayers together in the nighttime . . . [though] it's not really encouraged."

Taxi drivers keep mental maps of mosque locations in Manhattan. Several recited long lists. One Pakistani driver mentally mapped his places of prayer for us in relation to the routes he travels.

It depends on where my passenger is going at that time. If I'm near 96th Street, there is the mosque at 96th Street, Third Avenue. There's one on 72nd Street and York Avenue, but they've had some kind of problem there. Um—there is also one on Stanton Street, and . . . Street, and also one on 45 West Broadway, and—one is on Broad Street, on Broadway, . . . downtown, and, one is on 11th and 1st Avenue.

While the number of mosques in Manhattan has expanded rapidly in the 1990s (a current Muslim Student Association website lists twenty-two Manhattan *masajid,* both with and without imams), their number is still relatively small. Cab drivers feel this acutely on Fridays, when they try to fulfill the injunction to perform the Friday midday prayer at a mosque with an imam and forty Muslim men. After prayers, an imam or another person gives a talk (*khutba*), sometimes based on a Qur'anic passage. "The most important prayer of all is Friday prayer," a Pakistani driver impressed upon us. Others felt similarly, explaining that missing more than a few Friday prayers at the mosque would earn them God's punishment.

We asked the drivers how they make it to Friday prayers. Many day drivers take the day off or stop work early in order to return home in Queens or Brooklyn to attend services. One night driver likes his shift because it allows him to spend most of each Friday at the Islamic Cultural Center, Manhattan's largest mosque. He told us that he usually arrives at 11:30 A.M. for private prayers to "take a little time . . . [because] they read Al Qur'an for a while before the prayer" and then stays for most of the afternoon. He impressed upon us the importance of attending the *salah al-jum'ah*:

> I don't miss Friday mosque . . . I always go because God said, the Prophet said, that as a good Muslim, you can't miss unless you are sick. . . . If you just don't go to mosque, God will punish you . . . so Friday's a big day.

Those drivers who do not take Friday off but wish to fulfill this duty find parking to be "the toughest job," according to a Bangladeshi driver. Officials at the Islamic Cultural Center appear to be aware of this problem and apparently negotiated with the city to provide drivers with a special permit to double-park outside the mosque during busy prayer times. Some drivers find these parking permits to be a positive sign that the city government and police respect Islam. However, others stated that this goodwill is not shared by all of "New York's finest." Said one driver, we "still get a ticket. There used to be [more] allowance for having the [permit], but now [the police] give the ticket anyway."

Other drivers look for off-street parking: several have made a deal with the owners of a private parking lot behind the Islamic Cultural Center and pay a reduced fee during prayer periods. According to our informants, drivers also sometimes perform their prayers in this parking lot if there is no room in the mosque.

Other Strategies: Sidewalks and Prayer Places— Finding a Clean, Well-Lit Place

Despite the growing number of mosques in Manhattan, there are times when taxi drivers find that they cannot make it to a mosque in time to pray, or when they "forget" to pray until it is too late to make it to a mosque. (More than one driver noted that he misses the public reminders of prayer times announced from mosques' minarets in their home nations.) Two drivers reported that they had pulled over alongside the Brooklyn Queens Expressway after realizing they would not arrive at home or a mosque in time to complete their prayer. "Any time the time [to pray] comes you should stop right there and do your prayer." Another, following this dictum, said that he routinely prays in the back seat of his cab, even though this keeps him from performing the full, ritualized prayer. "God knows what is in my mind. . . . I can just take my shoes off in the back seat and I can perform, in the city, while I'm sitting in the car."

While several drivers state that they will pray on the New York City sidewalk, they exhibited varying degrees of comfort about performing their prayers in public. One Pakistani driver said that praying on the sidewalk, while completely acceptable, is not what he prefers, as the noise of the city makes it difficult for him to concentrate. Our West African respondent, in comparison, said that praying on the sidewalk does not make him uncomfortable "as long as [he] is not disturbing anybody and the place is clean." He sometimes becomes aware of the high noise level, which makes it difficult to concentrate, but nevertheless flatly stated that the street is often his choice, as "I can't lose the time" finding an adequate alternative. A Bangladeshi driver expressed a similar concern: time, rather than space, was of the essence. "It's not allowed to ever let the prayer time go. If you let the prayer time go, then you are guilty [before God]." Two drivers, however, refused to pray on the street under any circumstance. They prefer instead to miss the prayer, explaining that it is too difficult to find a clean place on the street, free from noise, to allow the concentration they feel is necessary to perform the prayers adequately.

Drivers likewise expressed some difference in opinion about ritual cleanliness of prayers that take place in the street. Espousing the most stringent position, one Bangladeshi driver related the rules, stating, "Anything you put on the floor should be clean and your body should be clean. Before you pray you have to [make ablutions] . . . gargle three times, three times water in the nose, water on the head, clean the arms and so on . . . then you are ready to pray." Accordingly, he believes that this makes prayer on the street difficult to conduct properly, as one would have to carry water and wash in the cab before praying on the street. Another driver, in contrast, told us that he performs his prayer on the street as long as he has not done anything to "break" his ritual cleanliness from the previous prayer. And yet another cited the rule that says that washing can be omitted where there is no water to be found (such as a desert or, he suggested, on the side of the Brooklyn Queens Expressway).

Two issues are at stake in drivers' considerations about praying on a New York City sidewalk. First, drivers expressed some concern over whether the street was clean, whether they could make themselves clean without a place to wash, or whether they could appropriately concentrate on the street. Better to pray on the street than in a space where activities prohibited by Islam might have occurred, one argued. He would not pray "in a bar because of the alcohol, and not in a motel either because other people have slept in that room." Another underlying concern centered on the problems of praying in a public space. We gathered from inferences drivers made that they were reticent to so publicly practice their faith by themselves. Every driver save our West African respondent expressed concern about how non-Muslims "perceived" them as terrorists at one point or another. They did not wish to individually attract more attention to their religion, if they could help it.

Taxi drivers face the reality of an inadequate number of mosques in which to pray, and find it less than satisfactory to pray on the street or in the back of their car. It is within this milieu that drivers (and in some cases, small business owners) create other semipermanent prayer spaces throughout the city. Drivers maintain prayer spaces at JFK and La Guardia airports, keeping prayer cloths and a Qur'an on hand for drivers to perform *salat*. One cab driver told us of a garage in downtown Manhattan that maintains space in a room where Muslim drivers regularly pray. Drivers also told us about semipermanent prayer spaces maintained in Bangladeshi, Pakistani, and other twenty-four-hour "ethnic" restaurants in Manhattan, some of which have been operating and known among drivers for more than fifteen years.

Restaurant prayer spaces are generally small, unassuming, and ad hoc. A "prayer space" might be the corner of a large stockroom, an area just inside the food preparation area, or a basement hallway. These sacred spaces coexist with the crumbling walls, boxes, crates, and cleaning supplies. A carpet may be kept rolled against a wall until needed for prayer and then unrolled and swept before the prayer. One exception to this model is the relatively extravagant space in one restaurant, where the owner completed a full basement renovation in 2000, installing an air conditioner, new carpeting and wallpaper, a bench, and prayer mats. While on vacation in Bangladesh he also purchased prayer caps and posters of translated Qur'an passages for the room. Renovations are also planned for the bathroom to facilitate ritual washing.

As far as we have learned, taxi drivers use these prayer spaces almost exclusively, and learn about them through word-of-mouth contacts. Restaurant prayer spaces are sometimes used by a regular group of drivers. At one Bangladeshi restaurant, a group of between fifteen and twenty Bangladeshi men conducts a nightly prayer session that begins at 2:00 A.M. On Thursdays, Fridays, and Saturdays, prayer is limited to the basic prayer ritual, taking between ten to fifteen minutes. During the remainder of the week, when business is a bit slower, the drivers spend more time at the restaurant, studying and discussing the Qur'an. Sometimes others will join them as well, particularly if there is a specific Qur'an text or issue that they are discussing, or if they are conducting a special "prayer for sickness."

Restaurant prayer places are certainly convenient, pragmatic solutions to the problem of where to pray in Manhattan. All the drivers we spoke to used restaurant prayer spaces from time to time. In all, we learned of the existence of more than a dozen restaurant prayer spaces in Manhattan. We imagine that there are more, given that such prayer spaces are easy to set up and, according to the drivers, are generally looked upon favorably by restaurant owners. Some drivers we spoke with used these spaces regularly, and even joined in Qur'an study groups with other drivers at these restaurants. Drivers, however, noted convenience as the main value of such spaces. Drivers can use the facilities, ritually wash, pray, and eat during the same stop.

Restaurant prayer spaces also "solve" other hurdles that Muslims (and other immigrants) face when they try to establish a regular meeting place in Manhattan, high rents being first among them. For instance, one mosque in midtown, funded largely by taxi drivers and street vendors, spends almost $10,000 per month to rent the basement of an office building (Sachs 1998). In comparison, restaurants and taxi drivers work out an arrangement whereby the space for prayer is "paid for" by the business that the drivers give the restaurant. One driver, speaking for others whom he knew also used prayer spaces, stated that they have "an unwritten agreement [with the owner] . . . that [the drivers] come here [to the restaurant], pray, use his space, and eat here . . . give him business." According to several drivers, this includes renting out the restaurants for birthday parties, celebrations, and even religious festivals. Drivers usually only purchase the carpeting, Qur'an, and maybe a bench or prayer caps that remain in the prayer space.

Restaurant owners view taxi driver business in a positive light and appear to be active participants in creating and maintaining these spaces. (Drivers explained that owners will benefit in heaven for helping taxi drivers find a place to pray.) Whatever the theological positions of owners, it is clear that taxi drivers provide a steady stream of customers throughout the early morning hours. In fact, there seems to be a small competitive market for attracting taxi drivers' prayers and business. One driver told us how for several years his prayer group used a stockroom at a restaurant a few doors down from the one where they currently meet. However, the space was a very small, narrow hallway in the basement and, as the group grew, they no longer fit in this space. Prayers became very difficult. Finally, the drivers began to look for a new place to pray, and the restaurant owner became angry, claiming that his business fell off.

One owner regularly allowed a group of men to stay at the restaurant during off-peak hours to play cards in order to maintain a constant group of customers. Many taxi drivers and other Muslims would not eat in the restaurant while the gamblers were there, our respondent told us, given that Islam forbids gambling. ("Gambling breaks up the community," he told us.) When the cook left and became the proprietor of a restaurant with an active prayer group, the other owner heard about the benefits that a prayer space might offer. He told the card players to leave and installed a prayer room in the basement. He has since attracted a sizable taxi driver business, more than compensating for the business lost from the card players.

Although drivers emphasize the practicality of the prayer spaces, they find more than a "practical" solution to the problem of finding a place to pray in these businesses. Eating and praying in these spaces reinforces the connections between community, national culture, and Islam for the drivers. The "taste" and flavor of home found in these small restaurants, particularly in the wee hours of the night, extend a kind of family to drivers. This becomes particularly true for drivers who live alone, or far away from their families. One driver drew the metaphoric connection between eating and praying concisely:

To keep yourself alive, you need to eat food. . . . The spirit [also] needs to stay alive with some kind of activity, and that is like saying prayer five times to keep your soul or spirit alive. The human being is a combination of body and soul and you have to take care of both. This is the meaning of ritual.

With few exceptions, drivers pray in restaurants of their own nationality. Restaurants themselves make their origins clear, both in the décor and food (they signal their Muslim origins by advertising "halal"). National sentiments were clearly displayed in one of the Bangladeshi restaurants we observed, for instance, as political posters in Bengali covered the walls. (The prayer space in the basement of this restaurant, likewise, contained signs that translated the "rules of Islam . . . from Arabic to Bengali," given because the drivers did not speak or read Arabic.)

In restaurants with prayer spaces, home, religion, and nationality come together in real ways. One group performed a wedding ceremony in its prayer space: the bride was a convert, and the group supported her conversion and helped arrange the party. "We work[ed] together, gather[ed] money, and made the festival." Another prayer space also provides room for a small but growing library of books on religious topics maintained by Bangladeshi drivers. Positioning prayer spaces in such close proximity to food seemed to underline the importance of hospitality within Islam for many drivers. As one Bangladeshi driver told us, over a plate of tandoori chicken,

[For] most of our culture, the food is very important. We have to have it; it is our culture, our custom. We are very happy to have good food. If we can entertain our guest with the food, we feel better.

Manhattan Mosques and Restaurant Prayer Spaces: Pan-Islamic and Cultural-Religious Institutions

Prayer spaces in ethnic restaurants are certainly interesting in their own right: they demonstrate the practical, innovative impulses of devout Muslims to continue their religious practices in spite of working conditions that make this difficult. Prayer spaces hold an important place in the lives of Muslim taxi drivers. They facilitate the practice of Islam in a crowded, busy city where it is sometimes difficult to reach a mosque during prayer hours. At the same time, prayer spaces provide nationally defined counterpoints to congregationally organized (and sometimes "multinational") mosques. In this light, prayer spaces emerge as an important aspect of drivers' full religious observance, experience, and identity.

According to the structural adaptation story, an immigrant Muslim group that wishes to establish a mosque must work within established legal parameters. At the very outset, issues of financing (Islam does not allow the use of loans or credit), incorporation, zoning issues, and so on present moments of "coercive" isomorphism that position the mosque within a field of (other) voluntary, relatively small, and autonomous religious groups (DiMaggio and Powell 1983). Groups wishing to establish successful mosques look to their American neighbors (both other mosques and other "religious" organizations) to see what works—that is, to see how a mosque is created where public prayers are not publicly announced and where the government does not fund congregational activities. Mosque leaders thus hire clergy (imams), formalize membership rosters and a weekly "schedule" of activities, place more emphasis on the Friday *khutba,* and offer social services and education (Badr 2000). Adopting (or adapting) a congregational structure allows Muslim groups to become "legitimate," at least when viewed from the perspective of the broader American culture. Such forms also help to dispel negative stereotypes (Williams 1988; Yang and Ebaugh 2001a).

These structural changes nevertheless alter the experience and reality of mosque participation for many immigrants. Within Muslim theology and practice, a mosque is a place where daily prayers are said, where teaching occurs in a weekly *khutba,* and where symbolic and practical understandings of Islamic universalism (the universal community of faith) are embodied. Mosques traditionally do not have formal membership rosters or professional "leaders" whose role it is to perform pastoral duties. Mosques are often maintained by the government or, in some cases, supported by a local community. A Muslim sense of "congregational" membership is, accordingly, quite broad. It is, according to Abusharaf, "exemplified by one's service to God, regardless of one's ethnicity . . . or class" (1998, 239). And, in the United States, mosques take on new purposes, meanings, and activities, which some immigrants consider antithetical to Muslim practice (Badr 2000). For instance, several researchers have commented on the growing participation of women as social service provision, education, and socializing frequently occurs within the vicinity of the mosque itself (Haddad and Lummis 1987; Badr 2000).

In addition to developing expanded purposes and drawing new groups of people (including women) into mosque activities, mosque officials in the United States often highlight or stress the heterogeneity of Muslim believers, even as they often emphasize the unity of Muslim practice. The Islamic Cultural Center, the most prominent and well financed of all New York City mosques, and a mosque that all cab drivers we spoke to attend from time to time, was founded by board members representing forty-six nationalities and consciously articulates a rhetoric of "pan-Islam." It uses English in all activities except for those that are conducted in Arabic. Even those mosques that are built and maintained by one national group can find themselves visited, or even overwhelmed by, newer immigrant groups from other nationalities. Many mosque communities, it appears, find themselves required to contend with issues of the relation of religion to national cultures, and insider and outsider status of various Muslim groups, in very close proximity (Ferris 1994; cf. Abusharaf 1998).

While scholars are correct that mosques in the United States embody the possibility of a universal brotherhood of Muslims (see Yang and Ebaugh 2001a), they also throw into relief some of the difficulties involved in enacting such a possibility. Practicing Islam with Muslims from diverse nations, observers have recently noted, forces Muslims to contend with the fact that different national groups have different habits in prayer, liturgy, and social organization—not to mention different spoken languages. Even though Islam stresses brotherhood and the universalism of its practice, local differences are apparent, and are often acutely experienced in local American communities. As one might expect, some interpretations of Islam and the role of a mosque within it are more conservative than others. A mosque's community thus often faces issues surrounding what constitutes orthodox practice and who determines such practice—issues that do not arise in more culturally homogeneous contexts. These issues are also often coupled with questions about what languages to use in services, in addition to Arabic (Badr 2000; Ferris 1994; Haddad and Lummis 1987; Abusharaf 1998; Kelley 1994).

One response within some mosques has been to work toward establishing distinctions between "authentic" Muslim and "cultural" practices. In other words, Muslims in the United States have taken up the work of separating "what is religious from what is cultural." Not surprisingly, however, any attempt to establish a true, authentic Islam inevitably creates a contentious arena wherein different groups lay claim to their own national and cultural practice as "legitimate" (Haddad and Lummis 1987). Thus,

while separating "the religious from the cultural" will undoubtedly continue as a rallying cry for uniting Muslim communities, it is also a rhetoric
highly charged with implications for social orderings within Muslim communities (Badr 2000; Ebaugh and Chafetz 2000a; Kelley 1994). Mosques,
like other religious communities in the United States, become sites where
multiple groups contend over the meaning of what actions and activities
are correct (Becker 1999; Marty 1994).

   While the rhetoric of separating the cultural from the religious in Islam
creates contention within a multinational American mosque, it also com-
bats negative American stereotypes of Islam as a violent religion and Muslims as violent people. Separating taints of national identity from "true"
Islam allows Muslims to develop a story of tolerance and openness. Practicing "brotherhood" often means employing English as a mosque's language, which constitutes both symbolic and practical steps toward creating a welcoming atmosphere for second-generation Muslims, Muslims
from other nations, and even curious onlookers.

   With such forces challenging "congregational" mosques in Manhattan,
restaurant prayer spaces become particularly notable. Unlike public
mosques, restaurant prayer places are unequivocally defined along national lines. Although there are no "rules" barring a Pakistani driver from
using a Bangladeshi prayer place, taxi drivers indicated that such uses were
exceptions rather than the rule. A Bangladeshi driver who only prays in
Bangladeshi restaurants commented that the space was "mainly made for
the Bangladeshi people, but anybody [is] welcome." On rare occasions, a
Pakistani or "Black Muslim" driver would use the Bangladeshi prayer
space, but only if that individual missed the prayer at a mosque and was
driving in the area. When we asked our West African respondent whether
he knew about, or had used, restaurant prayer places and mentioned the
name of a Bangladeshi restaurant, he replied: "Oh, yeah, yeah . . . it's for
Pakistanis . . . there's also an African restaurant [in Harlem] with a little
[prayer space]. . . . I go over there sometimes."

   Restaurant prayer places thus provide legitimate space for Muslim taxi
drivers to embrace both national and religious identities. Food and eating
practices are integral aspects of restaurant prayer spaces. Sharing food and
prayer recombines aspects of devotion and daily life that are parsed as separate parts of life (specifically, the "cultural" and the "religious") in
mosques. Likewise, drivers discuss and read the Qur'an in their native languages, socialize and discuss social news together, and eat food that is
most familiar to them. They can, thus, practice Islam and its rituals as they

know best, without having to think about separating the "cultural from the religious." These habitual practices and activities also include the de facto exclusion of women. There is no discussion or concern about whether women should or could participate in these spaces, which cater to members of an almost entirely male profession.

National exclusivity in prayer places does not indicate drivers' general unwillingness to gather with other Muslims. As we have noted, the drivers we spoke with constantly expressed pleasure in the diversity of the mosques they attended in Manhattan and the outer boroughs. The existence of such nationally demarcated religious alternatives appears to allow taxi drivers to better enjoy and participate in the pan-Islamic realities they encounter as they visit mosques throughout the city. In frequenting restaurants with dedicated prayer spaces, taxi drivers can immerse themselves in a sympathetic network of immigrants with whom they share ideas, experiences, and the study of religious issues. They can eat, talk, and pray in a space that is unequivocally identified with their national home. Some drivers we interviewed have used restaurant prayer places for more than ten years. These places have become a very important part of their ability to maintain a connection to their national identities.

By viewing the prayer places as an established strategy through which taxi drivers live their religion and culture, we see how complementary "lived religion" models can be to institutionally grounded structural adaptation models. Taxi drivers can commit themselves to developing pan-Islamic sensibilities and experiences while simultaneously maintaining homogeneous religious and national communities in which they can feel "at home." Prayer spaces and mosques thus supplement each other both religiously and culturally, and play off each other as taxi drivers make a place for themselves in Manhattan.

Further Considerations

The story that we tell calls scholars to pay greater attention to the range of religious practices immigrants negotiate through daily life and to incorporate such a view into studies of congregations. Our perspective extends the boundaries of discussion past the realm of immigrant congregations, which, while important and central in the lives of religious immigrants, nevertheless do not fully encompass the extent of immigrants' religious lives. Religious and national identities are clearly marked, although not so clearly or obviously practiced, within the myriad interstices of daily life. New York City's immigrant taxi drivers work hard to establish ways to continue to be religious in a country where they are by all accounts minorities in every sense. Their activities prompt further questions about the relationships between congregational and lived religious expressions of new immigrants. We address some of these below.

Are prayer spaces "nascent" congregations? We do not believe that restaurant prayer spaces are protocongregations. Rather, we understand these spaces as complementary institutions that will continue to have important value in the lives of Muslim taxi drivers. Several important differences mark prayer places as different from congregations or "nascent" congregations. First, as the spaces are maintained within the space of for-profit businesses, drivers view these spaces as a "service" that a restaurant provides. Drivers distinguish the restaurant prayer spaces both from congregational mosques and from "mosques without imams," a distinction that is well in place in Muslim nations. The drivers place "prayer spaces" in a different category from mosques proper, both in discussion with us and, it seems, in practice (for instance, one group performed a wedding in their prayer space, a ritual that is not typically held within a mosque) [Badr 2000]). All the taxi drivers we spoke with attend or are even members of congregational mosques. Aside from late-night prayer sessions that happen at the restaurants, drivers expressed a preference for praying in mosques. Restaurant prayer spaces are not suitable substitutes for the Friday afternoon prayers, which they are required to attend with a quorum of at least forty men. Furthermore, we have no evidence that taxi drivers see the prayer spaces as stepping-stones to establishing non-restaurant-based mosques.

Restaurant prayer spaces allow drivers to fulfill specific ritual obligations through their workdays. They are the product of drivers' conscious efforts to transfer and reinterpret the importance of ritual devotion in a country where they are members of a religious minority. All the restaurant spaces we learned of are located in Manhattan, where drivers find most of their business. While this does not "prove" the nonexistence of similar prayer spaces in the outer boroughs, it suggests that restaurant prayer spaces represent practical, innovative solutions to performing specific ritual requirements in a non-Muslim society. Thus, despite some superficial similarities to congregations, such prayer places present an alternative, divergent model of religious activity—that also happen to provide a counterpoint to the trends in congregational, pan-Islamic mosques throughout New York City.

Do prayer spaces provide cultural or social resources to drivers? Students of civil society argue that active participation in small groups and organizations (including congregations, sodalities, and mutual aid societies) allow participants to develop social capital that can be translated or transferred to other settings (Verba, Schlozman, and Brady 1995). Using this framework, the question arises whether restaurant prayer places help drivers develop resources for self-expression and action within the other "publics."

We believe that making a strong argument for flourishing social capital in these prayer spaces is premature. It is certainly the case that the restaurants act as important gathering points and places for exchange of information about the trade. Night drivers share information, such as tips on how to deal with the Taxi and Limousine Commission, while eating and socializing. Likewise, the prayer and study groups allow drivers to maintain aspects of religious identity and practice that are often curtailed in the "public sphere" of congregational, multinational mosques. We also sense that these spaces are particularly crucial for this subset of immigrants that has very few material or social resources to draw upon. Nevertheless, the taxi drivers we spoke with do not seem to actively participate (or wish to participate) in the agenda-setting aspects of the mosques they attend. Prayer spaces develop for ritual reasons, and thus are not easily compared with social clubs, small groups, or mutual aid societies adopted by earlier immigrant groups. Prayer spaces represent a novel organizational form in the United States.[2]

By the same measure, it is clear that taxi drivers' religious practices do more than preserve national differences within American Islamic communities. For instance, while restaurant prayer places construct certain kinds of national identity, various other activities, including maintaining and using prayer spaces in airports and praying at a number of different mosques through their weekly rounds, make Muslim drivers prime carriers of pan-Islamic ideals and practices. Taken as a whole, then, freestanding prayer spaces provide drivers with the ability to develop resources and innovations that complicate trends toward "Americanization" identified within the more familiar models of structural adaptation.

Do the peculiarities of New York City and its Muslim population limit the generalizability of these observations? While we have little evidence at this time about the existence of restaurant prayer spaces in other cities and towns, at least one Pakistani restaurant in Chicago allows taxi drivers to both eat and pray (Sheridan 1997). We have no further examples of this kind, but given that restaurant prayer spaces are not "public" mosques, we also do not take a lack of reportage to signal its nonexistence.

As necessity is the mother of invention, we expect that Muslim immigrants may also work to establish other innovative spaces and responses so that they can practice their religion in the United States, transforming it in the process. Restaurant prayer spaces hardly exhaust the possibilities for such innovations. We also expect that the more public of these, including those at airports, will be important locations for conflicts and education about public Muslim practice. For instance, a 1998 request by Muslim drivers to maintain an enclosed space for prayers in the waiting area of the Denver International Airport was met with opposition by airport officials. The airport stated that taxi drivers wishing to pray should enter the airport and use its prayer space (touted as the first Islamic prayer space in a U.S. airport). Otherwise, they could pray outside, in the elements. Denver taxi drivers, sounding like their New York compatriots, argued that this would take too much time from their workday, and was therefore not practical. Muslim drivers have faced similar opposition to constructing prayer spaces at Reagan International Airport in Washington, D.C., and at the Minneapolis airport (Davis, P. 1999; Furst 1999).

Conclusion

Muslim taxi drivers in New York are religious innovators, establishing, sometimes with the assistance of restaurant owners, a number of prayer places where they can fulfill their felt duties to pray five times daily. These spaces supplement immigrants' activities in mosques around the city and also subtly challenge the story of "pan-Islam" told by the drivers themselves. Prayer spaces represent, at one important level, drivers' attempts to negotiate and find space for religion and to redraw the boundaries between public and private practice.

This case of religious innovation viewed through the perspective of lived religion challenges the current focus in the literature on congregational adaptations by immigrants. This focus glosses over innovative aspects of immigrant religion that develop as immigrants engage and negotiate religious practice in public. If "religion" is an amalgam of conscious and unconsciously articulated rules, rituals, and expectations, all of which must be negotiated by immigrants, then our perspective on immigrants' religious lives necessarily extends beyond institutional walls. In other words, this perspective reinforces the interpretation of the congregation itself as public space where contention and struggle over appropriate practice occurs. In this case, while some mosques "look like" (Protestant) congregations seen from some (structural) vantage point, community discourse about the meaning of "authentic" Islam positions mosques as one particular site of discussion and practice of what it means to be Muslim.

Although it is beyond the scope of this chapter, future studies must investigate how innovations such as restaurant and airport prayer spaces alter the dominant congregational form—not just for the Muslims who adopt it, but also for observers outside the Muslim community. Daily religious devotions of the newest immigrants, insofar as they take place within daily life and outside the boundaries of congregational activity, will ultimately be a major site of religious learning and interchange for both immigrants and their neighbors.

NOTES

We thank John Stratton Hawley, John Schmalzbauer, Robert Wuthnow, and Neguin Yavari for their generous comments.

1. Any place where prayer is said by Muslims is technically speaking a mosque. Indeed, some of our respondents used the word (or the Arabic equivalent, *masjid*) colloquially in this sense. In this chapter, we mean "mosque" to specify an established space dedicated to prayer, as is typically found in Muslim nations and in the United States, and make note of the instances when our respondents mean otherwise.

2. The possible exceptions are the long-standing gatherings of *minyan* (ten Jewish men) for afternoon prayer (*mincha*). The Orthodox Union publishes a web directory of where the devout can gather for prayer in the New York region. *Minchas* in New York take place in temples and Jewish day schools, but also in law professors' offices and 47th St. jewelers' boiler rooms.

3

Paradoxes of Media-Reflected Religiosity among Hindu Indians

Ashakant Nimbark

This chapter explores some paradoxical and puzzling patterns of revived religiosity among nonresident Indians (NRIs). The focus of the chapter is on Hindu Indians in America. I critically review the ethnic media of NRIs to find out whether their media is a mirror or a modifier of their community. My general question is: Does the ethnic media simply reflect the shifting characteristics of a community or does it modify them? More specifically, does the NRI ethnic media serve as a mirror of the obvious shifts in the mind-set of Hindu Indians in America, or does it contribute to the process of this community's increasing desecularization?

I am inclined to say both, based on:

1. a content analysis of assorted NRI media in the New York City area; and
2. subsequent ethnographic observations and interviews at several Hindu temples in the New York City area.

The Asian Indian Media

More and more people belonging to multilinguistic ethnicities use their own intracommunity media (newspapers, magazines, radio, TV, VCR, and the Internet) to supplement or even substitute for the information they get from the mainstream American media (Hsu 2002). The ethnic media of newly arrived immigrants from non-Western societies differs signifi-

Lamp-offering (*arati*) for a memorial service at a small Hindu temple in Corona, Queens, New York City/Ashakant Nimbark.

cantly from the media of previous generations of Europeans. Whereas European immigrants followed similar Judeo-Christian faiths, spoke European languages, and were largely white, their non-Western Asian counterparts are racially, linguistically, and religiously quite different. Further, whereas previous generations of Asian immigrants mainly used the print media supplemented by postal correspondence for intracommunity communication, the present generation is truly multimedia savvy. The current Asian ethnic media incorporates both long-established formats and styles as well as more recent print technologies. The new media tends to be glossier, more colorful, and have more ads. The new radio, TV, and other computerized programs are more varied, more sophisticated, and more mass-produced than the older media, catering to the professional and cultural needs of their communities.

The media designed for South Asian, predominantly Hindu, immigrants fulfills the functions of informing, entertaining, and community networking for its users. What is remarkable is the extent to which this media has increased its religious content and intertwined religion with all its functions.

Religion and the Function of Informing

First-generation immigrants keep in touch with sociocultural and econopolitical developments back home, since for them being out of sight is not out of mind. This need seems to be both diminishing and intensifying at the same time. Many NRIs are professionalized, having neither sufficient time nor the desire to sift through the American print and electronic media to see how their homeland is being covered. According to recent observations, the overwhelming majority of Asians turn to their own ethnic media for news and views about Asia.

Over twenty newspapers and magazines in the New York City area cater to the information needs of NRIs. Other cosmopolitan areas such as Philadelphia, Chicago, Washington, D.C., San Francisco, and Los Angeles have their own Asian Indian media. This media has news summaries, editorials, letters to the editor, and above all advertisements for goods and services ranging from humble incense sticks to pricey late model TVs and from babysitting to religious services.

Ethnic groups such as Hindu Indians seem to be defying the traditional image of America as a great melting pot and instead rely on their own sources of information and advertising. According to a recent survey, a large majority (84 percent) of Asian Americans and other respondents said that they get their information not from the mainstream American media, but through ethnic newspapers, magazines, radio, and television (Chan 2002). The readers, viewers, and listeners of the ethnic media define themselves as a special ethnic community. The process of depending on the ethnic media seems to be intertwined with the process of underutilizing the supposedly more worldly secular and inclusive mainstream media partly because of insufficient time to use nonethnic sources of information but more importantly because of the ethnic media's ability to define their patrons in an exclusive way. This process relates particularly to the ethnicity-focused ads, notably the ethnic-language ads which are preferred over the English-language media ads. NRIs seem to be increasingly exposed to ads inviting them to religious celebrations and special weekend programs which feature "imported" religious leaders and dignitaries. Widely circulated publications such as *India Abroad* and *News India* (published in New York and read in Asia, Africa, Europe, the Middle East, and Australia) have been noticeably adding to the pages on religious worship, "spirituality," and ethnic festivals.

When I compared current issues with those twenty years back, I found that:

1. the pages and columns on religious and spiritual activities have more than doubled;
2. there is much more news about the increasing number of temples being planned and built, and the ads soliciting donations, tax free contributions, and pledges from their patrons have substantially increased;
3. the signatories for the "Appeals" to support religious celebrations have diversified and vastly multiplied and now include community leaders and successful professionals, whereas previously some publications drew a line between secular and sacred appeals and only hard-core believers signed the sacred appeals.

Likewise, the NRI media in one generation has gone from being lukewarmly religious to becoming enthusiastically faith-based. The letters to the editor and editorials reflect heated debates about "our rich religious heritage" and a preference for an unabashed Hindu identity over being a racialized U.S. minority and what is dismissively referred to as the "pseudo-secularism" of NRIs who are neither traditional nor truly modern in their beliefs but are blindly emulating the West at the expense of their own rich cultural heritage.

The Merger of the Entertainment and Religious Narratives

Previously, "entertainment" and "religion" dwelt in different columns, on separate pages, and aimed at specific targets. But they have been gradually merged so that today religious values dominate entertainment values. Music, dance, and theatrical performances are increasingly sponsored by desecularized community leaders and held in religious temples or spiritual retreats. Secular Indian Americans now have the nightmarish fear that all "cultural" events will have to take place in well-funded and spacious faith-based sites and be validated by their orthodox organizers who will reduce the secular elements to some "art for art's sake" program. A desecularized media is redefining "pure" or secular art forms as subservient to "purification" by much larger and more powerful "spiritual" religious organizations.

Religion and the Networking Function

While all ethnic media strive to network their audiences, the NRI media, mostly newspapers (as well as videoconferences and the Internet), are especially successful in providing religiously tinged "matrimonial" services. Aptly called the "chota bazaar," or mini market, these columns bring together single men and women searching for stable, permanent partnerships, though they have begun including short-time friendships. These print and Internet media-generated matrimonials present a set of ironies. True, they are very useful, but they are also extremely retrogressive. The retrogressive tendencies in the matrimonial ads include the revival of caste connections, a craze for light skin, and patriarchal authority. Many parents, especially fathers, continue to solicit detailed correspondence complete with recent full-length photographs and authentic horoscopes from the parents of prospective brides and grooms for an "early marriage" and "decent wedding."

In previous decades advertisers considered themselves to be progressively departing from the traditional norm of arranged and intracaste marriages. Ironically, current advertisers seem to be departing from the woes of nonarranged "love marriages" and re-embracing traditionally endogamous marriages as a retreat from secular, intercaste and self-chosen marriages which don't work. They are returning to the traditional practice of orthodox but predictably safe and retrogressively caste-based and religion-specific—and therefore (hopefully) more stable—marriages. These popular columns and on-line matrimonials may seem contemporary but a closer look at these "new" practices disclose the hidden—and not so hidden—messages of persistent promale double standards, fatalism, and the resurgence of racism ("fair skin is an asset"), religiosity ("high-caste Hindu from a respected family"), and class hierarchy (emphasis on income and status, deemphasizing open and free choice). In the matrimonial columns many male senior citizens refer to themselves as "experienced, resourceful, and youthful." Mature women describe themselves as "extremely fair and very beautiful" and "in the fifties but look like thirties."

As a major tool for ethnic networking, the NRI print media has come a long way from the lone weekly *India Abroad,* founded by Gopal Raju in New York in 1972, to at least fifty English-language news weeklies, magazines, and specialized journals currently published from different locations: California, Chicago, Washington, D.C., and Florida. Additionally, there are over twenty publications in regional Indian languages: Hindi, Gujarati, Punjabi, Bengali, and Telugu, to name a few. The specialized magazines discuss films, sports, matrimonials, and religion. More and more periodicals have been circulated among the devotees of various faiths such as the old and inclusive pan-Hinduism and the "new" sects which are increasingly fragmented and scattered, as are their followers. A wide array of monthly and weekly newsletters and colorfully illustrated magazines are being published by religious organizations and sent to their members. In a cyber-savvy community of Hindu Indians, numerous sects have their own web pages and radio stations.

The seasoned newspapers, like *India Abroad* and some of its close rivals—*News India, India Post,* and *India Tribune*—enjoy a broad readership. *India Abroad,* for instance, is printed in six editions and claims to be the largest Indian newspaper outside India. It is believed to have a readership of over six million, as its subscribers include NRIs "in at least twenty-five countries." The "Religion" pages of this paper have doubled and perhaps tripled. The "Letters to the Editor" column, too, has been expanded to include lively debates between the secular critics and their faith-based opponents who seem to be increasingly dominant.

After the first wave of print media, a second wave of radio programs appeared. Radio programs also contain a peculiar blend of religious-spiritual discourse and legal-commercial advice. The NRI-oriented radio stations offer firsthand home news and classical and movie music from old and new Bollywood films. Some long-standing radio stations have been run by faculty and students from India on major campuses such as MIT, Berkeley, Ann Arbor, Chicago, Columbia, and Philadelphia. Other radio programs are sponsored by South Asia–directed travel agencies, grocery stores, immigration attorneys, and investment advisors. Apart from worldly music and discussion, these radios offer their NRI listeners heavy doses of religious chants and hymns.

Among Hindu Indians there seems to be a great need for movie music as well as religious prayers. More and more devotional music has been influenced by the widely popular rhythms and tunes of Bollywood songs. Like old wine in new bottles, devotional prayers are presented in popular filmy musical scores. The nostalgic need for film lyrics in devotional music has increased remarkably among NRI listeners. More and more audiocassettes and audiodiscs are regularly used in their homes and automobiles, and a large proportion of this musical fare is devotional. Radio also provides guidance in nonmaterial matters such as auspicious days for religious celebrations, housewarmings, and weddings.

The third wave of television media presents unusual promise as well as problems for this ethnic community, as it does around the entire world. Television programs for the NRI community are of very uneven quality and coverage. The forty-year-old TV program *Vision of Asia,* started by a New York physician, Dr. Banad Vishwanath, and Satya Vishwanath, was a valuable source of information and provided abundant entertainment, in addition to popular movies and religious discourses. Subsequently there emerged a host of TV programs featuring elaborate religious rituals along with full-length Bollywood movies, fashion parades, cooking lessons, and VIP interviews. They featured the widely successful religious epic television serials—the *Ramayana* and *Mahabharata*—which were widely viewed in India during the 1980s and 1990s. These religious programs contain a very effective blend of ancient Hindu beliefs and modern television technologies. The ancient mythological stories of good versus evil were effectively produced for mass TV audiences by mixing old miracles with new electronic wizardry. Many media observers have pointed to a link between these successful TV serials and the emergence in India of a religious right-wing political party: the Bharatiya Janata Party, popularly called the BJP.

Television programming for NRIs has evolved from the one-hour-once-a-week of the 1960s and 1970s to around-the-clock presentations today with a smorgasbord of mega-multichannel cable networks and satellite dish televising of India-imported popular shows and music, music, and more movie music. The current growth of TV programs for the NRI community in America has obvious parallels to the phenomenal upsurge of this medium in India during the past twenty years. There, millions of viewers found the government-controlled and rationed token TV replaced by a virtual feast of more than a hundred channels. Ironically, though, senior citizens and weekend visitors in America who were previously engaged in social gatherings and outdoor activities might now be heavily absorbed in nostalgic (and solitary) viewing of old movies or religious dramas. Every grocery store in every town where there is a sizable NRI community carries inexpensive audio and videocassettes and legitimately prepared as well as pirated tapes on secular and sectarian subjects. Living in insulated suburban homes or crowded city apartments, such viewers have become addicted to TV in general and religious or quasi-religious programs in particular. They are responding to boredom, an unfavorable climate, nostalgia, and the resurgence of religiosity. The old orthodoxy of supernatural beliefs thus coexists gloriously with new electronic gadgets in this community.

A Content Review of Obsessions and Paradoxes Portrayed in NRI Media

A quick overview of the NRI ethnic media reveals three separate but interrelated obsessions among Hindu Indians. All the obsessions exhibit paradoxical attitudes and behavior, wherein the sacred coexists with the secular, spiritualism gets along with materialism, and otherworldly concerns intertwine with this-worldly ones. In each case the former seems to be taking over the latter.

I reviewed the news headlines, ads, editorials, and letters in well-circulated newspapers such as *India Abroad* and *News-India* from New York City, *India-Tribune* from Chicago, and *India-West* from California. I also assessed the content of elaborately published and attractively designed magazines such as *Little India* from Pennsylvania and *India Currents* from California, NRI radio programs and *desi* (native) TV. I also regularly checked websites such as http://www.hinduismtoday.com, http://www.hindunet.org, and http://www.templepujari.com. Additionally, I reviewed a few of the most important *desi* movies produced in India for overseas audiences and those produced in America. The Bollywood blockbusters produced in Bombay targeting the NRI include *Dilwale Dulhaniya Ley Jayenge* (wherein a rich but spoiled Indian playboy is won over by a religious country girl in rural India), *Lagaan* (wherein some humble villagers defeat the British in a cricket match), and *Devdas* (wherein a talented poet becomes alcoholic and self-destructive).

Recent Hollywood movies for NRIs include *ABCD* (American born, confused *desi*), *Monsoon Wedding* (wherein a joint family faces unforeseen conflicts while celebrating a lavish wedding party), and *Guru* (wherein an Indian con man presents himself as a savior).

I found at least three major obsessions among NRIs.

1. Sacred-Secular Contradiction

An older generation of social scientists assumed that modern technology and urbanization would weaken religious beliefs and orthodox practices in favor of rational and scientific attitudes and behavior. However, recent writers such as Raymond Williams and Peter Berger have challenged this precept and demonstrated that the shock of abrupt technological change and the alienation caused by modernization in fact create a *greater* need for religiosity (Berger 1999). Instead of abandoning their faith in the process of assimilation, recent immigrants are re-embracing their old beliefs and finding solace in religious worship and sacred rituals. Hindu Indians are a case in point. Although they are fascinated by their new experiences in this land, the fear of losing their roots and the overprojection of amoral and immoral behavior onto "Western" secularism causes them to reconnect with the traditions of the land they left. A review of the NRI media points to the fallacy of the sacred-secular dichotomy, especially in the "Letters" column. The letters consistently show that well-educated and widely traveled readers defend religious views and traditional practices. Likewise, the advertisements show redesigned artifacts of religious rituals side by side with new technological gadgets. Indeed, ads for the stores on the crowded streets of Jackson Heights (a community in New York City's borough of Queens) remind NRIs of the streets in India where one can go to a Butala Emporium and find all sorts of appurtenances for worship: *puja* boxes—the portable rectangular shrines for private homes, astrological charts, sacred sandalwood incense sticks, religious texts, and numerous audio and video cassettes of prayers and chanting. In a store adjacent to the Butala in Jackson Heights one can find the latest models of electronic gadgets. The ancient prayers and devotional songs will be played on pricey, ultramodern stereo systems in the homes of the many professionals of this community.

2. Spiritual-Material Dilemma

The NRI print and audiovisual media constantly reflects Hindu Indians' dual obsession with nonmaterialistic, spiritual, and broadly religious values together with their constant preoccupation with monetary matters. The lavish religious and commercial advertisements vouch for this dual preoccupation. In the print ads, there is a great craze for material possessions. Hindu Indians seem to be buying, owning, and hoarding more and more precious jewelry, bars made of pure gold and studded diamonds. Rows upon rows of jewelers do a brisk business in shops located near the temples and religious meeting places where great emphasis is placed on spiritualism, nonpossession, generosity, and the rejection of the evils of greed, competitiveness, and exhibitionism. As one approaches any of the dozen Hindu temples in Flushing, Queens, the antimaterialistic discourses of the especially imported priests and swamis are simultaneously assaulted by the screeching sounds of expensive automobiles and the vista of glittering jewelry. While entering or exiting these pious places, devotees seem to be busy showing off their latest acquisitions—from the latest electronic gadgets to the newest and finest fashions. While singing the songs of their antimaterialistic and spiritual values, NRIs seem to be preoccupied with making money and more money, planning their move from owning a Nissan to owning a Honda, and thence to a Lexus, a BMW, a Mercedes Benz, and, ultimately, a Rolls Royce. How do they do this? One witty but observable trait among many NRIs is to earn in dollars but spend in rupees—to work hard and save for the rainy day: a case of Protestant ethics among these non-Protestants!

These spiritual-material dilemmas are depicted in the recent colorful and eloquent PBS documentary *Desi*. After viewing the successful careers and rags-to-riches stories of many NRIs, you can't help but see that this community is obsessed with material possession while simultaneously it is glorifying its unique cultural tradition which is based on spirituality and the denial of materialism.

3. Otherworldly–This-Worldly Dichotomy

The NRI media is heavily preoccupied with images of the "other world," the state of Nirvana in which the endless cycle of birth, death, and rebirth finally ends. These images are seen in the movies when the hero and heroine, after a series of worldly setbacks, reach the point of ultimate resolution—no more worldly bothers, no more incarnations. Hindu holy men and women provide vivid images of this "end of the road" final step. They scoff at the worldly worries, anxieties, and other human frailties which afflict mortal men and women but melt away when one merges with the cosmic unity, the point of final liberation. Numerous plays, songs, dances, and stories portray the conflict between this-worldly evil versus other-worldly goodness, this-worldly temptation and hatred versus otherworldly selflessness and love. The print and electronic media regularly illustrate these themes through moralistic tales symbolic dramatizations of war in which otherworldly virtues conquer this-worldly vices.

The neo-Hinduized media directly reflects and indirectly justifies this conquest, depending on which medium we are approaching. The songs and stories depicted in colorful cartoons and CD-ROMs are in great demand by parents eager to expose their children to them. When I interviewed the owners of Butala, the largest multilevel store for Hindu paraphernalia, they told me that Hindu parents are worried that their children may lose their cultural roots by being overassimilated into American society, the source of the many "evils" depicted in the films and books sold in their store. Yet, they also told me that in addition to the religious publications they sell, other sought-after books and magazines pertain to real estate, investment, taxes, legal issues—and cooking.

This paradox of the otherworldly–this-worldly messages conveyed simultaneously makes me wonder whether these neo-Hinduized patrons are seeking success in this world by building an equity in condo and home ownership while searching for otherworldly peace by building elegant temples.

The NRI Media-Temple Circle

The NRI media has vastly increased its announcements of major fund-raising activities by NRIs for the planning, building, and maintenance of lavish Hindu temples on American soil. Further, the media claims that these temples have come to represent much more than places for worship. They perform a wide variety of functions for their devotees (Petievich 1999).

In interviews the NRI say that they initially used their media in a rather shallow way. They were entertained and only mildly interested in its religious dimensions. However, their visits to temples became crucial in moving them from being sympathetic viewers of religion in the ethnic media to being community-focused Hindus. Thereafter, the ethnic media served to intensify their temple experience.

At present, there are over fifty Hindu temples in the Greater New York area, and several more are being planned as the NRI community expands and diversifies. The Hindu temple in Flushing, Queens, is probably the oldest and most resourceful in this area, but other temples, such as the Swaminarayan temple, have been attracting increasing numbers of devotees from different language groups and/or regions. Temple-building activities require not only donations but also a steady supply of priests and caretakers who perform a wide variety of community functions ranging from childbirth ceremonies to funerals, from the cradle to the grave. A typical temple day might include morning, afternoon, and evening *pujas* wherein the idols of Hindu gods are offered sacred food and devotional prayers. Although temple structures and functions have to adjust to the local realities of climate, economy, and culture, the adjustment process is smoothed along by lavish donations from an affluent ethnic group.

Devotees visit the temples for nonreligious purposes such as bridal showers, birthday parties, weddings, and celebration of the Festival of Colors (Holi), the Festival of Lights (Diwali), and the birthdays of major deities. Even those who might have been nonbelievers and skeptics at the outset tend to be influenced by their temple visits and gradually become regular visitors and generous donors to the temples.

College and university students who are, of necessity, living apart from their families and friends are inclined to visit places where they expect to find others "sailing in the same boat." Professionals who wish to escape their busy work schedules, and housewives who want to socialize away from home, are also potential temple visitors. Some who were secular in India are lured to the cozy comfort of a "home away from home." And there are many cases of former nonbelievers becoming ardent believers, and skeptics becoming faithful devotees. This new affiliation, while involving a compromise with other secular values and this-worldly involvements, does offer some trade-offs—all of which come at a price.

First, there is the hope that temple visits will keep devotees away from worldly temptations and "unhealthy" habits. New devotees seem to have been influenced by their selective biases and exaggerated focus on features of modern Western and especially American society such as crime, drugs, and broken homes. Herein lies a real paradox: the nonproblematic and "desirable" aspects of the host society remain unknown to the new converts because the time and resources which could have been spent in exploring these areas are heavily committed to the temples. If weekdays keep them professionally busy, evenings devoted to an increasingly nationalistic and Hindu-orientated ethnic media and weekends spent with their own cohorts, there is simply no time, money, or other resource left for any extracommunity exploration. The price paid for their newfound faith is often a "new" mind-set which combines "old" orthodoxy, self-isolationism, and self-congratulation.

Second, there is an element of ambivalence and self-doubt, even among highly educated NRIs, who are often confronted with unnecessarily overdichotomized questions: "Why are you not helping the society which educated and supported you? Why are you, instead, simply becoming prosperous yourselves?" Those who lack the special skills, time, or resources to creatively confront such a question find themselves becoming members of an orthodox sect. The more NRIs believe and the more they donate to a temple, which symbolizes aspects of their early socialization, the better they can deal with their dilemma.

Third, collectively calculated self-interest lures numerous resourceful technicians, scientists, and doctors to megatemples such as Sri Siva-Vishnu temple in suburban Washington, D.C. (which, according to its devotees, is the largest Hindu temple in the United States), as well as a modest storefront temple in Corona, New York.

Interviews with a circle of physicians, their families, and friends who have recently become the followers of Sathya Sai Baba, reveal how the NRI media and temples are linked together in a totalistic world that leaves them relatively isolated and blind to the outside world. It also increasingly commits them to a fundamentalist Hinduism. Sai Baba is the more than seventy-year-old charismatic godman who presides over an affluent pilgrimage in south India. His followers consider him to be an incarnation of God and a man of miracles who simultaneously produces "holy ashes," Seiko watches, and diamond rings just by lifting his hand. Sathya Sai Baba now has a global organization that absorbs its followers' interest with web pages, newsletters, and branches in over a hundred countries.

Sai Baba followers have something in common with the followers of other godmen who own huge ashrams on many continents and are the beneficiaries of many ashram-run schools, colleges, and charities. Most of these places of Hindu worship are actually located outside India, a crowded and comparatively impoverished society. In a somewhat self-interested way, these devotees say that contrary to what may seem to be a logical assumption, many neo-Hindus are not retreating from a spiritual East to a materialistic West but are in fact escaping the contemporary East which is heavily influenced by Western and indigenously developed media full of illicit sex, violence, nonvegetarian fast food, drugs, and alcohol. Instead, they reside their "Indian" lives in the ethnic media and temples in the West. They say that their new-old American Hinduism represents a departure from a culturally contaminated and economically backward society where their salaries and incomes would be much lower than the ones available in the West. Here they can get the best of both worlds: a high-paying career, and a purer, more comfortable place of worship where they can live in a healthier environment.

This choice, however, has a hidden cost. Many Hindu Indians who have become more religious in America than they were in India have very little contact with other ethnic groups—and when such contact does occur, it is based on their own chauvinistic and exclusionary stereotypes of other communities, stereotypes which are continually reinforced by all the functions of the ethnic media and social interactions at their temples. Hence, old-fashioned religiosity and "desihood," no matter how regressive in their enviable new situation, are increasing. The more Hindu Indians pursue the "best of both worlds" in the media and at the temple, the less time, opportunity, and resources they have to become truly global citizens.

4

Global Hinduism in Gotham

John Stratton Hawley

The Lay of the Land

The global dispersion of Hinduism has ancient roots. Despite the brahmanical proscription against crossing "the black waters," Indian traders whose religious sensibilities would today be called Hindu have plied oceans west and east of the subcontinent for at least two millennia.[1] The worship of Shiva apparently dominated the Cambodian court in the fourth century C.E., and soon afterward there were settled communities of Hindus in Java (Coedes 1968, 49). Hindu traders were probably also a regular presence in East Africa since they were noticed there by Periplus in the first century C.E., though we know few specifics until large numbers of recruits from Punjab and Gujarat followed British railway-building projects in the nineteenth century (Younger 1999, 367). At that time new forces unleashed by European capitalism and imperialism spread Hindu religious forms even farther from India. Hindus from northern India were transplanted as far east as the Fiji Islands and as far west as Guyana, Jamaica, Suriname, and Trinidad. In the late twentieth century each of these communities began to send emigrants to the United States, and Emma Lazarus would have been pleased to see that a number of them were drawn to New York City.

Even without immigration, the twentieth century had already cultivated a healthy Hindu presence in New York. Americans who had grown up Christian or Jewish found themselves responding to the missionary efforts of charismatic Hindu leaders. Swami Vivekananda was the first such missionary. He made a sensational appearance at the Columbian Exhibition in Chicago in 1893 and soon traveled to New York, where he gathered a circle of admirers who became the first of America's Vedanta Societies (1894). For many years it has met in a handsome brownstone on the Upper West Side of Manhattan. Another Bengali, a retired businessman from Calcutta named Abhay Charan De, made a similarly deep impression three-quarters of a century later. His personal charisma as Bhaktivedanta Swami combined with his cultural moment to produce the Hare Krishna movement, whose singing, dancing entry into the East Village scene in 1966 has made it a countercultural legend ever since. Many other traveling gurus have had their impact, as well.[2]

Undoubtedly Americans attracted to leaders like Swami Vivekananda and Bhaktivedanta Swami have contributed substantially to the many-faceted religious history of New York, but the present mood of transnational Hinduism in the city owes far more to a second group, whose experience of the western hemisphere is much more recent. These are the immigrants from South Asia who have been touted as a model minority because their educational attainments and economic standing outrank those of all other ethnic groups in the American population today. They began to arrive in significant numbers after that watershed moment in 1965 when U.S. immigration laws barring non-Europeans were revised so as to assign priority to applicants not just on the basis of national origin but also in recognition of their educational and technical attainments that would make them useful in American society. Goodbye, Emma Lazarus! These are hardly "your tired, your poor." Some Hindu Americans feel the "model minority" billing conceals as much as it illuminates (Prashad 2000), but no one doubts that these Hindus have made a dramatic impact on the city's financial, professional, and intellectual life. Thanks to them—but also to Sikhs from the Punjab and Muslims largely from Pakistan and Bangladesh—the New York metropolitan area now hosts the second-largest concentration of South Asians living outside the subcontinent; only London ranks higher. The 1990 census showed there were just short of 100,000 "Asian Indians" in the city itself and twice that number in the greater New York metropolitan area (Jasper 2001, 17–20).

A third component of New York's Hindu population also comes from India, but not directly. These are the city's twice-migrant Caribbean Hindus, and reasonable estimates of their numbers hover around 100,000 (Carnes and Karpathakis 2001, 95–96; Jasper 2001, 7). A huge segment of that population arrived in the 1970s and 1980s, especially in response to the repressive politics of Forbes Burnham and his Peoples' National Congress Party in Guyana, which particularly targeted Guyanese of Asian descent. Nothing so vividly demonstrates their special ethnic identity among New York's Hindus as their eager participation in the boisterous, colorful West Indian parade that wends its way down Liberty Avenue in Queens every spring in celebration of the festival Carribeanites call Phagwa (i.e., *phalgun,* known more familiarly in India as Holi). There are other indices of this separate sense of identity, as well. Caribbean Indians have their own newspaper, *The Caribbean Indian Times,* and can listen to a specifically Caribbean radio station, WVOX (93.5 FM). Recently several of the Hindus in this wider Indo-Caribbean group—they constitute some 85 percent of the total—have established the Rajkumari Cultural Center to coordinate Caribbean Hindu information and activities. Given their separate history and their separate categorization in census data, it is perhaps not surprising that these Hindus are completely absent from the standard sources on Indian immigration into the city (Fisher 1980; Lessinger 1995; Williams 1988). But it is regrettable.

Taken as a whole, this new Indian American reality makes for an amazing scene, and Gotham's global Hinduism is an important part of it. New York's many Hindu temples serve as points of gathering, refuge, and concentration for vast numbers of ordinary Hindus resident in its five boroughs. The largest concentration of Hindu centers and temples, as well as 60 percent of the city's total number of Hindu residents, inhabit the remarkable borough of Queens, home to a kaleidoscope of immigrants from all over the world (Bogen 1987, 73–78; Khandelwal 1995, 181; Hanson 1999). We will visit four of these temples in the pages that lie ahead. Our purpose will be to see how each displays a transnational, even global identity while at the same time functioning as a local institution. They do so in strikingly different ways, yet there are signs that their individual styles increasingly interact, without necessarily converging.[3]

The Great Ganesh Temple, Flushing

The great Ganesh temple—formally the Sri Maha Vallabha Ganapati Devasthanam—is New York's best known Hindu temple. It has a mailing list that approaches fifteen thousand (Hanson 1999), and it is accessible on the Web to many thousands more (http://www.nyganeshtemple.org). This dot-com dimension is significant, but for the moment let's stay on the ground. The temple building is to be found on Bowne Street in Flushing, not many blocks away from the thirty-five-hundred-member Korean Presbyterian Church. The two buildings serve as anchors for this polyreligious street, but they look very different. While the Koreans have built a structure whose sloping roofs seem to soar into the future, the Ganesh temple strives to incorporate structural features that have been familiar to Tamil- and Telugu-speakers for many centuries: a golden pillar that culminates in an image of Vishnu's avian mount Garuda and a richly sculpted gopuram (gateway spire) that rises above the temple's main entrance.

The Ganesh temple's myth of origin is densely transnational. It focuses on the year 1970, when the temple is said to have been envisioned by Dr. Alagappa Alagappan, a Tamilian lawyer trained in London who became a career civil servant at the United Nations. Two years earlier, on a visit home in south India, Alagappan had received a communication from the sage Agastya, who spoke through a Nadishastra medium reading palmyra leaves. Agastya told him the god Ganesh would establish a small abode in a city whose name begins with the letter N, and that Dr. Alagappan would be his instrument. Later Alagappan learned from the same medium that he should have the new image of Ganesh fashioned of stone from Tiru-vannamalai, the major focus in Tamil Nadu for the worship of Ganesh. Thus the intercontinental religious bond expressed on Bowne Street is etched in stone.[4]

In much of India, Ganesh normally appears as a supporting member of the divine cast. His image is apt to be placed in an ancillary or introductory position in temples dedicated primarily to other gods—often near the entryway—or it may appear alone in a roadside shrine. In Flushing, however, Ganesh is definitely the central deity; the other gods circle around him. This is no accident. First of all, it matches Ganesh's position in several important temples in Alagappan's own native Chettiar region in the far southeast of the subcontinent. Second, it allows for the fact that Ganesh is a transsectarian figure worshiped by Hindus of many inclinations, and is therefore ideally suited to a temple that intended, at least in its origins, to appeal to Hindus whose religious backgrounds might have separated them back home. Finally, as the god of beginnings, furthermore, he was the ideal inaugurator of a whole network of temples in the United States. In this work, Ganesh was supported by another major transnational Hindu actor, the Tirumala Tirupati Devasthanam, India's richest temple, which made a loan of $150,000, and the Endowments Department of the government of the state of Andhra Pradesh, which played a supporting role. The Tirupati deity, a form of Vishnu, is also installed in the Flushing temple, further cementing the homeland connection.

The worship of Ganesh has been on the rise in India itself over the course of the last several centuries. In this he parallels Hanuman and certain forms of the Goddess (Lutgendorf 1997, 311–332; Waghorne 2001; Hawley 2001).

In part because these deities sometimes act as mediators to the "high gods" Vishnu and Shiva, they have an accessibility as loci of power that has caused them somewhat to displace their elders or superiors through time. But each of these is also transsectarian, and that role is especially important in New York, where Hindus—especially Hindus of the first immigrant generation—formed associations across boundaries of region, language, and sectarian association that would have been somewhat unusual in India. This new catholicity is often found in the broad selection of deities represented in diaspora temples, again by contrast to India itself.[5]

Ganesh also has a civic and even national meaning that deserves note. Beginning early in the twentieth century in Maharashtra, one saw an effort to turn the deity's annual celebration day, Ganesh Chaturthi, into a festival of corporate Hindu unity (Cashman 1975, 75–97; Courtright 1985, 234–238). That ritual has now begun to make its way to Tamil Nadu as well, and it is certainly at home in Tamil Queens (Fuller 2000). So when a portable image of Ganesh is paraded noisily through the streets on a huge temple cart around the beginning of September each year, a whiff of cultural nationalism is in the air. But is it "religious nationalism" in the narrower, more threatening sense? That seems unlikely. Hindus have long associated their understanding of what religion means with their community's geographical basis. India itself is regarded by Hindus as being in some way divine, and this sensibility has often flowed naturally into the veins of Indian nationalism. For this reason, when a date was selected for the ritual inauguration (*pranapratistha*) of the central image in Flushing, the date chosen was one that had a political significance. It was not India's Independence Day, however, but rather the fourth of July. Clearly nationalism matters here—nationalism in a religious sense—but in a complex and openly binational way.

American national consciousness is inscribed on the Ganesh temple in other ways, too. As links in the temple website indicate, this community sees itself as having been the genesis of a network of mostly Vaishnava, mostly south Indian temples throughout the United States. Unlike the others, however, the Bowne Street temple was not built de novo on a piece of suburban or urban property. In Pittsburgh or Atlanta it was possible to approximate the physical setting of the influential Tirupati temple by choosing from a set of American hillscapes, but on Bowne Street geo-graphic translation of this literal variety could not succeed (Narayanan 1992, 152, 160–162; Bhatia and Bhatia 1996, 245). Because of New York, because of the urban base of the Indian American community at that time, and doubtless because of financial limitations, the temple had to be built in a preexisting structure that had already gone through several churchly incarnations (elsewhere in the city, vacated synagogues were often the buildings of choice). Even with the recently completed annex for weddings, meetings, prayer sessions, and performances, the Ganesh tem-ple presents quite a contrast to the brand-spanking-new elegance of com-parable temples around the country. Here you leave your shoes in a rack next to the house next door—now part of the temple complex—or in the erstwhile church basement.

Actually, the basement and the sanctuary above it are not entirely sepa-rate. TV monitors downstairs enable overflow crowds on festival days to follow the ritual action that transpires in the immediate vicinity of the gods. And monitors have been suspended from the ceiling in the main sanctuary itself, permitting worshipers the same unhindered views—and incidentally, simultaneous access to more than one shrine area. It is a re-markably virtual, hypertext environment, favored by the heavily visual bias of Hindu temple ritual generally (Eck 1996; Babb 1981). In many ways, from the building of long vistas to the deft use of curtains to the shoving of the crowds, Hindu temple environments in India are closely at-tuned to the primacy of sight. Through priestly lineages and guilds of In-dian craftsmen, a sense of authenticity in the physical basis of *darsan* (see-ing the divine image) is maintained in New York City, but it is amplified simultaneously by this open adoption of an electronic medium. Nowadays it is a global medium as well, for static forms of the images one sees on the CRTs in the temple itself also appear on the temple website.

This website takes its place alongside hundreds, perhaps thousands of other Hindu websites. Given the astonishingly dense presence of Hindus, especially south Indian Hindus, in computer-related fields, this is no sur-prise: Tamil is among the languages most commonly used on the Internet today.[6] Little in Hindu ritual etiquette impedes the community's creativity in cyberspace. This is not an iconoclastic tradition. Hindus have always cultivated an awareness of the power of images and symbols, and they have a long history of recognizing alternate worlds or levels of conscious-ness in which it is possible to live simultaneously (e.g., Juergensmeyer 1991, 88–109). Hence the many disputes about one's proper relationship

to images in cyberspace: are they to be downloaded freely for home vener-
ation or not?[7] Must non-Hindu viewers become Hindu initiates (through
a few additional clicks) to access them?[8] Can the economy of *prasad*—the
offering and receiving of sanctified food—operate in this realm, as it does
through the medium of a regular temple image? What would it mean to
enliven such an image ritually, invoking the divine presence into this dot-
matrix form? These are some of the leading-edge questions in global Hinduism today.[9]

Such virtual media are familiar to many, perhaps most worshipers at
the Ganesh temple in Queens, and I suspect the fact that the temple oper-
ates in this virtual space adds to its value as a space in Flushing itself, increasing the number of visitors. The importance of bodily contact with
the deity, as mediated through *prasad,* has apparently not been sacrificed
in the process. People flock from miles around, especially the suburbs, and
take-home *prasad* is a major item for sale. At this point in the generational
history of Hindus around New York, to come to Bowne Street is to return
to some sort of center or source.[10] When I was there on the night of Shiv-
aratri in 2000, I heard a couple of teenagers say it was the only temple
around that *really* rocks all night long.

The temple was jammed that night, but there was in recent memory a
moment of even greater concentration, when fully global simultaneity was
achieved. This was the famous "Milk Miracle" of September 1995, when
Hindu images worldwide, especially Ganeshes, suddenly started accepting
and visibly ingesting spoonfuls of milk from their devotees. I say "suddenly" because news of the event spread like wildfire around the globe—
by phone and e-mail through networks of family and friends—well before
the public media picked up the story. Delhi (indeed, upper-middle-class
South Delhi) was apparently the point of genesis, so there was an implicit
political dimension as this seismic reality throbbed outward from the capital over telephone circuits and e-mail connections (Mehta 1996, 12–18,
28–31, 45–50; specifically on the phenomenon as experienced in Flushing,
23, 35–36).

Yet I believe the global content was at least equally important, a sense of
simultaneity that was not firmly anchored in national or even international space. Most who flocked to temples like the Bowne Street temple
had no idea that the pebble had dropped into the lake at Delhi. Moreover,
certain Hindu commentators saw the phenomenon as a clear and indeed
revelatory vindication of image worship to a world whose monotheistic
habits of mind were openly scornful of it. As a priest at the Mahalaxmi

temple in Bombay, India's most cosmopolitan city, put it: "God has a message for us. He is saying, 'This is not just stone. It is *me*'" (Davis 1998, 2).

For many people with whom I talked, the miracle itself took sustenance from and even consisted in the social fact of global Hindu synchronicity. Many who thought long and hard about the dispersive capillary effect created when spoonfuls of milk touched the stone nonetheless felt that thrill (see, e.g., Mehta 1996, 21, 37–38, 56–58).

The Swaminarayan Temple, Flushing

The Ganesh temple in Flushing, with its highly educated, overwhelmingly middle- or upper-middle-class constituency, illustrates some of the important vectors of transnational Hinduism. Yet very different versions of Hindu transnationalism can also be encountered within a five-mile radius of Bowne Street. One of the most notable of these is visible just down the street, in fact, at the Bochasanwasi Swaminarayan Sanstha. This temple was the first to be established in the United States by the worldwide network of Swaminarayan temples and ashrams headquartered at Ahmedabad, capital of the Indian state of Gujarat.

Originally unaware of the simultaneous presence of Hindus from south India who were gathered in the Russian Orthodox church down the street preparing to raze it and build the Ganesh temple, the Gujarati professionals who spearheaded the establishment of Bowne Street's Swaminarayan temple were responding to quite another call (Hanson 1999, 6). They were helping to spread a reformist brand of Vaishnava teaching and practice that had been developed at the beginning of the nineteenth century by a renunciant religious leader named Swaminarayan. The monastic order he established continues to provide the central infrastructure for the worldwide Swaminarayan community, but householders such as K. C. Patel, the medical doctor whose home near Bowne Street served as the first meeting place for the Bowne Street temple, provide far more than financial assistance in the cause. Through their energy, self-conscious missionizing, and example the Swaminarayan movement (as it calls itself) has expanded from its single location on Bowne Street to a whole network of other temples in the United States and Canada. These in turn are linked to Swaminarayan pilgrimage destinations of an international frame. They include not only the home sites in Gujarat—some venerable and some newly constructed with substantial donations from abroad—but also magnificent temple complexes in London and New Jersey that are intended to serve, in the words of a Swaminarayan pamphlet, as "spiritual oases" in a world habituated to other paths (*Swaminarayan Movement,* 1984).

The Swaminarayan religion has been studied extensively by Raymond Williams in a series of articles and books (especially Williams 1988, 152–185; Williams 1984),[11] but two aspects of its particular expression of transnational Hinduism in Queens should be flagged. These are the explicit global structure of the movement as a whole and its seemingly paradoxical counterpart: Swaminarayan's devotion to a Gujarati identity.

On the global side, Swaminarayan is interested in producing a tangible, well-articulated network of sites that will serve as magnets for travel and as resources abroad ("oases") for the extremely mobile Swaminarayan community itself. At the same time, somewhat after the fashion of the sparkling Baha'i temples that have been built on each continent, they are intended to display the brilliance of the Swaminarayan vision of humanity to others who might be attracted to it. When one visits the relatively humble Swaminarayan temple on Bowne Street, one hears of the greater glory of the temple being built in New Jersey and especially of the magnificence one can experience just outside London. The implication is that the London temple is not just an outpost; it is a new global hub.

Yet it is worth remembering that the presence of Gujaratis in England is even more marked than in the United States, so unlike the Baha'i parallel the London temple makes sense in local terms as well. Not only that, it makes sense in Gujarati terms. Swaminarayan is insistent in its devotion to the culture of Gujarat and its language, which was the medium of the founding guru. With the westward dispersion of Gujarati professionals, who constitute a large and influential segment of Indians recently immigrant to the United States, the Swaminarayan movement has taken a leading role in attempting to preserve Gujarati culture abroad. This is one reason why many immigrant Gujaratis whose families had not been connected with Swaminarayan back home have joined the community abroad. Summarizing this picture, Raymond Williams has spoken of Swaminarayan's particular brand of global religion as emphasizing "transnational ethnicity" (Williams 1984).

Not surprisingly, some of the most difficult issues that the community faces are connected to the loss of fluency in Gujarati on the part of the second generation, as is the case with Sikhs in regard to Punjabi (Mann 2000, 273–274; Mann, Numrich, and Williams 2001, 147–148). In both instances this is not just an ethnic but a religious issue, since scripture is involved. There is nothing wrong with being a second-generation American; quite the contrary. But the prospect of being a second-class citizen with respect to one's own religion—separated from its language—is an unhappy new development. This is especially so in traditions like Swaminarayan and Sikhism, both of which began by stressing the vivid, broad-based access to religious truth they provided by favoring the language commonly spoken in their religions. Swaminarayan's imaginative, carefully maintained, and officially supervised website plays on the reach of the medium itself to underscore the community's global identity, but that new sense of instant community only partially replaces the sense of deep belonging that comes from speaking a common language and hearing it used as the language of faith. Swaminarayan's "transnational ethnicity" still has to confront the threat of growing alienation from Gujarat and Gujarati on the part of its diasporic young.

The America Sevashram Sangha, Jamaica

Such problems of cultural alienation and reintegration have long been familiar to Hindus who have made their way to New York from the Caribbean. Members of the Sri Ram Mandir of Cypress Hill, Brooklyn, for example, continue to use Hindi in the devotional songs (*bhajans*) that form a major part of every Sunday morning worship service (*puja*), but many participants do so with the aid of hymnbooks that have the Hindi words transliterated out of their original Devanagari script and into the Roman alphabet.[12] The retention of Hindi, in part to permit real access to the celebrated *Ramayana* composed in the sixteenth century by Tulsidas, is a constant project (Hansbury 1999). Yet this degree of devotion to Hindi is not central to the practice of other Caribbean Hindu communities. Hindi bhajans may be overshadowed by chants using a basic Sanskrit, and the language of preaching and conversation is far more apt to be English than Hindi.

Such is the milieu of the America Sevashram Sangha, located in the Jamaica section of Queens. This neighborhood is a bit farther down the economic scale than Flushing. Here the most visible ethnicities are not Korean and Chinese, but African American, Latin American, Philippino, Pakistani, and Guyanese.

It was Hindus from Guyana who converted a good-sized synagogue building at 153–14 90th Avenue into the America Sevashram Sangha.

Their forebears had come to Guyana in the middle and late nineteenth century as indentured laborers from various locales in north India, especially Bihar, but this particular religious organization (sangha) owes its genesis to the missionary activity of an enterprising member of the monastic order established by the Bengali reformer-guru Swami Pranavananda (1896–1941) (Smart and Purnananda 1985). He is Swami Vidyananda. The America Sevashram Sangha is his handiwork. The congregation gathered to worship there on a Sunday morning comes primarily from the immediate neighborhood, but other Guyanese come from as far away as New Jersey. In Jamaica, Queens, education is a central focus both of the Swami and of his "parishioners." One member told me proudly that his son had been accepted at Columbia. Another young woman, enrolled at nearby St. John's University, waited patiently through a long conversation between the Swami and me to present him with a check to support the medical center his order is now building back in Guyana; she was acting on behalf of the Guyanese students' organization at St. John's. Especially at the aspiring socioeconomic level represented by many members of America Sevashram Sangha, education seems to provide the most basic sense of transnational security, and all the more so when it is framed in a religious context.

In such ways the America Sevashram Sangha both represents and enacts ties to the Guyanese homeland, playing exactly the sort of active role that religious centers often do for recently immigrant Americans.[13] Yet because it serves a twice-migrant community, the temple necessarily facilitates a sense of identification between Guyanese Hindus and their more distant South Asian homeland. Swami Vidyananda has promoted this process in recent years by taking certain members of his flock on an annual tour of various pilgrimage sites in India. Most of these destinations—Banaras, Hardwar, Rishikesh, Vrindaban, Kuruksetra—would figure in any standard religious journey around north India, but the itinerary culminates with a visit to the birth, enlightenment, and burial place (samadhi) of Swami Pranavananda in Bajitpur, now in Bangladesh. When these Caribbean Americans travel to South Asia in the company of their spiritual leader-cum-guide, they use a vocabulary provided by religion to close the India-Guyana-New York triangle that they and their forebears have otherwise traveled for economic reasons. In South Asia, pilgrimage routes have for centuries provided Hindus with an idealized yet flexible representation of what it would mean to encompass the whole (Eck 1981, 323–344; Eck 1998, 165–188; Das, Gupta, and Uberoi 1999; Bharati 1970, 83–126).

Here that pattern is adapted to global ends as Guyanese Hindus acquire the means to cross a border that was far more difficult for them to approach in Guyana itself: the border to India.

Yet there are features in the style of Hinduism displayed at the America Sevashram Sangha that are apt to seem unusual to Hindus of other backgrounds. Hindu students who take my introductory class on Hinduism at Barnard and Columbia come largely from Indian American families who migrated directly from South Asia, though a few have been reared by Anglo-Hindu converts. These students were intrigued by two features of the *puja* they witnessed on a class trip to Jamaica one Friday evening early in 2002. First, they were surprised to find that a cardboard image of Swami Pranavananda was the central focus of worship; both the medium and the subject seemed strange. Second, they found it unusual that the light-offering (*arati*) ritual through which the Swami was worshiped was performed individually by members of the congregation rather than mediated through a priest. It was Swami Vidyananda who did the *arati* first, but at that point he put down the tray of lamps and gestured to the rest of us to follow suit. One by one members of the class who wished to participate stepped forward and did the *arati* themselves.

I was struck by three things in the local-global process that ensued. First, Hindu students recognized the *arati* ritual as a basic feature of global Hindu practice, even though the particular inflection it was given in this Guyanese temple was new to them. Whatever their background, they had all done *arati* at home and they had participated in public forms of worship where *arati* was also performed. For the most part, they were ready to participate here as well. Second, by joining in the ritual they were further cementing the globalization of Hinduism right there on the spot, through the medium of a university class taught by a professor who grew up more or less Presbyterian. Among the transnational and transcultural formations one can observe along the spectrum of Hinduism as experienced in New York, this is perhaps one of the more unusual, though it is true that when students elect a class on a religious tradition with which they are already familiar, one of their primary motives may well be the desire to view the pie out of which their own particular piece was cut.

A third aspect of this *arati* experience was to me the most interesting of all. It was not just that the *arati* was individually performed, but that it was serially performed, and in a certain definite manner. This is not the case in every Caribbean Hindu temple: sometimes groups approach the deities (in image form) and gurus (in image or personal form) with the *arati* tray. But here a definite line was formed, single file down the center of the sanctuary. An obvious interpretation is that this practice emerged in the context of European public etiquette—particularly in its British expression, where the formation of a queue is an almost sacred duty. But I couldn't help noticing the strong parallel with specifically liturgical forms. As the temple's own devotees and my students joined the line and moved forward toward the altar, where Swami Pranavananda's picture stood at the center of a dozen or so deities, the procession looked to my eye like Christians moving toward the altar rail to receive the eucharist. Indeed, after doing *arati*, each student took *prasad*—food blessed by having been offered first to the gods—in the form of water, thus turning the analogy between the overall structure of eucharist and *prasad* into something that went beyond analogy. It seemed to me I was witnessing the result of a long process of accommodation between Hindu and Christian liturgical forms that had occurred since the first Hindu temples were established in British Guiana, the same process that focuses Guyanese corporate worship on Sunday morning from nine until noon in a more regular way than one encounters at American Hindu temples. Certainly this Sunday-morning form of congregational worship contrasts broadly with the account of Guyanese Hindu temple ritual that was published by H. V. P. Bronkhurst in 1883, where "worshippers stand outside in an area opposite the door belonging to the building" and only the priest can enter within "to perform the duties of his office in the presence of the idol" (Vertovec 2000, 50).

When I hinted at this interpretation to Swami Vidyananda, he held it at arm's length. To him the plotting of the ritual seemed instead to follow naturally from the observation of appropriate decorum and discipline. The latter term emerged frequently in his descriptions of what he thought was being achieved by the temple's programs and by the educational philosophy of the schools in Guyana that he had had so much to do with bringing into being. In this liturgical mode, he explained, the line formed as a simple solution to the fact that men sit on one side of the sanctuary, women on the other: they meet in a line that forms at the center so as to approach the guru, the officiating swami (himself), and the deities as a single body (Vidyananda 2002).

According to Swami Vidyananda, the introduction of the Vedic fire sacrifice (*havan*) into the *puja* ceremony served a similar purpose. Of course, it anchored the community's worship in the oldest surviving ritual practices of the Hindu tradition, as had been urged in India by the reformist

Arya Samaj toward the end of the nineteenth century and by Arya Samaj missionaries to the British West Indies beginning in 1910. Thereby the *havan* restored the tradition to a lost purity and authenticity, but its incorporation into the framework of a larger ritual frame (*puja*) focused on images meant that this was not done at the cost of throwing out the baby with the bathwater. Yet in addition to that, said Swami Vidyananda, the incorporation of the *havan* into a *puja* ritual centered on *arati* and *prasad* meant restoring a congregational focus to a ritual ambience that would otherwise be too scattered, too heterogeneous, too individual, too dependent on the ritual mediations of priests. In this way he articulated a complex but strictly Hindu explanation for changes in the direction of congregational worship that observers like myself might too hastily have attributed to the conditioning presence of British Christianity, especially as Guyanese Hindus became the targets of intense Anglican and Methodist missionary activity. Whichever way one sees it—and I would prefer not to choose—one is observing the fruits of a transnational and transsectarian past.[14]

Guyanese Hinduism has certainly not fossilized by virtue of its great distance from India. In fact, it has displayed a history of creativity all its own. On the one hand, this diasporic location has unquestionably encouraged efforts at internal reorganization and rerationalization that would better answer the kinds of criticisms directed against Hindus from the outside—or to put it more neutrally, better conform to models of religious behavior that outsiders (in this case, primarily Christians) tended to expect. On the other hand, efforts by Caribbean Hindu groups such as the Pundits' Council and the Sanatan Dharma Sabha tended to throw a more intense light on indigenous Hindu practices as they worked to create a semiofficial form of performed Hinduness. The lineage to which Swami Vidyananda belongs participates vividly in that history, as he does himself. Before we conclude, we will see how his own personal diasporization to New York produces new levels of transnational creativity—simultaneously pluralist and syncretizing.

Divya Dham, Woodside

The last site of local-global Hindu combustion that we will visit is located six or seven miles away at the corner of 37th Avenue and 56th Street in the Woodside section of Queens. This is a remarkable place called Divya

Dham, established in 1993 and expanded in 1996 as a project of the Geeta Temple (or more recently, Gita Mandir) which lies between Jamaica and Woodside in Elmhurst, Queens. The Geeta Temple, so called because of its dedication to the *Bhagavad Gita*, was established in the first wave of post-1965 Hindu activity in Queens, not long after Dr. Alagappan began envisioning the Ganesh temple in Flushing. The year of its incorporation as a tax-exempt religious entity was 1973, and its leadership came from a sweet and playful man known as Swami Jagdishwaranand. Now in his seventies, Swami Jagdishvaranand is also the person responsible for conceiving its much grander successor, Divya Dham.

You wouldn't guess these splendors from the outside. Divya Dham is sited not in a church or synagogue but in a former electronics factory. Yet the locale is significant. It's not just that a warehouse offers plenty of space for a modest price, but that such spaces have come to be a major venue of urban creativity in New York. Famously, they house apartments and artists' studios, but also clubs and movie studios, especially in nearby Astoria. Something along these latter lines is being shaped at Divya Dham.

The warehouse door is drab, but once inside, visitors find themselves in a vast, mysterious cavern. The language you are apt to hear is Hindi, or maybe Gujarati or Bengali, and many of the people who come here tend to be even more recent immigrants to New York than those one meets at the America Sevashram Sangha. Unlike the Caribbean Americans, however, their route from north India to the United States has often been direct. Some frequent visitors—and until recently even some of the *pujaris* who managed the temple and its rituals—are still a good bit more comfortable in Hindi or Gujarati than English.

As for the space itself, you find yourself walking among the primary deities of the modern Hindu pantheon. Near the door stands a whole wall of Shiva *lingas*—1,008, to be precise—and in front of them are several truly monumental *lingas* that capture the attention of most worshipers. Farther inside one encounters an impressive panoply. Hanuman, Ganesh, and Radha and Krishna define separate spheres, as do Rama and Sita, and there is a monumental three-headed image of Shiva as he appears in the spectacular Elephanta caves near Bombay[15] Back still farther, at the end of the L-shaped space, one finds a "Gujarat corner" comprising images of Krishna as Ranchorji and the nineteenth-century saint Jalaram Baba. These in turn abut a newly completed shrine dedicated to nine forms of the goddess Durga—nine life-size images which radiate from a single axis in individual wooden booths. Each booth displays a bronze plaque announcing the name of the donor, and in five of those booths the donors are women. Their names are listed first, then sometimes accompanied by the mention of their families.

The importance of goddesses is also evident at several other places in the temple. At the crux of the L stands the row of deities that serves as its main focus, if such a thing can be said for any of them in this huge warehouse-like space. At the center of that row stands the Great Goddess, here in her Gujarati aspect as Amba (Bhavani).[16] Not far away we see a diorama representing the descent of the Ganges—whom Hindus regard as a female divinity—into this world from her heavenly abode. A sign in English tells viewers that this is "Shri Bhagirath Ji praying to Lord Shiva when Ganga Ji is descending to Bhoolok (earth)." A model of a temple to her looms in the shadows above the fiberglass Himalayan peak where she made her earthly appearance, and the "cow's head" (*gomukh*) from which she is said to gush forth is also depicted, complete with an explanatory sign.

The generous array of deities one sees here would be unusual in India, but it is a familiar feature of the Hinduism on display in American temples; we meet it at the Ganesh temple and in Jamaica, as well. In diaspora, after all, there is far more need to summarize than in the homeland—a phenomenon we see analogously in the diaspora's disproportionate activity in generating primers of Hinduism and catechetical materials, and which doubtless reflects a heightened sense of multiple origins and of personal multilocality.[17] But Divya Dham also takes advantage of its potentially protean warehouse environment in a way that is quite special. It makes an attempt to transfer to the United States the actual landscape of the Indian subcontinent as conceived in religious terms.

Though it immediately grabs the attention of anyone who comes through the door, the tableau depicting the descent of the Ganges actually signals a more complicated geographical reality. The fiberglass mountain out of which the Ganges is seen to spring is also home—on its reverse side—to a deity known as Vaishno Devi. To reach her native Himalayan habitat in Jammu, pilgrims must undertake an arduous journey, yet in recent years some five million, mostly city dwellers, have made the trek. Here, however, all one need do is make one's way on coir mats down a fiberglass tunnel marked "one way," and one accomplishes the same purpose. One enters a back-room "cave" that grants a vision of Vaishno Devi: three coordinate personae identified in their image form as the goddesses

Kali, Lakshmi, and Sarasvati, and also present in aniconic form as three terracotta mounds, just as one would see in the cave shrine at Jammu itself.

Startling as it is to find Vaishno Devi's abode in industrial Queens—a window in her cave affords a glimpse of houses on 57th Street—this is spatial transposition in the classical Hindu way. For centuries Hindus have identified spiritual Gangeses and just-as-good Badrinaths for pilgrims who could only afford to go to pilgrimage destinations nearer by. If a city or region could boast all these sites in some sense—yet without losing its own particular draw—its efficacy was enhanced. Once again, then, the special needs of the diaspora are answered by patterns of thought and ritual action that developed in India itself, sometimes long ago.

This is not just mimesis: there is an actual sharing of physical substance. Like pilgrims worldwide, Hindus who travel to important pilgrimage sites have long made it a practice to bring back something with them. If the goal of one's pilgrimage is a city situated on the banks of a river, as so many are, then water from that river is the obvious prize. A bit of Ganges water, especially from a place like Banaras or Hardwar, is regarded as having sufficient sacrality that a mere drop can have a transsubstantiating effect on ordinary water. This explains at least partially the sign posted near the tiny tigers and fawns who rest at the river's source in Divya Dham's Himalayas: "May God Bless Gargi Pathak who fetched the holy water of the Ganges from its source 'Gomukh' Gangotri in her earliest age, first in the history of mankind." The six signatories to this touching message are celebrating the accomplishment of a little girl who was born in the same year as Divya Dham—1993. They are recalling her trip to the high Himalayas with her parents, and the remarkable fact that she was so young when it occurred. This girl, whose childhood made her a special object of respect and admiration, brought a vial of genuine Ganges water for the consecration of the Divya Dham site. In this way the sign points to a connection that goes well beyond analogy and representation: the Ganges really has come to Queens.[18]

The special signature of Divya Dham—"the Heaven on the Earth," as a recently produced guidebook portrays it (Pandey 2001),[19] is its focus on spatial transposition.[20] More than that, it attempts to represent the entirety of sacred space as Hindus have conceived it. The term *dham* means broadly "abode" or "dwelling," but carries religious overtones, such that it often refers to a place of pilgrimage.[21] Four of these *dhams* are regarded as having been divinely established at the four compass points of the Indian subcontinent, and pots representing these four pilgrimage destinations have newly been placed at the point in the L where one enters the central shrine area. A fifth representing Mount Kailasa, the mountain which stands at the very center of the Himalayas and serves as the abode of Lord Shiva, meets the visitor at the main door itself. Someone has hung lists of the "seven holy parvats" (mountains) and "seven holy puris" (cities) of India from two pillars that stand in front of the 1008 *lingas,* and the numerical fascination plays itself out on a series of placards that have been propped up along one long wall. These list everything from the four Vedas, the seven sages, the seven continents and oceans, to the nine "prominent serpents," the eighteen *puranas* (religious texts), and the twenty-eight hells. Notably, these lists branch into internal space as well—the eight supernatural faculties—and into the realm of time: the four sacred nights that occur in the course of a calendar year, the ancient sages and kings of the Surya lineage, and of course the various ages through which the universe has passed.

These placards are intended as a teaching tool, like the panels on stained glass windows of Gothic cathedrals, but it is hard to believe they have quite the same awe-inspiring effect on ordinary worshipers. Certainly not worshipers of a certain age. Underneath one of several signs forbidding eating, drinking, and audiography-videography, another of equal size has been appended: "No Running in Mandir." That in turn gives a hint of the enormous room that is Divya Dham's most distinctive contribution to the sacred geography of New York. Hidden in the middle of its vast layout, and not always open to visitors, is a three-dimensional representation of the center of the universe itself—the entire Himalayan range, with Mount Kailasa at the center. The four best-known Himalayan pilgrimage sites are marked in miniature, there's a catwalk for onlookers, and an electric train stands at the ready to make the circumambulatory circuit. "It's something for the kids," one family explained to me, and sure enough, the idea was born when the founding guru happened to meet an electric-train buff from New Jersey. Statues of this man and his wife, safe behind glass, welcome visitors to this interior exhibit.[22]

What is so intriguing to me is the thoroughly hybrid nature of the space as a whole. It's certainly transnational, but there's also something truly American here: "something for the kids," as my informant put it. It's Hindu—the transposition of sacred space writ large—and at the same time, by virtue of that very scale, it's Disney. Yet one sniffs traces of earlier hybridizations as well. At the Tulsi Manas Mandir in Banaras, for instance, one finds dioramas, an outdoor park with miniaturized versions of sacred landscapes, and images of Hanuman and Tulsidas that possess mechanical moving parts and speak recorded messages.[23] And while museums and sanctuaries may seem separate venues in American bourgeois culture, they might not seem so in the vast temple complexes of South Asia.[24] So hybridity is too simple. This is polymorphism, and polymorphism with a history.

Do the Ends Meet?

In this exploration of four different Hindu locales in Queens, I have emphasized the distinctive ways in which the reality and perception of transnational meaning are encoded into these several temple environments. Religiously, at least, one has to conclude that the sense of transnationality or globalism is anything but monolithic. It is subtle, layered, multidimensional, and it builds on histories of interregional interaction and perception that go back much farther than the sliver of time upon which we habitually focus when we claim that we are citizens of a newly dawning global age.

Yet there is some truth to that claim. Consider the second floor at Divya Dham. There, as if to further exemplify Swami Jagdishwaranand's overall fascination with goddesses as deities for our time, we find five rows of booth-type sculptures representing the fifty-one *sakti pithas*.[25] Female in form, these are the nodes of energy that were created all over India when the corpse of the goddess Sati, dismembered by her grief-crazed husband Shiva, was scattered throughout the Indian subcontinent. Her father Daksha had neglected to invite Shiva to a divine sacrifice he was superintending, and Sati, aggrieved on behalf of her husband, trumped her father's sacrifice with her own: she killed herself.

The tale is a gripping one, and images of *sati* have been marshaled by builders of the new Bharat Mata ("Mother India") temple at the base of the Himalayas in Hardwar to reinforce a sense of the embodiment of Mother India in real people, real women. Here, however, these *saktis*, laid out in five formulaic rows, seem strangely disembodied. After all, they are *not* quite Mother India. Instead, these divine women seem intended to evoke a sense that human women—mothers of India—have the power to transport an auspicious sense of religion and culture across national boundaries through their role as bearers of life and instruments of the deepest forms of socialization in their children. The sponsors' plaques that are beginning to appear beneath them, each recording the name of a woman, reinforce the message. Yet in the absence of the body of India "herself," they seem to speak to a sense of global superficiality as much as anything else, a fear of cultural deracination that seems especially appropriate to our time.

This is strictly my own reaction, not one I would attribute to any other visitor, and it is clearly not the main intention of those responsible for transplanting these *sakti pithas* to New York. A pamphlet available at Divya Dham and the Geeta Temple describes things quite differently. It associates the fifty-one *sakti pithas* with the fifty-one syllables (*aksaras*) that it considers to form the Sanskrit alphabet. The pamphlet goes on to claim that while "the people of Bharat" (India) worshiped these *aksaras* at specific locales in the ancient past, many of them are "either extinct or inaccessible now." It suggests that their power can be rediscovered in New York through their association with the *sakti pithas,* and that "the idea of bringing all of these fifty-one shakti-Peethas under one roof in New York is inspired and strengthened by the grace of Mother Goddess."[26]

This is a fascinating permutation of the mythology of the *sakti pithas,* leveraging their power for diasporic use through an intimate association with language itself. Language travels, giving it a universal utility that is not obvious in the case of geographic sites such as the *sakti pithas.* This would seem to be especially so in regard to Sanskrit, which is a learned language whose ascribed status as language of the gods also earns for it among many Hindus the reputation of being the origin of all other languages. When the conceptual architects of Divya Dham—Swami Jagdishwaranand first and foremost—associate the Mother and Language as divine principles, they evoke an ideal India that reaches out into diasporic and indeed global space. Without ceding a claim to physical space, which would vitiate the whole diasporic enterprise, they mix visible and invisible media to do so.

A second dimension in the recent history of Divya Dham pulls in a somewhat different direction. In the year 2001 Swami Jagdishwaranand, who came to the United States from the region around Banaras (via Calcutta and Burma), sent a message to Swami Vidyananda, who came from Guyana, asking him if he would be interested in taking over the management of Divya Dham. Various Hindi-speaking pundits whom he had attempted to enlist in that role had proved unsuccessful, and Swami Vidyananda's managerial reputation, together with that of the order to which he belonged, suggested a happy alternative. This proposal came as a complete surprise to Swami Vidyananda: the two men had never met and Swami Vidyananda had never so much as visited Divya Dham. Nonetheless, after immediately scheduling a trip to headquarters in Calcutta to seek official approval, he accepted, with the result that daily *havans* and *aratis* are now performed before a newly installed backlit image of Swami Pranavananda at Divya Dham.

It is hard to know what this change will mean in the long term, but it may indicate that an intermingling between Guyanese and north Indian streams of Hindu life in New York will come sooner than anyone might have thought. Already Swami Vidyananda has encouraged this to happen by sponsoring discourses on Tulsidas's *Ramayana* by a well-known Guyanese performer, Prakash Gossai, at Divya Dham. He glories in the healthy attendance—in January 2002, some seven hundred people gathered on a single night—and takes it as a sign of Hindu reunification. An assistant adds that Swami Vidyananda is trying to work on his Hindi. This need is not so urgent for some in his Jamaica congregation because they tend to pick up enough Hindi from their favorite Bombay-made films.

Obviously the serendipitous juxtaposition of these two swamis has had a great deal to do with bringing this new arrangement into being, yet older patterns of interaction are also at play. The two religious leaders are able to plot their connection to one another not just along the axes provided by the grid of streets that structures Queens, but by means of lines of guru-to-pupil succession they both trace back to the great philosopher-theologian Samkara, who flourished about 800 C.E. Samkara is famously believed to have established centers of learning and worship at the four compass-point *dhams* now represented as pots in Divya Dham, and in the mind of Swami Vidyananda, at least, he also intended to establish temples at the fifty-one *sakti pithas*. Alas, Samkara died young and was unable to fulfill this wish. But now, in the pan-Indian environment that America provides, it can be done—virtually (Vidyananda 2002). Swami Vidyananda sees India as having fallen victim to a process of gradual shrinkage as Nepal, Pakistan, and Bangladesh have been carved off as separate states. What is happening at Divya Dham, he thinks, is a sign that India can be somehow reconstituted in a global domain (Vidyananda 2002). Whether or not one shares this vision, one would have to note that its enactment at Divya Dham has not been immediate. Some of the people who worked hardest to make Divya Dham what it is worry that the temple has been turned over to people whose background is significantly different from their own. Time will tell whether the experiment succeeds.

Finally, let me report an encounter with another habitue of Divya Dham—this time not a person with Indian blood flowing in his veins. His name is Juan Marcini, and he was born in El Salvador. He often comes to Divya Dham of a Sunday afternoon to think and pray, and he too played a role in its construction. He was there several years ago when the Kailasa project was being conceived, and he allowed himself to be drawn in because of his background in architecture and what New Yorkers call landmarking: preserving historic buildings and restoring them to their original condition. Marcini's job was to manage the task of producing the little temples that adorn Divya Dham's Mount Kailasa and represent the temples that actually exist at the four *dhams* that mark the most salient points in the Himalayas themselves. These four dhams (Kedarnath, Badrinath, Yamunotri, and Gangotri) are distinct from the other set of four that mark out the sacred geography of the Indian subcontinent.[27] Marcini did his job carefully, working with photographs of the original temples and involving small teams of Hindu students at various colleges and universities in the New York area. Thus the man who had the idea for the circumambulatory train—a pure fantasy—was Italian American and the man who built the mountain *dhams* to scale was Hispanic.

As I said before, this is a notable expression of diasporic complexity, but what is most interesting about Juan Marcini is his conception of himself in relation to Divya Dham. He praises the British for adopting a policy of religious toleration in its colonial domains that he thinks contrasted sharply to what the Spanish did in Central America. There, he says, "the monsignors burned all the manuscripts the Indians possessed," whereas Hindu religion survived the colonial regime intact (Marcini 2002). Yet he also believes one can trace the major outlines of a submerged common history of human religion by excavating the pre-Constantinian history of Christianity with the help of documents such as those unearthed at Qumran and paying attention to analogues between, say, the Mayan calendar and various mandalas that appear in Buddhist temples of Southeast Asia. Hindus' sense of the unbroken historical depth of their tradition feeds into Marcini's conviction that the cosmic geography being projected at Divya Dham is actually ecumenical in a larger sense. It represents a vision of global coherence and historical integrity whose truth we are only beginning to discover. For Marcini, Divya Dham is much more than Hindu.

Many readers will find something quaint about such conceptions. Their appeal to cosmic consciousness seems far less straightforward than the realities of global politics and simultaneous electronic communication worldwide. But there is an architect's devotion to modeling the whole that is admirable. I also read here an intuition about the importance of actually touching something amid our global virtualities, which I associate with the miraculous sensation Hindus experienced back in 1995 when Ganesh drank milk worldwide. One of the most exquisite aspects of the Hindu tradition is its ability to prize the specific, the local, the bodily, the imagistic in a context that is dramatically universal. Extreme forms of other religious traditions, particularly the monotheistic ones, may devote themselves to a vision of the global that reduces many to one. But among Hindus, characteristically, the globe's abundantly evident plurality is interpreted as a sign that there is value in every part. In the crunch of life in Queens, this message comes across as plainly as it could anywhere on earth.

NOTES

It is a pleasure, in beginning, to acknowledge the efforts of a number of students and former students who have helped me understand the temples explored in this essay: Jamie Berk, Michelle Caswell, Virginia Cromie, R. Scott Hanson, Gregg Hansbury, Glenn Kaufman, Vikas Malhotra, Douglas Peters, Anne Murphy, Shrivani Persad, Rovika Rajkishun, Alvino Sarran, and Shana Sippy. I also wish to express my gratitude to the many people who welcomed me and cheerfully answered my questions as I traveled in Queens, several of whom are cited in reports of interviews below. In particular I am indebted to Swami Jagdishwaranand of the Geeta Temple, Swami Vidyananda of the America Sevashram Sangha, and Kuldip Bahl of the Bharat Sevashram Sangha. I am grateful to Scott Hanson, Lindsey Harlan, Peter Manuel, Rachel McDermott, and Shana Sippy for helpful comments on a draft, and to my wife, Laura Shapiro, as ever, for her consummate skills as an editor.

1. A handy resource for understanding debates about the proper use of the term Hinduism and its history is David Lorenzen (1999, 630–659). Also see J. S. Hawley (1991), and Wendy Doniger (1991, 20–41).

2. For a short digest, see Eck 2001, 96–120. On Bhaktivedanta Swami in New York, see Brooks 1989, 74–78.

3. Generally helpful background for approaching the subject of transnational religion is provided by Susanne Hoeber Rudolph in her introduction and conclusion (Rudolph and Piscatori 1997, 1–24, 243–261).

4. Information on the Bowne Street temple can be had from a number of sources, but I am particularly grateful for help from R. Scott Hanson, both in personal communication and in his essay "Sri Maha Vallabha Ganapati Devasthanam of Flushing, New York," and to publications of the temple itself. Hanson's dissertation explores the phenomenon of Bowne Street as a whole (2002).

5. This phenomenon has been widely noticed (e.g., Waghorne 1999), 117–118.

6. It had been reported to my colleague E. Valentine Daniel in 1999 that Tamil was the third most frequently used language on the Net, but Charles Kurzman pointed out subsequently that the statistics quoted at www.glreach.com/globstats.index.php3 do not appear to confirm this claim. However, South Asian languages other than English are explicitly omitted from the abstract given there, leading me to propose "the top ten" as a safe estimate of Tamil's relative frequency of usage on the Net.

7. A cautionary view is that of Mani Varadarajan, the designer of www.best .com/~mani/temples.html, who requests on each page, "out of respect for the Divya Dham dampatis, please do not print or download these images." Vasant Nayak, designer of a Shiva *darsan* website (www.charm.net/~nayak/shiva .html), had a much more liberal perspective. According to Michelle Caswell—to whose undergraduate thesis "Hinduism on the World Wide Web: Darshan, Diaspora, and the Body in Sacred Cyberspace" (1997) I am grateful for information about both Varadarajan and Nayak—in an e-mail conversation Nayak expressed the view that since "we live in such a simulated world anyway, [where] all experience happens within," the medium of external access to the gods makes no real difference.

8. This is the case on the Shri Yantra site at www.hubcom.magee/tantra/9mandal.htm.

9. Michelle Caswell has continued her earlier work, "Hinduism on the World Wide Web," by assembling a website on the subject labeled "Hinduism Online," which is dated January 3, 2001, and is posted at http://www.asiasource.org/news. One of its links enables the viewer to arrange for the delivery of *prasad* offerings to deities in various locations by means of a service called ashramonline.com, based in Chennai.

10. Khandelwal singles out Flushing and Elmhurst as "*core areas* of ethnic life" in view of the fact that many recent immigrants to the New York City area settle there first (1995, 185–186).

11. The Bowne Street temple in particular has been studied by Hannah Hea-Sun Kim (2000).

12. This is true in Trinidad and Guyana as well, but less so in Suriname (see Manuel 2000). A contrast to the Ganesh temple in Flushing is instructive in this regard. Recently the America Sevashram Sangha produced a book to accompany liturgical use called Vedic Mantras, Saswaras (with Swara) (Manuel 1998). In that book only the one-page introduction and the table of contents appear in Roman

script; the remainder is Devanagari. Especially for a congregation most accustomed to English, Tamil, and Telugu—the latter two have scripts of their own—this seems significant. In fairness it should be mentioned that the temple also makes available a four-page listing of some of the chants in frequent liturgical use in Roman transliteration.

13. In saying this I do not mean to imply that these enacted ties reproduce exactly either the form or the range of religious life among Hindus living in the Caribbean itself (see Klass 1988/1961, 137–183; Vertovec 1992, 106–130).

14. On the history of Sanatanist organizations in the Caribbean, see Vertovec 2000, 52–57.

15. A very interesting card available at Divya Dham entitles this image Trimurti. The word literally means, "having three forms [or images]" and normally refers to the triad of supreme divinities comprised of Brahma, Shiva, and Visnu, but the card points out that more than one triune representation of the divinity has been under worship in the history of Hindu religion. It goes on to discuss an earlier misidentification of the Elephanta Shiva as the Trimurti and then mysteriously adopts that very title as the identification for this reproduction of the Elephanta image. The card is entitled "Trimurti: Masterpiece of Indian Sculpture."

16. On the issue of how one should speak of the relation between the Great Goddess (Devi, Mahadevi) and a goddess such as Amba, see Hawley 1996, 1–28; Pintchman 2001.

17. On the latter, see Vertovec's discussion of various possible meanings of "diaspora" (Vertovec 2000, 141–159, especially 146–149).

18. For this information I am grateful to an interview with Gargi's parents at the Geeta Temple (January 18, 2002). The same physical connection to India also exists in another medium: fire. A flame (jyot) stands before the goddess Amba, centrally placed in the tableau of deities that receives regular worship when a congregation is assembled at Divya Dham. This flame, which is carefully tended so that it never dies out, was ignited by a flame brought overland to Europe and then by sea to New York from the mountain shrine of the goddess Jvala Mukhi in 1996. Jvala Mukhi's magnetism for pilgrims from all over north India stems from the constantly burning fire that emerges from the earth there, and is sometimes taken to represent the tongue of Sati among the sakti pithas. Swami Jagdishvaranand told me it had been merged with a flame from Vaisno Devi before being transported to the United States, which gives particular appropriateness to the fact that flames are also kept burning in Divya Dham's shrine to Vaishno Devi (Jagdishvaranand 2002; cf. Cromie 2000).

19. The bilingual and binational quality of this book is a subject worthy of attention in its own right. It was written by a professor of astrology (jyotisa) at Banaras Hindu University; its introduction is given both in Hindi and in English; and although its publisher is located in Queens, it was printed in Banaras.

20. Diana Eck's term is "transposition of place" (Eck 1982, 40–41, 144–145,

283–284). In "The Imagined Landscape" Eck has revisited the idea as a "process of duplication and multiplication" that contributes to the construction of a landscape that "is a system of reference in which each tirtha functions as part of a whole fabric of tirthas" (ibid., 167–170).

21. The most extensive and erudite discussion of this concept is provided by Jan Gonda (1976).

22. He is Bruce Williams Zaccagnino of Flemington, New Jersey, and is named in an undated temple pamphlet soliciting donations for the "Kingdom of Himalayan Gods" he has helped construct. The pamphlet, acquired in 1996, says he "is famous for making Railway Museums, Doll Museums, and Art galleries."

23. A brief description of the Tulsi Manas Mandir is provided by Philip Lutgendorf (1991, 51).

24. Basic reading on this subject in regard to the modern West would include Tony Bennett (1995) and Barbara Kirschenblatt-Gimblett (1998). On the question of whether these domains correspond to distinct milieux in an urban setting such as contemporary Chennai, see Waghorne (2001), yet it is clear that Divya Dham veers far more in the direction of the museum than either of the other temples I consider in this essay.

25. On the appeal of goddesses in a contemporary diasporic frame, see Waghorne (2001). The enumeration of the *sakta pithas* (seats of sakti) as fifty-one is relatively frequent, although the number of *sakta pithas* (i.e., *sakti pithas* [seats pertaining to sakti]) listed by D. C. Sircar in his survey of textual sources for the tradition varies from 4 to 108 (Sircar 1973, 11–31). Sircar believes the number fifty-one is to be traced to the seventeenth-century Tantrasara (ibid., 23, cf. 74–80).

26. "Divine Celebration at Divya Dham! Ekyavan Shakti-Peeth Devi Names," pamphlet announcing the inauguration of the fifty-one *sakti pithas* on May 25–27, 2001. Gary Tubb points out that this association of the number fifty-one with the Sanskrit *aksaras* is a difficult jump (personal communication, January 17, 2002). While no standard number can be assigned to the Sanskrit syllabary, it is hard to arrive at fifty-one by any means. That number would correspond accurately to the Tamil alphabet instead, and may indirectly reflect that awareness, but Divya Dham's pamphlet cites instead a text called the *Meru Tantra* as its source for the concept of fifty-one *aksara devis*.

27. Diana Eck discusses the applicability of the concept of "four dhams to various locales (1998, 180–182), and Ann Grodzins Gold refers to its flexible usage in this light by Rajasthani villagers and pilgrims (1988, 36).

Part II

The Boundaries of Time
Events, Generation, and Age

5

Negotiation of Ethnic and Religious Boundaries by Asian American Campus Evangelicals

Rebecca Y. Kim

On a southern California campus an African American student started attending an Asian American Christian club. But after three meetings he stopped coming. Two white men walked into another Asian American Christian meeting after hearing the praise music from the outside. After ten minutes, they walked out. Incidents like these are profoundly disturbing to local Asian American Christians, who believe that their religion should be inclusive. One Korean American campus leader reflected, "It is kind of a shame if we can't go beyond our little circle. I don't even have any Christian friends who are not Korean, so it is like, what the heck am I doing?"

West Coast University (a pseudonym) is a large and fairly typical public university in California. It has an ethnically diverse student body with a sizable Asian American population. Asian Americans make up 40 percent of the students on campus, with Chinese Americans making up 14 percent of the student body and Korean Americans 10 percent. Promoting itself as the center of diversity and multiculturalism, one of the university's highest priorities is to advance and promote the ethnic diversity of its students, faculty, staff, and administrators. This does not mean that there is ethnic and racial harmony on campus. But the pressure to conform to a presumably unified white majority has declined and students have more freedom to express and explore their ethnic identities and affiliations. This kind of changed social milieu—along with changes in ethnic and racial density and diversity that make separate ethnic associations possible—encourages students to participate in a variety of ethnic student organizations, including separate ethnic religious groups.

The growth of separate ethnic religious organizations, however, conflicts with the fact that most ethnic religious organizations in the United States appeal to some form of universalism and ecumenism—the belief that their religion should be inclusive and transcend ethnic and racial boundaries. Despite such beliefs, the majority of them remain ethnically and/or racially segregated.[1] Thus, when an African American or a white person comes knocking at their church door, Asian American evangelicals are troubled. Their tension is an example of the larger tension between wanting the comfort of ethnic habitation and the desire to strike out into the greater ethnically diverse world as their evangelical religious tenets teach. As Raymond Williams (1988, 279) writes, based on his observations on immigrant religious communities in the United States, "the ecumenical is always in tension with the national and the ethnic, as most religious groups appeal to some form of universalism."

This tension between ethnic separatism and religious universalism is not as strongly felt by newly arrived immigrants who are unfamiliar with American culture and the English language. But it is strongly felt by the later generations who do not have the same language and cultural barriers and could be more inclusive in their religious participation. Members of ethnic congregations that attract a native-born population must at one point or another grapple with the tension of being ethnically exclusive in their religious participation while claiming to adhere to a broader and more inclusive religious identity.

Although this conflict between ethnicity and religion continues, little research has been done on how the tension is understood and negotiated by the individuals involved in separate ethnic congregations. Most of the studies on ethnic congregations focus on how ethnicity and religion mutually reinforce one another; few examine how the two identities may conflict and how the conflict in identities may be negotiated to maintain separate ethnic group boundaries. And as most studies on ethnic religious organizations focus on the first generation, studies on how ethnic and religious identities interact for the second and later generations are even more sparse.

Understanding how this tension is worked out by individuals in separate ethnic congregations can shed light on why America's religious communities remain so segregated—why separate ethnic congregations continue to be the most popular (cp. Emerson and Smith 2000)—while also contributing to the increasing debate in America's religious communities over the merits of having ethnically separated versus integrated multiethnic congregations. This chapter focuses on the participation of growing numbers of Asian American college evangelical Christians, particularly second-generation Korean American evangelical Christians, in separate ethnic campus ministries.

Asian American evangelicals adhere to the same evangelicalism practiced by mainstream American evangelicals. Second- and later-generation Asian Americans' ethnic campus ministries are conducted in English and are led by American-trained pastors or staff members. Like mainstream American evangelicals, Asian American evangelicals believe in the inerrancy of the Bible and in the divinity, resurrection, and salvation found in Jesus Christ (Alumkal 2000).[2] They also emphasize preaching the "gospel" and proselytizing *all* nationalities.

Unlike other conservative Protestants, evangelicals are also known for being more engaged in the larger society about social issues such as racism. There is a growing movement among evangelical Christians (e.g., the Promise Keepers, InterVarsity Christian Fellowship) to promote "racial reconciliation"—the breaking down of ethnic and racial barriers through an overriding faith and unity in Jesus Christ. Moreover, as college students in major universities, Asian Americans have greater opportunities to interact with people from various ethnic and racial backgrounds and to make their religious participation more inclusive. Accordingly, the tension between ethnic separatism and religious universalism can be especially strong for them.

Campus Multiculturalism

While the university prides itself on being a center of diversity and multiculturalism, its commitment to multiculturalism is somewhat perfunctory. As a large public university serving a diverse student population, its leaders are focused primarily on meeting the pragmatic concerns of its students. The purpose is to help them function and survive in an increasingly diverse setting, not necessarily to instill a multicultural ideology in them. This conforms with the Asian American Christians' attitude. Their campus Christian groups are a pragmatic adjustment or reaction to first-generation religious practices or a practical extension of their churches; students hardly ever refer to multicultural arguments to justify founding and maintaining their monocultural ministries. Thus the multiculturalism that the Asian American Christians are concerned about is a pragmatic one. They know that their campus and the larger society are diverse; so they desire a pragmatic multiculturalism—practical skills in dealing with people across ethnic lines. Their multiculturalism is not ideologically driven.

Asian American Campus Evangelicals

The majority of religious groups on campus are evangelical Christian organizations. Out of fifty to sixty Christian groups, twenty-five to thirty are evangelicals. The largest groups are all evangelical. InterVarsity Christian Fellowship has about two hundred weekly attendants. Korean American Mission for Christ (KAMC, a pseudonym) and Christian Student Fellowship (a pseudonym) start in September with a hundred regular attendees and have about fifty in the spring.

Much of our knowledge about the growth of Asian American campus evangelicals is anecdotal due to the recent nature of the phenomenon and the lack of systematic research on the topic. However, the news media concurs with campus evangelical leaders that Asian Americans, especially Korean and Chinese Americans, predominate in the major campus evangelical organizations of many top colleges in the United States, particularly in the West and Northeast (Busto 1996; Chang 2000; Ch'ien 2000). For example, about 80 percent of the members of more than fifty evangelical Christian groups at UC Berkeley and UCLA are now Asian Americans. At Yale, one of the largest campus Christian organizations, Campus Crusade for Christ, was 100 percent white in the 1980s, but now the members are 90 percent Asian. At Stanford, InterVarsity Christian Fellowship, another large campus organization, has become almost entirely Asian. On some West Coast and Northeast campuses and in parts of the Midwest, the percentage of Asian Americans in a given InterVarsity chapter can be as high as 80 percent (Chang 2000; Ch'ien 2000). Responding to this growth, two of the major campus evangelical organizations, Campus Crusade for Christ and Navigators, have formed separate Asian American ministries within their organizations. Independent ethnic organizations like Korean American campus evangelical organizations as well as pan-Asian campus evangelical organizations have also proliferated. Asian American campus evangelicals have now become a common sight on many college campuses (Chang 2000).

As the numbers of Asian American and other ethnic students have increased on college campuses, the debate over the merits of having ethnically separated versus integrated campus ministries has escalated. Most of the mainstream campus ministries currently prefer to have separate ethnic campus ministries in those campus ministries where the numbers of ethnic minority students have increased. The Asian American ministries wouldn't advise excluding anyone, but they do not actively recruit non-Asian students as they do Asian students. If a non-Asian wants to join an Asian American campus Christian group, he or she is expected to adapt to Asian American culture. But some among the campus evangelical community want to pursue integrated multiethnic or multiracial campus ministries in lieu of separate ethnic ministries.

Methods

For two years I was a participant observer in a variety of different ethnic campus ministries at West Coast University. I particularly focused upon two Korean American campus ministries. However, I also spent a great deal of time at five other campus evangelical Christian organizations: two Asian American, two multiethnic, and one white-majority campus evangelical Christian organization. The members of both the Korean American campus ministries, which I will refer to as Korean American Mission for Christ (KAMC) and Christian Student Fellowship (CSF), were Korean Americans who were either born in the United States or received most of their primary education in the United States.[3]

During my time at WCU, I conducted over one hundred personal interviews with the students, directors, staff, and pastors who were involved in campus evangelical organizations.[4] Fifty of the interviews were conducted with second-generation Korean Americans in the Korean American campus ministries.

I had numerous opportunities to observe how members of Korean American campus ministries reconciled the conflict between the ethnic nature of their religious participation and the universality of their religious beliefs. In particular, there were several occasions when those from other ethnic and racial backgrounds expressed an interest in participating in the Korean American campus ministries; at such moments members wrestled with the theological onus to evangelize "all nations" and be inclusive in their membership. Without sounding like the voice of conscience, I asked the members of Korean American campus ministries if they felt any conflict about being part of an ethnically separate campus ministry while professing more inclusive religious beliefs. If they felt such a conflict, I asked them what, if anything, they did to mitigate ("deal with") it.

A Case Study of Korean American Campus Ministries: KAMC and CSF

The tension between ethnic separatism and religious universalism is evident in the history and development of Korean American Mission for Christ (KAMC) and Christian Student Fellowship (CSF).

Korean American Mission for Christ

KAMC was founded in the 1970s by a group of first-generation Korean pastors. It was established to encourage a "mission movement" among the growing number of Korean college students while also helping them to build social networks and sort out their bicultural identities as both Koreans and Americans. Because it was started by first-generation Koreans, the worship services in KAMC were originally conducted in Korean and consisted of members who were more comfortable speaking Korean than English.

In 1993, however, the ministry began to conduct their services mostly in English, and currently all the worship services and Bible studies are conducted in English alone. A student commented on the change, "You would not know it now, but KAMC was considered *fobbie* [a word used to characterize those newly arrived in the United States] before, but it became more Americanized in the 1990s." This change came about as KAMC's membership began to consist of a greater number of second-generation Korean Americans who were more comfortable speaking English than Korean. Thus, KAMC soon became a predominately second-generation Korean American campus ministry.

With this shift in membership, some of the members began to feel uncomfortable about being part of a separate ethnic campus ministry. Their pastor was trained in an American seminary, their worship services were conducted entirely in English, and their campus ministry focused on "evangelizing" nonbelievers (regardless of ethnic or racial background). Consequently, although the leadership as well as the membership remains predominately Korean American, KAMC has made efforts to be more inclusive. Their evangelizing "outreach" activities are held for all ethnic and racial groups who may be interested in Christianity. And a few Korean terms carried over from the ethnic church that were used during the weekly worship services are now no longer used. Coinciding with these changes, several non-Korean Americans started attending KAMC's weekly gathering. Yet KAMC remains a distinctively Korean American campus ministry, 99 percent of whose regular members are Korean American.

Christian Student Fellowship

Unlike KAMC, Christian Student Fellowship (CSF) was not started by first-generation Korean pastors. It was started by Korean American college students who were interested in forming an English-speaking Bible study group. Originally known as "Korean Christian Fellowship," CSF began with nine members and sought to attract Korean American students interested in Bible study who were more Americanized and comfortable speaking English than Korean.

In the late 1990s, however, CSF took a major step in loosening its ethnic boundaries. A few of the leaders of CSF say that they recognized that a ministry that is conducted entirely in English and that endorses a universal gospel message should be open to all ethnic and racial groups. To reflect this understanding, CSF, which was originally called "Korean Christian Fellowship," changed its name in 1999 to "Christian Student Fellowship." The leaders felt that the new name would better indicate their openness to students of different ethnic and racial backgrounds. One of the founders of CSF, Pastor Ron, envisioned CSF as a multiethnic-multiracial campus ministry for all college students. Following this vision, he tried to make the leadership of CSF more diverse and invited pastors from various ethnic and racial backgrounds to provide the weekly sermons at CSF. However, 95 percent of its members are Korean American, and CSF is still known to the West Coast University evangelical community as a "Korean American" campus ministry.

The Tension

Today, Korean American campus evangelicals say that they feel a moral guilt over the possible ethnocentrism of their religious practice. They

Do white every. groups feel this tension?

wonder whether they are living up to their names of "evangelical" and "Christian." This moral quandary leaves them feeling ambivalent over what norms should govern their actions. On the one hand, their religion proclaims universal acceptance of all people. On the other hand, they believe that being "comfortable" is an appropriate emotional quality in intimate settings, and they don't feel as comfortable in cross-ethnic settings.[5]

Both KAMC and CSF are trying to be more inclusive in their worship services. They have stopped using particular Korean terms; they have "outreach" and "witnessing" events that target all college students; and they have several "mission trips" to non-Korean countries in an effort to "preach the gospel to all nations." A few Korean Americans also occasionally bring their non-Korean American friends to their campus ministry. Despite such attempts to be more inclusive, however, both KAMC and CSF continue to have predominately Korean American members and are known as distinctively Korean American campus ministries.

One student noted, "It is not like there is going to be a Korean section in heaven . . . so I don't think it is right for us to all have our own separate thing." Another student reflected, "You have to think . . . what would Jesus do? He is not going to let ethnicity or race divide people. He was all about breaking down barriers, not putting them up." A Korean American student from CSF talked about this tension by expressing his concern over how non-Christians may view the Korean American Christian groups on campus:

> We were all talking in our suite and one of my white roommates asked me, "Why do all of you guys have all these separate Korean Christian clubs?" He was kind of like asking why can't you Christians all just get along? You would think if anyone could get along it would be [the Christians].

Other Korean American students referred to specific passages in the Bible that encourage Christians to unite under a broader religious identity despite differences in cultures.

Christians of other ethnicities also talked about the tension of having various separate Asian American campus ministries, particularly the relatively large Korean American campus ministries. A white Christian student from a diverse campus ministry was critical of organizations such as KAMC and CSF:

I can understand why they want to have a Vietnamese culture club or KSA (Korean Student Association) . . . but I don't know why they have to attach Christianity to [a particular] ethnicity. Would Jesus do it? If he came back today where would Jesus go? If he came back as a twenty-year-old white guy at WU, would he be accepted in these Korean Christian fellowships?

The tension between ethnic separation and religious integration is especially strong among second-generation Korean Americans because they do not "have to be" ethnically segregated to practice their faith. In contrast to the mainly first-generation alumni of the fellowships who are adamant about maintaining a monoethnic identity, many of the second-generation students grew up in diverse neighborhoods with ethnically and racially diverse friends. Their services are all in English, they meet in a convenient location on campus, and they adhere to a universal religion that strongly emphasizes proselytizing nonbelievers. A Korean American student leader of KAMC lamented:

> We have no excuse like our parents. I don't see the point of organizations like KAMC and CSF for second gens. I mean I like my [Korean American campus fellowship], but just because you are in it does not mean you think it is OK. You are not doing what Jesus said you should be doing.

This tension can be heightened when Korean American students attempt to evangelize to different ethnic groups. For example, two Korean American students from KAMC said they were conflicted when they evangelized a white woman who not only wanted to hear "the gospel message," but also wanted to join their campus ministry. If a Korean American woman had expressed an interest in joining their campus ministry, the two students would have readily and eagerly invited her to KAMC. But because the student was white, they were hesitant and troubled. One of the two students explained how she felt, "I felt awkward . . . embarrassed, because I didn't want to invite her out to KAMC because I knew that she would feel like an outcast or feel different because everyone basically looks the same [at KAMC]." The other Korean American student who had also evangelized the white woman said he went ahead and invited her to KAMC but forewarned her that most of the members are Korean American. The student suspected that this was the reason why the white woman did not contact him again and come to KAMC. Thus, the ethnically separate nature of

Korean American evangelicals' religious participation conflicts with their more inclusive religious identity.

The leaders are usually the ones who talk about the tension. Further, the professionally trained clergy leaders have been the most adamant about moving toward a multiethnic ministry. The clerical leader for CSF trained at local evangelical institutions (Biola University and Fuller Theological Seminary), which emphasize cross-cultural evangelism. His advocacy of a multiethnic approach generated a lot of conflict with the other staff. The biggest conflict came over substituting "Christian" for "Korean" in the name Christian Student Fellowship.

This tension, however, is not equally experienced by all second-generation Korean Americans in separate ethnic ministries. Some occasionally talk about it but say it is not something they dwell on. Others claim never to have experienced such tensions (though they recognize that they do or could exist). As a Korean American student put it, "Most people do not think about it. . . . For most people having intellectual or theological coherence is not an issue." Some campus evangelicals also pointed out that the majority of people do not have the time to think about such conflicts when faced with the everyday practicalities of being part of a campus ministry as busy college students. A student leader of KAMC said:

> We can barely keep up with the people that are in our own campus ministry. Trying to help them as students ourselves is hard enough. . . . So we don't have time to even begin to think about things like [the tension] even though I admit it is a problem.

For some, this tension was a not even an issue. Another Korean American student leader pointed out:

> Do you think the average freshmen coming here, maybe just looking for a few friends, a good time, hang out . . . nervous about if he is going to fit in or not is going to think about that? . . . Nah, man. At the maturity level of people coming here, as freshmen, their first opinion is not going to be like "OK, I am going to worship God with the whole family of Christ." Instead it is like [CSF] is cool, I am going to try it out.

Thus, the tension between separation and integration may not be equally experienced by all the members, and some may not experience it at all. But it is a tension that some, particularly those in leadership roles, clearly recognize and sense. It is a conflict that all Christian ethnic congregations, on or off campus, that attract a native-born population will face in today's increasingly diverse society.

Negotiating Boundary Tensions

"We are all sinners." Several Korean Americans explained the seeming contradiction between their religious beliefs and their ethnic exclusivity by noting that people are naturally weak and "sinful" and often fail to do what is right. "How do we deal with it? I don't know. . . . It is just sin, we are weak," one student said. "We know what is good, what is right, but we don't do it."

Thus the tension between ethnic separatism and religious universalism is negotiated by noting that segregation within the Christian community is only one of man's many weaknesses, inconsistencies, and hypocrisies. In the face of this fact of life some noted that they could only "pray" and "turn to Jesus for help." Talking about his friends in his Korean American Christian Fellowship, a Korean American student lamented, "We have to pray that Jesus will move their hearts and inspire them to change . . . that the Holy Spirit would work in them . . . otherwise, unless Jesus changes people's hearts, change is not going to happen." The conflict between ethnic separatism and religious universalism is therefore partly alleviated by seeing the problem as a deeply entrenched "spiritual" one that can only be resolved by divine intervention.[6]

The members in these ethnic religious organizations also negotiated the tension between their ethnic and religious identities in two other ways: by referring to the salience of choice and comfort involved in individuals' religious participation; and by making a distinction between private and more public religious participation.

Choice and Comfort

While Korean Americans feel conflicted over the discrepancy of "sharing the gospel message" with others while not inviting them to their own campus ministry, these sorts of conflicts are sometimes alleviated by the knowledge that non-Korean American students can attend other campus ministries. As a Korean American student put it simply, "So long as we are not the only campus ministry out there . . . I think it is OK." Another explained:

> I mean it is best that they go to the campus group where they feel the most comfortable and where they think they can grow. . . . So if this is not for them, then they can go somewhere else. . . . It is not like KAMC is the only campus ministry around.

Claiming that religious needs can be fully met through a variety of organizations, the leaders and members of campus ministries say that the most important factor determining participants' choice of ministry is where they feel most "comfortable." Given the choice, Korean Americans and non-Korean Americans alike responded that individuals will choose to participate in campus ministries with which they are the most culturally familiar, where they can be part of the majority group, and where they are likely to have the easiest access.

People want to participate in a religious organization where they can be with others who can best share and understand their cultural background, norms, and beliefs. They want to be where their ethnic group can be the majority in power—where they do not have to feel discriminated against or deficient because of their ethnic or racial background. In an all-Korean organization, the students feel that they don't have to second-guess themselves because of their ethnic or racial minority status. Related to these two factors, individuals will go where they have the easiest and most ready access, where they have the most social ties, which for many tend to be with their own ethnic group. Thus, given the choice of participating in an ethnic, multiethnic, or traditional white campus ministry, most Korean American students (and other ethnic minority students) will participate in an ethnic campus ministry where their ethnic group is in the majority.

The way Korean American students date, relate to others, and participate in group activities also reinforces a sense of belonging to a group rather than being an individual. Highly relevant for young singles, many Korean American students feel more comfortable dating as a group where a group of men and women go out together rather than in pairs. Even when two people eventually go out on their own, the opinions and concerns of their peers and parents play a significant role in their relationship. Further, students in the Korean American fellowships enjoy ways of socializing and interacting with others with special group games and singing to a degree not usually found in mixed ethnic groups. The style of their Bible studies is also more subdued and no one is "put on the spot" by being asked to contribute to the discussion. Being more group-oriented, Korean Americans are also more likely to be respectful and deferential toward their parents and to maintain closer ties with them than most other Americans.

The group emphasis is also noticeable when students discuss what film they want to see or what place they want to visit after the weekly fellowship meetings. The purpose of the discussion is not so much to decide on a goal, as to allow everyone to feel that they were part of the decision, part of the group. Thus one can find Korean American students "hanging out" for a significant amount of time after the weekly services not because they have not decided where or what to do next, but because they are trying to take everyone's preferences and opinions into account. Given this kind of tendency, some Korean campus staff members maintain that Korean Americans would not have as many opportunities to be heard in a white-majority or mixed ethnic group setting.

Recognizing the needs of the average religious consumer, the leaders of campus ministries noted that a culturally "contextualized" ministry that targets particular ethnic groups is simply a smart and efficient strategy for ultimately satisfying the greatest number of religious consumers. Having specialized ethnic campus ministries is said to be the best strategy for drawing the maximum number of religious consumers into their respective organizations and ultimately "spreading the gospel" to all ethnic and racial groups. Without such ethnic campus ministries, the leaders of campus ministries reason that they would lose many potential religious consumers. Indeed, the best path for success for a Korean American staffer is following the contextualized ethnic ministry model. One Korean American leader justified this approach by referring to Apostle Paul in the Bible when he said that Christians should "become all things to all men" so that they may be able to "save" and lead people to Jesus.

A campus pastor explained further:

> Most people coming into campus ministry are not spiritually mature. So when you are trying to reach them . . . you want to make sure that you do not place any unnecessary obstacles, barriers in their way. For example, if you have an African American student who is interested in learning more about Christ, you don't want to bring him into a Korean American campus ministry setting where he is obviously going to be uncomfortable. . . . But if he was placed in a contextualized campus ministry for African Americans, you can see how he would have an easier time and grow.

In these ways, it is reasoned that if they did not cater to the average religious consumer and offer more comfortable contextualized ethnic campus ministries, they would lose potential members. Ethnic campus ministries thus minimize the conflict that they may have over their exclusivity by noting that ethnic campus ministries are necessary to reach the largest number of ethnic and racial groups.

Private and Public Religious Participation

The leaders and members of ethnic campus ministries also negotiate the tension between separation and integration by making distinctions between private life and the more public and socially integrative aspects of religious participation. For example, engaging in more private and intimate religious activities with other coethnics is acceptable so long as there are other religious activities that are more socially integrative. This was most evident in the evangelical Christian campus ministries' involvement in the Intercollegiate Christian Council (ICC).

Led by student representatives of the various Christian groups on campus, the ICC holds several events throughout the school year that seek to unite the Christian students at WCU and thereby have an impact on the larger campus. For example, at one of the ICC events, many of the campus Christian groups pooled their resources to invite Christian intellectuals to come to campus to speak to a broad student audience on topics related to the Christian faith. In another event called "Servant Evangelism" (or "Love-WCU Day") the various Christian groups provided free food and drinks to students on campus in an effort to express "Jesus' love." These activities enabled the members of the separate ethnic campus ministries (along with other multiethnic campus ministries) to publicly unite to work together to positively influence the larger campus. Several student members of KAMC, CSF, and other campus ministries spoke favorably about their experiences with the ICC—how it helped them to "worship" and positively experience what it was like to be part of a larger Christian community:

> The first time [an ICC event] was held . . . you walked in and there was this room full of Christians from all the fellowships . . . and most of them were represented. The major ones were all there and we were worshiping and praying together as an entire body. There was so much power

in that . . . thousands of voices praising God. It was an awesome experience.

ICC is where you can get out of your bubble . . . do something crazy for this campus . . . like on Love-WU day, we passed out food and drinks to whoever as a group.

I was really excited with [one of the events supported by the ICC] . . . it was so good to see groups getting together to repent and worship together. I really loved meeting non-Korean Christians.

It is cool to have your own personal fellowship where you can get along better. . . . But I really like something like ICC . . . where you can see God work as a whole body of Christians at school instead of just at CSF. . . . It definitely helps you to think bigger . . . it gets you out of your little niche.

Being part of the ICC enables students to extend beyond their particular Christian ministries and have part of their religious participation be more inclusive. It enables students to unite and take part in the broader Christian community without leaving their more intimate ethnic Christian community.

The tension between ethnic separatism and religious universalism is also negotiated by having some activities *within* each of the separate ethnic campus ministries that are more inclusive. For example, while both KAMC and CSF are separate ethnic campus ministries for Korean Americans, they also have religious activities within their organizations that include other ethnic and racial groups. They feed the homeless, work at local charities, and go on short-term mission trips to foreign countries (e.g., to Mexico, Russia, and Africa) that are not ethnically exclusive. By participating in these activities, students within separate ethnic campus ministries have several opportunities to go beyond their ethnic communities and decrease the tension that results from being part of a separate ethnic campus ministry. A student leader of KAMC described it as trying to go beyond the "Korean Christian bubble":

We are trying to help people to have a bigger vision . . . look beyond the Korean Christian bubble . . . so like now, the core [the KAMC leadership] is trying to get together with this environmental group on campus and do like

a homeless thing. . . . We also want to do stuff for the community in general
and also the WU community for us to say, at least we are trying. At least
people can see that as a Christian group we are trying to break down barriers and not have these walls so strong and so big. It is tough, but I think that
it is something that we have to press.

Such public and inclusive religious events thus help Korean Americans
deal with the tension that comes from adhering to an ethnically exclusive
religious organization.

Conclusion

We have seen how individuals negotiate the enduring tension between
ethnic separatism and religious universalism. The leaders don't have a
road map to the future, and resolutions so far have been unplanned and
unsatisfactory. They throw up their hands declaring, "We can't help it if
our members don't want it," while the members claim that their wills are
weak and their desire for comfort too strong. Yet, in practice as the fellowships compete in the local religious market, they are generating innovations that are further integrating them into the local religious economy.
Pretty soon their leadership in religious innovation may open up new
ways of integrating them into the multiethnic market. Their success may
breed their own demise.

Thus far, Asian American evangelicals on campus have reached across
ethnic boundaries through ethnically defined cross-cultural innovations.
For example, to introduce their groups to new students they have developed a Chinese food take-out box filled with erasers, pens, pencils, and the
like. Taped to each eraser is a Bible verse written like the fortune found in
a fortune cookie. Here and elsewhere across the United States, Asian
American groups have pioneered a revival of a capella singing. At West
Coast University Korean American evangelicals have become known for
their cutting-edge music. Students of other ethnicities commonly tell interviewers, "Oh, the Koreans have a great worship team." The KAMC also
made a movie about their year on campus. They filmed students waxing
nostalgic over their past year. Other ethnic ministries interpreted the film
as very hip and are planning to emulate it. Most of the Asian American
evangelical groups have also been very active in creating skits and other
small dramatic presentations.

As a result of the Asian American evangelicals' innovations, the religious marketplace has become more competitive. This may lead to further innovations that reach across ethnic lines so as to maintain or improve religious groups' market positions. One example of this market-driven cross-ethnic boundary crossing is the formation of a new multiethnic ministry by a defector from the KAMC. A 1.5 generation[7] founder of KAMC came into conflict with other KAMC leaders over his desire to change the ethnic boundedness of the group. Finally, he left to form a multiethnic ministry reaching the "postmodern generation." He hired an African American to help him monitor the new group's inclusiveness and invites speakers of diverse ethnicities. So far, the group remains small, but it is closely watched by other Christian groups on campus.

Two years of study suggest that if integrated congregations are the desired goal, ethnic congregations must be willing to give up some of their cultural comforts, negotiate power relationships with different ethnic groups, and extend their social ties to other ethnic groups. In some diverse evangelical groups on campus white leaders stepped down so that other ethnics could assume leadership positions. One of the few successful multiethnic campus ministries at WCU, InterVarsity Christian Fellowship (IVCF),[8] does exactly this. IVCF actively recruits diverse students and aims to provide an environment where different ethnic groups would feel welcome. The staff expects all members to show an appreciation of other cultures.

Although their practices seem to be isomorphic to the liberal multiculturalism of the university, the leaders feel that their multiculturalism is transformative in its goal of social unity, not celebrated segregation. IVCF has monthly gatherings where members talk specifically about ethnic and racial issues and students can discuss and explore their ethnic identities. They also have ethnically diverse speakers come and provide the weekly sermons. Their "praise team" is also ethnically diverse and the members occasionally sing some of their "praise music" in Spanish (with English subtitles). Even though their worship activities are integrated, IVCF also provides opportunities for the different ethnic students to establish closer social ties with other coethnics. They do this by occasionally having separate dinners, Bible studies, and retreats for the different ethnic groups. Trying to balance the comforts and needs of a number of different ethnic groups without making any one of them feel marginalized within the group, however, is not an easy task. Thus, integrated multiracial campus ministries continue to be the exception rather than the norm.

NOTES

1. About 90 percent of American religious congregations are comprised of at least 90 percent of one racial group (Emerson and Smith 2000).

2. The term "evangelicalism" covers a wide canopy of definitions. It originates in the Greek word "evangelion" which means "good news" or "gospel." Martin Luther adopted the term during the Reformation as he broke away from the Catholic Church. The term has been subsequently used to connote religious movements and denominations that swept the North Atlantic Anglo-American world in the eighteenth and early nineteenth centuries. "Evangelicalism" is now commonly looked at as a socioreligious movement and tradition, which denotes a particular style of Christianity as well as a set of beliefs.

Whereas the term "evangelicalism" is used as a socioreligious movement and tradition, the term "evangelical" is commonly used to describe those conservative Protestant "Christians" who affirm several theological principles. These include: (1) belief in the complete reliability and authority of the Bible; (2) belief in the divinity of Christ and the efficacy of His life, death, and physical resurrection for the salvation of the human soul; and (3) the importance of conversion or being "born again," having personal faith, and proselytizing nonbelievers.

3. I found out whether the organization identified itself as "evangelical Christian" or not through the organization's mission statements and by talking to the members and leaders. I categorized an organization as "evangelical" if it fit the traits common to contemporary evangelicals: believing in the sole authority and reliability of the Bible, emphasizing individual faith and salvation of the human soul solely by faith in Jesus Christ, and proselytizing nonbelievers. I categorized a campus organization as a Korean American campus evangelical organization if the pastor and staff of the organization are Korean American and if the majority of its members are Korean Americans who were either born in the United States or received most of their primary education in the United States.

4. The real names of the Korean and Asian campus evangelical organizations that I observed have been changed and/or excluded in the discussion.

5. Tensions can also exist between Asian Americans' ethnic and religious identities because Christianity can be viewed as a "white man's religion." However, because Korea had a relatively positive historical relationship with Christian missionaries and more than a quarter of its current population identifies itself as Christian, most Korean Americans did not view their Christian religion as a "white man's religion."

6. These religious rationalizations suggest that those who are more religious and within high-authority religions will be able to overcome such inconsistencies and actually have more integrated religious organizations. Interestingly, the most diverse Christian groups on campus were those that were labeled "cultic" and considered religious extremists. One of them is a well-known cult led by a leader who

deviated from one of the Protestant denominations. Another is a zealous group that focuses heavily on world evangelism. Their explicit and main purpose is to raise missionaries to "all nations." With such an ambitious goal, even dating between members is not allowed. Because these groups are so extreme, they get most of their members through outreach and evangelizing on campus instead of by word of mouth. It may be that their extreme religious beliefs override any differences in ethnicity and race.

7. Someone not born in the United States, but who has received most of his or her primary education in the United States.

8. Not all IVCF chapters are alike; WU IVCF is exceptional in its diversity.

6

Christian by Birth or Rebirth?

Generation and Difference in an
Indian American Christian Church

Prema A. Kurien

Dissatisfied with the way the church was meeting their needs, some of the younger generation members of the St. Thomas church of Bethelville[1] formed a youth focus group in 1998 to analyze the problems and come up with suggestions for reform, which they then planned to present before the congregation.

"We met in the classroom behind the church every month. We started with the basics, what is our church about, what is the purpose of a church? We also went on field trips to a few churches. I kept the *Achen* [pastor] closely informed about everything. But the adults in the church kept asking, 'What are they doing, what are they doing?' Then all of a sudden the rumors started flying, it is a secret group, Johnny is a cult leader. They couldn't wait and wanted us to present immediately. We said, fine, we will present what we have up to that point. I had all these transparencies prepared and rather than just saying this is what we want, I tried to give some background. I said, 'We need to have a vision for the church.' As I am trying to water the soil before planting the seeds, people are saying, 'get to the point, get to the point.' People are interrupting . . ."

Johnny, the leader of the focus group, laughed as he narrated what had happened that day. In a separate interview, George, another of the youth members, described what happened next.

"We were being shot down by the congregation, left and right. Then Sam started talking about the importance of being a true Christian, of having a personal relationship with Christ. As he was talking, you could see the steam rising in church. Finally, one of the uncles in the congregation jumped up and shouted, flailing his arms vigorously to make his point, 'How can you imply that we are not Christians? We are all Christians in this church. My father was a Christian, I am a Christian. I was baptized by the *Thirumeni* [Bishop] himself. My son was born a Christian and will be a Christian all his life.'"

Indian immigrants and their children at St. Thomas, a reformed orthodox Indian church located in the suburbs of a major metropolitan area in the United States, were confronting each other with very different models of religion and the role of the church. Members of the immigrant generation wanted to maintain a largely traditional church and theology according to which membership was attained through ascribed religious and ethnic criteria. This was in complete opposition to the second generation's universalistic, achieved, and individualistic model of evangelical Christianity. As a consequence of this conflict, many of the adult children were leaving the immigrant church.

What is interesting about the case of Indian Christian immigrants and their American-born children is that three types of cleavages—the intergenerational gap, the fundamental differences in worldview between immigrants and their American-born children, and the different models of Christianity of those who are part of a traditional denominational church and those who are members of postdenominational parachurches (see Miller 1997) were superimposed upon each other. In this chapter, we will see how these conflicts played out in the church and their practical and analytical implications, both for the ethnic church in question and for immigrant religion more generally.

Intergenerational Relationships in
Immigrant American Churches

Within the sociology of religion, it is now well understood that religious institutions play an important role in immigrant adaptation since they often become the means to create community, construct ethnic identity, and transmit homeland culture and values to children (Ebaugh and Chafetz 2000a; Warner 1993; Warner and Wittner 1998; Williams 1988; Yang and Ebaugh 2001a). However, to really understand what role the religious institutions founded by the new wave of immigrants will play in the lives of the second and later generations, we have to look at the involvement of the American-born youth in such institutions.

There are indications that the second generation obtains several social, psychological, and economic benefits from participation in ethnic religious institutions. In particular, such participation seems to help second-generation Americans deal with the identity issues they have to confront, focus on educational achievement, and avoid assimilating to popular American teenage norms that emphasize social success over academics (Busto 1996; Ebaugh and Chafetz 2000a; Kurien 1998; Zhou and Bankston 1998). In the absence of continued, high levels of new immigration, how intergenerational tensions are addressed will determine whether or not ethnic churches will survive the first generation. Since ethnic religious institutions are frequently the primary ethnic organizations for immigrants, the survival of ethnic churches is also critical for the reproduction of ethnicity over time.

Although this chapter is based on a case study of the Bethelville church, the available literature indicates that the intergenerational problems facing the church were ones that many immigrant churches in the United States have confronted (see Cha 2001; Chai 1998, 2000; Ebaugh and Chafetz 2000a; Yang 1999b; Williams 1996, 189–194). The descriptions of Niebuhr (1929, 200–235) and Herberg (1983/1960) show that early immigrant European churches faced problems of generational transmission not very different from what contemporary immigrant churches are having to deal with. Unlike the ascribed character of religious affiliation in their home countries, in the United States religion was "voluntaristic," and thus in many cases, established American denominations were able to woo immigrants, and particularly their children, away from their own "ethnic" churches (Ebaugh and Chafetz 2000a). Herberg (1983/1960) has argued that European immigrants gave up their ethnic identities over time, but maintained their religion—Protestantism, Catholicism, and Judaism—as a marker of their distinct identity in American society. However, he has also noted that although many of the second generation abandoned their religion in addition to their homeland identities in order to become "American," members of the third generation overwhelmingly returned to the religion of their grandparents as a way of locating themselves within the social landscape of America. Other scholars have pointed out that ethnic identities were not completely abandoned as Herberg would have us believe, but were maintained within the denominational structure of Protestantism (Marty 1972; Niebuhr 1929) and within the regional ("quasi-denominational") or parish level in the case of American Catholicism (Greeley 1972, 119).

The growing literature on Korean and Chinese American Christians (Cha 2001; Chai 1998, 2000; Yang 1999b) indicates that there are many parallels between the intergenerational dynamics in the Bethelville church and what is taking place within these churches. Even among groups like Korean American Christians where two-thirds of the immigrant generation attended an ethnic church service every week with their families (Min 2000, 130), very few of the second generation adults (as low as 5 percent according to one study in New York City)[2] remained in the immigrant ethnic church. However, many such second-generation Korean Americans went on to second-generation Asian American churches.

An important factor affecting the shape of the second-generation Korean and Chinese American church appears to be the confrontation of its members with the process of racialization. Busto (1996) speculates that Korean and Chinese American students are attracted to evangelical campus groups in large numbers because such groups help them affirm a nonracial identity. The literature indicates that the consequent "conversion" of many of the second generation to evangelical Christianity resulted in very similar intergenerational conflicts over the role of religion in Korean and Chinese American churches as in the Indian Christian church that I studied, and that a large number of second-generation members initially dropped out or joined nonethnic parachurches. However, many of these members started returning to the immigrant church as they experienced racism and exclusion in the wider society and in the parachurches. These individuals then worked to obtain more autonomy for the second-generation church and in some cases even broke away to form independent ethnic churches that followed most of the practices of American evangelical groups (Cha 2001; Chai 1998, 2000; Yang 1999b). Thus, Korean and Chinese American Christians have been successful in resolving the tension between the particularism of ethnicity and the universalism of religion that the immigrant church faces by institutionalizing an ethnic church (theoretically a universalistic church with a majority ethnic congregation) that practices a generic American Christianity.

There are hints in the literature that indicate that the gendered religious practices of immigrant groups might also be important in shaping their religious institutions in the long term (Kim, A. 1996; Park 2001; Rayaprol 1997). In many cases, the greater degree of congregationalism and lay leadership of immigrant religious institutions has resulted in women obtaining more significant religious roles in the diaspora. However, in groups where men have experienced downward mobility as a consequence of immigration, religious institutions become an even more fiercely guarded male arena (Min 1992; George 1998). This in turn might lead to more second-generation women leaving the church than men.

The Mar Thoma Church

The Mar Thoma denomination is part of the Syrian Christian church, the name given to the church in the state of Kerala in southwestern India that traces its origin to the supposed arrival of Apostle Thomas to the Kerala coast in 52 A.D. According to tradition, the Apostle Thomas converted several upper-caste Malayalee Hindus to Christianity and was subsequently martyred in south India in 72 A.D. It is called a Syrian church because it was initially under the control of the patriarch in Syria and used a Syrian liturgy. Over the centuries, the church split several times and there are now several denominations—Orthodox, Catholic, and Protestant—that claim a Syrian Christian heritage. The Mar Thoma church is a reformed Orthodox church which has incorporated many Western Protestant elements into its theology and worship service. The denomination is now headed by a patriarch in Kerala.

Christians comprise less than 3 percent of the population in India but are a much higher proportion of Indian Americans. One study of Queens borough of New York City estimated that they might make up 12 percent of the population (Min 2000, 130).[3] According to Raymond Williams (1996, 93), Christians from the state of Kerala are the largest group of Indian Christians in the United States.[4] Within this group, the churches of the Mar Thoma denomination generally tend to be the largest, best organized, and most active (Williams 1996, 137).

The North American diocese of the Mar Thoma denomination was established in 1972. Initially it came under the Episcopal church of America because of the similarities in liturgy. However, in 1998 it was recognized as an independent American denomination. Despite this, the North American diocese remains under the control of the synod in Kerala. The church functions on a principle of pastoral rotation. Priests are sent from Kerala to each North American parish every four years. After this period, they are assigned to a parish back in Kerala. The pastor and his family are fully supported by the local parish, which pays for his housing, utilities, car and gas, medical insurance, and a monthly salary. At the time of my fieldwork, the pastor's monthly salary was about $1,400 a month. In addition, the Bethelville congregation supported several projects in India and also had to contribute to the mother church in Kerala. Thus, the financial demands on parishes, particularly smaller ones like that of the church at Bethelville, were quite high and were often a source of conflict. At the Bethelville church, each family was expected to contribute a minimum of $35.00 a month, in addition to the special collections round the year. In 1999, a church membership of over a hundred families provided the entire income of the church, almost $100,000. Most of this money came from about 60 percent of the membership and the average contribution of these families was around $1,500 a year. Every year the church sent out the annual accounts indicating the contribution made by each of the member families for the different causes. Being high on the list was an important source of prestige for the congregants.

Since the social composition of the Bethelville congregation determined many of the characteristic features of the church, I will discuss this briefly before addressing the issues on which the first and second generation differed. The St. Thomas church in Bethelville was established in 1976 and met in rented facilities until 1988, when it was able to buy a church in Bethelville. All the members of the church were of Malayalee heritage. The majority of those who attended services on any regular basis were immigrants who had grown up in the largely Christian areas of rural Kerala. Many had gone to other parts of India to study and work before immigrating to the United States. Around 80 percent of the women in the older generation (forty-five years and older), were nurses and had been the primary immigrants. Since nursing was considered a low-status occupation in Kerala, most of the women who went into the profession (and the men who married them) hailed from lower-middle-class families. Generally, the women came to the United States alone. Their families joined them a few years later when the women had obtained the necessary sponsorship papers and had saved enough money to pay for their passage and to support them when they arrived in the United States. The majority of this group arrived in the seventies when there was a big shortage of nurses in the United States. The husbands did not have a job waiting for them and many initially worked in factories before obtaining the qualifications for better positions. Several of the men subsequently obtained clerical or postal service jobs.

A second, smaller group was comprised of men who had migrated to the United States seeking professional education, and their families. Most had arrived in this country between the late sixties and the late seventies. They had either come with their wives or had gone back later and got married to Malayalee women. This group was very well established economically. Some were doctors or engineers, others were in management positions. At the time of my fieldwork, very few from this group attended the Bethelville church on a regular basis, most preferring to attend a local nonethnic church. The majority of those who did attend came just once every few months.

A third group of men (eleven in the St. Thomas church) had come to the region through church contacts in the 1970s in order to study at a local Christian university that had an affiliation with a Bible college in south India. Some of these men had married nurses. These were the three subgroups of pioneers who came together to establish the Bethelville church. Subsequently, some of the relatives sponsored by the pioneer groups arrived in the United States and joined the church. There was also a smaller group of more recent, younger generation immigrants who worked largely in the computer field.

The traditional liturgy of the St. Thomas church was in ornate, ceremonial Malayalam (very different from the colloquial, everyday language) with some Syriac and Aramaic words woven in. It was mostly sung in a sonorous chant, with congregational responses. If the pastor has a deep voice and good intonation, the liturgy has a particularly soothing and uplifting quality. To cater to the second generation, who for the most part did not know much Malayalam (and certainly not the formal Malayalam used in the liturgy, prayers, and sermons), the Bethelville church also offered English services on the second and third Sundays of the month. Although most of the congregation knew English quite well, in general fewer people attended the English services. Because of the schedule of the nurses (most of whom had to work on alternate weekends), many families could not attend every Sunday and thus chose to attend on the Sundays that there was a Malayalam service.

Between July 1999 and August 2000, and again in the fall of 2001, I conducted ethnographic fieldwork in the St. Thomas church of Bethelville. I chose to study this church since I am a Syrian Christian belonging to the Church of South India (CSI). Because the CSI has full communion with the Mar Thoma church, I was "eligible" to attend and even become a member (which I have not done so far). Besides attending church services, general congregational meetings, some Sunday school classes, and other church functions, I also conducted interviews with thirty-four members of the congregation of the first, second, and 1.5 generations. I had lived in and conducted research in a Syrian Christian rural village in Kerala for an earlier project, and my familiarity with the background of most members was very helpful, since the first generation often found it difficult to articulate what their identity or religion meant to them. The youth, on the other hand, brought up in the talk-show secular culture and the testimonial-oriented evangelical culture of the United States, were much more articulate.

My research showed that Syrian Christians who were a long-established and insulated minority in India, had to face several challenges in their attempts to establish and institutionalize an "ethnic" church in the United States (see also Yang 1999a; Chai 1998, 2000; Cha 2001). An important issue was how to retain the allegiance of the second and later generations to the distinct liturgical, ritual, and ecclesiastical practices of the traditional denomination. In the Mar Thoma case, not only did these practices seem alien to the American-born children, but the parents found it difficult to explain and justify their particularistic, ascriptive, and communal model of Christianity in the face of the universalistic, achieved, and individualistic model of evangelical Christianity to which their children were being exposed in school and college.

Of course, not all first- and second-generation members fit neatly into these two categories. Some of the older members, who were influenced by Billy Graham and other American television evangelists, did acknowledge the importance of having a "conversion" experience and a personal relationship with God. The church was also divided into several factions and some members always opposed the proposals of their rivals. The nature and extent of intergenerational conflict present at any particular time depended partly on the qualities of the pastor, who was replaced every four years. The conflict was particularly intense between 1996 and 2000 because the pastor at the helm had a reputation for being uninterested in the youth and only catering to the older generation. Yet it is fair to say that most members of the immigrant generation (with the possible exception of some of the younger immigrants) shared an understanding about the meaning of being Christian and the role of the ethnic church that fundamentally differed from the perspective of the majority of the second generation.

Of course, some of the second generation were apathetic about religion and only came to church because of parental pressure. But at the time of the study all the youth leaders of the church (who were all male) shared the evangelical model of Christianity. Since these were the youth who were in charge of teaching high school and college students and organizing the youth Bible studies, cottage meetings, and retreats, their model was very influential and dominant among the second-generation youth who were active in the church.

Generational Differences in the Meaning of Being Christian

The Immigrant Generation

For the immigrant generation, being Christian was inextricably intertwined with being Syrian Christian Malayalees. Except for those women who had become a part of the St. Thomas denomination by marriage, it also meant being a St. Thomas Christian. In other words, for most of this group, heritage, faith, and denomination were bound together and conferred by birth, as was the case for most other social groups in India. As Sam, one of the youth leaders noted, "I did some reading about the St. Thomas church—it was just another caste in the Hindu system instead of being about the worship of God." He meant this as a criticism, but for the immigrant generation, being part of the honored, successful, upper-caste Syrian Christian group was a matter of pride. In India, Syrian Christians had a clear subcultural identity as Christians belonging to an ancient Middle Eastern church. Besides preserving their religious heritage, Syrian Christians maintained their distinct identity through the practice of prescriptive endogamy within the larger community (interdenominational marriages were frequent), and through their characteristic names, cuisine, clothing, and jewelry as well as their inheritance, marriage, and death customs, all of which differentiated them from the groups around them.

The older generation told me that they had been taught about Christianity by their parents, grandparents, other members of their extended family, and the local church. For the immigrant generation, being a good Christian in India or the United States meant attending the local church of one's denomination every Sunday, participating in its activities, reading the Bible, praying every day, and being a "moral" person. Parents were expected to send their children to Sunday school, make them read the Bible, memorize verses from it, and to pray. Parents, particularly mothers, also periodically exhorted their children to live good Christian lives, a practice that they said they continued with their American-born children. "My mom would always tell me that I should be religious and follow the 'right way.' That was her big thing. 'Follow the right way.' I don't know what that means to this day," said Biju, a member of the second generation who rarely attended the church any more. Members of the first and 1.5 generation indicated that part of being Christian in India meant that their parents had often been more strict than those of their friends. Several mentioned that they had not been allowed to watch movies at all or had been heavily restricted regarding which movies they could watch. Parties and dances (in the case of those individuals who grew up in metropolitan areas in India) had also not been permitted.

The St. Thomas denomination (in contrast to the orthodox Syrian Christian denominations) has traditionally emphasized the importance of supporting humanitarian causes. Thus, some of the older generation mentioned that to them an important part of being Christian was the call to perform service to the community and indicated that their choice of profession—as a doctor, nurse, social service worker, or missionary—had been dictated in part by this call. They also said that they felt an obligation to "give back" to the poor and needy in Kerala and in other parts of India. Every year, the Bethelville church sent money to support several social service projects in many parts of the country. While the church also supported some missionary work, the pastor told me that unlike more evangelical churches, St. Thomas and the Mar Thoma denomination generally donated more for humanitarian causes.

The Second Generation

All the youth who told me that religion played an important role in their lives indicated that their primary sources of information about Christianity were not their parents, the pastor, or even the Sunday school (as had been the case for their parents). Many had attended private Christian schools where they had learned about Christianity through its classes and speakers. School and college friends and campus Christian groups were an even more important source of knowledge and of support. A few had done a lot of reading on their own. They also mentioned television programs and websites. Some of the younger members of the youth said that the youth cottage meetings of the St. Thomas church (which were led by the youth leaders) had been helpful as well.

Although there were differences in some of the specifics, largely on gender lines, being a committed Christian instead of a "nominal" Christian seemed to involve three primary components. The first was a personal relationship with Christ, often initiated as a result of a fairly dramatic "conversion experience." Frequently this happened at a Christian revival meeting organized by the school, where a particular speaker had seemed to be "speaking to me directly." So, most of the youth could give me the exact date on which they were "born again in Christ," "accepted Christ," or "gave my life to Christ." Having such a personal relationship with Christ in turn meant that "Jesus is the center of my life and the one that directs me in all that I do, in all areas of my life," in the words of one of the youth leaders. It meant knowing the Bible well and knowing how to apply it to everyday life decisions and problems. For some of the youth it meant that God was controlling every aspect of their lives. "For instance, I believe that if my car didn't break down on my way to church, it is not because of mechanical reasons but because God is watching over me," said Joshua, a youth in his early twenties.

A second component which was stressed particularly by some of the youth leaders, was the importance of having an intellectual understanding of Christianity. At a youth cottage meeting, the discussion was about a video they had just watched where the speaker emphasized that Christians should eschew the relativism of many American youngsters and believe without any hesitation that Jesus was the only God. One of the teenage girls asked, "But people of other faiths believe with equal certainty that their religions are true. So how can we know which is the true religion?" She answered the question herself saying, "Well, I guess beyond a point, it has to be a matter of faith." Another of the girls followed up by saying that it was largely because of her upbringing as a Christian that she believed in the religion. Maybe if she had been born into another religion, she would not have believed in Christianity.

But Philip, the youth leader, replied, "It is not just a matter of irrational and blind faith or upbringing. Faith should be belief based on logic and evidence. For instance, take George Washington. We were not there, we never met him, but we know and believe that he existed because of all the evidence we have." He talked about how there was sufficient evidence "proving" that the Bible was true and concluded by exhorting the group, "So, we should not just inherit our beliefs but actively study and educate ourselves about Christianity and make the personal commitment on this basis." In one way or another, all the youth leaders of the church expressed this point of view.

The third component was the importance of evangelism, "spreading the word of God and bringing others to Christ." Some of the youth members, particularly the males, argued that this was the central mission of a committed Christian. The four key youth leaders in the church told me that they felt a calling to particularly focus on the youth of the church— those still in church and those who had "fallen out." Johnny, the Sunday school principal and the teacher of the seniormost class (high school students) told his group, after a particularly gruesome account about the horrors of hell, "This is why I am doing this, to save as many of the youth of the church as possible. I know I am headed for heaven. Hope to see you there too."

There are substantial gender differences in the meaning of being Christian. The young women that I interviewed spoke about how Christianity provided meaning and motivation for life and how prayer had helped them get through the hurdles they had to face. They too spoke of the importance of reading and knowing the Bible. But unlike the young men, none of the women emphasized the importance of evangelism. Instead they seemed to see religion as a personal choice that should not be imposed. Sheila spoke about how she had initially been very judgmental after her conversion experience. "But later on, as I grew older, I began to be more accepting. Not that it's condoning anything . . . but we're all there [i.e., we are all imperfect] and no one is better than the next person. We all make mistakes." Sheila told me that she came to this position as she recalled her own experiences with racism when many of her schoolmates taunted her "and pointed fingers at me, just for being different." Similarly, the teenage girls who spoke up at the youth meetings and Sunday school classes seemed to subscribe to a much more relativistic model than that of the youth leaders.

Generational Differences in the Role of the Church

The differences in the meaning of being Christian also meant that immigrants and their children had very different conceptions about the church, its mission and structure, the role of the pastor, the types of sermons they wanted to hear, the language that should be used for worship services, the importance of liturgy, and even the types of worship songs sung in church.

The Immigrant Generation

Since the church that St. Thomas Christians traditionally attended was the one that they were "born into," there was no question about which church to go to when they came to the United States (provided of course that there was a church of the denomination in the area). When I asked Mr. Thomas Mathews (who had moved to the Bethelville region from another part of the country) how he had found the church, he said, "The first thing St. Thomas Christians do even before getting to a new place is to find out where the [nearest St. Thomas] church is."

As the primary community center for immigrants, diasporic religious institutions take over a variety of functions not performed by religious institutions in the homeland. As the Vergheses, one of the couples in the church, emphasized, "Since our families are around in India, we are not so close to friends or members of the church. The church community here substitutes for the family we had in India." Thus the social lives of the members of the immigrant generation were closely tied in with the church. Indeed, most of them indicated that their close friends were other church members. Although many of the first generation were critical about many aspects of the current situation in the church, particularly the "groupism and infighting" and the pastor, they said that they attended because it was a "comfort zone" where they felt at home. A few members had previously been members of local American churches but had left and started attending the St. Thomas church despite having to travel a great distance, because although the congregation had been friendly, they had never felt part of the community. Another member mentioned that an important reason why people drove all the way was that they knew that they could have a say in church matters. "People can speak their minds, which you can't do if you were part of an American church."

Many parents indicated that they drove the long distance to St. Thomas with their families several times a month because they hoped that this would help them maintain their culture and language and transmit it to their children. They also wanted their children to associate with other families from the same background. "It is important to maintain one's identity and culture. Maintaining the church language and traditions is an important part of this," Mr. Verghese told me emotionally after narrating a story about a Punjabi Indian man they had known in Canada who on his deathbed had asked his sons to promise that they would teach Punjabi to their children.

Perhaps not surprisingly, the St. Thomas church was a male-dominated sphere. This has traditionally been the case even in India, but in the United States the church became even more fiercely guarded "male turf" since it was the primary arena within which downwardly mobile husbands try to reclaim the social status they lost as a result of immigration. Several scholars (Min 1992; George 1998) have also made this point, namely, that an important function of an ethnic church is to serve as an avenue for social status for downwardly mobile men. Recall that a substantial proportion of the older generation men were married to nurses and had arrived in the United States as secondary migrants, sponsored by their wives. In this context, the church community became the only platform where the men could assert themselves and obtain leadership positions. Consequently it became the staging ground for a "status struggle" between those members who had been considered "low status" in Kerala (nurses and their families) and those who had been considered "high status" (professionals).

Although the financial situation of the husbands was not particularly strong, the nurses were able to earn a good income (particularly in the 1970s and 1980s) by working at night and doing double shifts. So the families had become affluent. As the largest group in the church, they were trying to redefine traditional Malayalee conceptions of status. The Mathais observed that one of the reasons the current pastor was unpopular among many in the congregation was that he did not treat everyone equally but made distinctions between people on the basis of their occupation. "For instance," Mr. Mathai said, "I don't have a doctorate, but that does not mean that he should treat me differently from someone who has a doctorate." Mrs. Mathai (who was a nurse) added, "In India doctors have a high status. But here we are all equal."

There was a constant battle between the "high-status" families (who were in a minority in the church) who saw church leadership as their right and prerogative, and the "low-status" families, who were mounting a challenge to this authority. This cleavage (and the other divisions in the church) often manifested themselves at the General Body meetings which were consequently emotional and conflict-ridden and sometimes degenerated into a shouting match between the different sides.

When I asked the older generation what they liked about the church, several mentioned the liturgy. It is something that they had been used to from their youth and had come to associate with spirituality. They found it comforting and it also put them in the "mood" to say their personal prayers. The same was the case with the traditional hymns, sung to the accompaniment of the organ. Many said that although they did come for the English service—for the sake of their children or because it was the only Sunday they were free—they did "not get anything out of it" and it did not make them feel "spiritual."

The Second Generation

In general, the American-born members said that they did not believe in the concept of an "ascribed" denomination but instead felt that it was important to "shop around" until they found a church that fit their requirements. All but one of the thirteen youth I talked to were very critical of the St. Thomas church. Following from their individualistic, evangelical model of Christianity, the committed Christians among the second generation wanted to separate their faith from their heritage and indicated that their faith was more important. Sarah was a young woman in her late twenties and her response was typical. She indicated that for her, "More than cultural identity, is the identity in Christ. I will still do things with the Indian group—I have cousins, relatives. But you need to be grounded in the word of God." The youth leaders argued that the church should be an inclusive faith community, not a "default ethnic community" and that it should be a house of God, a place to learn God's word, regardless of racial and ethnic background, not an ethnic center or a place to learn language and culture.[5] According to them, the main problem with the St. Thomas church was that instead of being focused on the worship of God, it was more concerned about other things.

"For them [the older generation] it is just a ritual. They are not necessarily there to worship God. It is part of their tradition," commented Philip. Another young man made a similar remark: "It feels like, Malayalees congregate together once a week and simply because it is a Christian gathering, they call it a church. And they have traditions they feel they have to follow." Several of the youth criticized the excessive focus on fundraising. "It is just a business. The focus is always on money, money, money." Others criticized the "hypocrisy and fighting" among first-generation members. According to Sarah, "You see adults fighting and you don't feel you are in a church when that happens. You don't feel you are in a holy place. You have service and then right after, we forget everything we've just heard." Sarah said that she and her husband now came to the St. Thomas church just once a month, primarily to see her relatives and friends.

Most of the youth also indicated that the service, liturgy, and sermons were not meaningful for them. Biju said,

> It took a long time for them [his parents] to understand that I didn't really get much out of the entire thing [the Malayalam church service]. Then they started the English service and my parents were like, go to the St. Thomas church now, there's an English service there. But it really didn't do much for me at all. To me it was like reading a script when we were there. One person reads, and another person says something else, and then I know, okay three more pages and I get to sit down!

Vinay, a young man in his midthirties who had grown up in Kuwait and had then moved to the United States in his late teens, thought that the church should encourage the congregation to get directly involved in causes (social and spiritual) rather than delegating such work to others (such as church workers and missionaries in India) and then collecting money for them. Three of the youth argued that the church should give money to help the poor in the United States and not just in India. Joshua, who had had a "conversion experience" the previous year, criticized the fact that there was no support or "checking up" mechanism to keep those like him, who were "new Christians," on track.

Most of the youth felt that the church needed to abandon its "archaic, meaningless rituals" and focus on making the service and message relevant to the congregation, particularly the growing number of second-generation members. Johnny, the Sunday school principal, said passionately, "Pastors should focus more on the youth since they are the future of the church. Currently pastors are very oriented toward adults. Look, they attend the area prayer meetings, and the women's meetings, but not the youth cottage meetings. Shouldn't it be the other way around, I am asking." Five of the youth mentioned that they would like the pastors to be more youth-focused in their sermons and that they should "at least periodically address the concerns of the second generation such as the pressures they face growing up here—dating, drugs, drink." The youth also wanted pastors from the United States who could understand the American context and communicate well with the youth, not pastors from Kerala who spoke a halting, accented English. They were also against the four-year term of the pastors since they felt it was too short to accomplish anything.

Several particularly criticized the liturgy, which they thought should be "done away with." "Right now, no one focuses on the meaning. They just sing it from habit. I feel we should at least rewrite it so it is shorter and more meaningful," said Sam, one of the youth leaders. Some of the youth preferred to have all the services in English. According to Jacob, "Everyone can understand English—the older generation and the younger generation—so why not have English services all the time? At least give the sermon in English during the Malayalam services and have a few English songs."

Rather than the traditional hymns sung to the accompaniment of an electric organ, the younger generation indicated that they preferred singing "praise songs" with a guitar, since they found singing that way to be "a very spiritual experience." In 1998 a few of the youth had done this regularly before the English worship service (they still did it but only sporadically). But there had been a lot of criticism from the older generation. Joshua, one of those who had been involved in the singing, said: "I would look out into the congregation and the expressions on people's faces alone told me that they did not like it. Some of the uncles even came up to us and told us that. They said that they did not want to add to the length of the service with the singing. And there was one uncle who asked the *Achen* sarcastically, 'Did the *Thirumeni* appoint them to sing before the service?' This kind of criticism really tore me up, since we had to put in so much effort to keep the singing going. I had to get there early, before the Sunday school, to practice and set up the mikes."

All the youth leaders in the church were male. There were several girls in the high school group who were active members of the youth group, but there were very few in the older group (college age and beyond). Most had apparently dropped out. Even the wives of two of the highest-ranking youth leaders attended nonethnic parachurches. Three of the women who still attended the church alluded to the fact that they sometimes felt marginalized as women. Manju, a young woman who was in her first year at college, said she had stopped attending the youth activities since she felt that it was "boy-dominated" and also dominated by "computer freaks." Lizzy, who was going through a divorce, spoke bitterly about how the church members had pushed her out of her Sunday school teaching position but had supported the continuing involvement of her husband in the church. But she said that the *thirumeni* had been supportive of her, and that she was planning to fight to get her Sunday school position back. Sarah, who had been a youth leader and a member of its executive committee, said that she had quit after being spoken to rudely by some of the men on the committee.

But three others seemed to feel that the congregation was open to more participation by young women and that it was their own busy schedule that prevented them from doing so. In general, although it was never explicitly voiced, there was the sense that the girls and unmarried women in the congregation did not feel the same sense of ownership and responsibility toward the church as did the boys and young men. This probably had to do with the fact that they were members of the church through a male link—their fathers or their husbands. Since intermarriages within the St. Thomas congregation were rare, most members ended up leaving the church and often even the Mar Thoma denomination upon marriage. Thus it was not surprising that they were less motivated to put in the time and effort it took to be a youth leader.

In the interviews, many of the youth kept comparing the St. Thomas church unfavorably with the nonethnic American churches that they had attended. For instance, Sarah, the young woman who now only came once a month to St. Thomas with her husband, talked about how much they enjoyed the American megachurch that they normally attended. "I feel that I am going to church when I go there. When I am there, I feel like I am at a church. I feel that I have come to worship and wholeheartedly can worship, can get something out of it. I understand the service, I feel refreshed." She continued, "It is a very large church . . . smaller prayer groups make it more personal. But even with the thousands of people there, we find it so meaningful and that they are talking directly to us. Going to the St. Thomas church, that one Sunday that we miss, we feel that we miss a lot."

Intergenerational Conflicts over Religion

Since the first and second generations had such a different understanding of the meaning of being Christian, the two groups were often at odds, both in the church and at home, on the subject of religion. The second-generation youth were very contemptuous of the "automatic Christianity" model of the older generation. Several of them talked about the fact that the older generation did not really know the word of God well or how to apply the Bible to their lives.

For instance, when Johnny, the Sunday school principal and one of the oldest of the second-generation members in church, preached one Sunday, he named three young men (he himself pointed out that they were all men, and said, "where are the girls, I am asking") as the only committed Christians in church, angering several of the older members.

As in the case of the confrontation with which I began this chapter, the older generation were deeply offended when the youth stated or implied that they were not true Christians because they had not had a "born again" experience and did not personally evangelize. Williams (1996, 58) points out that Syrian Christians have traditionally avoided active evangelism, "which may have contributed to their peaceful relations with their Hindu neighbors" and was probably also important for their survival as a minority group in Kerala. The importance of tolerance and of getting along with non-Christians seemed to be a philosophy that even the prelate of the denomination upheld, since he wrote in one of his pastoral letters from Kerala (which was read aloud in church) that "St. Thomas Christians have to realize that we live among those with different faiths and we have to live in harmony with them." Thus, while the second generation was right in saying that their parents' religion was basically about following traditions and rituals, they did not appreciate the context within which these traditions had taken shape. Dr. Peters, one of the founding members of the church, summed up the perspective of many of the older generation when he said, "We are a traditional church. We are not like the Pentecostals who go after people. We believe that it is the obligation of those who are Christians (by birth) to go to their church and become part of the church. And though we may not personally evangelize to non-Christians, our church supports the activities of missionaries who do."

In interviews many members of the older generation spoke passionately about the hardships that they had experienced, and continued to experience, due to immigration and relocation. In most cases, they justified these hardships by saying that it had been for the sake of the children (although it was not always clear that this was the original motivation for the migration). Thus, they found it particularly upsetting when the youth in the church were trying to take away the one place where they could re-create home and be validated, and when their children were rejecting all their cherished traditions and becoming strangers to them. The youth, on the other hand, felt that their parents were placing an undue burden on them. As one young man put it, "We didn't ask them to come here. But now that they are here, they can't expect us to act like we are still living in India in the 1960s."

The tensions between the two sides often came to a head over the issue of marriage. Many of the youth felt that there was a contradiction in their parents' emphasis on the importance of being Christian and having "Christian values," and their insistence that they should marry a Malayalee Christian. Some parents whose children had married non–Indian American Christians told me that this was the trump card that their children had used in their attempt to persuade them to agree to the marriage. Mrs. Cherian reported, "My daughter asked me, 'Isn't it hypocritical to say that we are Christians and that being Christian is important and then saying that only an Indian Christian is worthy of being married? Aren't we all equal in the sight of God?'" They had subsequently agreed to the marriage and had come to like their son-in-law. During a visit to the home of the Chacko family, the topic of marriage also came up for discussion. Philip, the twenty-two-year-old son and one of the youth leaders in the church, told me that the most important consideration for him would be that his wife should be Christian. "The rest is not so important." But his mother interrupted from the other side of the room to say, "I am very strict about this. I tell them, I love them and will love them until I die but that they must marry a Christian from India." She paused and then added, "A Malayalee."

Conclusion

In India, Syrian Christians are able to maintain a distinct subcultural identity based on their religious affiliation. In a majority Christian country like the United States, however, it becomes more difficult for them to use religion as the locus of their ethnicity. Indian American churches also face intense competition from evangelical groups in schools and colleges for the allegiance of their children. As a consequence, most of the adult children of Syrian Christian immigrants are leaving the church and denomination of their parents.

Gender is a differentiating factor in the exit patterns. More young women leave the Mar Thoma church than men, while more of the female dropouts join nonethnic churches than the male dropouts. These differences seem to be due to the fact that women are not given a meaningful role within the ethnic church.

Surprisingly, there does not seem to be as much focus on racial marginality among second-generation Mar Thomites who have joined parachurches when compared with East Asian American groups (see Cha 2001; Yep et al. 1998; Park 2001; Yang 1999b) and even other Indian religious groups. Do Indian Christians face less racism than these other groups? Or are they less aware of it? Either way, the Mar Thoma case indicates that the process of racialization is complex and that the outcome cannot be predicted on the basis of skin color alone.

The absence of a strong minority consciousness may mean that unlike Korean and Chinese Americans, religiously inclined Indian Christians will eventually become part of nonethnic churches. This outcome is also likely because Indian Christians are not in a position to form separate second-generation churches, at least at the present time. Indian Christians are a much smaller group in the United States than Chinese or Korean Christian Americans and are also dispersed throughout the country. Again, since Christianity has existed for much longer in India than in either China or Korea, there are well entrenched Orthodox, Protestant, Catholic, and Pentecostal denominations which make it difficult for the youth to unite together to form separate churches.

Mullins (1988) has pointed out that ethnic churches that rely on priests from the homeland are likely to lose their membership over time as the second and later generations become more assimilated. Thus, the *transnational* character of many of the denominations may hasten the demise of the American dioceses in the long term. This demise may also be hastened by a fundamental contradiction that the church faces. Leaders of both the first and second generations recognize that the church needs to make some changes to accommodate to the American environment. At the same time, the church faces the possibility that if it accommodates too much, it will lose its distinctiveness and disappear. As Abraham, one of the youth pointed out, "If St. Thomas became like any of the other churches, we could just go down the road to the nearest church. There would be no need to drive sixty miles every Sunday."

Today, unlike in the past, multiculturalism is institutionalized and "fashionable" and emphasizing ethnicity has become an asset, particularly for nonwhite immigrant groups. Given the racial diversity of the contemporary wave of immigration, it is likely that ethnicity will be maintained for a much longer period than in the case of the earlier waves of immigrants. In this context, what will happen to groups like second-generation Indian Christians who seem to be abandoning their ethnic church and community? Will they be able to integrate into the mainstream? Will they suffer downward mobility over time? Or will Herberg's thesis regarding the third generation returning to ethnic churches hold true?

A lot will depend on immigration patterns in the future. If immigration continues, Indian Christian American churches may be revitalized by the newcomers and gradually accommodate the changes that are taking place in both India and the United States, thus retaining many more of their youth. At the time of my fieldwork, around one-sixth of the regular attendees in the congregation had arrived over the past five years, most as computer programmers. Many of these individuals were in their late twenties and thirties and had grown up or studied in cosmopolitan urban areas outside Kerala. Thus, their worldviews and perspectives on religion and the church were often rather different from that of the older generation. By the time I returned to the church in the fall of 2001, this group seem to have developed as a buffer between the older-generation immigrants and the American-born youth. Much of the conflict that I witnessed earlier was muted, aided also by the presence of a pastor whose mission was the mending of the rifts within the congregation.

NOTES

This research was funded by grants from the Pew Charitable Trusts and the Louisville Foundation. I thank R. Stephen Warner and Tony Carnes for their helpful comments.

1. The name of the church, its location, and its members have been changed to protect confidentiality.

2. Study by Stephen Linton, cited in Chai 2000, 157.

3. This figure is likely to be an underestimate since the study used the most common Indian last names to obtain respondents and many Indian Christians do not have distinctly Indian last names.

4. Although only 19 percent of the population of Kerala is Christian, according to Williams (1996, 63) they comprise the majority of Keralite immigrants to the United States.

5. They felt that language and culture should be taught at home.

7

"Korean American Evangelical"

A Resolution of Sociological Ambivalence among Korean American College Students

Soyoung Park

Today, second-generation immigrants are engaged in innovatively constructing their identities. In *Legacies* (2001), Portes and Rumbaut consider second-generation success under an explanatory scheme of either doing poorly in school life because they become Americanized too quickly or succeeding because they hold onto the relationships and values of the first generation. However, their own evidence indicates that second-generation immigrants are innovating multiple "successful" resolutions. Religion, which Portes and Rumbaut have tended to overlook, is often a key ingredient in these resolutions. Some are socially effective, some are not. In fact most carry a degree of ambiguity that signals success while at the same time posing further dilemmas.

On college campuses and in churches second-generation Korean American evangelicals position their unique identity as a resolution of sociological ambivalence (see Merton 1976; Merton, Merton, and Barber 1983; Janis 1980; Coser 1979; Room 1976). It resolves what Pai (1993, 257) called "the tangled web of conflicting norms." When Korean American evangelical college students are asked about their religious and racial-ethnic identity, they consistently name being Christian as the foundational part of who they are. In doing so, they separate their religious identity from their ethnoracial Korean and American identities. Their American identity is also ascribed by their parents' presence in the United States. Their religious identity is achieved by accepting Jesus as their personal savior, while their ethnoracial identity is ascribed by virtue of their Korean ancestry, as well as their status and social experiences as nonwhites in the United States. For these students, therefore, being an evangelical Christian seems distinct from being Korean, American, or Korean American. In reality, however, these three threads of their identity are in balance.

College students use their evangelical Christian identities to achieve a bounded social space between their parents, nonevangelical students, and the larger American society (Coser 1975), thereby creating an identity, time, and energy for themselves. Their status as evangelical Christians and their values act as governors controlling the rate and tensions of their disaffiliation from their parents, other students, and their assimilation as Americans. Consequently, their inner contradictions, the conflicting answers to the question, "Who am I?" are fitted together into the unique social identity of "Korean American evangelical" (see Merton 1976; Linton 1945).

Korean American Evangelical College Students

Korean American evangelical college students are the children of Korean immigrants who came to the United States following the liberalization of immigration laws in 1965. Consequently, their social identities are in transition. As they become more involved with various American institutions, they balance, redefine, or withdraw from some of the social statuses and identities of their parents while accumulating new ones (see Coser 1966; Coser 1964). Indeed, they believe that their parents occupy a transitional status of immigrant middlemen entrepreneurs that does not have a long-term functionality in American society. The parents themselves encourage this notion of status transition because they are usually college-educated immigrants who took retail store jobs for the sake of their children's future integration into the professional occupations of America.[1]

According to the official count of the 1990 census, about 800,000 Koreans resided in the United States, compared to 69,130 in 1970 and 350,000 in 1980 (Min 1995, 204). However, most observers believe that there are about one million Koreans and Korean Americans in the United States, including students, visitors, and others (ibid.). Similarly, the number of Asian Americans enrolled in American colleges has increased from 197,900 in 1976 to 286,400 in 1980, 572,400 in 1990, and 797,400 in 1995 (*Chronicle of Higher Education* 1997, 18).

Furthermore, Korean American college students are mostly the children of Korean immigrants who are extensively involved with Korean ethnic churches. The numerical increase of Korean ethnic churches accompanied that of Korean immigrants. For example, compared to the four churches in the New York City area prior to the 1970s (Min 1991, 253), the 1995 Korean Churches Directory of New York State listed about three hundred churches.

While Christians in Korea comprise a little over 20 percent of the entire population, about 75 percent of Korean immigrants in the United States are now Christians (Min 1995, 214). About 50 percent of Korean immigrants were already Christians when they immigrated (Min 1991, 251) because Christians in Korea are more urban-oriented, educated, westernized, and willing to immigrate to the United States (ibid., 251–252). Another 25 percent of Korean immigrants convert to Christianity upon coming to the United States, partly because the majority of their fellow ethnic immigrants are Christians and Korean ethnic churches provide a ready-made social network.

Most Korean ethnic churches are conservative in their religious orientation, focusing on separation from the world, biblical inerrancy, and a born-again experience, that is, a radical moment of confessing one's own sins and accepting Jesus as a personal savior. Spending their childhood and adolescence in Korean ethnic churches, most second-generation Koreans acquire a conservative Christian religiosity. This chapter broadly uses Korean American evangelical college students or second-generation Korean evangelicals to refer to those who were born to Korean immigrants either in Korea or in the United States, have acquired a religious orientation of conservative Protestant Christianity, and are currently in college.

In fact the children of the first generation are divided between 1.5 and second generations. The 1.5 generation were born in Korea and came to the United States before graduating from high school. They are usually more familiar with the Korean language and culture and feel somewhat uncomfortable with the second generation. The second generation (commonly called "ABKs" for American-Born Koreans) were born in the United States; they are less familiar with the Korean language and culture and distinguish themselves from the 1.5 generation. If the second generation predominates in a campus or church fellowship, the 1.5s usually won't join. At the time of this study Korean Christian Fellowship was a strictly second-generation fellowship, though I also observed fellowships made up of exchange students from Korea and the 1.5 generation.

Downtown University and Its
Korean Christian Fellowship (KCF)

Downtown University (DU) is a large private university in New York City that has become a "name-brand" among Asian Americans.[2] The university is an easy subway commute for the 69,718 Koreans (out of 512,719 Asians) in the city (U.S. Census Bureau 1994). In 1996–97 about 21 percent of DU's students were Asians and Asian Americans, and there were many Asian and Asian American clubs, the largest being evangelical Christian ones. Because of its urban location, many of the Korean American students either live at home or commute home over the weekends. Consequently, they are in continual contact with first-generation Korean culture and churches. However, an increasing number of Downtown University Korean American students attend Redeemer Presbyterian Church, a majority Anglo multiethnic church, and its branches or Remnant, a pan-Asian American church.

The parents are intensely proud of their children's acceptance at Downtown University and make quite clear their expectations of high performance and big success. One source of conflict with their children is that the parents emphasize career goals over Christian activities.

The Korean Christian Fellowship (KCF) of DU is an ethnic evangelical parachurch organization of Korean Americans which may be found on many U.S. college campuses. Each KCF is a club organized and operated by a group of Korean American students on a campus with a volunteer pastor or a seminarian. KCF does not have any affiliation with a local church, denomination, or higher governing body. The KCFs in the New York City area interact through local clubs' revival meetings and their loosely organized umbrella organization, the Korean Intercollegiate Christian Fellowship, which is mainly responsible for planning their annual retreat "Unity."

KCF is part of the rise of evangelical parachurch organizations on U.S. college campuses. The cultural and social changes in the 1960s and 1970s brought about a crisis of values within colleges and universities (Ferm 1976, 54; Tipton 1982; Guinness 1973). Consequently, evangelical organizations provided a distinct worldview and life plan as a resolution to the crisis in values. By making use of students' cultural idioms, American evangelical groups attracted a large following among Asian American students (see Busto 1996, 135; Roof 1993, 103). At the evangelical college missions' national conference "Urbana '93" Asian American students comprised more than 25 percent of the attendees (Kennedy 1994, 48). The mainline Protestant denominations declined in campus significance (cp. Warner 1994, 74) and attracted few Asian Americans to their campus ministries.

Having celebrated its seventeenth anniversary in April 1997, the DU KCF consisted of officers, pastoral staff, alumni staff, and forty to forty-five students regularly in attendance. While conducting interviews with DU KCF members, I also observed and participated in their weekly meetings, retreats, and revivals for about one year from 1996 to 1997. For the sake of comparison the research encompassed other evangelical organizations on campus such as the Asian American Christian Fellowship (AACF) and Multi-Ethnic Fellowship (MEF), which are the chapters of the international InterVarsity Christian Fellowship (IVCF). Further, my observations are based on the meetings and events of other ethnic groups such as the Korean Campus Crusade for Christ (KCCC), the Korean ethnic chapter of CCC, and the Korean Students' Association (KSA), a nonreligious ethnic organization. Korean Americans are heavily involved in all the evangelical organizations. Finally, this chapter draws on interviews with volunteer pastors, officers, and regular members from KCFs at other schools in the city.

Religious Identity

Throughout U.S. history, religion has been important to immigrants who use their religious traditions in the process of formulating their self-identity in a new social world (Williams 1988, 293). Religion functions as "a powerful scheme for sacralizing the elements of identity and preserving them through the identity crises that are endemic to emigration" (ibid., 278). It is one effective way of helping immigrants construct and maintain their ethnic identities (Sheth 1995, 185).

The U.S. social structure designates ethnic and religious membership as normal, even expected. Further, because of the disestablishment of religion from the political-legal structure and the widespread plurality of religions from which to choose (Greeley 1971, 117), new immigrants have structurally and symbolically assimilated to American life through their ethnoreligious identities. Therefore, denominations often play "ethnic" or "quasi-ethnic" roles by providing their members with a sense of self-definition through a social location in the larger society (ibid., 108). Thus, there are Irish Catholics, Greek Orthodox, Dutch Reformed, and so on. Ethnicity (and race) in the United States have also become the skeletons of religion, providing the supporting frameworks, "the bare outlines" or "main features," of religion (Marty 1972, 9).

Korean immigrants have followed this pattern of bringing ethnicity-race and religion together. They have established their own social space through ethnic churches and denominations in the United States, such as Korean Presbyterian Churches in America (KPCA), or their own ethnic structure within American denominations, such as Han-Mi, which is the name for all the Korean American presbyteries in the Presbyterian Churches in U.S.A. (PCUSA).

Korean American ministers also intertwine a messianic Korean identity with moral strictness. Faced with what they see as the disintegrating moral fabric of the United States, church leaders see Korean immigrants as bearers of the Puritan heritage (also see Kim 1981, 206). Although most American-born evangelicals also see themselves as the keepers of Puritanism (Ammerman 1987, 17), Korean American ministers believe that only the Korean church has the necessary relentless moral discipline.

The second generation has also continued to intertwine conservative Christianity, morality, and ethnicity-race through the founding of campus ministries, parachurch organizations, and ethnic second-generation churches. In doing so they have created an American-evangelical style of religion that clashes with their parents' traditional Korean style of Christianity. Second-generation evangelicals also maintain a sense of their unique destiny. At the pan-KSF Unity '97 the speakers claimed that God had chosen Korean Americans for the special purpose of evangelizing the world. God had brought them to the United States to learn English and get American citizenship so that they could more easily go to any other country. The second generation, one speaker said, was like the Apostle Paul who used his Roman citizenship to protect himself and open the door to further travel.

Strictly speaking, most second-generation Korean American evangelicals would not say that their religious identity was a self-achieved status. The dichotomy of achieved versus ascribed statuses is an ideal type which contrasts self-orientated Western societies and group-orientated non-Western ones. Rather, most Korean Americans would say that their faith identity is the result of individual choice plus group encouragement and divine intervention. However, Korean American evangelicals are still very group-oriented and often interpret decisions as a Self deciding with group help. Yet, relative to the first generation, the second generation believes that it is much less group-bound, and that it favors individual freedom. The second generation tends to see the first generation's professions of faith as a product of Korean tradition and collective experiences. KSF member Hong contrasted the two types of faith as follows: "Korean American identity is more cultural and political. I think Christian identity is more spiritual and pure, or more toward ethics, your spiritual and religious beliefs."

However, in relation to Anglo-Americans, some members of the second generation feel more comfortable with the group processes of Korean ethnic ministries, though Korean American evangelicals also attribute their faith to divine intervention at the individual level. Their typical sentiment about their faith is that they are grateful that "God came down and met me where I was at."

Racial-Ethnic Identity

DU's Korean American evangelical college students don't understand race and ethnicity in isolation. Instead, they always intertwine the two, because they themselves are both a racial and an ethnic minority in the United States. Their race and cultural and linguistic Korean backgrounds are different from those of the dominant group in the United States.

Indeed, ethnicity alone cannot address the experiences of most Asian Americans (Omi and Winant 1994, 16). Although some scholars define ethnicity inclusively, as determined by common origins such as religion, language, and nation as well by common biological characteristics (Petersen 1980, 235), U.S. discussions tend to distinguish ethnicity from race. Whereas race is widely applied to physical and biological differences, classifying Asian Americans as nonwhites, the term ethnicity is reserved for Americans of European ancestry (Petersen 1980, 235–236).

On the one hand, the racial-ethnic identity of second-generation Koreans is inherited and primordial. Because they were born to Korean immigrants in the United States, they inherit a specific racial-ethnic identity as Korean Americans. Their individual sense has a historical continuity with Korean history and culture (De Vos 1975, 17). On the other hand, their racial-ethnic identity is emerging within the U.S. social structure

(Morawska 1990, 214; Kivisto 1993, 99; Roosens 1989, 19; Yancey et al. 1976, 392).

As second-generation Korean Americans assimilate to the U.S. ethnoracial social structure, they are also changing it. The dynamic interplay between first-generation identity, American identity, and the emergent Korean American second-generation identity creates tensions that redefine what each identity means and how each is activated in social life. Accordingly, the racial-ethnic identity of second-generation Koreans cannot be understood without considering their social contexts (ibid., 393; Yinger 1985, 162). Since the development of an identity is located in "a set of social relationships" (Gordon 1978, 229), this study examines the relation of second-generation evangelical Koreans to different reference groups on and off campus: the Korean Students' Association (KSA), first-generation Korean Christians, and U.S. society (cp. Hurtado, Gurin, and Peng 1994).

Identity and Sociological Ambiguities

KCF Ethnic Evangelicals versus KSA Ethnic Nonevangelicals

In constructing their evangelical Christian identity, Korean American evangelical college students make the KSA, a nonreligious ethnic club, their major negative reference group (Merton 1968, 354–355). Almost every Korean American student has some experience with the KSA. Typically, the KSA invites first-year Korean American students to an initiation by drinking beer at a local bar. The occasion is heralded as an opportunity to maintain one's Korean identity while also better assimilating to American campus life.

At Downtown University the initiation took place at a local bar a couple of blocks from campus. Before the initiation, the first-year evangelical students didn't know what to expect. However, as soon as they started to smell the thick cigarette smoke at the entrance to the bar, they quickly began to size up the KSA. Through round after round of beer, the students got to know each other. Some became staggeringly drunk. During the process, committed evangelical students became convinced that the KSA was not for them. Although some evangelical students smoke, drink, and go to *karaoke* bars, few would admit it. No one shows up at the campus ministry meetings smoking or with alcoholic breath telling about the hot dance party the night before. Highly committed Korean American evangelicals don't drink or go to dances where people drink and smoke.

The contrast between the two clubs is stark. At freshmen orientation the KCF played contemporary evangelical songs and sang gospel songs in deaf sign language. The KSA had its dance team do hip-hop dances. While the KCF did a skit on the church as one family, the KSA's skit gave advice on finding dates and love. At the pan-KCF Unity '97 retreat, skits portrayed rituals of repentance for drinking and dancing. Every weekly DU KCF meeting has about twenty minutes of praise and prayer. As the music dies down, the praise leader prays for strength against the "temptations" of "sensual immorality," "worldliness," and the like. When second-generation Korean evangelicals participate in such "worldly" activities, they feel guilty and try to keep them secret. Thus, evangelicals consider group KSA members to be secular, social, and permissive about drinking, smoking, dancing, and partying, and thus antithetical to an evangelical moral stance. By constantly highlighting the difference between themselves and KSA members' activities and events, Korean American evangelical college students try to distinguish Christians from non-Christians and faithful Christians from opportunist Christians (Lamont and Fournier 1992, 289–308).

However bad second-generation Korean American evangelicals may feel about their parents' criticism of their Americanizing ways, they derive solace, identity, and some respect from their parents by comparing themselves to KSA cultural norms. It is as though the evangelical students are saying, "However bad you may think we are, the others are worse" (cp. Merton 1968, 296–299, 337).

KSF member Tiffany depicts this distinction as follows:

> I think [the] difference is . . . KSA is known to be a social club because . . . it doesn't have that Christian aspect. . . . [I]t would be kind of negative to call KCF a social club . . . because . . . Korean Christian Fellowship, [its] emphasis is often Christian. . . . [S]ocial has that . . . negative connotation. So . . . KSA being [a] social club, they just meet together and have fun. And that's it. That's their purpose. But, for KCF, I think people will think that it's not social, because we do meet, but we have more important, our basic purpose [is] to come together, worship God, and then, through that, we are socializing.

Regular KSF attendees usually say that "opportunistic Christians" go to the KSF irregularly and to their churches only when they go home. The "opportunistic Christians" are also more interfaith-oriented, saying that every religion has basically the same values. Perhaps "opportunistic Christians" alternate their social memberships as a way of satisfying everyone, but they don't gain much praise from the Korean American evangelical reference group. The evangelicals are more concerned with drawing boundary lines between themselves and the KSA, so they strongly recommend that KSF members drop their participation in the KSA (see Merton 1959, 185; Grodzins 1956, ch. 1–3, 10). The KSF sees alternation between organizations as a sign of nonconversion by "opportunistic Christians" (see Atal 1970).

Furthermore, the exclusivist claim of conservative Christianity on salvation leads the KSF to consider coethnic nonevangelicals to be "the other," the subjects of their evangelism. Korean American evangelicals consider nonevangelical Koreans to be part of the "world" that is rife with bars, alcohol, drugs, nightclubs, hanging out, not going to church, and missing classes. In short, in their view, the KSA is part of the "undisciplined," the "immoral," and the "chaotic." One member, John, says the campus setting is a testing ground where one chooses which organizations and practices will exemplify one's life and shape one's identity. He concludes, "[College] is a place where you test where you stand and how strong you are in your walk with God."

However, KSF students seldom try to evangelize, influence, or otherwise socialize with KSA students. In fact the Korean American evangelicals seem to be using their religion to withdraw from their status as Koreans through the KSA in favor of a status as "ethnic Koreans" through membership in the KSF. Consequently, KSA members often feel that Korean American Christian club members fail to appreciate their efforts to learn about Korean culture and stigmatize them as merely a partying and drinking crowd. Regular participants in the KSA say that the evangelical KSF are "very exclusive of others." KSA students also have a pretty good knowledge about the KSF, as some are articulate rebels against their parents' churches. Jennifer, one such rebel and the president of the KSA, upon finding out that KCF and KCCC members told new students not to go to the KSA, comments, "How dare *they* criticize *us*." In effect Jennifer is saying that KSF leaders are structurally incapable of comprehending the KSA (compare Merton 1976). However, both groups know each other pretty well.

Although the racial-ethnic background of both evangelical and nonevangelical students is the same, the religious faith of the evangelicals leads them to develop a distinct identity from that of the nonevangelical

Korean American students. Their focus on a born-again experience and the strict personal morality of evangelical Christianity creates an us-them dichotomy and thus leads them to stand apart from the nonevangelical Korean Americans on campus. The evangelicals also use the religious divide as a means of striking a balance toward an American identity rather than a Korean identity. Yet they still belong to a Korean fellowship. This way of drawing social lines and defining their identity resonates with the way evangelical Korean Americans deal with their parents.

Second-Generation Korean Evangelicals versus First-Generation Korean Christians

EVANGELICAL CHRISTIANITY VERSUS KOREANNESS

Many parents come to the United States with a romantic conception of America and the possibilities for their children's assimilation, but they also want their children to have a high esteem for Korea and its culture.[3] Parents insist that their children politely bow to adults while saying, "An Nyung Ha Se Yo?" (How are you?). An American "Hello" would fall to the ground with a thud as impolite, frivolous, and an alarming sign of moral deterioration. In order to prevent such selfish behavior, adults shame their children so that the children do not cause the parents to lose face (see Shon and Ja 1982, 214; Ha 1995, 1114–1115).

The parents expect their children to remain connected to their identity as ethnic Koreans. Although the first-generation adults generally have no plans to return to Korea, they retain a deep sense that Korea is the mother country from which they originated and to which they in some sense belong. This feeling is partly class-determined, with lower-class Korean immigrants feeling insecure and consequently having a deeper attachment to Korea as their lifeline. Based upon current participant observations, upper-class Korean immigrants like those residing in the affluent suburb of Bergen County, New Jersey, feel confident of their lives here and are less likely to maintain an emotional dependence upon their home country. These parents may thus be a little less insistent that their children maintain Korean identities, social ties, and values.

Still, for almost all members of the first generation their churches are a safe space to be Korean. They bring their outside experiences into the church where they are collectively reintegrated and symbolically presented to the second generation as the correct way of understanding the world and one's role in it (cp. Durkheim 1965/1915). Consequently, first- and second-generation relations are not just personal but symbolically and interactionally institutionalized.

On the other hand, U.S. society demands that the second generation assimilate to an American identity. Consequently, the second generation feels a socially caused ambivalence. Second-generation Korean American evangelicals often have a love-hate relationship with their parents. They love them and are deeply attached to them through reciprocal bonds of respect and care. Yet, the second generation's orientation to the American culture of individualism and universalism means that they are often irritated by their parents' group-orientated, formalistic culture (on Korean versus American cultural values, see Lee and Cynn 1991; Chung 1992). The structural dilemma creates an emotion similar to what Eugene Bleuler called a love-hate ambivalence (Bleuler 1910, 1911). To resolve the tension the second-generation youth hold onto the Christian identity that they share with their parents while also redefining it in a way that brings them closer to an American-style identity. They redefine their Christian identity toward American evangelicalism and prioritize it over their parents' ethnic claims. The second generation asserts its brand of Christianity as a superior form purified of ethnic distortions.

Korean ethnic churches have separate worship services for different age groups (such as nursery, kindergarten, and elementary students), a youth group (junior high and high school students) and young adult group (college students and singles). In particular, the high school and college youth groups and the English ministry as a whole develop their own identities distinct from the first-generation congregation. By high school the second generation has developed an Americanized cultural style within a church-based network of Korean American friends. According to Min and Choi's study of Korean American high school students in the New York City area, the students do not display a strong attachment to ethnic culture but do have a strong attachment to an ethnic social network (Min and Choi 1993, 169). Mostly, this network resides within the Korean churches. Each cohort of second-generation youth has continuous, intense experiences with each other through the church youth groups. They do Friday fellowships, Saturday morning cleanups, and a long Sunday together, as well as group dates, trips, events, conferences, and retreats. For years afterward participants of the church youth groups remember their experiences as alumni of "New Hope," "New Covenant," "Firm Foundation," and other groups.

This intense cohort identity formation continues into college. At the KCF current members act as a tight-knit extended family. A newcomer is immediately celebrated by becoming the subject of a playful song sung to a popular tune like "Jingle Bells." For example, Arnold Lee was introduced as follows:

> Arnold Lee, Arnold Lee
> Arnold is his name!
> One request—he has for us:
> No more Schwarzenegger jokes!

Gradually, the KCF becomes the center of identity and life. The rhythms of the school year are demarcated by the club's fall retreat, Christmas banquet, spring retreat, April anniversary banquet, and the May Senior Send-Off. As the KCF student walks through campus, he sees his cohort, remembers the rich pungent smell of Bul-go-gi, a marinated Korean barbecue, and shares the latest pictures from their events. There is a deep sense of historical continuity and personal connection that carries over for years after college.

Although the entire Korean ethnic congregation usually comes together for special occasions such as Easter, Thanksgiving, and Christmas, the assemblies scarcely establish a shared religious bond between parents and their children. In addition, first-generation parents are not usually involved in the religious education of their children due to language barriers and cultural differences. Instead, they try to find English-speaking Korean pastors or Americans to work with them. This strict separation of the parents and their youth leads them to develop different religious experiences. The parents' religious experiences more often deal with their sense of exile and migration. Many of them pine for the return of Jesus, especially when they witness serious crimes, natural catastrophes, sudden weather changes, and the like. Reflecting on her struggles and sufferings, one parent said, "I cannot wait until Jesus comes back."

The second-generation children are more concerned about finding an identity and managing their new interpersonal relations. Their rhetoric tends more toward their personal experiences of Jesus as one who saves, gives strength, and benevolently controls their lives. At DU KCF's regular meetings, speakers often urged the students to abandon merely habitual worship in favor of "personally meeting God." God should be like their best friend or "Daddy." In one popular song "There is none like you," KCF members proclaim, "No one else can touch my heart like You do."

The second generation is also restive about the first generation's use of hierarchy based on seniority as a standard to evaluate the fellowships and prestige of individuals within the church. By contrast, the church youth fellowships and KCF are more egalitarian. Indeed, at the KCF the pastoral leadership is peripheral to most of the fellowship's functionings. One member put the prestige of the younger students' leaders above that of the older leaders. "Many people think that ministers are just pastors and youth pastors. But the best minister we can have is a student," he said.

Denied prestige and formalized recognition in the greater American society, first-generation Korean Americans invest great personal pride in being recognized within the formal prestige structure of their churches (see Hurh and Kim 1990). However, the youth don't understand or appreciate very well the dynamics and conflicts of "face" (Shin and Park 1988, 241; Chong, K. 1998, 281). As a result, the second generation is surprised and aghast at the bitter conflicts over insults to face that sever parent-child relations and the church. In the eyes of KCF students these conflicts are "cliquish," "political," and "hypocritical." One KCF member commented, "I don't think they are focused on what is right. They always fight and break up."

Also, entirely different worship styles come between the two groups. Korean-language services are relatively ornate and formal, including the recitation of the Apostles' Creed, a Psalter reading, pastoral prayers, and traditional hymns accompanied by organ and piano. In contrast, English-language services are composed of mainly two parts: singing contemporary gospel songs accompanied by guitar, keyboard, and drum, and the delivery of a sermon. Indeed, the liturgical style of second-generation Korean evangelicals often becomes one of the avenues through which they express their generational and cultural conflict with their parents (McGuire 1997, 62).

For many Korean American youth, the format of the adult worship service appears superficial and less edifying than their fervent, emotion-filled gospel singing worship service. The formal style seems a part of the parents' investment in the formalized prestige hierarchy in the church. As KSF member Min Kyu recalls the difference, first-generation worship is seen as "formal" and "hypocritical" while second-generation worship is regarded as "true" and "spiritual." Second-generation Koreans feel "disconnected" and "bored" at the adult worship service. And when the adults come to English-speaking services, they also feel out of place.

By dissociating themselves from the religious rhetoric and worship style of their parents, the youth can distance themselves from Korean culture and language. By adhering to their own brand of evangelical Christianity, second-generation Korean evangelicals create an identity of their own as an Americanized generation apart from first-generation Korean Christians. In short, the foundation of their identity is, as Karen J. Chai found in her study of a second-generation Korean congregation in the Boston area (Chai 1998, 309), no longer Koreanness, but religion. They try to detach themselves from first-generation Korean communities without abandoning their common religious faith (Lee et al. 1993, 247). After all, evangelical Christianity also emphasizes family values and treats the crossing of cultural barriers with critical respect. Second-generation evangelical Korean Americans, then, live in a social world that balances the normative universalism of evangelical Christianity with its counternorm of loyalty to parents and respect for cultures.

KOREAN AMERICAN VERSUS EVANGELICAL CHRISTIAN: KOREANNESS VERSUS AMERICANNESS

The racial-ethnic identity of second-generation Koreans indicates their socialization in the two worlds of the United States and Korea from which they often feel alienated and marginalized (Lee, S. 1996). On the one hand, they are not Korean enough for first-generation Koreans. As they are primarily socialized in American educational institutions, their knowledge and socialization about Korean culture and language are tenuous and hardly sufficient to initiate them into the world of their parents and Korean society.

On the other hand, second-generation Koreans often believe that they are not American enough in the eyes of some Americans who "are still unaccustomed to thinking of Asians as part of the national landscape of humanity" (Kim, E. 1997, 70; Sung 1967, 267). Their physical appearance as Asians always makes them stand out. On the way to a retreat in rural upstate New York, one carload of KSF students became conscious that a local gas station attendant was looking at them as if they were "weird" sights never seen before. The realization that "looking Asian" sets them apart as "strangers" can even lead to a sense of despair. As one evangelical student commented, "I am physically Korean. I have a Korean family. I will never escape it."

Korean American college students also feel that U.S. racial dialogues render them invisible. In particular, the KCF staff faces the invidious invisibility of being "in between." Claire, an alumna of DU KCF and now one of its pastoral staff, describes the Korean American college students' sociocultural position as follows: "American culture is so based on black and white. They are forgetting that it's no longer black and white. You have multicolor going around. But they are so into this bipole society that they make everything into that. [If] you are in between, you feel invisible. No one talks about you. And I think that's where we are. We are in between."

Korean American college students are also not as comfortable with non-Koreans as they are with Koreans. KCF member Tiffany observes that she, like others, prefers to be around Koreans to let her hair down. She says, "When I came to KCF, I stayed there because they were Koreans. And it's wonderful to be around Koreans! So, I do admit that I feel [more] comfortable being around Koreans than Americans." To the Korean Americans non-Korean students, even evangelical ones, practice an American individualistic way of relating that feels narcissistic, pushy, and inconsiderate.

In this context, their religious identity as evangelical Christians is the most salient, informed, uncontested, and familiar part of their identity. Whereas they have to juggle their ethnoracial identities, that is, how to be Korean as well as American, their religious identity clearly tells them how to be evangelical Christian. Wade Clark Roof claims that conservative Christians view their lives as a "series of concentric circles, with a person's own relationship with God at the center and expanding outward—to family, to church, to others" (Roof 1993, 92).

By valuing their religious identity more than their racial-ethnic identity, second-generation Korean evangelicals also gain a sense of control and achievement as to who they are. While their Christian identity is achieved and controllable, their ethnoracial identities are given and uncontrollable (Phinney and Rosenthal 1992, 149). The Christian dimension of their identity is not "inherited," "taken-for-granted," or "ascriptive," but "chosen," "aggressively proclaimed," and "achieved" (Warner 1988, 72). At the same time, they come to know God's love and plan for salvation, which are not conditioned by any ethnic and racial categorization, but offered to everyone. As Song explained:

To me, Christian identity is different. It's much more important, I think, because I guess ethnic, we really don't have control over it. It's who you are. It's

a part of you. Christianity, you chose to do it. And it's beyond ethnic. It's beyond race. It's about searching, seeking out God. . . . God loves everybody. I
think it matters.

By the same token, their religious identity can function as a mechanism
to deal with their negative experiences as members of a racial-ethnic minority in the United States. By believing in a supreme being who loves
them regardless of their race and ethnicity, they earn a sense of a new
identity as the "children of God." In this sense, a religious identity is more
appealing to them than a racial-ethnic one because it provides them with
"refuge" from their marginal social status and "along with it, positive social identity and empowerment" (Chong, K. 1998, 262).

Second-generation Korean American evangelicals emphasize a hierarchy of norms and counternorms: relation to God comes first, then come
loyalties to family, church, and others. Their faith balances out the claims
of American and Korean identities in a way that honors their Christian
parents and other Americans without being dominated or diminished.
However, their relation to secular Korean American classmates seems to be
so low on the scale of normatively valued relations as almost to be at the
breaking point. Unlike their parents, secular Korean Americans lack the
religious commonality of the evangelicals' parents and the certified status
as "Americans" that white students have.

A Middle Path: Korean American Evangelical

Second-generation Korean American evangelicals use their religious status
to simultaneously resolve the tension with their parents and non-Christian Korean expectations, and U.S. society's rejection of their Koreanness.
In the process the second generation creates a new master status of "Korean American evangelical." This new identity prioritizes Korean and
American norms as second to Korean American evangelical norms. However, some socially generated discounting is necessary for this social balancing act to work.

But while Korean American evangelical college students claim that their
Christian identity is the most essential part of their identity, they do not
necessarily go to just any evangelical organization on campus. Since campus parachurch organizations share a common evangelical subculture in
terms of their theological focus on born-again conversion experience and

worship style, they could attend any fellowship without much theological difficulty. Whether they attend the meetings of the KCF, the KCCC, or the AACF, they sing the same gospel songs and listen to similar messages. Therefore, second-generation Korean evangelicals have to find ways to explain why they prefer to practice their universal religious confession within the context of their own racial-ethnic groups, a practice which actually integrates their religious and their racial-ethnic identities.

In explaining the gap between their religious confession and their organizational affiliation, second-generation Korean evangelicals take advantage of normative contradictions within the doctrines of evangelical Christianity (Mitroff 1974; cp. Thumma 1991). By selectively focusing on individual salvation and fellowship rather than evangelism as their organizational goals, they legitimate an exclusive association with other Korean Americans. Their mission statement advocates strengthening faith, fellowship in Christ, and "spreading the word" to others.

At "Friendship Night" and the "Ice Cream Social," the students' goal is ostensibly evangelical. Yet the crossing of ethnoreligious boundaries poses an acute structural tension for the students. How can they bring the non-Christian or the non-Korean into a club that is designed to support a certain type of unique Korean American identity? Club vice president Song's describes the dilemma in the following terms, "The hardest part is to bring non-Christians to the club and make them comfortable. . . . It's also our duty." Thus, they use the evangelical doctrinal emphasis on fellowship among believers to explain their homogeneous membership and culture at the KCF, and their lack of interaction with other racial and ethnic groups.

Hyo Jin discusses how the average member's concern for personal relationships translates the boundary-crossing evangelism into boundary establishing as follows, "I think we can change one person's life each semester, that counts. Rather than going out to Central Park and doing nothing." Song describes how the club's resolution is the firmament of their identity: "We are a little more down to earth, more on the college student level. And I know it doesn't sound as glamorous as evangelizing, but yet . . . God wants us to . . . encourage one another. Anyone [who wants to get trained to go out to Washington Square Park to evangelize its homeless people or go to Ethiopia, KCF is not the place to be."

A major theme in KCF conversations is "serving God." This usually means serving other KCF members. Tiffany reports that serving God can be an intensely unifying experience. "I think to serve God means to serve people. And when you serve people, you are giving yourself to members, to people, and saying, Wow, it shows you care!" They also seldom evangelize non-Christian Korean Americans on campus. Fellowship members point out that socializing with KSA non-Christians would entail making moral compromises.

Additionally, they support their concentration on Christian fellowship by finding a parallel concept in their ethnic culture, that is, the Confucian ethic of taking care of the young and respecting the old. Confucian and Christian ideas of family powerfully comfort KCF students who are separate from family and church. One member, Justin, describes KCF as a close-knit family, a home away from home. "It's kind of true the way they say about KCF trying to be a family. It introduces you to a brotherhood," he says.

KCF fliers remind Korean American students of the group-oriented support of the ethnic church holding "one another accountable to ensure the spiritual and physical well-being of each member." Justin reflected how KSF gave him familial care, "While it's giving you spiritual guidance, it also has people that watch out for you and help you to grow up." In the familial setting of KCF, older "siblings" look after their younger "siblings," a pattern that reflects Confucian teachings on seniority and Christian teachings on family and brotherhood. Hong explains, "The bottom line is creating a Christian family and taking aspects of Korean culture, like the big brother and little brother relationship." Hong further comments that the familial hierarchical pattern was "feedback from my Korean roots, Noo-Na, Un-Nee type of thing. So much of it is built upon big brother, little brother, big sister, little sister relationships. That is so important to our club."[4]

Although, being an Americanized generation, they find it confusing to apply this Korean tradition, nevertheless they use their ethnic cultural practice to support and enforce their ethnicity-bound fellowship at the KCF. In doing so, they give the flavor of their Korean ethnicity to evangelical Christianity. By creating a Korean American version of evangelical Christianity, they can reduce the gap between their religion and their race-ethnicity.

Korean American evangelical college students also find a way to interpret their orientation toward race-ethnicity through their religion. Since God created them as Koreans, they can celebrate their racial-ethnic identity as God's gift. This way, their race-ethnicity claims its place as God's creation in their evangelical confession. Moreover, for these students, it is precisely because of their racial-ethnic identity that they can reach out to other Korean American students on campus and witness to them more effectively and easily than to people of other races and ethnicities. They are aware that there are still many Korean Americans who have not yet found Jesus Christ as their personal savior, and that a Korean American racial-ethnic identity links them together. By regarding their race-ethnicity as an instrument for evangelizing coethnic students, they attach a positive value to this identity.

At the same time, these explanations accompany the keenly felt acknowledgment that they cannot completely assimilate into dominant American society. As one student asserts, "Koreanness is my limit, reaching out to other non-Koreans . . . this is not easy. I don't socially fit in." In the process, they create a version of evangelical Christianity that contributes to constructing and maintaining the boundaries of their racial-ethnic identity (Swierenga 1991, 182). Their appeal to their "Korean otherness" also gives them some solidarity with their parents while simultaneously invoking the Christian ethic of being "strangers" to the world.

A number of the students attend Redeemer Presbyterian Church, which is a multiethnic megachurch headquartered on the East Side of Manhattan. The sermons are very collegiate, and the church is very "established" as an American denomination. Yet, the students' primary focus of identity remains the KCF, which bridges evangelicalism and Korean ethnicity and provides personal intimacy.

This example of religio-racial-ethnic group identification occurs when a religious group is composed of individual believers sharing a common ancestry based on similar physical characteristics and shared sociocultural experiences (Dashefsky 1972, 242–243). Claire, the KCF pastoral staff, admits, "If you are a Christian and a Korean, it might bind you closer to them. If you are a Christian, Korean, and American that will truly help me sync with them a lot more." In negotiating their religious identity as evangelical Christians and their racial-ethnic identity as Korean Americans, second-generation Korean evangelicals engage the three components of their identity in a mutual dialogue.

Conclusion

The formation of the religious-racial-ethnic identity of Korean American evangelical college students is a response to their own social location as both Korean Americans and evangelicals in the United States. The two aspects of their identity are not far removed from each other, as they claim, but rather are closely interrelated. Their relation to different reference groups such as both coethnic evangelicals and nonevangelicals, first-generation Koreans, whether Christian or not, and the larger U.S. society often overlaps and intersects, creating a complex web of social networks and thus influencing the formation of their identity. By negotiating and rearranging their experiences as Korean Americans and evangelical Christians, they formulate a unique identity for themselves.

One possible social identity for the second generation would be duality, an identity that takes the best of the both worlds. Rose (1967) concluded that Jews in small towns of upstate New York in the 1960s were not "strangers" characterized by marginality (Stonequist 1937), but by a duality in which they felt that they had the best of both Gentile and Jewish America. Second-generation Japanese Americans (Nisei) claim that they are in the comfortable position of not being "too Japanese" or "too American" (Lyman 1970, 151–176). However, the second-generation Korean American evangelical identity doesn't usually seem to occur as a duality or a golden mean. Although it is an identity still in formation, "Korean American evangelical" is more of a stand-alone identity defined in terms of rejection of the first generation and mainstream American culture. Undoubtedly, the emphasis on a stand-alone identity and definition by negation draws upon the evangelical conception of Christianity as the one unique way to truth.

All second-generation Korean Americans face similar cross-cutting structural pressures. Some resolve the sociological ambiguity by withdrawing from their religious status and becoming hard-drinking, smoking, dancing fraternity and sorority types. They alternate between secular ethnic and American identities, which keeps them relatively distinct at least for a while. If they attend church, they do so by redefining it as part of their sociality as a Korean. An appropriate name for their identity might be Korean American church attender. Others withdraw from their Korean status by joining white or multiethnic fellowships. They use their Christian evangelical identity to withdraw from most participation in the KSF and the Korean church. One could call them "American Korean evangelical."

However, a large number of second-generation Korean Americans are using evangelical Christianity as a gyroscope to balance the structural pressures of America and first-generation Korean American society into a unique "Korean American evangelical" identity. At "Uptown University" in New York City the same structural issues are also resolved as a "Korean

American evangelical." Most likely, this social process is repeated at college campuses across the United States.

As second-generation Korean Americans graduate from college, get married, and have families, the ways in which they resolve these social structural ambiguities will likely create different structural outcomes for Korean American religion. One can easily imagine KSA members becoming stalwarts of more tolerant, liberal mainline churches that emphasize an ethnic identity. They will be religious but not sectarian. The members of American-orientated Campus Crusade for Christ and InterVarsity Christian Fellowship might be more likely to join majority white evangelical churches like New York City's Redeemer Presbyterian that also has large numbers of Asian Americans. KSF alumni may be inclined to energize both the Korean churches and a pan-Asian church movement.

The second-generation "Korean American evangelical" is a type of "adhesive identity" described by Fenggang Yang (1999a). This chapter reveals how this identity is a unique outcome, but not the only outcome, of the sociological ambiguity of Asian Americans. The social structural analysis undertaken here also allows us to fill in some of the details about the dynamics of "adhesive identities" and to forecast some likely outcomes. Of course, in the end, Justin, Julie, Min Kyu, John, Claire, Hong, Tiffany, Arnold, Hyo Jin, and Song will steer their own paths through the structural pressures they face, perhaps in ways that will surprise us all and leave us analysts thinking, "Ah hah! Why didn't we think of that!"

NOTES

1. Temporality as a social property includes the "socially expected duration" of statuses (Merton 1984; De Lellio 1985; Westie 1973). Second-generation Korean Americans pick up the professional careers that their parents often had to abandon. Long ago, Paul Lazarsfeld noted that the individual motivations of youth are patterned by their parents' occupational distribution. Among Korean Americans, it is the parents' occupations and educations in Korea that color expectations. Milton Friedman factored in the way expectations of profession and income may be relatively permanent through various social statuses in his "permanent income theory." College students spend much and save little because they expect to eventually earn more (see Lazarsfeld 1953; Friedman 1957).

2. The names of the university, informants, and interviewees have been changed.

3. Compare Merton's study of the "instability and lack of consensus" because

of an incongruence between the romantic complex and taboos on intermarriage in the United States (Merton 1976, 227).

4. In Korean society every relationship has a hierarchical name. Noo-Na is the name used by a younger brother for his older sister. A younger sister, however, calls her older sister Un-Nee.

8

Gender and Generation in a Chinese Christian Church

Fenggang Yang

Women's leadership roles in the Chinese American Christian church have been a controversial issue. The immigrant generation at the Chinese church usually goes the extra mile to try to avoid this controversy, whereas the younger generation of American-born Chinese sometimes stumbles upon it in anxiety. This was what happened at the Chinese Fellowship Church, a midsized, nondenominational, evangelical church in a metropolitan area on the East Coast. It was founded in 1958 by a group of Chinese immigrants and has received several waves of new immigrants of diverse sociocultural backgrounds. In 1986 it began a separate English Sunday service and later hired an Anglo assistant pastor to meet the needs of the young adults of the second generation. Tensions between the American-born or American-raised Chinese and older adult immigrants have been clearly present since the early 1970s. But other conflicts in this heterogeneous church, which caused a bitter split in 1976 and the forced departure of several pastors in its history, have often overshadowed them.[1]

The young people of the second generation finally won a contentious battle in the summer of 1996. At a congregational meeting, the search committee presented a candidate for the senior pastor's position. Just the previous year, the congregation had voted out the senior pastor Daniel Tang. The process of voting on the pastor frustrated the youth, and the result of the vote led some immigrant members to worry that the notoriety of this church for treating pastors harshly might hamper their search for a new senior pastor.

After a year's hard work, the search committee, composed of immigrant men in their fifties, enthusiastically recommended a man who seemed very qualified in terms of his seminary credentials, ministry experiences, and multilingual capability. The immigrant members expressed their relief and gratitude that such a qualified candidate was willing to serve their church. Surprisingly, however, the young people of the second generation firmly opposed the candidate. They did so for a single reason: his wife was an ordained minister. "If the biblical principle of no female spiritual leadership can be broken," a young man around twenty years old stood up and said challengingly, "is any biblical principle unchangeable?" Several young people supported him by arguing that to protect the integrity of the faith, Christians should not accommodate to worldly trends in this matter. The search committee and some members expressed their anxiety about not being able to find a capable senior pastor to lead this heterogeneous church, but they failed to offer any theological rebuttal to the arguments against ordained women ministers voiced by the young people. The candidate was dropped.

This incident is very puzzling, but not isolated. Both commonsense and scholarly expectations suggest that immigrants from underdeveloped societies are more conservative in regard to gender equality whereas people who are more Americanized, especially the American-born generation, are more egalitarian (Ebaugh and Chafetz 1999). However, this incident shows the contrary: it was the more Americanized young people who took a fundamentalist position against women's leadership roles at the church. Moreover, this is not an isolated incident. I have noticed the same pattern in several other Chinese American churches that I have studied, and some Chinese Christian leaders and scholars also share the same observation (Yau, Wang, and Lee 1997; Chong, M. 1998; Tseng 2002). Why is the younger generation more conservative on this issue? Where does their fundamentalist standpoint on women come from? Why do their arguments seem so persuasive to the congregation?

In this chapter I explore the dynamics of gender and generation in this Chinese Christian church. I will argue that (1) the major source of the conservative standpoint against women's leadership roles at the church is the fundamentalist subculture of the United States, not the Christian subculture of China, nor the Chinese traditional culture of Confucian patriarchy; and (2) women's leadership is a victim of power struggles between the immigrants and the second generation at the immigrant church: the American-born or American-raised young people who desire recognition and influence use biblical authority to undercut the traditional authority of their seniors.

Key Terms

Some of the words used here are loaded with complex emotions for various people. It is beyond the scope of this essay to sort out all the dimensions and meanings of these terms, but it is necessary to clarify their meanings to reduce any misunderstandings.

Sex, Gender, Patriarchy, and Equality

In the current sociological literature, whereas *sex* commonly refers to the biological characteristics of males and females, *gender* refers to the social characteristics of males and females, and *patriarchy* to the system of males dominating over females. I use these terms with such meanings. Patriarchy has been the dominant gender structure in many societies over many centuries, just as inequality structures race and socioeconomic class. Gender equality or egalitarianism is a modern idea, although its roots may be traced to ancient times and texts. The ideal of *gender equality* is not necessarily to deny biological differences between men and women, nor necessarily to mean that men and women must perform the same roles, either at home or in society. However, sociologists recognize that equality between men and women, or the lack of it, is a social construction that varies in different societies and different times. *Equality* can mean both equal result and equal opportunity. In this essay my emphasis is on equal opportunity. More specifically, I have no intention of measuring gender equality at the church by counting the proportion of women among ordained ministers. The issue is whether women are allowed to be ordained at all. Although gender equality has been the agenda of contemporary feminist movements,[2] this chapter doesn't advocate a position. Rather, my purpose is to provide an objective and dispassionate sociological interpretation of what is happening in the Chinese American church in regard to women's leadership roles.

Fundamentalism and Evangelicalism

Most Chinese American churches are conservative in theology (Yang 1999a). However, there is an important distinction between two major camps within conservative Protestantism: evangelicals and fundamentalists (Ammerman 1991; Smith 1998). Fundamentalists and evangelicals share many characteristics: including insisting on orthodox or "traditional" interpretations of Christian doctrines, believing in the Bible as the revealed word of God, actively evangelizing or spreading the gospel to nonbelievers, and often speaking of their life-changing experience of conversion as being "born again." However, conservative Christians diverge in their ways of responding to modernity and the larger society. For example, while fundamentalists and most evangelicals believe in the inerrant Bible, fundamentalists are more rigid:

> As fundamentalists see the situation, if but one error of fact or principle is admitted in Scripture, nothing—not even the redemptive work of Christ—is certain. . . . They insist that true Christians must believe the whole Bible, the parts they like along with the parts they dislike, the hard parts and the easy ones. (Ammerman 1991, 5)

However, having made this rhetorical proclamation, interpreting the Bible is still a tough challenge:

> Such contemporary use of ancient texts requires, of course, careful interpretation. Studies of fundamentalists invariably point to the central role of pastors and Bible teachers in creating authoritative meanings out of the biblical text. (Ibid., 5)

In other words, while accepting the principle of the inerrancy of the Bible, in practice fundamentalists have to rely on the interpretations of certain pastors or theologians who command authority. By extension, fundamentalists trust certain institutions. These include the Moody Bible Institute, Biola University, many small Bible colleges, Dallas Theological Seminary, and many independent churches. They accept some individuals such as Jerry Falwell as leaders with charisma.

In contrast, Billy Graham is seen as the primary representative of the evangelicals, and Fuller Theological Seminary is one of the primary evangelical institutions. In 1941 fundamentalists formed the American Council of Christian Churches (ACCC) to set itself apart from both the liberal-leaning Federal Council of Churches (today known as the National Council of Churches of Christ) and moderate conservatives, Pentecostals, Anabaptists, and Holiness groups. Separatism is an essential characteristic of fundamentalists, who are highly sensitive to any appearance of cooperation with nonfundamentalists. Consequently, they hardly tolerate any disagreement. In 1942, the evangelicals organized the more inclusive National Association of Evangelicals (NAE), which has grown to be the largest Protestant association in the United States. The NAE affirms the principle of "in essentials unity, in nonessentials diversity, in all things charity." The organization says, "Founded on a common acceptance of the infallibility and plenary authority of Scripture, we shelter without offense varieties of biblical understanding. . . . We affirm that our diversities result from our human fallibility and that one day when we know as we are known we shall more adequately see the proper coalescence of all things in the unitary truth which is of God."[3]

Sources of Gender Conservatism

There are three major possible sources for the gender conservatism of the Chinese immigrant church: traditional Confucianism that holds to an ideology of patriarchy; a Chinese indigenous Christianity that may have adopted Confucianism; and Christian fundamentalism in the United States. My ethnographic research shows that neither Confucian patriarchy nor Chinese Christianity are responsible for gender inequality in today's Chinese American churches. The major influence comes from the American subculture of Protestant fundamentalism.

Confucian Patriarchy

Because of its association with foot binding and other oppressive practices against women in traditional China, critics have pointed to Confucianism as the source of gender inequality in China and other East Asian communities. In their studies of women in Korean American Christian churches, Ai Ra Kim (1996) and Jung Ha Kim (1997) observe that women are commonly excluded from leadership roles at the Korean church. They argue that Confucianism is a major factor for this gender inequality. If this is true, we should expect that a person who is more Confucian would also be more patriarchal. Because the immigrants are supposedly under a greater influence of Confucianism than their American-born children, we would expect them to be more conservative than the latter. However, the incident described at the beginning of this chapter shows that the American-born Chinese are more conservative in matters of women's church leadership.

Doubtlessly, Confucian patriarchy had great influence among Chinese immigrants who came from peasant villages of Guangdong (Canton) in the late Qing Dynasty and early Republican era. The Chinese American women's movement struggled against this heritage in the first decades of the twentieth century (Yung 1995). However, since the May Fourth Movement in 1919, most educated people in China have rejected Confucianism in general and Confucianism-endorsed patriarchy in particular. This is not to say that Confucian patriarchy has completely ceased to exist among the Chinese. In fact, women continue to be devalued in Chinese societies, especially in the villages, and in Chinese American communities, especially those in the ghettoized Chinatowns. Even among educated people, patriarchy persists as a cultural habit to a certain extent. Still, generally speaking, patriarchy and education are negatively correlated. Those who have received a higher education, especially a modern Western education, either in China or America, tend to be less patriarchal in terms of gender roles. Although we do not have equal results in terms of familial and social roles, equal opportunity between similarly capable men and women has become a mainstream ideology among the educated Chinese, especially in the public social sphere. Moreover, one of Christianity's appeals to the Chinese is its emphasis on greater equality between men and women. Christian influence has liberated people from the bondage of traditional customs and practices.

In the United States, over 90 percent of Chinese Protestant churches have been founded by post-1965 immigrants, a majority of whom are educated Chinese from all over China and Southeast Asia. In fact, most of the churched Chinese immigrants are people who came to the United States with their family members to attend college or graduate school. At the Chinese church both the wife and husband commonly have college or graduate degrees and hold professional jobs. The Western educational achievement of immigrant church members limits the influence of Confucian patriarchy among contemporary Chinese immigrants in the church. Of course, well-designed survey research is needed to validate or invalidate this proposition.

Neither the ethnographic data nor published research reveals justifications of women's status and roles in the church based on Confucianism or Chinese tradition. Of course, there has been some integration of the Christian faith with Confucian ideas. Elsewhere (Yang 1999a), I have argued that many *Chinese* Christians in America indeed can be called *Confucian* Christians because Confucian identity is somewhat synonymous to

Chinese cultural identity. However, the Chinese Christian acceptance of Confucianism is both selective and transformative. Selectively preserved and transformatively integrated are Confucian moral values and virtues that are perceived to be compatible with Christian beliefs, including love (*ren*), filial piety (*xiao*), hard work, thrift, temperance, delayed gratification, and the like (see Yang 1999a, ch. 4; also see Constable 1994). As in the larger Chinese community, Confucian patriarchy is subject to criticism and rejection, not acceptance.

In the public discourses at the Chinese Fellowship Church that I observed, members never invoked Confucianism to make women subordinate to men. From the early days of the church, women have served as deaconesses on the church council or united board. At rituals with high symbolic significance, women were sometimes put ahead of men. For example, at the baptismal ceremony, when both men and women were to be baptized, a common arrangement was for the women to walk into the baptismal pool before the men. However, the traditional age hierarchy was maintained: the usual order was that older women went before younger women, then older men before younger men. Despite the age hierarchy, traditional Confucian patriarchy was not a significant source of gender conservatism in women's leadership roles in the Chinese church.

Indigenous Chinese Christianity

One might ask whether indigenized Chinese Christianity unconsciously integrated Confucian patriarchy, which in turn affects gender inequality at the Chinese immigrant church. The answer seems to be a qualified no. Actually, indigenized Chinese Christianity is less patriarchical than Western Christianity, and the Christian gospel has been a liberating force for Chinese women as well as men.

Some feminist scholars have noted that the core symbolism of Christianity is androcentric and can be used to legitimate male domination and belittle women (Daly 1968, 1973; Ruether 1983; Morton 1985). Two of the three persons of the trinitarian God are male (Father and Son), and God is generically referred to as He. While Chinese Christians inherit the trinity of God the Father, God the Son, and God the Holy Spirit, they also use a written Chinese character *ta* that denotes neither male nor female but divine. In the Chinese language, the third person pronoun is uniformly pronounced *ta,* which can be either male (he) or female (she). Moreover, the traditional Chinese notion of the divine can be both masculine and feminine, as reflected in the Dao (Tao) that manifests itself through the interplay of the yin and the yang. Bible translators have used the word Dao in place of *logos* or "Word."

In fact, the nineteenth century saw the "feminization of Christian symbolism" when Christian symbolism and concepts were transposed to the Chinese context. Pui-lan Kwok (1992) shows that in the nineteenth and early twentieth centuries, Chinese Christianity emphasized the compassion of God, inclusive metaphors for the divine, and Jesus' relation with women. It downplayed the sinfulness of Eve. Kwok argues that "the image of God as father could also be used to challenge the hierarchical and patriarchal kinship relations" (ibid., 56). Instead of the absolute authority of the patriarch, all Christians were now equal brothers and sisters under the same heavenly father. Today, Chinese churches in North America are continuing the feminization of Christian symbolism and Christian teachings. Chinese Christian sermons and evangelistic discussions often highlight God's love and forgiveness instead of judgment and condemnation. The Christianity that appeals to contemporary Chinese immigrants is one that provides comfort, not one that makes prophetic demands or kingly commands. What are highlighted, then, are the soft, tender, feminine characteristics of God.

Historically, Christianity has been a liberating force for Chinese women. This includes the campaign against women's foot binding from the nineteenth through the early twentieth centuries, the role models of missionary women outside the home, and missionary schools for the education of girls (ibid., 1992). Judy Yung (1995) also argues that Protestantism was a significant catalyst in the awakening of Chinese women's consciousness in the United States before World War II. Churches in China even began to ordain women in the 1930s (Chong, M. 1998), much earlier than the missionary-sending churches in the United States. Given this tradition of Chinese Christianity as a liberating force for women, it is no surprise that immigrant women have often actively sought ordination in Chinese churches in the United States (Tseng 1999). Moreover, the very few writings calling for women's leadership roles (Kwok 1992; Yau, Wang, and Lee 1997; Chong, M. 1998) are by women who were raised in the churches of greater China. The *Ambassadors* bimonthly, a popular Chinese-language Christian magazine published by the Ambassadors for Christ, Inc. in Lancaster, Pennsylvania, published a series of articles in 1999–2000 discussing women's leadership roles in the Chinese church. Again, women's advocates, supporters, and sympathizers are those who either live in greater China or had grown up in churches in greater China before coming to the United States. Some observers are bewildered by the fact that Chinese churches in North America are more conservative than their counterparts in China and Southeast Asia (Yau, Wang, and Lee 1997; Maak 2000).

Of course, some Chinese Christian sectarian groups, such as the Little Flock, have insisted on patriarchy in church leadership. However, the influence of Watchman Nee, the founding leader of the Little Flock, and similar sectarian charismatic leaders, is mostly limited to first-generation immigrants. Moreover, their strong influence is probably limited to the sect and the churches led by the direct spiritual heirs of Watchman Nee. Watchman Nee was well respected by many Chinese Fellowship Church immigrant members, as reflected in their preaching, talks, and discussions. One of Watchman Nee's spiritual heirs was a frequent and popular guest preacher at the Chinese Fellowship Church. However, there were also open disagreements about some of Watchman Nee's ideas. Despite the influence of the Little Flock among immigrants at the Chinese Fellowship Church, the search committee, which was composed entirely of immigrant men, did not see the ordained wife was a theological problem. They recommended the candidate to the congregation. In short, indigenous Chinese Christianity cannot be held responsible for the gender conservatism of the Chinese Christian church in the United States.

American Fundamentalism

The rapid increase of Chinese Christian churches in the United States since the 1970s has occurred at a time when fundamentalism has become a significant force in American politics and society (Ammerman 1991). Chinese American Christians have been under the broad influence of the Christian Right, parachurch organizations with specialized ministries such as Focus on the Family, and, most importantly, conservative seminaries such as Dallas Theological Seminary, Moody Bible Institute, and Westminster Theological Seminary. Chinese Fellowship Church records show that in the early 1970s, a young deacon proposed to the church that it take action against a legislative bill regarding women's equality. He specifically cited an alarming article in the *Moody Monthly* magazine on this issue. On another occasion, another deacon proposed joining a letter campaign to support astronauts reading verses of the Bible while in an orbiting spaceship, again citing fundamentalist magazine articles.

American fundamentalism's most penetrating influence at the Chinese American church comes from seminaries. In the metropolitan area where the Chinese Fellowship Church is located, a small seminary is fondly dubbed the little DTS (Dallas Theological Seminary) of the Northeast. This is in part because most of its instructors are graduates of the DTS, but there are theological reasons as well. Chinese Christian laity who desire more theological training are often constrained by their jobs and family life. Few can afford full-time seminary study. However, this "little DTS" is very flexible in its curricular design and sends out teachers to teach at receptive churches. Some CFC lay leaders have taken its courses intermittently for many years. These lay leaders in turn pass on what they have learned to other members through Bible study meetings and Sunday school classes.

An incident illustrates the conservative impact of these courses on women's leadership roles. In 1994, an evangelistic fellowship group of the church elected a woman as its chairperson. In the course of a successful career she had been head of a laboratory at a national institute of health research. She was passionate about evangelism and enthusiastic about this ministry opportunity. To better equip herself for this ministry, she took some theological courses with the "little DTS," along with other church leaders. However, before long she was taught that according to the Bible women should not be spiritual leaders. She started pondering several questions: is the chair of the fellowship group a spiritual leader? and can a woman be the head of such a church group over men? The men who attended the same courses reduced or stopped supporting her leadership. She became confused, frustrated, and increasingly ineffective in her leadership. Consequently, after her term, this fellowship group gradually died out. Although other conflicts were present, the fundamentalist influence added its weight in causing the collapse of this once effective outreach ministry.

A more direct influence of fundamentalism came from Assistant Pastor Allan Houston, who came to serve the English-speaking young people in 1989. Reverend Houston holds degrees from a small Christian college in the South and from the "little DTS" in this metropolitan area. He also studied at Dallas Theological Seminary and later became an adjunct professor at the "little DTS." One year after Houston came to CFC, the Chinese senior pastor left for a Chinese church elsewhere in the United States. So, for a time, Houston became the only pastor at CFC. To maintain normal operations, he assumed greater responsibility and pushed to hire another Anglo man as the youth pastor. Some senior members opposed hiring more non-Chinese-speaking pastors. That young Anglo man left after a few months' service at the church without a pastor's title. Houston said that the young man left because he disagreed with the policy of having women as deaconesses and felt the church was too liberal. Actually, CFC has had women deaconesses almost since its inception. In 1990, Houston, together with some conservative lay leaders, succeeded in nominating only men as candidates for deacon. When they found out, some women who had served as deaconesses protested but later accepted the election results in order to preserve a harmonious climate. The following year, however, some women were elected to the church council or united board. The second Anglo man reacted to this by leaving, whereas Houston changed his position from opposition to reservation, justifying his compromise by saying that deacons and deaconesses were not really spiritual leaders. Pressed by senior members, Houston confined his ministry to the English congregation.

However, after eight years of continuous nurturing, fundamentalism had already made a clear mark on the young people. In the 1996 congregational meeting they strongly opposed the candidacy of the senior pastor because his wife was also an ordained minister. Houston had been part of the search committee, but other committee members rejected his suggestions. They considered his advice too American and impractical for their Chinese church. Consequently, Houston made clear to the English congregation his opposition to the candidate and announced his resignation from the church. The English-speaking young people nurtured by his fundamentalism took up the cause and effectively blocked the candidate.

American fundamentalist influence is common in Chinese American churches. In *Following Jesus without Dishonoring Your Parents* (Yep et al. 1998) published by the InterVarsity Press, Jeannette Yep recounts her own painful experience at a Chinese immigrant church. She was teaching a college-age Sunday school class for her church on inductive Bible study methods.

> Things proceeded well for a time, until the ten-week quarter was nearly over. Then, after class one day, Tim, a graduate student member, came to me and said that I couldn't teach Sunday school anymore. He had chatted with the pastor and they agreed. Tim would be taking over, and he would finish out the quarter.

In shock, I asked why was I being pulled. He said it was because there were young men in the Sunday-school Bible study class. "The Bible doesn't allow you to teach young men—see 1 Timothy 2," Tim said with authority. So I was relieved of my duties midstream! I passed on my notes to Tim, and he finished teaching the quarter's curriculum. (Ibid., 110)

Similarly, at a large Chinese church in Houston, English pastors who were trained at Dallas Theological Seminary opposed women's leadership roles in the face of a more moderate stance by the immigrant pastors. In the 1980s, a newly elected young Deacon of Christian Education threw the church into a crisis by dismissing all the female Sunday school teachers (see Yang 2000). Cecilia Yau, the leading author of a Chinese-language book calling for women's leadership roles in the Chinese church, had a more shocking experience. A Chinese church in a city on the East Coast had her preach to the Chinese congregation. Afterward, a young man from the English congregation came over and asked for her address. A few days later, she received a postcard without a signature but with words of warning, saying that she was breaking God's law by preaching because she was a woman. Such disruptions are commonly initiated by English-speaking young people under the influence of fundamentalism.

Generations and Authority

Tensions between the immigrants and the American-born or American-raised generation have been a chronic problem at many Chinese American churches. Young people of the second generation growing up in the immigrant church often feel frustrated by their lack of input in church decision making and lack of attention to their needs. Other conflicts and concerns, such as absorbing new waves of immigrants of diverse social, political, and cultural backgrounds and preserving the harmony and unity of a heterogeneous membership, have often taken priority over the needs of the second generation (Yang 1998a). At the CFC, the immigrant generation believes that it has already met the particular needs of the second generation by holding a separate English Sunday service with an Anglo pastor.

Houston, the Assistant Pastor since 1989, did not speak the Chinese language and had little interest in learning about Chinese culture. He was hired specifically to minister to the English-speaking members, most of them children of immigrant members. Why would a Chinese immigrant church want an Anglo pastor to minister to the young people? In part the reason was a lack of American-born Chinese (ABC) in full-time ministry. Not only have few ABCs become pastors, but the few that do often become burned out after serving the Chinese church and drop out of the ministry. In the 1970s, the senior pastor handpicked a young man who had grown up at this church and ordained him as youth pastor, though he was opposed by some immigrant members. Before long, in 1976, the church split when half the members walked out to form another Chinese church. In 1986 CFC finally hired an ABC youth pastor to start up the English Sunday service, but about a year later he quit the ministry to go to law school.

A major difficulty for the ABC pastor is the language and culture. Chinese immigrant members commonly hope that the ABC pastor will serve as a role model for their children and they expect him to speak Chinese and be deferential and polite toward seniors. However, such ABC ministers are rare. As an Anglo American, Houston was not expected to pass on Chinese culture to the young people. Although some senior members complained about his lack of deference to seniors and general politeness to everyone, the immigrant parents liked his firm Christian faith and effective ministry to the youth.

New immigrants commonly worry about the bad moral influences on their youth emanating from American society (Ebaugh and Chafetz 2000a). Chinese Christians who are influenced by Confucianism especially want their American-born or American-raised children to follow cherished traditional moral values and virtues. However, Americanized young people do not easily accept tradition or parents as sources of authority. They react negatively to common parental arguments such as "You should do this because we have done it for generations" or "You must listen because I am your parent." In this regard, the authority of God can be a substitute for the preservation of such Confucian moral values. At CFC, for a period of time several parents were very worried that their teenage youth in high school seemed to be dating. "But we didn't know what we could do," a mother said. She also recounted:

> These are youth at a rebellious age in this free American society. But God is really wonderful. Right then the assistant pastor [Allan Houston] gave a sermon: "True Love Waits." It was an excellent sermon. My boy understood the preaching very well and liked it very much. The pastor asked these young people to make a commitment to God, write it down, and keep it for themselves, that they would wait for the true love.

Because of his effective ministry in inculcating the youth with strict moral standards, Houston was well respected and generously treated by church members. The church repeatedly renewed his term without a problem.

Although Confucian patriarchy is not prevalent in the Chinese American church, there is a problem of "Confucian seniorarchy." Rule by age is an implicit or even explicit rule in the daily operation of the church. Young people are expected to defer to senior people, both their parents and others. Indeed, the parents regard propriety as very important, usually more important than the actual issue in a discussion. In 1993 a young man who had once served as a deacon on the church council circulated a six-page letter among church leaders about his frustrations. He complained that young people had few opportunities for church leadership and that their opinions were never taken seriously. Some immigrant members responded that it was not that young people's opinions were never taken seriously. Rather, the first-generation elders said, the young people did not make their point clearly in a good and respectful manner. At deacons' board meetings, some immigrant members frequently complained about how spoiled and irresponsible the ABCs were. After an ABC deaconess protested, she was brushed off. Respectful disagreement by the young people is fine, but confrontational protest is not acceptable. Consequently, some young people feel resentful about the "politics" of senior members.

Before the 1995 congregational meeting that refused to renew senior pastor Daniel Tang's term, as described at the beginning of this chapter, there were quiet campaigns for or against removing him. In informal discussions long before the congregational meeting, some young people expressed their opposition to voting on the pastor. They argued that the church should be ruled by a theocracy, not by a democracy. They said that the members are not the boss, because God is. Pastors are servants of God. They are called to lead the flock, not to be led by the congregation. But the immigrant members insisted that there was nothing wrong about voting on the pastor and argued that "We are in America, where democracy rules." Unable to change the church constitution in a short time, some youth then urged their own parents to vote for the pastor. Some parents were baffled, and brushed it off by telling them, "You do not understand the complexity of the matter, you do not know the situation of the Chinese-speaking congregation." At the congregational meeting that voted on the pastor, before ballots were distributed the chairman of the church council first asked youth under age eighteen and nonmembers to remove themselves from the main sanctuary, and then requested those who were not familiar with the situation of the whole church or issues facing the Chinese congregation to refrain from voting. Some youth complied, but they later expressed their anger and frustration at the immigrant members for "firing" the senior pastor.

Reverend Tang lost his position for complicated reasons,[4] but women's status was not a major issue. After he became the senior pastor of CFC in 1991, he circulated a position paper in English calling for greater roles for women in church ministries. Although some immigrant members influenced by fundamentalism questioned it, most church members did not have a clear position on the issue. Most people did not think it an urgent issue, for no woman pastor had been called to serve or invited to speak at the pulpit. Further, some women deaconesses, including some ABCs, had already served on the deacons' board. Young people never took issue with Reverend Tang regarding women's roles at the church. So, in light of the young people's campaign for keeping Reverend Tang, it was surprising that women's ordination suddenly became the major and only issue at the 1996 congregational meeting discussing the new candidate for the senior pastor position. The young people opposed him simply because his wife was also an ordained minister. The immigrant members, especially those on the search committee, were thinking of practical matters, such as whether the church should hire both the husband and wife to minister to the church, or help his wife find a ministry of her own, and were debating whether that would hinder his service to their church. However, the young people opposed the candidate from the fundamentalist principle of opposition to women spiritual leaders. They quoted verses of the Bible[5] to support their arguments.

Given the history of the church and the circumstances during that period, it seems that the real issue revolved around the voice of the young people, not women's ordination. After being repeatedly put down, the young people finally found an opportunity to dissent from the senior members in a way that made their arguments unanswerable. By referring to the absolute authority of the Bible, they successfully thwarted the authority of the seniorarchy. No longer could the seniors argue that the young people did not understand the situation, for the literal interpretation of the Bible was assumed to be clear and absolute. Since the immigrants had not undertaken a theological study of such biblical verses they were unable to offer a rebuttal based on alternative hermeneutical principles. Further, even if they had offered a rebuttal putting these biblical verses in their cultural context, they might be perceived as relativizing the Bible and thereby allowing for other compromises, such as justifying homosexuality or other unbiblical lifestyles.

By referring to the danger of the slippery slope of one compromise leading to the next, the youth utilized a most effective argument for maintaining the literal interpretation of biblical verses against women's leadership roles at the Chinese church.[6] Out of their concern for moral issues in the lives of the young people, immigrant parents conceded to such fundamentalist arguments. In this power struggle between the immigrant parents and the second generation, women's leadership roles evidently became the victim. However, the church may have missed a good opportunity to have a capable pastor. The church finally hired a senior pastor in 1998, but about a year later he abruptly resigned. Since then, the senior pastor position has been vacant.

Conclusion

Chinese Protestant churches in the United States tend to be conservative in theology. Whereas many Chinese Christians are evangelicals, some have been influenced by American fundamentalism. The fundamentalist influence clearly manifests itself in regard to women's leadership roles.

Women's leadership roles in the Chinese American Christian church have been a controversial issue. Because Chinese culture emphasizes harmony over confrontation, immigrant members at the church usually try hard to avoid this controversy in their conversations, discussions, and sermons. Meanwhile, given the Chinese evangelical culture of humility, few women have asked for a serious examination of the issue at their respective churches. Consequently, many Chinese Christian women who may have been well qualified for leadership roles have not been able to serve.

Women's leadership roles at the Chinese church are also sidelined by other controversies. At CFC they became victim to the power struggles between the immigrant seniors and the American-born young people. The immigrants worry greatly about moral problems in American society, and out of their concern for the moral education of their youth they have accepted American fundamentalist claims of absolute certainty and clarity. Few church members have taken the time to study this issue and come to a position of their own. Unless some women members put the issue on the agenda, it will continue to be sidelined in favor of other more pressing concerns.

Since the late 1990s, some Chinese Christian women have begun to speak and write about this issue. Some male pastors and well-known spiritual leaders have given their support to their efforts. However, most of these efforts have been made in the Chinese language, which fails to reach most Americanized Chinese Christians who have been assimilated into American fundamentalist culture. Without effectively reaching them and replacing their fundamentalism with evangelicalism, the situation cannot be changed in favor of promoting women's leadership roles. But this in turn requires change on several important fronts: the way of caring for and nurturing the spirituality of American-born and American-raised Chinese; alternate sources of theological training for the clergy and laity; and most important, the development of an indigenous Chinese Christian theology. These are profound problems facing the Chinese Christian church. Women's leadership roles may be one of the specific issues that will serve as a catalyst for great changes in Chinese Christianity.

NOTES

1. I thank Tony Carnes, Cecilia Yau, and Lai Fan Wong for their helpful comments on earlier drafts. However, I am solely responsible for the views and arguments in this essay.

Pseudonyms are used in this chapter. For detailed descriptions of this heterogeneous church and of a previous congregational meeting in which the members refused to renew the senior pastor's term, see "Tenacious Unity in a Contentious Community: Cultural and Religious Dynamics in a Chinese Christian Church" (Yang 1998b).

2. Regarding religion and women's status, there are a variety of feminist positions. Rosemary Radford Ruether (1983) identified three major approaches. The "liberationists" see patriarchy as inherent in the text of the Bible but choose to overcome it through criticism and selective rejection. The "Evangelical feminists" believe that the message of scripture is fundamentally egalitarian, but has been misread by traditional theologians and that better exegesis will clean up the problem. The last approach is to abandon Christianity in favor of alternatives, such as goddess worship. Simply put, feminism does not necessarily mean rejecting traditional Christian beliefs. Evangelical feminism is one of the major approaches.

3. See the NAE's website www.nae.net.

The NAE, Fuller Seminary, Graham's crusades, and *Christianity Today* were only a few of the important organizational initiatives taken to institutionalize the

budding evangelical movement. . . . The emerging evangelical educational establishment, for example, eventually came to include not only Fuller Seminary, but,
at the graduate level, also Gordon-Conwell Theological Seminary, Trinity Evangelical Divinity School, Calvin Theological Seminary, North Park Theological
Seminary, Covenant Theological Seminary, and Asbury Theological Seminary.
(Smith 1998, 12)

4. There were personality conflicts, cultural tensions, and theological disagreements. Reverend Tang failed to understand the complexity of the contentious subgroups and their diverse social, cultural, and political backgrounds, and offended
too many people. For a full analysis, see Yang 1998b.

5. A literal reading of some biblical verses seems to support the fundamentalist position. For example, "But I would have you know, that the head of every man
is Christ; and the head of the woman is the man; and the head of Christ is God" (1
Corinthians 11, 3); "Let your women keep silence in the churches: for it is not permitted unto them to speak; but they are commanded to be under obedience, as
also saith the law" (1 Corinthians 14, 34); "Wives, submit yourselves unto your
own husbands, as unto the Lord. For the husband is the head of the wife, even as
Christ is the head of the church: and he is the savior of the body. Therefore as the
church is subject unto Christ, so let the wives be to their own husbands in every
thing. Ephesians 5, 22–24); "Let the woman learn in silence with all subjection.
But I suffer not a woman to teach, nor to usurp authority over the man, but to be
in silence. For Adam was first formed, then Eve" (1 Timothy 2, 11–13).

But some hermeneutics would put these verses in their cultural context and
argue that the Holy Spirit has broken the boundaries of race, class, and gender, as
expressed in the verse, "For ye are all the children of God by faith in Christ Jesus.
For as many of you as have been baptized into Christ have put on Christ. There is
neither Jew nor Greek, there is neither bond nor free, there is neither male nor female: for ye are all one in Christ Jesus" (Galatians 3, 26–29).

6. A passage from Ammerman 1991, quoted in the body of the present chapter, is worth noting here:

> Fundamentalists also claim that the only sure path to salvation is through a faith
> in Jesus Christ that is grounded in unwavering faith in an inerrant Bible. As fun-
> damentalists see the situation, if but one error of fact or principle is admitted in
> Scripture, nothing—not even the redemptive work of Christ—is certain. . . .
> They insist that true Christians must believe the whole Bible, the parts they like
> along with the parts they dislike, the hard parts and the easy ones. (Ammerman
> 1991, 5)

In sermons, lectures, and articles in church magazines, Chinese fundamentalists
often argue that some people relativize biblical verses in order to justify homosexuality. In other words, a comprise on women's roles at the church would lead to a
slippery slope leading to moral chaos, which is not compatible with the immigrants' desire for certainty.

9

Faith, Values, and Fears of
New York City Chinatown Seniors

Tony Carnes

"The morning wind is from Heaven. So, I do taichi in the morning," Mr. Chou says. "Then, I feel good."

Chou is one of the earliest immigrants from Fujian Province on Monroe Street in New York City's Chinatown. In his old age he wants to have a morally good heart and a body refreshed by the wind from Heaven. He is typical of Chinese American elderly in Chinatown. Every day, he practices a taken-for-granted spirituality that only occasionally brings him into a temple or church. But don't misunderstand—religion is important for him as it is for 41 percent of Chinatown seniors. They attend over forty-eight religious temples and churches as well as practice religious exercises, rituals, and customs at home and work. About one-third of the seniors are active attendees of religious services.

Monroe Street stretches its nondescript way in south Chinatown from one housing project on the East under the Manhattan Bridge past another housing project, terminating finally in the Smith Housing project on the West. Old tenements string in between the big projects. Mr. Chou and three hundred other Chinatown seniors from one of the projects worked with our survey research team to produce a statistical profile of their beliefs, values, fears, and social lives. Very few studies have been done documenting the religious beliefs and practices of the Asian American elderly. But Monroe Street's seniors gleefully (well, mostly) took part in recounting their lives to a team of twenty-eight interviewers.[1] Mr. Chou summed up the experience in a moral proverb, "If you talk to someone, you will be happy. You talk, you have happiness in the heart."

Immigration is a "theologizing moment" for many immigrants, and immigrant incorporation often occurs through religious groups (see Smith 1978). It is also clear that older people are more likely to be religious (Donahue and Benson 1995; Idler 1987; Koenig 1995; Moberg 1997; the National Institute of Health 1998; Missine 1985). Among Chinatown seniors, the oldest are more likely to be religious than younger seniors.[2] Eighty percent say that religion plays an important role in their lives. Older Chinatown seniors are about twice as likely as younger ones to attend religious services. For example, 36 percent of the seniors aged eighty to ninety attend religious services at least once a week while only 17 percent of seniors aged sixty to seventy-nine do the same. It is not completely clear why this is the case.[3]

Likewise, in the general population, those above age 80 report the strongest religiosity (combined 1973–98 General Social Survey, s = 33,609). Fifty-six percent say that their religiosity is strong, compared to the strong religiosity reported by 28 percent of eighteen- to twenty-nine-year-olds and 34 percent by thirty- to thirty-nine-year-olds.

The more religious a Chinatown senior is, the more satisfied that person is with his or her life.[4] The most religious are more than twice as likely than the irreligious to be satisfied with their lives. The type of religion associated with life satisfaction is religion that is deeply and personally felt.[5]

In recent years the social sciences have belatedly come to recognize that religion plays an important role in the elderly's social, intellectual, emotional, and physical well-being (Crowther et al. 2002). Studies have shown

TABLE 9.1
Survey of Congregants

What role does religion play in your life?*

Very important	20%
Important	21%
Not very important	20%
None	24%
Hard to say	14%

On the average, how often do you attend religious services?

Several times a week	7%
Once a week	12%
Several times a month	9%
Once a month	5%
A few times a year	14%
Once a year	3%
Almost never	30%
Never	21%

* Excludes 4% that didn't answer.

Monroe Street neighborhood church: The House Church in New York City's Chinatown/Tony Carnes.

Monroe Street seniors coming back from church and temple, New York City's Chinatown/Tony Carnes.

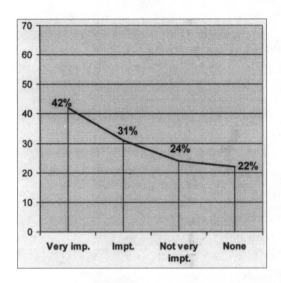

Religion in Chinatown
I am completely satisfied with my life and the role
religion plays in my life is . . .

that the most common coping mechanism that seniors use is religion
(Courtenay at al. 1992; Krause and Tran 1989; Williams et al. 1991). In
particular, turning to religion for consolation during a health crisis is the
coping practice most often cited by seniors (Ferraro and Kelley-Moore
2000). Most studies show that religion enhances health among the elderly
(Ferraro and Abrecht-Jensen 1991; Idler and Kasl 1992).

In sum, there are strong indications that professional care for the Chinese elderly must include a religious component. Indeed, outside their immediate block on Monroe Street, the seniors give most of their top ratings
for senior services to religious organizations.

Recent U.S. laws, executive mandates, and Supreme Court decisions
also make quite clear that there is legal endorsement for taking religious
considerations into account in the process of providing social services.
The question is how to do this in a sensitive way that maximizes the seniors' wishes. For example, nonreligious seniors in crisis are not more
likely to turn to religious pathways for coping. Rather, they turn to friends,
counseling, and other religiously neutral alternatives (see Ferraro and Kelley-Moore 2000). Because Chinese American seniors are significantly less

religious than seniors in the United States as a whole, secular service options also must be plentiful.

What is remarkable is how many of the seniors are products of the post-1965 immigration boom sparked by the change in immigration laws. Few people have realized that we are witnessing the beginning of retirement of the (relatively) new immigrants. Eighty-three percent of elderly Chinatown immigrants came in 1965 or later (He 2002, 4, reports similar figures). The Chinese American seniors also represent the coming predominance of Asians and Latin Americans among the foreign-born elderly (ibid., 3–4). The elderly foreign-born population is increasing by 1.5 percent per year.

Also noteworthy is how many seniors came to the United States as seniors or at least near to senior age: 16 percent of immigrant seniors arrived between 1992 and 2002. Undoubtedly, they came to be reunified

Monroe Street neighborhood temple: Shi Zhu Shan Xian Buddhist Temple/Tony Carnes.

Monroe Street neighborhood churches: First Chinese Presbyterian Church and Ling Liang Church/Tony Carnes.

with their children. That motive also means that these seniors have arrived with a commitment of care from their children. In turn, they are also likely to be caretakers of their grandchildren.

Gender

Religion plays a far greater role in the lives of older Chinatown women than among the elderly men. However, almost a third of the men say that religion plays an important role in their lives. Furthermore, many men engage in practices relating to good health, luck, and relationships that have seeped into folk wisdom from Chinese religion. Chinatown seniors don't usually see these practices as religious.

TABLE 9.2
Importance of Religion in Lives of Chinatown Seniors by Gender

	Very Important/Important	Unimportant/No Role
Men	29%	51%
Women	50%	38%

Cantonese and Fujianese Americans

One of the most important relationships for Chinese immigrants is based on the home village, town, city, or province they come from. These particularisms profoundly affect patterns of religious growth, settlement, and incorporation in Chinatown. Chinatown seniors tend to relate to religion through worship centers that are associated with their locality group. Opinions of Cantonese and Fujianese Americans tend to be mutually antagonistic.[6]

Seniors from Canton and Fujian do often have relationships (*gwanxi*) with each other,[7] but they seldom say that those relations are pregnant with emotional feeling (*gwanxi ganching*; see Jacobs 1979; Vogel 1965).[8]

Rather, Chinatown seniors are largely drawn from two important, competitive, first-generation immigrant waves: the Cantonese, and the new wave of Fujianese. Most of the Chinese American seniors were born overseas (cp. data in Administration on Aging 2000; Angel and Hogan 1992).

Seniors born in Hong Kong or Guangdong Province make up 41 percent of Chinese Americans. The great majority come from the Pearl River Delta between Hong Kong and Guangdong (Canton). The Cantonese American seniors who came earliest to the United States tend to be from the hilly Toisan (Taishan) area. Seniors who immigrated later come from a variety of large and small localities in the Pearl River Delta, like Xinhui (Sanmoy), Fetsan (Foshan), and Mongsan (Mengshan).

The older power structure of Chinatown, which is centered on the Chinese Consolidated Benevolent Businessmen's Association, is Cantonese American. The rival power structure located in the modern social service centers is also dominated by Cantonese Americans.

The Cantonese brought with them an effusive religious panoply of gods, ghosts, ancestors, luck, and Christianity. However, over time the public worship of Buddhist, Taoist, and folk religions declined while the Christian churches grew. Even though many Cantonese Americans continued home and work rituals, others became more or less secular with occasional religious inclinations during special events or crises.

Many Cantonese Americans have left Chinatown, though often returning to work, worship, and shop. As Chinatown has expanded eastward, a
new rival to the Cantonese Americans has settled in large numbers. A
number of years ago, I was surprised to hear a man get up in the mainly
Cantonese-speaking megachurch Overseas Chinese Mission Chinese service and announce, "Wo shih Fujian ren," he said. "I am a Fujian person
and want to meet other Fujian people after the service." Afterward, a number of Fujianese warmly gathered around. Out of interactions such as
these have arisen one of the fastest growing groups in the city. A significant number of elderly Fujianese live on Monroe Street.

A remarkable 44 percent of the Chinese American seniors were born in
Fujian (about 40 percent of the Fujianese American seniors speak the
Fuzhou dialect, probably indicating that they are from Fuzhou City and its
environs). This is surprising because immigrants from Fujian arrived later
than the Cantonese. Since most of the Chinatown social service agencies
are staffed by English or Cantonese speakers, there is an immediate need
to add the capacity to understand Fujianese-origin seniors. Mr. Cheng Lin,
a direct descendant of the famed fighter against the opium trade Commis-
sioner Lin, said shortly before his death in 2002, "The social welfare of the
Fujian seniors is one of the most neglected topics in Chinatown." Mr. Lin
was also the architect of the beginnings of the retirement benefits system
emerging in the People's Republic of China, and before his retirement, he
was a high-level official in the government-run Protestant church in
China. Mr. Lin found that the Chinese church was his key resource to surviving in the United States. He said that a local pastor took Mr. Lin into
his home after his own family turned him away. The Fujianese are very active in using religious organizations to confront the problems of their existence as mostly illegal immigrants in the United States (Guest 2003).

The seniors from Fujian are a little more likely than the Cantonese to
give weight to religion in their lives. Forty-seven percent of the Fujianese
say religion plays an important role in their lives while 42 percent of the
Cantonese say this. However, the difference is not great and the immigrants regularly go to religious services in similar proportions, about 30

TABLE 9.3
Natal Provinces of Chinese American Seniors

Fujian	44%
Guangdong/Hong Kong	41%
China	7%
Other Countries	5%
NA	4%

percent going at least several times a month. Fujianese are much more likely to practice home rituals, with 32 percent doing them most of the time while only 16 percent of the Cantonese do. It seems that overall the Cantonese have a more secular profile.

Religious and Ethnic Identity

Religious Chinatown seniors are much more likely than the nonreligious to fuse their religious and Chinese ethnic identities. This is particularly true for Fujianese American seniors. For those Chinatown seniors who say religion is important to them almost three-quarters say that they feel strongly that their ethnic identity means observing Chinese customs and traditions. Only 42 percent of the nonreligious agree. Most of the religious seniors also say that their ethnicity means confessing a traditional Chinese religion.[9] Forty-two percent of those who say religion is very important in their lives also feel strongly that their ethnicity includes knowing the history of China. The nonreligious are much less likely (26 percent) to root their ethnic identity back into Chinese history.

The very religious are also twice as likely as the nonreligious to feel that they are surrounded by other hostile ethnic groups. The more a Chinatown senior attends religious services, the more he or she is likely to say that one's ethnicity means feeling a hostile separation from other ethnicities. Thirty-two percent of those who attend services several times a week feel this way, compared with 15 percent of those who never attend.

Even so, only a minority of the religious seniors reference their ethnic identity to discrimination or estrangement from American society. This probably means that unlike African American seniors in New York City they have not experienced any sharp, recent hostility from groups outside Chinatown.

The very religious seniors are also somewhat more likely (43 percent) than the nonreligious (35 percent) to feel that Chinese ethnicity means marrying a Chinese. However, we should note that most religious and nonreligious Chinatown seniors understand their ethnicity as belonging to an open group.

Nominal Buddhists are more likely to be nationalistic (being Chinese means to be "proud of my nation" and "to support my nation") than Buddhists who do home rituals or Christians. This is largely because they are more often recent immigrants from China.

Although religious Chinese American seniors might appear not to be very far down the road toward calling themselves "American," there is a striking bit of evidence that most have firmly latched onto an American identity. Almost one-third of the religious and nonreligious Chinese American seniors stopped our interviewers over the ethnic meaning questions that said "my ethnicity means to support my nation" and "to be proud of my national history." These seniors instructed our interviewers to write in "America" for these questions (37 percent and 32 percent respectively).

Religious Denominations—Buddhists, Christians, and Seculars

Thirty-four percent of Chinatown seniors say that they find Buddhism most attractive. The majority of Buddhists are from Fujian. Forty-nine percent of the Fujianese find Buddhism most attractive, while only 20 percent of the Cantonese do. Indeed, two-thirds (67 percent) of the Cantonese find Buddhism unattractive while only 36 percent of the Fujianese share that opinion.

Three-quarters (77 percent) of Buddhists say that their religion is important or very important to them. However, nominal Buddhists, those who say that Buddhism is partly attractive to them, are also likely not very interested in religion. Sixty-six percent say that religion has little or no importance to them.

Nominal Buddhists are also not very likely to regularly attend religious services. Most never do. Seventeen percent of those who consider Buddhism to be only partly attractive do go to the temple at least a couple of times a month. However, these temple-goers probably don't deeply believe in what they are doing but go to make offerings just in case they work and perhaps out of a sense of tradition. One temple-goer, Mr. Li, observed, "Hey, maybe it works! You don't know, but many old timers go [to temples]."

Religious Orientation of Chinese American Seniors

Chinese seniors who are strongly attracted to Buddhism are divided into two groups, depending on how often they attend religious services. About half (57 percent) of the strong Buddhist identifiers don't go to services more than once a month. Most seldom go to temple services. Their strong interest in Buddhism is mainly satisfied through home rituals.

However, 41 percent of strong identifiers with Buddhism are very active in temple-going. This group itself seems to be split into two groups. On the one hand, half of them appear to follow the traditional Buddhist pattern of going to the temple on the first and fifteenth of the lunar month. The other half have adopted the typical Christian congregational pattern of attending services at least once a week, probably on Sunday. They most likely look forward to seeing friends at the temple, hearing the Buddhist scriptures read and taught, and having lunch afterward.

About one in five elderly Chinatown residents are Christians. Cantonese American seniors (15 percent) are a little bit more interested in Christianity than the Fujianese American seniors (12 percent). Further, the Cantonese seniors are much more likely than the Fujianese seniors to receive social services from well-known local Protestant Faith-Based Organizations (FBOs) like the Salvation Army and the Chinese Christian Herald Crusade. Cantonese seniors are also generally much more knowledgeable about these agencies.

Seventy-nine percent of the elderly Chinatown Christians are Protestants. Most of the Protestants say that their religion is important or very important to them. Protestants who are strongly attracted to Protestantism are highly likely (75 percent) to attend church services at least several times a month. Sixty-three percent fall into the weekly worship pattern of Protestantism.

Seventy-five percent of nominal Protestants attend church services only once a month at best. Most seldom attend. Still, those who are only "partly attracted" to Protestantism also report higher church attendance rates than other seniors. Further, about half (44 percent) are more likely than nominal Buddhists to say that religion is important to them. Recent

TABLE 9.4
Religious Orientation of Chinese American Seniors

	Most Attractive	Partly Attractive	Not Attractive
Buddhism	34%	14%	52%
Christianity (total)	18%	—	—
Protestantism	14%	6%	81%
Catholicism	4%	4%	92%
Judaism	0%	3%	97%
No Religion	6%	4%	90%
All Religion	<1%	6%	94%
Other Religions	1%	<1%	<1%

studies that indicate a trend toward greater religiosity that starts out as church attendance with a friend before religious commitment seem to apply to a greater proportion of nominal Protestants than to nominal Buddhists.

About one in five elderly Chinatown Christians identify with the Catholic Church. Chinese seniors who are strongly attracted to Catholicism also emphatically state that religion is important to them. Very few who strongly identify with Catholicism are tepid about their religiosity. In China rural Catholics are said to have "hard bones" because of their unbending devotion to Catholicism (see Madsen 1998). Nominal Catholics are much like nominal Buddhists in attaching less importance to religion in their lives. Catholics seem divided into either wholehearted Catholics or nominal Catholics who want little to do with religion. The Chinese seniors who are attracted to Catholicism are also almost all Cantonese (90 percent). However, there are elderly attendees with a Fujianese priest at a small congregation at the Transfiguration Roman Catholic Church on Mott Street.

Home and Work Religious Rituals

In order to find out about the practice of much popular Buddhism, which is centered around daily rituals performed at home or work, we asked the Chinese American seniors if they performed home rituals. About one in five Chinatown seniors regularly do so.

The question sharply distinguishes Buddhists from Christians. Three-quarters (74 percent) of those Chinese seniors who are most attracted to Buddhism do home rituals. Even two-thirds (67 percent) of the nominal Buddhists do home rituals, though in a less active manner than the strong Buddhist identifiers.

Eighty-one percent of strong identifiers with Protestantism don't do home rituals. As we have noticed with church attendance, the Chinese American seniors who are somewhat attracted to Protestantism are divided between those who are probably on their way to converting and those who are likely to retain only a nominal interest. Fifty percent of the seniors who are partly interested in Protestantism also don't do rituals and are perhaps the group that is closest to assimilating to Christianity. Catholics are somewhat more likely than Protestants to do home rituals, with 30 percent doing them. However, 70 percent of Catholics do not do rituals.

Seculars

Twenty-four percent of Chinatown seniors say that religion presently plays no role in their lives.[10] Most of these seculars don't go to religious services or have any interest in any of the Chinatown religions. Only one in five (12 percent) has a passing interest in one of the religions. Seculars are more likely to be Cantonese Americans than Fujianese Americans.

Values and Fears

Every week, many Chinatown seniors uncharacteristically raise their hands, hop, turn, and glide with big smiles to the tunes of the "Senior Healthy Dance." Introduced around 1992 by a Mainland Chinese immigrant, the dance was an instant success. "Being healthy," seniors say, "is the most important value on our value scale."[11] More seniors (76 percent) rate this as more important than being with family, having no financial worries, being active, or losing control of their own lives. The seniors' greatest fear is that they will get ill. Undoubtedly, in their eyes the ability to do the other things that are important to them depends on being healthy.

In dealing with health and illness as well as other issues, all seniors regardless of religious leanings tend to frame their concerns more often than non-Chinese seniors in terms of their care and their fear of being a burden on their families. However, religious Chinese American seniors are more likely to emphasize affective relationships than secular seniors. Their values lean more toward being with family, friends, and being appreciated by others. When one gets sick, a religious senior is more likely to be concerned about how the illness impacts his or her close social relationships.

Secular Chinatown seniors are more likely to emphasize either instrumental relationships or circumstances that don't require help from others. More than the religious seniors they value getting help when they need it, having no financial worries, and being healthy. If one gets ill, the secular senior is more focused than the religious senior on self-recovery than on the social disruptions of being ill. These values seem somewhat rooted in necessity, since secular Chinatown seniors have fewer family and other social relationships upon which to draw in times of crisis. The difference in values between religious and secular Chinese seniors is independent of origins, income, and gender.

Chinatown seniors of all religious inclinations are much less likely than other senior New Yorkers to place emphasis on having fun, being active, informed, and appreciated. They esteem to a lesser extent the actual emotional contents of their lives. They are pragmatic doers rather than sunny optimists. If they are healthy enough to do things, they are satisfied. Chinese American seniors don't place as much emphasis on "having fun" as other seniors in New York City do. This deemphasis of subjective well-being in favor of objective well-being is in fact characteristic of Chinese culture, where nature and the social others tend to define the self rather than vice versa.

Religious and nonreligious Chinatown seniors are also very concrete and action-orientated, particularly in personal relations (cp. Bond 1986). Commonly, Chinese American seniors respond to concrete examples (often historical) and to actions that are beneficial to themselves that signify that the interactor really has goodwill. They often distrust abstract notions and proclamations of goodwill embellished with smiling faces. They say, "Show me, don't tell me." Some Chinese American seniors respect traditional words like Confucian texts and more use proverbial wisdom, but all believe that relationships are based on interpersonal adjustments over a long period of time. They dislike contracts among friends as signs of distrust and the evil intent of people with "wolf hearts and dog lungs," as one senior put it.

What is feared can also become the focus of a religious reflection. Religion is about the acceptance of spirits, values, and a way of life as well as a rejection of those things that can create chaos and meaninglessness in life. Asian American seniors' religious notions often focus on warding off things that could disrupt their families, living or dead.

Indeed, Asian American seniors may fear social death more than physical death. Their cultural values emphasize the continuity of family, regular family contact, and acceptance and interaction within a network of friends.[12] In particular, mothers value continuing interaction with their sons.[13] So, they aren't as worried about their own deaths as they are about how much grief and trouble their deaths will cause their family. They don't want to get deathly ill, causing their family to spend money and become traumatized.

For seniors, being active and having self-control and autonomy is largely defined in what seems to be a negative sense of not being a burden on their families. Their family concerns far outweigh their value of being active, having fun, losing control over their lives, and being alone. This hierarchy of values is rooted in a sense of self that is more social than individual. A typical Chinatown senior is happiest when he or she is either with family or is in active orientation toward his or her family by "not being a burden" or worrying about losing a family member to a terrorist attack.

Next to illness, Chinatown seniors most fear losing someone close to them. The fears that they have after September 11 are also closely tied to their fears of losing a family member or of losing their ability to get treatment for health problems, which would affect their relations with their families as well as other activities.

Chinatown seniors are also physically close to their families. Chinese American seniors are more likely than other New Yorkers to live with adult children, with one-third living with them (cp. Liao 1999; Goodman and Silverstein 2002; Salari 2002). Moreover, Chinese Americans are much less likely to depart the area where their extended families live and leave for the "sunbelt states" (Kritz and Nogle 1994; Zavodny 1999).[14] Fujianese seniors (43 percent) are much more likely than Cantonese (27 percent) to live with their children.

We were able to see how fears, family, and religion interplay through discussions about how the Chinatown seniors dealt with September 11. This challenge has acted as a significant disruption in the lives of the elderly so that their previously settled minds, habits, and customs were at least temporarily unsettled (Mahler 1995). Three families in one housing project lost a son or daughter in the terrorist attacks. Though this is a small number, everyone in the houses seems to know about the loss, and they are daily reminded of it by the shrine in the courtyard. A couple who lost their son in the attacks are not fearful for themselves but are most worried about losing anyone else close to them.

Yet, paradoxically, in some ways the seniors' fear of September 11 or of losing a family member has been healthy because it reinforces their social sense of self. They have an important role in their children's lives: they must worry for them! Which, of course, is what they have done all their lives (sometimes a little too unctuously for their children!).

Further, the social self-orientation goes hand in hand with an other-directed activism rather than talking. These seniors feel best when they are worrying for their family and can do something to help. Additionally, to paraphrase just a little, they typically comment, why should they worry about being bored as long as they have their family to worry about? Nor are they worried about not having anyone to talk to about their problems.

As one senior said, "Who else am I going to talk to but my daughters?" As long as they can also *do* something to help their family, they don't feel as great a need to talk about their problems with someone else in a therapeutic setting. Indeed, they don't want to burden their families by talking about their problems.

Of course, maybe the seniors do actually need someone to talk to about their problems. Indeed, at the 1995 White House Conference on Aging, it was concluded that of the 32 million Americans age sixty-five and over, nearly five million suffer from persistent symptoms of depression, and over one million have major depression. Depression is a serious but relatively unnoticed problem among elderly Chinese immigrants (Mui 1996a, 1996b; also see Mui 1997). Chinese American seniors have one of the highest suicide rates among ethnic U.S. elderly (Baker 1994; Lester 1994).

However, our interviews point out that trying to get seniors to talk about their problems has to be done in a way that doesn't make them fear it will get back to their families or weaken their ability to do things that keep their burdens off their children. "Active-listening" for these seniors has to be "active-listening-doing." That is, these seniors will just feel worse by sharing their fears unless it allows them to relieve the burdens on their families, to gain their families' attention, and to do things that makes them feel more connected to others (for a complete discussion of this point, see Chen 1997; also cf. Yeo and Hikoyeda 1993).

Religion makes a big difference in the Chinatown seniors' responses to September 11. Protestants, in particular, and Buddhists as well were much less likely to worry a lot after the attacks. The number of Protestant seniors expressing a lot of fear after September 11 was 40 percent less than would be expected based on their numbers. Buddhists with a lot of fear were 30 percent less than would be expected based on their numbers.

The Protestants and Buddhists cite their beliefs as a reason. However, it is also possible that the lower fear level is a result of the modestly better social integration into the United States that results from the Chinese elderly belonging to a religious group. For example, Fujianese American seniors who go to the Buddhist temples are significantly less fearful about the post–September 11 situation than Buddhists who only do home rituals. On the other hand, American-born seniors had higher fears after 9/11 precisely because they are highly integrated into U.S. society. The Chinatown seniors who most value patriotism as part of their ethnic identity quite naturally had more fears (7–8 percent) after the attacks. So, the Chinese Protestants and Buddhists are not as anomic—poorly integrated—as secular Chinese because they belong to local religious organizations. However, because of language and more recent immigration, they are not so highly integrated into U.S. society that they identify themselves as personal targets as do native-born Americans.

Doing home rituals doesn't change the levels of fear, except for a distinct rise in the fear of being ill or of losing a family member. Ritual practitioners also have some elevation of fears about losing control of their lives. Doing only home rituals is also inversely related to the level of personal life satisfaction.[15] At best, ritual practice seems to be a place some seniors turn to when they or their families are sick. Dying of cancer, a Chinese American senior in the neighborhood became intensely ritually oriented and donned numerous copper bracelets to ward off evil forces. He was hopeful about the outcome of his actions but his level of fear seemed to be unchanged. However, much mystery remains about how the rituals helped him emotionally.

The Chinatown socializers among the seniors were significantly more fearful (5–13 percentage points higher) than the other seniors. These are the people who love to talk with friends and be with family. Those who most value being with their families or friends were more likely to have post–September 11 fears. Yet, if the socializers are Buddhists or Christians who are regular worshipers at their temples or churches, their fears are much lower. It appears that going to Buddhist temples or Christian churches can somewhat offset the disruptions to social life that the attacks brought.

A Last Word

The last word on the faith, values, and fears is well said at the Lucky Bakery, across the street from the Lucky Newsstand which is next to the allegedly luckiest stop for taking a bus to the gambling halls of Atlantic City.

"Don't get on that bus with your family money! Your luck has run out!" an elderly man tells Old Lee.

A white-haired Christian pastor observes, "He has just got off work and has no place to go. I wonder if he would listen to me. Let me sit with him."

As everyone heads for the bus after *youtiao* (Chinese donuts) and tea, someone from the big Mahayana Buddhist Temple across the traffic square hands out a flier announcing a famous priest speaking about "the fortune is golden peace" of Buddhism.

Lucky's is just an ordinary, though joyous, tea and bakery place in Chinatown that is favored by the seniors. But all the gods and fortunes go through it with the seniors. Everybody got on the bus, including Mr. Lee with his family money, the pastor with his prayers, and a few with the Buddhist flier in their hands for good luck. On this day you cannot understand the Chinatown seniors, help them, or enjoy them deeply without understanding their destinies. One elderly woman said, "Being old is like being in a rocker—you go up and you go down but heaven is the biggest up."

NOTES

1. The respondents' ages range from fifty-five to ninety-seven years. Forty-seven percent are aged sixty to sixty-nine, 31 percent are seventy to seventy-nine and 15 percent are over eighty. The average age is seventy. However, the Cantonese American seniors are older on average than the Fujianese American seniors. Sixty-five percent of the Fujianese seniors are younger than seventy while 52 percent of the Cantonese seniors are older than seventy.

The interviews took place between May 9, 2002, and July 19, 2002. During this period of time, the news media carried stories about ongoing terrorist fears, the economic difficulties of Chinatown, and the economic jitters caused by corrupt corporate management. On the other hand, the news media also reported that there was a near certainty that seniors would be receiving some sort of help with payments for prescription drugs.

A simple random sample was taken of all the seniors, over one thousand of them, in a large housing project on Monroe Street in Chinatown, New York City. The sample is nearly identical to the demographic profile of seniors in the Chinatown census tracts. The questionnaire was drawn from previous national questionnaires that provided valid data or was based upon an analysis of previous literature and interviews with social service workers in Chinatown. The questionnaire was available in both English and Chinese. The translation was tested by the translation—retranslation method, and it was examined and discussed by the survey team. Additionally, professional translators of Mandarin, Cantonese, and Fujianese were consulted. The biggest challenge to the questionnaire was the attempt to be user-friendly to a population with a grade school education and little experience with survey research. The Principal Investigator and several social workers worked with the interview team to perfect standardized explanations of the questions.

Twenty interviewers, who are mostly first- or 1.5–generation Chinese immigrants, conducted a total of 340 completed interviews. In general the seniors were friendly and eager to take the survey. They also undoubtedly liked the eager, friendly interviewers. Several respondents did say that they were worried about giving out confidential information, particularly information that the housing administration or city social workers might use against them. Interviewers explained the confidentiality of the survey and the fact that the personal survey responses would not be individually tabulated.

Six percent of attempted surveys were not completed. Most of those were never begun because the respondent was not at home even though we visited him or her up to six times, or we had the wrong address. Probably, about half were unwilling to participate or complete the survey. This is a remarkably low refusal rate. Ten percent of the interviews were done by proxy, with the respondent being helped by an intermediary (usually a family member) during the interview. The reasons for the proxy interviews were mental or physical disability or need for translation.

Hamilton Madison Houses and Project Liberty funded the study.

2. We have set the lower limit of "old" at age fifty-five because the number of retirees at that age was quite large in our population. However, it is not easy to define "old" according to objective biological criteria. Although we may say a person is "old" when the body starts to lose significant functions, this definition could apply to anyone acutely ill regardless of age. Further, eleven-year-old victims of progeria and twenty-year-old victims of Werner's syndrome die of biological old age. People may become psychologically "old" at age thirty following a major trauma, or they may remain psychologically "young" at age seventy. There are grandparents in their twenties and seventy-year-old fathers of infants.

Another common standard is to say we are old when we approach the biblical "three-score and ten," that is, seventy years. Mainly, this standard has meant that at this age every new day alive is unpredictable. So, under this standard, old age is when you are in the deathwatch period, regardless of your physical abilities. Because this is not a very cheery perspective, many people prefer to think about the fact that in the modern world our average life expectancies and time of physical well-being are increasing. This fudges up the time of the deathwatch.

Indeed, bodies break down and sooner or later give out. Because aging is so intimately and visibly tied to the body, many analysts make the assumption that aging is part of an inevitable life cycle. However, the model of a biological life cycle is seldom the way individuals age. Some die "prematurely," while others seem to be ageless in disposition and appearance until death suddenly strikes. Of course, it is undeniable that in the aggregate certain maladies and practices are more common among biologically older humans. (For an overview, see Olshansky and Wikins 1998; Freedman and Martin 1998; Crimmins, Saito, and Reynolds 1997; Reynolds, Crimmins, and Saito 1998; Allaire et al. 1999; Ferrucci et al. 1998; Simonsick, Guralnik, and Fried 1999; Anderson et al. 1998; Guralnik et al. 1999.) But there is a plurality of exceptions, and how people age varies widely.

There are at least three variables that shape how biology affects aging. First, there are the specific physical dysfunctions of the seniors' bodies. Typically, physical dysfunctions come in clusters, so that one impairment either causes or appears together with other impairments (Guralnik and Simonsick 1993; Fried et al. 1991). These impairments may be temporary, repairable, or presage further problems.

Second, physical dysfunctions may or may not lead to disability. Seniors have a resilient resourcefulness that propels them to hide, repair, or work around their physical dysfunctions (among the many studies of the relationship between physical dysfunction and disability, see Katz and Akpom 1976; Katz, Ford, and Moskowitz 1963).

Still, the patterns of relationship between physical dysfunction and disability can be quite strong (Benvenuti et al. 1995; Ensrud et al. 1994; Fried et al. 1994; Gill, Williams, and Tinetti 1995).

Third, the relation of physical dysfunction and disability is strongly affected by the senior's response and the sociocultural context.

The more active, catastrophe theory of aging, which this chapter uses, looks at the wide variability of aging and asks, How do people actively shape their lives after sixty-five? Do they practice strategies of "aging successfully" or strategies of self-destruction? (Rowe and Kahn 1998; Katz et al. 1983; Leveille et al. 1999; Courtenay et al. 1992; Mirowsky 1997; Van Doorn and Kasl 1998; Van Doorn 1998). Individuals and societies vary greatly in the way they define and utilize their "disabilities" (Lawrence and Jette 1996; Jette et al. 1998; Glass 1998; Fried and Guralnik 1997).

3. The greater religiosity of older Chinese and non-Chinese may be partly a generational characteristic rather than a function of age per se (Markides, Levin, and Ray 1987). Twenty-two percent of Chinatown seniors are widows (a majority) or widowers. Seventy-three percent of Chinatown seniors are married (cp., the virtually same figures as for U.S. seniors in He 2002, 8; Kinsella and Velkoff 2001). Cantonese American seniors are less likely to be married (68 percent) than Fujianese American seniors (80 percent).

4. Studies of the life satisfaction of Chinese elderly include Chinese Americans (Chan 1998) and Beijing residents (Zhang and Yu 1998).

5. Poorer Chinese American seniors are less satisfied with their lives. However, the effect of deeply and personally felt religion on life satisfaction is similar for all income levels. The importance of religion and attendance at religious services is roughly the same for all income levels.

The seniors report very low income levels. Twelve percent say they are living on less than $300 per month. However, most have some form of public or family assistance. The Fujianese Americans report the lowest incomes.

The 1990 U.S. Census showed that 21 percent of New York City's Asian American elderly live below the poverty level on employment (see the discussions on the Senior Community Service Employment Program by the National Asian Pacific

Center on Aging 2002). In 2001 the poverty rate among persons sixty-five and older rose from 9.9 percent to 10.1 percent, according to the U.S. Census. Also, the median annual income of householders sixty-five and older dropped 2.6 percent to $23,118. The poverty line is set at $10,700 a year for a couple older than sixty-five and $8,494 for a single older person.

6. Also cp. Kim 1983.

7. Liang (1974, 94) asserts that Chinese society is not socially based (*she-hui-ben-wei*) but relationship-based (*gwan-xi-ben-wei*). See the comprehensive study by Yang 1994.

8. All cultures value relationships, but the Chinese place much more emphasis on the relationships' existential importance for life and business (Chu and Ju 1990; Kipnis 1997). A relationship with a Chinese is a bond of dependency, exchange, and familiar feeling. The first thing the Chinese do when meeting one another is to establish whether they have any relationship through personal, regional, school, religious, or other networks.

For more on *gwanxi,* see Jankowiak 1993; Thaxton 1975; Folsom 1968; Nathan 1983; Ch'i 1976; Eastman 1974; Whitson and Huang 1973; Sullivan 1984; Perry 1976; Selden 1971; Lewis 1987; Rocca 1991.

9. Not surprisingly, few (17 percent) of the nonreligious would say this.

10. "Seculars" are those who say that religion is not important to them.

11. The values offered to the seniors on the questionnaire were taken from other value surveys, an analysis of the literature on which values are important to Chinese American seniors and a modeling of the social and cultural resources which Chinese American seniors use to make significant decisions. The modeling was based on several years of testing of survey questions with Chinese American seniors attending six churches and an intensive qualitative study of the Zhung family.

12. Chinese culture includes a tendency toward emotional and social dependency or interdependency. There are two interpretations. One group of scholars identifies a sense of dependency as a primary cultural value. They point to Confucian ethics of hierarchy. Cf. Eisenstadt 1980; Pye 1992/1968; Solomon 1966; Muensterberger 1951, 37–69. Metzger (1983) leads another group of scholars who say that this Chinese cultural value is one of interdependency. De Bary 1983, 10, 27, 161 rejects both views in favor of a strong defense of the Chinese sense of self-autonomy promoted by neo-Confucianism. This means that the Chinese feel emotionally most at rest and socially satisfied when they have entered into dependent or interdependent relations with others. As Confucius said, "I seek to integrate rather than to be a man of much learning. When friends come from afar, isn't that delightful?"

13. For a broadranging discussion, see Sokolovsky 1997.

14. In fact, CAREN, a Chinese American retirement home co-op in the D.C. area, has found that Chinese American seniors, who could afford such a facility,

were discouraged by their children or children's spouse (to whom the seniors had transferred their life savings) from moving to a retirement home in order to "save money" (cf. CAREN 2000, 2; also cp. Lee, Woo, and Mackenzie 2002; Steinberg, Ansak, and Chin-Hansen 1993).

15. Only 20 percent of those who regularly do home rituals are completely satisfied with their lives, compared with 35 percent of those who don't do home rituals. This difference doesn't seem to be effected by our SES variables.

Part III

Political Boundaries

10

Religious Diversity and Social Integration among Asian Americans in Houston

Stephen L. Klineberg

There is a new way of doing religion in Houston.[1]

The demographic revolution has transformed this Anglo-dominated biracial city into one of the most ethnically and culturally diverse metropolitan areas in the country. This diversity is vividly displayed in the Asian American houses of worship from the Houston Chinese Protestant megachurch to a little bit of Saigon at St. Mary's Catholic Church. Drawing on the most comprehensive survey ever undertaken in all four of Houston's major ethnic communities, this chapter explores the distinctiveness of the Asian experience in urban America. It documents the striking religious, socioeconomic, and political differences among Asian Americans. Religious institutions have a seemingly paradoxical role in facilitating the integration of Asian immigrants into their coethnic communities while also integrating them into the wider Houston and American society.

The Houston Context

During most of the twentieth century, and particularly in the years after World War II, Houston was America's quintessential "boomtown." Hand in hand, up went the petroleum skyscrapers along with the traditional mainline church colonial edifices, the kettledrum Baptist churches, the modernistic synagogues, and old world-styled Catholic churches. While the rest of the country was languishing in the long national recession known as the "stagflating seventies," this city's prime industrial products were becoming several times more valuable with no lessening of world demand. The price of a barrel of Texas oil rose from $3.39 in 1971 to $31.77 in 1981. Local bank deposits tripled in value, and Houston led the nation in housing starts and the growth of manufacturing (Feagin 1998). The traditional American religious organizations had overflowing coffers and blueprints for new buildings tacked up in the sanctuaries. Oil and religion business was good. Between 1970 and 1982, almost one million people moved into the greater metropolitan area. They were coming at the rate of some thirteen hundred per week. Few suspected that the end would arrive so abruptly and definitely. The era of "Boomtown Houston" suddenly ended.

Global recession was reducing the demand for oil just as new supplies were coming onto world markets, and in May 1982 the oil boom collapsed. Buildings emptied out and religious leaders pulled in their belts to keep their doors open for the stricken. The price of Texas crude fell to less than $28 per barrel at the end of 1983, but Houston had been borrowing in the expectation of $50 oil. By late 1986, with the price of oil falling to less than $12 per barrel, the recession had spread from the energy sector to the entire economy (Smith 1989). One out of every seven jobs that were in Houston in 1982 had disappeared by early 1987, making this the worst regional recession in any part of the country at any time since World War II. The city recovered by the early 1990s, only to find itself in the midst of a restructured economy and a demographic revolution.

Houston's Ethnic Transformations

After economic collapse in 1982, the number of Anglos in the county declined. In 1980 the population of Harris County (Houston) was still almost two-thirds Anglo. Only 2 percent were Asian. Yet, as Harris County's total population expanded, the Asian numbers grew much faster, by 76 percent in the 1990s. By the year 2000, Houston had joined New York, Los Angeles, and Chicago to become one of the nation's premier "multiethnic melting pots" (Frey, Abresch, and Yeasting 2001). All four of America's largest cities now have majority minority populations. The 2000 census counted 3.4 million people in Harris County, of whom just 42 percent were European Americans. The county's population now included 7 percent Asian or other: 174,626 residents of Harris County checked an Asian nationality on the "race" question, and an additional 18,433 checked

"Asian" in combination with one or more other races, for a total of 193,059 Asian-origin Harris County residents. A 1990 cover story in *Time Magazine* (Henry 1990) portrayed Houston as the new America; it is even more true now. "At the Sesame Hut restaurant in Houston," the author wrote, "a Korean immigrant owner trains Hispanic immigrant workers to prepare Chinese-style food for a largely black clientele."

The New Asian Immigration

Counting those who checked only "Asian" on the race question, the census found that the Vietnamese and the Asian Indians recorded the most rapid growth, at 79 percent and 70 percent, respectively, followed by the Filipinos (at 48 percent), the Chinese (39 percent), and the Koreans (33 percent). In 1980 the Chinese were the largest Asian community in Harris County. By 1990 they trailed the Vietnamese, and by 2000 they had slipped into third place, now numbering just slightly less than the region's Indian population.

The Houston Area Surveys

The data reviewed in this chapter are drawn from the 1995 and 2002 expanded versions of the annual Houston Area Survey, a telephone survey of public opinion conducted each spring since 1982.[2] By May 23, 2002, five hundred randomly selected Asians living in these households had completed the interviews (for a response rate of 67.5 percent). One-fourth (24.8 percent) of the interviews were conducted in Vietnamese, Mandarin, Cantonese, or Korean.

The Importance of Religion

Religion is very important to a majority of Asians in Houston, and a majority regularly attend religious services. Both immigrants and American-born Asians place roughly equal emphasis on the importance of religion.

Combining the Asians in the 1995 and 2002 surveys, we find that 57 percent of Asians say that religion is very important. However, immigrant

Asians are much more likely to say that they don't have a religion. Twenty-three percent of immigrant Asians say that they don't have a religion compared to 10 percent of American-born Asians.

The lower proportion of immigrant Asians identifying with a religion seems to be consistent with other indicators that they are less integrated into the wider Houston community than the American-born Asians. Fewer foreign-born Asians report close Anglo or African American friends and were more worried about being victims of crime.

The Young Asian American Religionists

The Asian American religionists are much younger as a whole than the Anglos or African Americans. As a consequence, Houston religious organizations are as likely to be divided along generational lines as they are along ethnic ones. Forty-two percent of all the Anglo respondents in the Houston surveys were fifty or older, compared to 24 percent of Asians. At the other end of the spectrum, 30 percent of the Asians were under the age of thirty, compared to just 13 percent of the Anglos.

Immigration is generally undertaken by younger adults, who are more often prepared to brave the difficult journey in pursuit of better opportunities for themselves and their children. The median date of arrival for Asian immigrants was 1988, at the median age of twenty-four. Of all the Asian immigrants living in the Houston area in 2002, 40 percent moved to the region since 1992.

Fully 86 percent of all the Asian adults are first-generation immigrants, and 69 percent grew up outside the United States. Almost half (48 percent) of the Asians immigrated to Houston directly from abroad, without having lived anywhere else in America. Moreover, 96 percent of all Asians report that *both* their parents were foreign-born.

This means that in contrast to Asian American religious organizations in the country as a whole, Houston's are overwhelmingly made up of first-generation immigrants. The first- and second-generation issues have hardly started here.

Types of Religion

A plurality (41 percent) of Houston Asian Americans are Christian. Over half of the Christians are Catholics because of the numbers of Vietnamese and Filipinos in the county. Forty-six percent are Protestant.

One in five (21 percent) of Asian American Houstonians are Buddhists. Almost as many Asian Americans (18 percent) say that they have no religion.

The South Asian American community is evenly divided between Muslims and Hindus, each making up 9 percent of the Asian Americans.

TABLE 10.1

Demographic Correlates of Church Attendance among Asians in Houston (2002 Survey)

		Attended Religious Services in Past 30 Days?		
		Yes (N = 267)	No (N = 227)	Chi Square
1. What is your religious preference, if any?	Protestant	23.4%	6.7%	
	Catholic	33.3	6.7	
	Hindu	9.6	9.3	
	Muslim	10.0	9.3	
	Buddhist	13.8	31.1	
	Other, no religion	10.0	36.9	118.240***
2. Were you born in the United States?	Yes	16.5%	10.6%	
	No	83.5	89.4	3.606+
3. Highest grade of school or year of college completed?	High school or less	19.5%	23.8%	
	Some college	19.5	20.3	
	College degree	61.0	56.0	5.897
4. [If Working:] What is your specific occupation?	Prof., Managerial	50.6%	42.2%	
	Tech., Sales, Serv.	40.2	40.8	
	Prod., Laborers	9.2	17.0	5.016+
5. [If Working:] Income you personally earned in the year 2001:	Less than $25,000	26.7%	32.6%	
	$25,000 to $50,000	29.7	38.6	
	More than $50,000	43.6	28.8	7.076*
6 Total household income during the past year:	Less than $25,000	14.8%	23.1%	
	$25,000 to $50,000	27.8	30.1	
	More than $50,000	57.4	46.8	6.034*
7. Language of the interview:	English	80.5%	70.0%	
	Other language	19.5	30.0	7.328**
8. Would you call yourself a Republican, Democrat, Independent, or something else?	Republican	24.3%	17.6%	
	Democrat	21.7	13.2	
	Independent, Other	35.2	44.9	
	Don't know	18.7	24.2	12.268**
9. Do you think of yourself as conservative, moderate, or liberal in your politics?	Conservative	33.0%	23.8%	
	Moderate	33.3	32.2	
	Liberal	20.6	23.3	
	Don't know	13.1	20.7	8.330*

+ $p < .10$, * $p < .05$, ** $p < .01$, *** $p < .001$ (two-sided tests).

Church Attendance

The Christians were disproportionately likely to say that they had attended a religious service, other than a wedding or funeral, in the past thirty days.

Buddhists, in contrast, along with those who indicated no religious affiliation, were disproportionately unlikely to have gone to a religious experience in the previous month.

There was a slight tendency for U.S.-born Asians to be more likely than first-generation immigrants to have recently attended a religious service. Among the Asian immigrants, however, the surveys reveal no relationship at all between church attendance and the length of time these newcomers had been in this country.

There is a weak but consistent relationship among Asians in Houston between church attendance and higher incomes, more prestigious occupations, and greater fluency in English, although there is only a nonsignificant association with educational attainment.

Church attendance may be particularly helpful in facilitating the integration of middle-class immigrants into the wider Houston and American society. Churchgoers were significantly more likely than nonattendees to affiliate with *both* the Republican and Democratic parties, whereas nonchurchgoers were more likely to choose "Independent," "Other," or "Don't know" when asked to give a political affiliation. Similarly, 21 percent of the nonchurchgoers could not identify their political ideology, compared to only 13 percent of those who had recently attended religious services. The latter (by 33 percent, compared to 24 percent of the nonchurchgoers) were also more likely to think of themselves as "conservative" in their politics.

Asian Religious Diversity

The Vietnamese are equally divided between Catholics (40 percent; who are more likely to have come in the 1970s) and Buddhists (44 percent; who generally arrived more recently).

When asked what it was that brought them or their parents to this country, almost three-fourths (72 percent) of the Vietnamese respondents said they immigrated because of political persecution, as a result of war, or in search of freedom.

Those in the "first wave" of Vietnamese refugees were far more likely than later arrivals to be members of the economic elite in war-torn Vietnam. Further, their social and economic integration into American society was facilitated not only by material advantages, but also by their affiliation with mainstream American religions. More than half (54.5 percent) of the Vietnamese who came to America in the 1970s were Catholics or Protestants; just 38 percent were Buddhists. Among the more recent arrivals, in contrast, 59 percent are Buddhists and only 29 percent are Catholics or Protestants.

Unlike most of the other Asians who came as immigrant professionals under the occupational provisions of the Immigration Reform Act (AKA the Hart-Celler Act) of 1965, the Vietnamese and other Southeast Asians immigrated primarily as victims of persecution after the fall of Saigon in 1975. Along with the Cambodians and Laotians, they were part of the largest refugee resettlement program in American history.

Like most refugee communities in the United States, the Vietnamese came in several waves. Many of the early arrivals were highly educated professionals, politicians, or military officers who had served in the former American-backed government in Vietnam. Many more came in the 1980s and 1990s with little formal education and few resources, having survived horrible conditions in refugee camps and terrifying voyages across the seas. Often they speak little English: 47 percent of the Vietnamese respondents completed the interviews in their native language.

The Chinese are the least likely of the Asian communities to express strong religious commitments. When asked about their religious preference, 39 percent of the Asians from Mainland China, Taiwan, and Hong Kong declared that they had no religious affiliation. At twice the rate for Asians in general, 36 percent of the Chinese said that religion was "not very important" in their lives, and 65 percent (compared to 47 percent of all Asians) had not attended a religious service during the month preceding the interviews. Only 13 percent of the Chinese gave politics as a reason for immigrating.

The Indians and Pakistanis are evenly divided between Hindus (38 percent) and Muslims (37 percent); only 10 percent are Christians.

The Filipinos are the most likely of the major Asian communities to be strongly religious. Almost 90 percent asserted that religion was very important in their lives. And 81 percent said that they had attended a religious service, other than a wedding or funeral, in the past thirty days. Almost three-fourths (74 percent) of them are Catholic. The Filipino

Catholics are also disproportionately female. They emigrated with far more education under the occupational provisions of the 1965 Hart-Celler Act—conspicuously, the surveys suggest, for jobs as health technicians and nurses at Houston's Texas Medical Center (the world's largest medical complex) and at other area hospitals. Seventy-eight percent have a college degree.

Patterns of Asian Assimilation

The Asian immigrants had achieved remarkably high levels of education before their arrival in this country (59 percent have college degrees). Further, the Asian immigrants are generally fluent in English even before they set foot on this continent. The success that so many Asian immigrants have achieved in America has given rise to the "model minority" stereotype. However, Asian success is attributable primarily to the educational and occupational backgrounds these immigrants experienced *before* they came to America (Snyder 2002). When asked what occupation their fathers had when they themselves were sixteen years old, 42 percent of the Asians in the Houston surveys said their fathers were doctors, lawyers, professors, engineers, corporate executives, or other professionals.

Half of the Asian immigrants (51 percent) already thought of themselves as "equally Asian and American," another 16 percent said they were "primarily American," and only a third saw themselves as "primarily Asian." Moreover, 62 percent of the Asian immigrants were already American citizens, compared to just 25 percent of foreign-born Hispanics.

By 51 percent to 27 percent, the Asians as a whole were far more likely than the Latinos to report having participated at least occasionally in meetings of their ethnic group, or by 79 percent to 50 percent in an ethnic holiday or cultural event. They were also somewhat more likely than the Hispanic respondents to report having made a special effort to teach younger members of their community about their ethnic background (by 60 percent to 50 percent) and to have contacted friends or relatives in their country of origin (84 percent versus 79 percent).

The stereotype of the "model minority" overlooks the class advantages enjoyed by the high proportion of Asian immigrants who come from upper-middle-class families in their countries of origin, and diverts attention from continuing discrimination. It also lumps together into a single image individuals from twenty-seven different nationalities, who speak different languages, follow different religious and cultural traditions, and may be recent immigrants or fourth-generation Americans. Above all, the "model minority" myth glosses over the fact that large segments of the Asian population in Houston and America are far from prosperous, and makes it less likely that impoverished Asians will be given the help that others receive.

The Asian Diversity

The various Asian nationalities have come to America under contrasting circumstances, for divergent reasons, and with vastly different levels of resources.

Filipinos (by 64 percent) said they came primarily for work opportunities; they were also (at 26 percent) more likely than the other groups to cite marriage or family reasons for immigrating.

TABLE 10.2
Differences on Indicators of Social Integration between U.S.-Born and Immigrant Asians (1995 and 2002 Surveys, Combined)

		Asians		
		Born in the U.S. (119)	Immigrants (878)	All Asians (997)
1. Participated in meetings of your ethnic group?	Often	17.4%	14.4%	14.7%
	Occasionally	30.4	37.5	36.7
	Never	52.2	48.1	48.6
2. Participated in ethnic holiday, cultural event?	Often	36.5%	32.0%	32.5%
	Occasionally	36.5	47.6	46.3
	Never	27.0	20.4	21.2
3. Made special efforts to teach background?	Often	24.1%	29.5%	28.9%
	Occasionally	26.8	31.1	30.6
	Never	49.1	39.4	40.6
4. Contacted friends, relatives in your country of origin?	Often	35.5%	49.8%	48.1%
	Occasionally	30.9	36.7	36.1
	Never	33.6	13.5	15.8
5. How worried about being a victim of crime?	Very worried	28.0%	56.7%	53.8%
	Somewhat	46.0	31.1	32.6
	Not very	26.0	12.2	13.6
6. In past 30 days, went to church?	Yes	64.7%	52.3%	54.0%
	No	35.3	47.7	46.0
7. What is your religious preference, if any?	Protestant	35.5%	18.8%	20.8%
	Catholic	23.4	24.8	24.6
	Other religion	30.8	33.8	33.4
	No religion	10.3	22.6	21.1

Both the Chinese and the Asian Indians cited education and employment in roughly equal proportions, but the Chinese (by 43 percent to 32 percent) were more likely to mention education, and the Indians (by 48 percent to 36 percent) more often cited work opportunities.

The Religion–Social Integration Paradox

Religion simultaneously produces greater integration in the immigrants' own ethnicity and in the greater society.

The data consistently point to a seemingly paradoxical effect of church attendance. Religious organizations facilitate integration *both* into the co-ethnic community and into the wider Houston and American society at the same time. When respondents were asked about their sense of national identity, the Asian churchgoers were significantly more likely than nonchurch attendees (by 59 percent to 44 percent) to think of themselves as "equally Asian and American," whereas the nonchurchgoers were more apt to see themselves either as "primarily Asian" (by 32 percent to 23 percent) or as "primarily American" (24 percent versus 18 percent).

These seemingly contradictory effects are confirmed in the other differences. Asian churchgoers were more likely to report that they had close personal friends who were African American or Anglo. At the same time, they were more involved in activities that contribute to the "reproduction of ethnicity" (Ebaugh and Chafetz 2000a). Compared to the nonchurchgoers, they were more likely to have participated in the past year in the meetings of an organization of people from their ethnic community and to have made special efforts to teach younger members of the community about their ethnic background. When more sophisticated statistical analyses are used to isolate the effects of churchgoing while controlling for differences in country of origin, religious preference, English fluency, and socioeconomic status, the pattern of relationships with church attendance remains significant and consistent.

The key to this dual impact of religious institutions may well be the decisive importance of church attendance in encouraging and facilitating participation in volunteer activities, since these are contexts that often bring people from varied communities together. More than 70 percent of those who attended church said they had personally contributed some of their time in the past year to a volunteer activity. This was true of just 43 percent of the nonchurchgoers.

Finally, our results confirm that social conservatism is associated with religious outlook. The Asian churchgoers were not only more likely to think of themselves as generally conservative in their politics, but they were also more opposed to homosexuals being legally permitted to adopt children, or to having birth control counseling and supplies available to teenagers in the public schools. By 53 percent to just 34 percent among the nonchurchgoers, they were far more likely to disagree with the suggestion that "It should be legal for a woman to obtain an abortion if she wants to have one for any reason."

TABLE 10.3
*Social and Attitudinal Correlates of Church Attendance
among Asians in Houston (2002 Survey)*

		Attended Religious Services in Past 30 Days?		
		Yes (N = 267)	No (N = 227)	Chi Square
1. Do you think of yourself as *primarily*:	Asian	22.9%	31.9%	
	Both equally	58.9	44.4	
	American	18.2	23.6	9.818**
2. Have a close personal friend who is Anglo?	Yes	73.8%	64.4%	
	No	26.2	35.6	5.024*
3. Have a close personal friend who is black?	Yes	58.4%	40.5%	
	No	41.6	59.5	15.722***
4. Have a close personal friend who is Hispanic?	Yes	56.2%	49.8%	
	No	43.8	50.2	2.019
5. Participated in meetings of an organization from your ethnic community?	Often	21.0%	11.4%	
	Occasionally	35.8	36.4	
	Never	43.2	52.3	8.736*
6. Made special effort to teach young people about their ethnic background?	Often	21.9%	17.2%	
	Occasionally	35.5	26.7	
	Never	42.6	56.1	8.718*
7. Participated in a holiday or cultural event in your ethnic community?	Often	37.7%	27.6%	
	Occasionally	42.4	50.2	
	Never	19.8	22.2	5.581+
8. Contributed your time to a volunteer activity?	Yes	70.3%	43.2%	
	No	29.7	56.8	36.958***
9. Gays being legally permitted to adopt children?	For it	35.2%	46.9%	
	Against it	64.8	53.1	6.024*
10. Abortion should be legal for any reason.	Agree	47.0%	65.9%	
	Disagree	53.0	34.1	16.680***

$+ p < .10$, $* p < .05$, $** p < .01$, $*** p < .001$ (two-sided tests).

Asian American Politics: Political Party Preferences

Houston's Asian communities also diverge in their political orientations, which means that their religious commitments are often intertwined with differing political commitments.

Respondents were asked if they would call themselves "a Republican, a Democrat, an Independent, or something else." Those who did not give an affiliation were asked if they thought of themselves as closer to the Republican or Democratic Party.

The Filipinos were more likely than other Asians to name the Republican Party. This means that Filipino politics will likely carry a Catholic prolife, profamily flavor. The Vietnamese, too, favor the Republicans by a two-to-one margin. The flavor of their politics will likely also be prolife and profamily for at least the Catholics and religious anti-Communists for both Catholics and Buddhists. The Chinese were more likely to choose "Independent" or "Other" when respondents were asked about their party preference. The Chinese were also more inclined, by margins of almost two to one, to favor the Republicans over the Democrats.

The Indians and Pakistanis, by equal margins, were more likely to be Democrats. This reinforces a national trend for Hindu and Muslim Asian Americans to be Democratic and liberal in ideology.

Despite their overall preference for the Republican Party, Asians as a whole are significantly *less* likely (at 28 percent) than Anglos (46 percent), African Americans (40 percent), or Latinos (38 percent) to think of themselves as "conservative" in their politics. The most likely explanation for the general Asian tendency to support the Republican Party lies in foreign policy considerations.

The immigrants from China and Vietnam were more likely than other Asians to cite religious and political persecution from Communist regimes as their reason for coming to America. Like the Cubans in Miami, they may be especially attracted to the Republican promise of a firmer anti-Communist foreign policy. If this is the case, one might expect some lessening of that Republican preference in recent years, as anticommunism has gradually faded in its political importance (Fong 2002).

Summary and Conclusions

The survey findings reviewed in these pages offer a compelling picture of a major American metropolis in the midst of fundamental redefinition. This Anglo-dominated biracial boom city emerged from the economic collapse of the mid-1980s with a demographic revolution and a whole new set of religious institutions.

As a major immigrant destination since the 1980s, Houston has become one of the nation's most ethnically and culturally diverse metropolitan areas. In the census of 2000, only 42 percent of the 3.4 million people living in Harris County were Anglo. The Houston area population was now 33 percent Hispanic, 18 percent African American, and 7 percent Asian.

The two Houston Area Asian Surveys, conducted in 1995 and in 2002, reached large representative samples of respondents from Houston's rapidly growing Asian communities. The data make it clear that the various Asian nationalities differ importantly in their religions, circumstances of their coming to America, and their socioeconomic backgrounds.

The Filipinos, overwhelmingly Catholic, are the most likely to be church attendees and to say that religion is very important in their lives. The Asian Indians are generally either Hindus or Muslims, the Vietnamese either Catholics or Buddhists. The immigrants from Mainland China, Taiwan, and Hong Kong are far less likely than other Asians to be members of *any* religious community, and they are the least likely to have recently attended a religious service.

The Asians in the 2002 survey who said they had attended a religious service during the previous month were of slightly higher socioeconomic status and more likely to be fluent in English. The attitudinal and behavioral correlates of church attendance suggest that religious organizations are playing a dual role in the lives of these immigrant populations. Church attendance seems to facilitate integration not only into the wider Houston and American society, but into the coethnic community as well.

The Asian churchgoers were more likely than nonchurchgoers to think of themselves as "equally Asian and American." They were more prepared to identify their political affiliation (as Democrat or Republican) and their ideology (as liberal, moderate, or—more often—conservative). They were more likely than nonchurchgoers to have African American and Anglo friends. At the same time, they reported more frequent participation in meetings of organizations from their ethnic community and in efforts to teach younger community members about their ethnic background.

The church appears to have its most decisive impact in facilitating involvement in volunteer activities. Fully 70 percent of Asian churchgoers said they had contributed some of their time to a volunteer activity during the preceding twelve months, but 57 percent of the nonchurchgoers indicated they had not volunteered. It may well be as a result of experiences such as these that church attendance not only encourages the integration of Asian immigrants into their coethnic communities, but also facilitates their assimilation into the wider Houston and American society.

Houston's various Asian communities differ importantly in their political affiliations, and this will coincide with their distinct religious differences as well. In the 1995 survey, the Filipinos, Vietnamese, and Chinese were far more likely to express a preference for Republicans rather than Democrats, whereas the Indians and Pakistanis were more likely to be Democrats. In recent years, anticommunism has faded as a political issue, while concerns about restrictive immigration policies and about anti-Asian discrimination have increased. By 2002, the Asian respondents in the Houston surveys were significantly less likely than they were in 1995 to prefer the Republican Party.

The Asian newcomers appear to be following the path of previous generations of immigrants, toward the rapid adoption of the political perspectives and cultural values of the American nation as a whole (Lind 1995). Today, as in the past, America's religious institutions are demonstrably contributing to that acculturation process.

NOTES

1. This research was supported by a consortium of contributing sponsors, including the United Way of the Texas Gulf Coast, the SBC Foundation, Gallery Furniture, the Greater Houston Community Foundation, the *Houston Chronicle,* the Houston Endowment Inc., Southwest Bank of Texas, and the JPMorgan-Chase Texas Foundation. Thanks are also due to Professor Lamia Karim, now at the University of Notre Dame, for her assistance in an earlier phase of this project. The data analyzed in this chapter and all other materials necessary for replication are available from the author.

2. Respondents from Houston's metropolitan area (Harris County) are selected each year through a two-stage random-digit-dialing procedure. In every

household reached by computer-generated telephone numbers, the respondent is selected randomly from all residents in the household aged eighteen or older. The interviews for the basic surveys are conducted during February and March in each year by Telesurveys Research Associates, the Houston research firm. In nine of the ten years from 1992–2002, the surveys have been supplemented with "oversample" interviews to enlarge and equalize the number of Anglo, African American, and Hispanic respondents. In 1995 and again in 2002, the oversamples included systematic surveys of Houston's Asian communities.

As the numbers were dialed, the ones that were disconnected or not in service, that reached business or government offices, or that turned out to be faxes, modems, beepers, children's phones, and the like were removed from the list. The interviewers eventually dialed a total of 65,000 numbers, from which there remained 40,083 that were potentially connected to Harris County households. By the end of three months of data collection, more than 24,000 interviews had been conducted with a randomly selected respondent in each household reached with these numbers. In February 2002 the interviewers began with groups of randomly generated numbers serving Harris County telephones.

The 650 interviews for the basic 2002 survey, reaching a representative sample of all Harris County residents, were completed between February 21 and March 8. The sample consisted of 335 Anglos (52 percent), 151 Latinos (23 percent), 118 African Americans (18 percent), 23 Asians (3.5 percent), 18 "others" (2.6 percent), and 5 individuals who did not report their ethnicity. To conduct the oversamples for specific groups including Asians, the interviewing process continued until at least five hundred surveys were completed with randomly selected individuals from each of the four ethnic communities.

These additional surveys used identical selection procedures and the same opening questions to screen for eligible respondents. The interviews were terminated after the first few questions if the respondent was not of the "correct" ethnicity. Out of the initial 24,267 screening interviews, the research staff identified 741 households (3.1 percent of the total) in which there was at least one Asian adult.

The interviews, averaging twenty-four minutes apiece, encompassed a wide array of attitudes and beliefs, and probed deeply into backgrounds and life experiences. This chapter presents only a small sampling of the research findings. Further analyses of the data as they become available will be posted on the survey web site (www.houstonareasurvey.org), and other aspects of this research will be presented in subsequent reports. The distributions by countries of origin in the census parallel the distributions among the respondents in the Asian surveys. Thus, 30 percent of the survey respondents were Vietnamese (as were 32 percent in the 2000 census), 23 percent were Indians (compared to 21 percent in the census), 26 percent were Chinese (versus 20 percent), and 8 percent (9 percent in the census) were Filipinos.

This close correspondence with the census figures, in combination with the high response rates obtained in both the Asian surveys (67.5 percent in 2002, 82.1 percent in 1995), strengthens confidence in the reliability of the data. The careful procedures that were undertaken here should provide about as accurate a picture as it is possible to obtain through scientific survey research of the experiences, attitudes, and beliefs of Houston's varied Asian communities.

Generating Representative Samples from Houston's Four Major Ethnic Communities (Field Period: 21 February through 23 May 2002)

A. Total Random Phone Numbers Assigned	65,000
1. *Less:* Nonexistent or disconnected numbers	12,699
Business or government telephones	8,621
Children's phones, faxes, modems, etc.	3,597
Total unusable numbers	24,917
2. *Net sample* (phone numbers that are presumably reaching Houston area households)	40,083
3. *Less:* Refusals, break-offs	6,388
Other (e.g., no answer after repeated tries)	9,428
B. Screening Interviews	24,267 (60.5%)
1. Anglo interviews completed (by 11 March 2002)	504
2. Hispanic interviews completed (by 26 March 2002)	50
3. African American interviews completed (by 8 April 2002)	500
4. Other non-Asian interviews for HAS2002 (completed, 8 March 2002)	33
5. *Less:* Other non-Asian households	19,016
Call-backs (inability to reach the designated respondent)	2,495
Other (e.g., no answer after repeated tries)	474
Total unusable screens	21,985
C. Asian Households Identified	741 (3.1%)
1. *Less:* Refusals, break-offs	164
Others (e.g., inability to reach the designated respondent; no answer after repeated tries; etc.)	77
2. Asian interviews completed (by 23 May 2002)	500 (67.5%)

11

Religion and Political Adaptation among Asian Americans

An Empirical Assessment from the Pilot National Asian American Political Survey

Pei-te Lien

According to the most comprehensive survey of the religions and politics of Asian Americans, most Asian Americans are religious and their religiosity often makes a difference in the way they define their ethnic identity and participate in American politics. Yet scholars of Asian American studies have been slow to systematically study the religious factor in Asian American politics.[1]

A cursory review of the Asian American studies literature suggests that the study of religion in the political adaptation of Asian Americans is a doubly marginalized research frontier. Generally, scholars of Asian American religions have not adopted the quantitative approach, and quantitative studies on the religious factor in political behavior have not included Asian Americans. This chapter uses the 2000–1 Pilot National Asian American Political Survey (PNAAPS), to help bridge the gaps in both fields by providing an empirical map of the religious world of Asian Americans at the dawn of the twenty-first century and by exploring the political implications of religious preference and of attending religious services.

Does religious preference influence ethnic identity and adaptation to the U.S. political system? Does more frequent attendance of religious services lead to higher levels of incorporation in citizenship and participation in voting and activities beyond voting? Does religion play a role in Asian American political preferences?

Religion and Immigrant Political Adaptation:
A Brief Literature Review

Theories of assimilation and secularization have traditionally predicted that religion would decline in importance over time as immigrants gained acceptance and access to American mainstream society and culture (for a review, see Warner 1993). However, recent studies focusing on immigrant communities have found that religion remains central in shaping immigrants' sense of identity and community (Warner and Wittner 1998; Ebaugh and Chafetz 2000a). Because migration itself is "often a theologizing experience" (Smith 1978, 1175), some scholars maintain that the religious association may become even more salient for individuals regardless of their prior affiliation with a religious institution in their home countries (Greeley 1971; Smith 1978; Williams 1988; Yang and Ebaugh 2001a).

A major reason why religious institutions are central in the settlement and incorporation processes of immigrants is that social services are provided primarily through informal social networks of coethnics within the ethnic church (Ebaugh and Chafetz 2000a). For example, Ai Ra Kim (1996, 67–68) lists four significant sociological functions of the Korean American church:

  it provides fellowship for immigrants and serves as a social center for meeting people and making friends in the new land;

  it provides social services and information regarding host society functions such as on health care, employment, business operation, housing, and children's education;

  it confers social status and positions of leadership upon adult members, especially for men, who may find themselves otherwise marginalized in the new land; and

  it strengthens the Korean identity of members by maintaining Korean cultural traditions in the church.

Similarly multifaceted functions of ethnic religious institutions are reported in various studies of Asian immigrant communities and in Christian and non-Christian congregations (e.g., Hurh and Kim 1984b; Rutledge 1985; Williams 1988, 1996; Min 1992; Numrich 1996; McLellan 1999; Yang 1999a, 1999b; Yoo 1999; Kwon, Kim, and Warner 2001). Furthermore, because many immigrants are part of a multiethnic and/or multilingual social network, some congregations are beginning to stress a panreligious identity and a set of practices to broaden their appeal, especially to the young generation (Ebaugh and Chafetz 2000a).

Scholars on Asian American religions generally agree that religion can play a crucial mediating role in simultaneously reaffirming and creating ethnic identity. Their findings lend support to the adhesive identity theory proposed by Hurh and Kim (1984b) and question whether assimilation to Christianity is necessary to gain power and privilege (Yoo 1996). Yang (1999a), for example, found that Chinese American Christians of all generations may attain or retain multiple identities, and selectively assimilate or reject certain elements of mainstream- or ethnic-based cultural systems. There is thus evidence against the straight-line assimilation and unidimensional model of immigrant adaptation. Rather, a pluralistic reading would see religion in immigrant-majority communities as a bridging institution to the ethnic homeland, the U.S. mainstream society, and the creation of a new panethnic identity in America. The diversity of religion in Asian America also calls for attention to the way religion may help to distinguish between various ethnic identity preferences based on denominational differences within the immigrant community.

Religious association may also help to shape political orientations, incorporation, and participation. So far, most of the empirical evidence between religion and politics is based on observing non-Asians; the specific implications for Asian Americans are therefore far from clear.

In the realm of American political discourse, religion has been seen, paradoxically, as both declining and resurging, as a means of both suppressing and sparking political action and legitimizing and shaking up the status quo (Billings and Scott 1994). Still, a review of white votes in presidential elections between the mid-1960s and mid-1990s suggests that religion-based voting and partisan cleavages remain substantial, ranking second only to race cleavages. The religiously based cleavages have remained relatively stable for Catholics and conservative Protestants (Manza and Brooks 1997).

One main interest of this study is to see whether or not the political behavior of Asian Americans can be understood by using the theories and models developed from studying whites, blacks, and Latinos. However, the richness of the PNAAPS dataset also permits an exploration into the empirical relationship between religion and other dimensions of political adaptation not addressed in the literature. Studies that incorporate the views of nonwhites and non-Christians generally affirm the mobilizing role of religion for providing the resources, leadership, social interaction, and communication networks necessary for individual and collective political action (McAdam 1982; Morris 1984; Wald, Owen, and Hill 1988; Wilcox 1990; Harris 1994). For racially subordinated groups, religious institutions may be especially potent in giving them faith in the justice of their cause and the inevitability of its triumph (Warner 1993, 1069). The dual function of religion in political mobilization is illustrated by two recent studies in Los Angeles and New York which found that Catholic and other Christian institutions are instrumental in incorporating immigrants into American politics either by organizing demonstrations in defense of immigrant and workers' rights or by urging congregation members to apply for citizenship, register to vote, and cast their ballots in a certain way (Miller, Miller, and Dyrness 2001; Wong 2002).

However, the evidence for the role of religion in encouraging political participation is muddied by research using church attendance to measure religiosity. This research has produced contradictory conclusions on the relation of religion and political participation. Generally, the studies report a positive, direct effect of church attendance on voting turnout (Milbrath and Goel 1977; Macaluso and Wanat 1979; Hougland and Christenson 1983; Martinson and Wilkening 1987; Strate et al. 1989; Peterson 1992; Harris 1994; Verba, Schlozman, and Brady 1995; Alex-Assensoh and Assensoh 2001; Jones-Correa and Leal 2001). Some argue that church attendance promotes voting because it gives citizens a sense of civic obligation. Others argue that involvement in church organizations may give citizens the opportunity to cultivate civic skills. A recent study found that the associational membership function of the churches serves as a conduit for political information and recruitment, which were more important than any civic skills gained at the churches in mobilizing Latino turnout (ibid.).

However, several studies have found that church attendance is unrelated to more demanding forms of political participation such as campaigning and contacting public officials (Hougland and Christenson 1983; Martinson and Wilkening 1987; Harris 1994; Verba, Schlozman, and Brady 1995; Calhoun-Brown 1996; Jones-Correa and Leal 2001; McKenzie 2001).

Charting the Religious Dimension: Report from the PNAAPS

The Pilot National Asian American Political Survey (PNAAPS) is the first publicly available national survey focused on the political opinion of

Asian American adults. The Asian American political action committee has done some exit polling during elections, but their results have not yet been made public. Some exit polling and surveys have also been large enough to generate Asian American samples, but necessarily the surveys didn't ask the type of questions that would be deeply relevant for understanding Asian Americans. Nor were most of the studies conducted in multiple languages, as PNAAPS was.

The hubs have both central city Asian Americans and significant numbers of the fast-growing suburban Asian Americans. This chapter is based upon a survey of the adults of the six largest Asian American ethnic descent groups who reside in five major population hubs of the Asian American population, making up about 40 percent of the U.S. Asian population. A total of 1,218 adults of Chinese, Filipino, Japanese, Korean, South Asian, and Vietnamese descent residing in the metropolitan areas (SMSAs) of Los Angeles, New York, Honolulu, San Francisco, and Chicago were interviewed by phone in English as well as in four ethnic languages of preference between November 16, 2001, and January 28, 2002 (see Appendix A for a detailed description of the sampling and survey methodology).

Religious Preference and Ethnic Self-Identification

Asian Americans in the five metropolitan areas professed five major religious identifications: Christian; Catholic; Buddhist; Hindu; and Muslim. Quite a few said that they had no religious identification.

Does Religion Influence the Adaptation of Asians to the United States?

One way to answer this question is to look at the role of religion in assimilating Asians to an American identity. Indeed, religious preferences are associated with differences in identifying oneself as "Asian ethnic" (e.g., Chinese American, Filipino American, etc.), "Asian American," and "American." "Asian" and "Asian ethnic" (e.g., Asian Chinese, Asian Filipino, etc.) are not associated with differences of religious preference.

Mostly, "Asian ethnics" (e.g., Chinese, Filipinos, etc.) have the same religious profile as their fellow ethnics. However, the Asians without a religious identification are more likely to identify themselves as an "Asian ethnic."

About 34 percent of Asians identify themselves with a hyphenated "ethnic American" identity like Chinese American or Filipino American. However, Catholics (42 percent) and Muslims (42 percent) are much more likely to offer this identity while Hindus (30 percent) and the nonidentifiers (29 percent) are less likely to do so.

Hindus (27 percent) and Muslims (21 percent) are more likely to offer the panethnic "Asian American" identity. Only about 15 percent of all Asians offer this as their identity.

At present, perhaps because of their relatively recent immigration to the United States, only 12 percent of Asians identify themselves as unhyphenated "American." However, Asian Christians (17 percent) are a little more likely to have this identity.

Deciphering the Religious Factor with Multivariate Results

Of course, relationships between religious preference and ethnic identity choice may be attributable to a number of factors other than a person's religious preference. Ethnic identity may be influenced by factors such as a respondent's religiosity and degree of social, cultural, and political integration. To decipher the role of religious identification in ethnic self-identification among Asians, we have used multivariate analysis to control for the effects of various factors other than religious identification. The factors we have taken into account are: the respondent's political integration;[2] the respondent's concern with ethnic group issues;[3] the respondent's level

TABLE 11.1
Religious Preference by Ethnic Self-Identification
People think of themselves in different ways. In general, do you think of yourself as
an American, an Asian American, an Asian, a [R's Ethnic Group] American,
or a [R's Ethnic Group]?

	Christian (Protestant)	Catholic	Buddhist	Hindu	Muslim	None	All
American (%)	17	8	9	9	13	14	12
Asian American (%)	17	14	12	27	21	16	15
Asian (%)	5	4	5	5		1	4
Ethnic American (%)	33	42	36	30	42	29	34
Asian Ethnic (%)	26	30	34	23	12	36	30
Not Sure (%)	2	1	3	4	12	4	3
N	320	249	184	77	24	226	1218

of acculturation into the United States;[4] and the respondent's socialization in the United States.[5] In addition, we also controlled for a respondent's sociodemographic background.[6]

Self-identified religious denominations often predict respondents' ethnic identity choices. Specifically, holding other attributes constant, Catholics or Buddhists are more likely to self-identify as "ethnic Asian" than as "American."

Being Hindu is associated with a higher likelihood of self-identifying as "Asian American" than as "ethnic Asian." And being Muslim or Other believer is associated with a higher likelihood of self-identifying as "American" and "ethnic American" than as "ethnic Asian."

However, being Christian may not make a respondent significantly more likely to self-identify with any of the three American-based identities.

Interestingly, we find religiosity to have no impact on identity assimilation after controlling for religious denomination and other factors.

Religion and Political Adaptation

Does Religion Influence the Political Adaptation of Asians in America?

Table 11.2 shows that the relationship between religious preference and political adaptation as indicated by respondents' levels of political participation and the adoption of mainstream political ideology and partisanship in the aggregate may vary by the spheres of political participation and types of religious identification.

Respondents' levels of political participation are indicated by five measures: citizenship status, citizenship intent, voting registration, voting turnout, and participation beyond voting.

In terms of the acquisition of U.S. citizenship, Catholics have the highest rate of having U.S. citizenship. Moreover, Catholic noncitizens have one of the highest rates of expectation of acquiring citizenship. Muslims have the lowest rate of having U.S. citizenship.

The citizenship rate for nonidentifiers is about the same as that for the average identifiers. Among noncitizens, nonidentifiers have the lowest rates of expected citizenship.

Over eight in ten Christians, Hindus, and Buddhists who are U.S. citizens have registered to vote; the registration rate for religious nonidentifiers is the same as that for identifiers.

An average of over eight in ten registered Asians turned out to vote in the 2000 presidential election. The turnout rates among the registered are lowest among nonidentifiers and highest among Muslims; the turnout rates for Christians, Hindus, and Buddhists are about the same.

Relative to voting participation, there is more variation in the rates of participation in political activities beyond voting across religious denominations, with Hindus and Muslims being more active than Buddhists and nonidentifiers, whose participation rate is lower than the Asian average.

In the United States citizens have become accustomed to thinking in terms of liberal, moderate, and conservative ideologies, which are loosely associated with the organized politics of political parties and voting. Among Asians variations in religious preference are strongly related to variations in these mainstream political ideologies and parties. Asian adherents to different religions often have different political ideological profiles. Some Asian religions are associated with more liberal ideologies. A much higher percentage (18 percent) of Hindus than of Asians in general (8 percent) report being "very liberal." Further, 43 percent of Hindus say they are "somewhat liberal." Muslims, too, lean toward the liberal side though a little less emphatically than the Hindus. Fifty percent of Muslims say that they are "somewhat liberal" as compared to 28 percent of all Asians.

The "middle of the road" is occupied by Buddhists (41 percent) more often than by Asians in general (32 percent).

TABLE 11.2
Religious Preference and Political Adaptation

	Christian (Protestant)	Catholic	Buddhist	Hindu	Muslim	None	All
Base N	320	349	184	77	24	226	1,218
Political Participation							
U.S. Citizenship (%)	70	77	66	57	33	67	68
Expected Citizenship (among Noncitizens) (%)	70	84	75	67	87	65	72
Voting Registration (among Citizens) (%)	82	76	80	84	62	80	80
Voting in Election 2000 (%) (among the Registered)	85	77	87	86	100	74	82
Other Participation (%)	47	49	36	58	67	37	45

TABLE 11.3
Political Ideology
"How would you describe your views on most matters having to do with politics?
Do you generally think of yourself as very liberal or somewhat liberal or
middle of the road or somewhat conservative or very conservative?"

	Christian (Protestant)	Catholic	Buddhist	Hindu	Muslim	None	All
Very Liberal (%)	4	8	6	18	8	10	8
Somewhat Liberal (%)	27	32	21	43	50	22	28
Middle of the Road (%)	33	24	41	17	12	36	32
Somewhat Conservative (%)	25	24	12	14	17	15	18
Very Conservative (%)	4	4	6	—	8	3	4
Not Sure (%)	7	7	14	8	4	13	10

More "Christians (Protestants) (25 percent) and Catholics (24 percent) lean to the "somewhat conservative" side than do Asians as a whole (18 percent). Indeed, only 4 percent of "Christians (Protestants)" would say that they are "very liberal."

Asians who identify themselves as Buddhists seem to be less oriented than other Asians to the American political party system. A higher percentage (26 percent) of Buddhists claim that they don't think in terms of "Republican," "Democrat," and "Independent." Further, even Asian Buddhists who think in these partisan terms are more likely to be unsure where they fit.

In contrast very few Hindu (5 percent) and Muslim (4 percent) respondents have trouble thinking of themselves in traditional partisan terms.

More liberal than Asians as a whole, Hindus (49 percent) and Muslims (42 percent) are relatively strong identifiers with the Democratic Party. Further, their non-Democrats are less likely to side with the Republicans but more often than Asians as a whole (13 percent) to say that they are "Independents" (Hindus 20 percent, Muslims 25 percent, Christians (Protestants) and Catholics are more likely to identify themselves as "Republicans," 19 percent and 18 percent respectively.

Political participation such as voting, registration, and even more active forms is significantly higher for Asian religionists who go to a religious service every week. Their rate of participation is much higher than that of

TABLE 11.4
Political Partisanship
"Generally speaking, do you usually think of yourself as a Republican,
a Democrat, an Independent, or of another political affiliation?"

	Christian (Protestant)	Catholic	Buddhist	Hindu	Muslim	None	All
Don't Think in These Terms (%)	17	14	26	5	4	29	20
Republican (%)	19	18	14	12	17	5	14
Democrat (%)	38	39	26	49	42	30	36
Independent (%)	11	14	11	20	25	13	13
Not Sure (%)	13	13	21	9	13	22	16

Asians who don't go to any religious services. However, the level of political participation by Asian religionists doesn't seem to have much association with levels of attendance at religious services less than once per week.

Deciphering the Religious Factor with Multivariate Results (Appendix D)

As in the case of estimating the religious influence on making ethnic self-identity choices, we can distinguish the influence of religion from other factors on the political participation and orientation of Asians with multivariate regression procedures (Appendix D).

Three measures[7] are used to gauge respondents' adaptation to the U.S. political system: citizenship status,[8] voting in elections,[9] and participation beyond voting.[10]

At first the results seem to show little evidence of a relationship between religious preference and political incorporation through U.S. citizenship, participation in voting, and other political activities. The one exception is that being Muslim or follower of "Other" religion may be associated with a lower likelihood of acquiring U.S. citizenship.

However, controlling for religious preference and other conditions, more frequent attendance of religious services may be associated with greater political adaptation, indicated by the incidence or plans of obtaining U.S. citizenship. Importantly, consistent with the observations made by studying non-Asians, a higher level of religiosity as indicated by one's frequency of religious service attendance may also be associated with a higher frequency of election turnout of registered voters. On the other hand, consistent again with the literature on non-Asians, more frequent attendance of religious services may not be related to a higher level of participation in political activities beyond voting.

We also explored the relationship between religion and the acquisition of mainstream political orientations in terms of political ideology[11] and political partisanship.[12] The results (Appendix D) show that both religious preference and religiosity may help predict the adoption of liberal ideology. Other conditions being equal, those who self-identify as Hindu, Muslim, or followers of "Other" religions may hold a stronger liberal ideology among Asians. However, one's frequency of attending religious services, regardless of religious denominations and other social and political experiences and background, may be negatively associated with the acquisition of a liberal political outlook. In other words, those Asians who participate more frequently in religious services are also more conservative in political outlook regardless of denomination. Nevertheless, one's frequency of participation in religious services has no significant effect on the acquisition of Democratic partisanship. Instead, religious preference matters for the acquisition of political partisanship among Asians. Specifically, Buddhists may be less likely, Hindus may be more likely, but Catholics or Muslims and Other believers may not be more likely than those who have no religious preference to develop a stronger identification with the Democratic Party among Asians, even if differences in the frequency of attending services and other factors are controlled.

TABLE 11.5
Religious Attendance and Political Participation

	Voting in 2000			Voting Registration			Other Participation		
	No	Yes	Total	No	Yes	Total	No	Yes	Total
Every Week (%)	26	34	33	24	33	31	26	33	29
Almost Every Week (%)	8	7	7	8	7	7	7	9	8
1–2 Times/ Month (%)	11	11	11	13	11	11	12	13	12
A Few Times/ Year (%)	27	25	25	24	25	25	22	25	23
Never (%)	25	18	20	27	20	21	27	16	22
N	121	537	658	166	658	824	673	545	1,218

Summary and Conclusion

This research represents a preliminary effort to empirically assess the relationship between religion and political adaptation among Asian Americans. Using a new and unique large-scale survey, this study gauges the religious landscape with questions on self-identified religious denominations and frequency of attending religious services. The direction and degree of political adaptation to the U.S. mainstream political system is assessed in terms of adopting U.S.-based identities, citizenship status and orientation, voting and other political participation, and the acquisition of major political ideologies and partisanship.

The summary findings present a pluralistic religious landscape with five major denominations ranging from 2 percent Muslim to 26 percent Christian as well as 19 percent nonidentifiers. Respondents also vary widely in terms of their habits of attending religious services as a whole and along specific denominations. About three in ten Asians report having attended services on a weekly basis, but close to one in four report no attendance at all. Although as high as 63 percent of Muslims report attendance on a weekly basis, only 4 percent of Buddhists would attend with such frequency.

Religious preference appears to shape ethnic identity preferences and political alignments in ideology and partisanship. Over one in four Catholics and Muslims prefer to self-identify as "Ethnic American"; about three in ten Buddhists and Catholics choose to self-identify as "Ethnic Asian"; close to three in ten Hindus prefer to self-identify as "Asian American," and over two in ten Other believers prefer to call themselves "American" over other ethnic labels.

About six in ten Hindus and Muslims describe their political ideology as very or somewhat liberal; about three in ten Catholics and Christians are either very or somewhat conservative; and more than four in ten Buddhists consider themselves "middle of the road." Respondents are overwhelmingly more Democratic than Republican as a whole and among identifiers for each denomination. However, as high as one in four Buddhists do not think of their political affiliation in conventional partisan terms.

Not all these differences can be explained away by differences in respondents' religious, social, political experiences, and demographic background. Being Catholic may lower one's likelihood to self-identify as

"American"; being Buddhist may lower one's likelihood to self-identify as "American" or "Asian American"; but being Hindu may increase one's likelihood to self-identify as "Asian American"; and being Muslim or Other believer may increase one's likelihood to self-identify as "American" and "Ethnic American."

We also find that Asian Americans, like other Americans, are more likely to become incorporated into the U.S. political system in terms of citizenship acquisition and voting participation when they attend religious services on a more frequent basis. Further, more church attendance may be associated with having a more conservative political ideology. However, we find that being Hindu and Muslim/Other may increase the adoption of a liberal ideology. Being Hindu may increase the acquisition of a Democratic partisanship, but being Buddhist may have the opposite effect.

These statistical renditions are advantageous in more accurately charting the diverse religious landscape within the Asian American population, in identifying the unique contribution of religious preference and church attendance to political adaptation. However, to better explain the underpinnings of the ethnic identification and political adaptation patterns, future research will need to incorporate ethnographic research and in-depth interviews. This qualitative information will help account for the roles of the character, belief systems, and religious traditions and practice in the processes of ethnic identity formation and political adaptation.

APPENDIX A: SURVEY METHODOLOGY

This multicity, multiethnic, and multilingual survey is a preliminary but unprecedented attempt to measure the political behavior and attitudes of Asian Americans. A total of 1,218 adults of Chinese, Korean, Vietnamese, Japanese, Filipino, and Asian Indian or Pakistani descent who resided in Los Angeles, New York, Honolulu, San Francisco, and Chicago metropolitan areas were randomly selected to be interviewed by phone between November 16, 2000, and January 28, 2001. Telephone households in these five metropolitan areas—chosen for their Asian population size, geographic location, and Asian ethnic group makeup—were sampled using a dual-frame approach consisting of random-digit dialing at targeted Asian zip-code densities and listed-surname frames. Only telephone households with surnames associated with the top six Asian ethnic groups in population size were included in this study. The listed-surname approach was the only method used to generate samples in New York and Chicago. Within each sampling area, the probability of selection for each ethnic sample was to approximate the size of the ethnic population among Asians according to the 1990 census. However, the Vietnamese and Asian Indians were over-sampled to generate a sufficiently large number of respondents for analysis. Within each contacted household, the interviewer would ask to speak with an adult eighteen years of age or older who most recently had a birthday. To increase the response rate, multiple call attempts made at staggered time and day of week and to recontact break offs and refusals were used.

The resulting sample contains 308 Chinese, 168 Korean, 137 Vietnamese, 198 Japanese, 266 Filipino, and 141 Asian Indian or Pakistani Americans, or an average of 200 completed interviews from each MSA and an additional 218 interviews from the Los Angeles Metropolitan Area. Based on the English proficiency rate of each Asian subgroup and practical cost concerns, English was used to interview respondents of Japanese, Filipino, and Asian Indian descent; respondents of Chinese, Korean, and Vietnamese descent were interviewed in their language of preference. Among the Chinese, 78 percent chose to be interviewed in Mandarin Chinese, 19 percent in Cantonese, and 3 percent in English. Close to 9 out of 10 Koreans (87 percent) chose to be interviewed in Korean. Nearly all Vietnamese respondents (98.5 percent) chose to be interviewed in Vietnamese.

The average interview length is 27 minutes for interviews conducted in the respondent's non-English language and 20 minutes for interviews conducted in English. The average incidence rate for interviews drawn from the listed surname sample is 41 percent, with a range from 14.5 percent for the Filipino sample to 81 percent for the Chinese sample. The incidence rate for RDD interviews is 15 percent, which ranges from 4.6 percent for Korean to 24 percent for the Japanese sample. The average refusal rate is 25 percent, with 34 percent in the listed sample and 3.5 percent in the RDD sample. The margin of sampling error for the entire sample is plus or minus 3 percentage points.

This survey is sponsored by a research grant from the National Science Foundation (SES-9973435). The KSCI-TV of Los Angeles donated money to augment the Los Angeles portion of the project. Samples were developed by Survey Sampling Inc. of Fairfield, Connecticut. Interviews were conducted by the Interviewing Services of America, Inc, of Van Nuys, California. Any opinions, findings, and conclusions or recommendations expressed in this material are those of the principal investigator and do not necessarily reflect the views of the National Science Foundation or the KSCI-TV.

Political Integration Strength of Party Identification

"Generally speaking, do you usually think of yourself as a Republican, a De-mocrat, an Independent, or of another political affiliation?" [IF REPUBLI-CAN OR DEMOCRAT] *"Would you call yourself a strong (Republican/De-mocrat)?"* [IF INDEPENDENT] *Do you think of yourself as closer to the Re-publican or Democratic Party?*
0 = no party identification, 1 = Independent, closer to Democrat or Re-publican, 2 = Democrat or Republican, but not a strong Democrat or Re-publican, 3 = Strong Democrat or Republican

Citizenship Status [IF NOT A CITIZEN]

"Are you planning to apply for U.S. citizenship or to become a U.S. citizen?"
0 = no, 1 = not a citizen, but expect to be one, 2 = citizen

Ethnic Group Action and Concern

Participation in Activities Involving Asian Americans

"Which of the following activities, that you participated in, involve/d an Asian American candidate or issue affecting Asian Americans?" [read all re-sponses from a previous question on participation beyond voting reported in note 9]
0 = no participation in any Asian American activity, 1 = participation in one Asian American activity, . . . 8 = participation in eight Asian American activities

Panethnic Linked Fate

"Do you think what happens generally to other groups of Asians in this country will affect what happens in your life?" [IF YES] *"Will it affect it a lot, some, or not very much?"*
0 = No, 1 = Yes, will affect but not very much, 2 = Yes, will affect some or not sure how, 3 = Yes, will affect a lot

Ethnic Linked Fate

"What about the [R'S ETHNIC GROUP] people in America, do you think what happens generally to [R'S ETHNIC GROUP] Americans will affect what happens in your life?" [IF YES] *Will it affect it a lot, some, or not very much?*
0 = No, 1 = Yes, will affect but not very much, 2 = Yes, will affect some or not sure how, 3 = Yes, will affect a lot

Acculturation Language Use (Business/Home)

"What language do you usually speak, when at home with family?" "What language do you usually use to conduct personal business and financial transactions?"
1 = Something else (language other than English), 2 = Mix of English and other language, 3 = English Media Use
"Compared to your usage of the English media, how often do you use [R'S ETHNIC GROUP'S] language media as a source of entertainment, news, and information? Would you say, all of the time, most of the time, about the same time, not very often, or not at all?"
5 = not at all, 4 = not very often, 3 = about the same time, 2 = most of the time, 1 = all of the time

Racial Interaction

Attitude toward Intermarriage

"How would you feel if someone in your family married a person of a different ethnic background than yours? Would you strongly approve, approve, neither approve nor disapprove, disapprove, or strongly disapprove?"

1 = strongly disapprove, 2 = disapprove, 3 = neither approve nor disapprove, 4 = approve, 5 = strongly approve

EXPERIENCE WITH PERSONAL DISCRIMINATION

"Have you ever personally experienced discrimination in the Unites States?"
2 = yes, 1 = not sure, 0 = no

ETHNIC DISCRIMINATION
[IF EXPERIENCED DISCRIMINATION]

"In your opinion, was it because of your ethnic background?"
1 = yes, 0 = otherwise

VICTIM OF HATE CRIME

"Have you ever been the victim of a 'hate crime,' that is, have you had someone verbally or physically abuse you, or damage your property, specifically because you belong to a certain race or ethnic group?"
1 = yes, 0 = otherwise

Immigrant Socialization

Nativity

"Were you born in Asia?"

Place of Education

"Were you educated mainly in the United States?"
1 = No

Sociodemographic Background

Education

"What is the highest level of education or schooling you have completed?"
1 = less than high school, 2 = high school graduate, 3 = vocational/technical training beyond HS or some college, 4 = bachelor's degree, 5 = some graduate school, 6 = postgraduate degree (beyond college degree)

Income

"If you added together the yearly incomes of all the members of your family living at home last year, would the total of all their incomes be less than $20,000 . . . or more than $40,000 . . . or somewhere in between?" [IF LESS THAN $20,000] *"Would the total of all their incomes be less than $10,000?"* [IF IN BETWEEN] *"Would the total of all their incomes be less than $30,000 or more than $30,000?"* [IF MORE THAN $40,000] *"Would the total of all their incomes be between $40,000 and $60,000 . . . or between $60,000 and $80,000 . . . or more than that?"*
1 = less than $10,000, 2 = $10,000 to $19,999, 3 = $20,000 to $29,999, 4 = $30,000 to $39,999, 5 = $40,000 to $59,999, 6 = $60,000 to $79,999, 7 = $80,000 or over. (Because of the large number of missing cases, we use the grand mean of 4.47 to substitute the "not sure" and "refused" response categories)

Age

"In what year were you born?"
(raw score = 1 + year of interview—birth year)

Employment Status

"What were you doing most of last week: working full-time, or working part-time, or were you self-employed, or keeping house, or going to school, or are you looking for work, or retired, or what?"
1 = working full-time, part-time, or self-employed, 0 = otherwise.

APPENDIX C

Multinomial Analysis Predicting Ethnic Identity Choice with Religion*

	Ethnic American		American		Asian American	
	b	s.e.	b	s.e.	b	s.e.
Religious Preference (ref = no preference)						
Christian	.072	.494	.167	.425	.313	.359
Catholic	−1.042*	.524	−.585	.443	.078	.362
Buddhist	−1.309*	.549	−.905*	.437	−.033	.327
Hindu	.218	.810	1.188*	.538	.363	.507
Muslim/Other	1.962*	.720	1.006	.643	1.076*	.561
Religiosity (5 = every week)	−.071	.495	.055	.417	−.118	.349

N = 825   −2 Log Likelihood (Intercept only) = 2161.35   Model Chi-Sq = 473.04
Nagelkerke R-sq = .471; McFadden = .219

* Because the dependent variable, ethnic self-identification, is categorical and has more than two values, we apply multinomial regression procedure (see below) to estimate an Asian's likelihood to adopt a certain ethnic self-identity mode over the category of reference ("Asian ethnic"). The effect of a specific religious preference on the adoption of a certain ethnic identity is assessed by a series of dummy variables created by assigning a value of 1 and 0 otherwise to each of the response categories shown in Table 11.1. For reason of parsimony, we combine Muslim and Other identifiers into one category. The results are the same when each religious category is entered separately. The reference category is "No Religious Preference." Cell values in are logistic coefficients (b) or log odds; standard errors (s.e.) are in the columns to the right. The "American" columns report respondents' likelihood to prefer the "American" identity to an "ethnic Asian" identity. The "Asian American" and "Ethnic American" columns report respondents' likelihood to prefer either of the two identity modes to "ethnic Asian."

Multinomial regression procedure is a variant of the maximum likelihood-based estimations (MLE). It requires that one of the dependent variable categories be selected as a referent point. Effects are then computed and assessed in comparison to that category. This procedure has the advantage of helping assess if and how the possible correlates of ethnic identity may influence a respondent's decision in selecting his/her preferred ethnic identity mode while considering simultaneously the effects of all other variables on a range of alternative identity choices. Because the impact of any given factor in an MLE model is not constant across values and cannot be interpreted independently of other factor scores, discussion of results and comparison of effect size are facilitated by estimating the parameters with rescaled independent variables with scores varying between 0 and 1.

The dependent is a categorical variable with 4 possible responses. The reference category is R's self-identity as "ethnic Asian." The parameters are estimated using multinomial regression procedures with re-scaled independent variables where scores are to vary only between 0 and 1.

b = unstandardized logistic coefficient, s.e. = standard error, ** $p < .005$, * $p < .05$
Source: Multi-Site Asian American Political Survey (MAAPS), 2000–1.

APPENDIX D

OLS Regression Analysis Predicting Political Participation and Preferences with Religion

	(1) Citizenship Status		(2) Voting in Elections		(3) Participation beyond Voting		(4) Liberal Ideology		(5) Democratic Partisanship	
	b	s.e.	b	s.e.	b	s.e.	b	s.e.	b	s.e.
Religious Preference (ref = no preference)										
Christian	−.113	.068	−.051	.103	−.019	.110	.020	.108	−.020	.136
Catholic	.010	.072	.015	.108	.022	.115	.109	.114	.107	.143
Buddhist	−.069	.067	.049	.105	−.066	.109	−.083	.107	−.273*	.134
Hindu	−.162	.095	−.049	.153	.018	.152	.471**	.151	.492*	.189
Muslim/Other	−.238*	.099	−.187	.169	.203	.160	.529**	.157	.140	.198
Religiosity (5 = every week)	.035*	.017	.064*	.025	.018	.027	−.074**	.026	−.024	.033
Citizenship Status					.081	.055	−.063	.054	.114	.068
Strength of Partisanship	.039*	.017	.042	.027	.085**	.028	.093**	.028		
Ethnic Participation	.033	.022	.096**	.031	1.022**	.035	.094*	.035	−.024	.044
Sense of Linked Fate	−.012	.020	−.027	.030	.083*	.032	−.033	.032	.093*	.040
English Language Use	.094**	.031	−.051	.050	.097*	.050	−.065	.050	.107	.062
Support Intermarriage	.013	.023	−.009	.035	.053	.037	.128**	.036	−.005	.046
Experienced discrim.	.064	.058	.153	.087	.145	.093	.111	.092	.324**	.115
Education	−.043*	.012	.085**	.019	.028	.019	.046*	.019	−.002	.023
Family Income	.021	.013	−.051*	.021	.064**	.022	.020	.021	.017	.027
Female	.005	.040	−.072	.060	−.174*	.064	−.014	.063	.114	.079
Age	.007**	.001	.014**	.002	.004	.002	.001	.002	.005	.003
Employed	.073	.045	.109	.072	−.113	.072	.049	.071	.033	.089
Foreign Born	−.195**	.058	−.208*	.084	−.217*	.094	.020	.093	−.180	.117
Non-U.S. Education	−.254**	.051	−.135	.080	−.244**	.084	−.026	.082	.105	.103
Constant	1.359	.129	.330	.204	−.214	.220	.786	.217	.178	.272
N	882		488		861		882		882	

Note: The model estimating voting is for the subsample of the registered.
Source: MAAPS 2000–1.

NOTES

1. This survey is sponsored by a research grant from the National Science Foundation (SES-9973435). Pei-te Lien is the principal investigator. The KSCI-TV of Los Angeles donated money to augment the Los Angeles portion of the project. Samples were developed by Survey Sampling Inc. of Fairfield, Connecticut. Interviews were conducted by the Interviewing Services of America, Inc, of Van Nuys, California. Any opinions, findings, and conclusions or recommendations expressed in this material are those of the principal investigator and do not necessarily reflect the views of the National Science Foundation or the KSCI-TV. The author thanks colleagues Janelle Wong, M. Margaret Conway, Taeku Lee, KSCI-TV research director Alice Lee, and Pacific Opinion president Christian Collet for their generous advice and support.

2. Political integration is indicated by his/her acquisition of U.S. citizenship, expectation of citizen status, and strength of identification with a mainstream political party.

3. Ethnic group concern is indicated by his/her level of activism in Asian American organizations, political campaigns involving Asian American candidates or issues, and sense of linked fate with other Asians.

4. Acculturation into the United States is indicated by his/her reliance on English to communicate at home, in business settings, and to receive information and entertainment from the mass media, and everyday interracial interactions—as indicated by experience with ethnic discrimination and attitude toward intermarriage.

5. Socialization in the United States is indicated by whether one was born outside the United States and if his/her primary education was received outside the United States.

6. Socioeconomic background is indicated by education, family income, gender, age, and employment status. We do not, however, control for one's ethnic origin because of its affinity with religion and its tendency to knock off the significance of religious preference in predicting political behavior.

7. Because the dependent variables in this table are continuous in nature, we report ordinary least squares-based (OLS) regression results with b for unstandardized slope coefficients and s.e. for standard errors.

8. We assign a value of 2 to respondents with U.S. citizenship, 1 to those noncitizens who expect to become citizens, and 0 to those noncitizens who have no plan to become citizens.

9. The two questions on voting are: *"Thinking about the November 2000 presidential election when Al Gore ran against George Bush, did you vote in the election?"* *"Did you happen to vote in the 1998 Congressional elections, or didn't you get a chance to vote?"* We assign a value of 2 to those who reported voting in both the

1998 and 2000 national elections, 1 to those who reported voting in either one of the elections, and 0 to those who did not participate in either.

10. The wording of the question is: *"During the past 4 years, have you partici-pated in any of the following types of political activity in your community? (ACCEPT MULTIPLE ANSWERS)"* Response categories were:

wrote or phoned a government official;
contacted an editor of a newspaper, magazine, or TV station;
donated money to a political campaign;
attended a public meeting, political rally, or fund-raiser;
worked with others in your community to solve a problem;
signed a petition for a political cause;
served on any governmental board or commission;
took part in a protest or demonstration;
worked for a political campaign.

Each respondent is assigned a participation score according to the number of ac-tivities mentioned. Thus, a value of 0 equals no participation in any activity, a value of 1 equals participation in one activity, and a value of 8 equals participation in eight activities.

11. Because of our interest in the direction and strength of a certain ideology, we assign a value of 3 to "very liberal," 2 to "somewhat liberal," 1 to "middle of the road," and 0 to all other responses.

12. Because the focus is on predicting the acquisition of a major U.S. main-stream political partisanship, we assign a value of 3 to "Strong Democrat," 2 to "Democrat, but not a strong Democrat," 1 to "Independent, but closer to the De-mocratic Party," and 0 to someone with no party identification.

Part IV

Transcending Borders and Boundaries

12

Creating an Asian American Christian Subculture

Grace Community Covenant Church

Russell Jeung

I want to go to a place where it's not about being Korean, but being a Christian. It's the question of which is the adjective—being a Korean Christian or being a Christian Korean. At Grace, you don't see a particular culture emphasized, but it's just a community of believers.
    —Cameron Kim, a 1.5–generation Korean American

I started the church search looking for a multiethnic church, because that seemed to be more aligned with my perspective of what God desires for His community. But I felt that if I went to a multiethnic church or a primarily Caucasian church, then I wouldn't get plugged in as fast. It would eventually happen. But I joined an Asian American church.
    —Nic Chan, a second-generation Chinese American

These two evangelical Christians[1] espouse two separate discourses regarding their Christian identity and racial-ethnic background. Cameron suggests that one's religious identity is primary—not a mere descriptor—and that the ethnic church is often too culturally bound. Complaining about churches that are too exclusive and focused on cultural preservation, he asserts, "In Korean churches, unless you're Korean, you're going to feel like an outsider. Korean culture comes out a lot."[2] On the other hand, Nic believes that the church should acknowledge people's backgrounds and differences so that members can learn from one another. In promoting racial reconciliation and Christians of all backgrounds meeting together, he continues, "Going through college, it's all about diversity. It's all about being together, building each other up."[3]

Ironically, both Cameron and Nic attend Grace Community Covenant Church, a congregation that intentionally identifies as an Asian American panethnic church.[4] Cameron left the Korean American immigrant church because of its overemphasis on cultural practices, but he still purposely chose to attend a church organized around racial lines. Nic wanted to be part of a more diverse congregation, but he ended up joining Grace Community which is primarily East Asian, and becoming one of its leaders. What drew both these individuals to join an Asian American church, when, paradoxically, their values should have led them to different congregations?

This chapter is an ethnography of Grace Community Covenant Church, a new evangelical church designed to serve "second and third generation Asian Americans and their friends in Silicon Valley."[5] Within four years of its founding in 1998, the church had a worship attendance of almost two hundred and hosts eighteen home groups where people meet weekly for fellowship. I argue that panethnic churches like Grace Community form to meet the *organizational needs* for affiliation of Asian Americans. As a formal organization, the Asian American church can be analyzed in terms of its structure of authority, its use of resources, and its emergent culture (Ammerman 1997b). In creating institutional space for a new church subculture, Grace Community meets members' needs for acceptance, belonging, and expression of their own values and beliefs. Panethnic churches are also organized to accommodate a rejection of the hierarchical and authoritarian structure of Asian ethnic ones. On the other hand, Asian Americans may find the culture of Caucasian congregations uncomfortable.

To learn about the unique institutional subculture of Grace Community, I attended its church services, reviewed church documents, and conducted in-depth interviews with eight members about their involvement.[6] In addition, I have interviewed forty-four ministers and conducted ethnographies of other Asian American congregations as part of a larger research project.

Theories of Panethnic Organizations:
Instrumentalism and Primordialism

Panethnicity is the creation of a supraidentity among a collection of previously distinct ethnic groups (Lopez and Espiritu 1990). This process also involves racial formation, in which groups become categorized by the state and mobilize around identities and meanings surrounding different phenotypes (Omi and Winant 1994). One example is the creation of the category "Hispanic," in which groups as diverse as Cubans, Puerto Ricans, and Mexicans have been lumped together. Since the 1970s, the grouping of "Asian American" has also become an official state census category. Ethnic groups with different linguistic, religious, and cultural heritages have taken advantage of this lumping categorization to organize as Asian Americans to garner greater political clout, government funding, and professional networking (Ho 2002; Espiritu 1992).

Of course, the diversity among Asian Americans makes organizing along one common identity, culture, and values difficult. According to some theorists, membership of panethnic groups is primarily an affiliation for instrumental, political purposes, in which Asian Americans identify as such because they share common material interests. For example, Nazli Kibria (1996) suggests that panethnic consciousness is fostered by successful pan-Asian political efforts, such as revisions of census designations and campaigns against anti-Asian violence. Furthermore, Yen Le Espiritu suggests that panethnic organization for political and economic reasons precedes group solidarity.

Establishing congregations that are Asian American does create a larger target population around which churches can grow. By expanding beyond a Chinese or Korean ethnic market, ministers act as cultural entrepreneurs by catering to more religious consumers. Yet drawing together different Asian American ethnic group members as church family requires calling upon a deeper loyalty than simply a political coalition. I contend that panethnic churches form for reasons beyond mere political alliance or economic interest.

Pyong Gap Min (2002) argues that individuals affiliate with Asian American congregations because they share primordial common ties of culture, history, and phenotype. He observes that those attending Asian American churches are primarily Chinese and Japanese Americans who share Confucian values and American racial experiences. In contrast, Southeast Asians, South Asians, and Filipinos rarely attend these congregations because they are separated by differences in class, generation, and physical appearance. Min concludes that the qualifiers "East Asian" and "South Asian" are more accurate in describing panethnic congregations.

However, primordial explanations of ethnicity and panethnicity cannot readily account for *varying* degrees of primordial group solidarity. Despite the fact that East Asians—Japanese, Chinese, and Korean Americans— plant most pan-Asian churches, only some of the believers in these ethnicities attend panethnic congregations; many continue to attend ethnic ones. Further, many Asian Americans no longer see their primordial roots as important as their common experiences in the United States.

Like Yen Le Espiritu (1992), I argue that neither instrumentalist nor primordialist theories provide a full explanation for the emergence of Asian American panethnic congregations. Instead, I suggest that these congregations establish such churches in response to the religious institutional landscape. The need for organizational space, where new congregational subcultures might develop, acts as the main impetus for these new churches. As this chapter will show, Grace Community's Asian American organizational subculture is a distinct and unique response to Caucasian- and immigrant-dominated organizational forms.

The Context: The Politics and Economics of Race

Grace Community targets the growing Asian American community in the Silicon Valley, the birthplace and largest concentration of high tech corporations in the world. Recognizing the increasing numbers of Asian Americans in the area, the church saw that many of the newcomers also needed a church home. Large numbers of Asian Americans have recently moved to Silicon Valley in California's Santa Clara County, where no racial group makes up the majority. In 1980, Asians and Pacific Islanders (APIs) made up only 7.4 percent of Santa Clara County. With the boom in the computer industry and increased immigration, APIs increased to 16.8 percent of the county in 1990 and to 25.7 percent in 2000. Currently, 430,095 Asians make their home in the county (Kim 2001; Mangaliman 2002).[7]

New immigration has complicated and diversified the grouping of "Asian Americans" as well. The Chinese population, numbering 110,632, is the largest API ethnic group in the county and grew by 73 percent in the

1990s. The Vietnamese community grew by 84 percent to total 99,986, and the Filipino population includes 76,060 residents. The Asian Indian population in the county saw the largest net increase of all groups—231 percent—and now numbers 66,741.[8] Other large API groups include Japanese, Korean, and Cambodian ethnic populations. However, like most "Asian American" churches, one ethnicity predominates at Grace. Eighty-five percent of the congregation is Chinese, 12 percent other Asians, and 3 percent whites.

Beyond their ethnic diversity, Asian Americans also represent a range of occupations and class backgrounds. In Silicon Valley, the high tech industry has created a "digital divide" within the region, with high-income professionals on one side and low-paid service sector employees on the other.[9] Asians fall on both sides of this divide with a large percentage of people in low-income and working-class occupations.[10] In contrast to these households, 16.0 percent of Silicon Valley Asian Americans have graduate degrees and 11.6 percent of Asian American households earned over $100,000 in 1990. Grace itself has almost no low-income members. These professional Asian Americans often become racialized during their college years, as they become more connected to ethnic and racial student groups, take courses in Ethnic Studies, and find themselves categorized as Asian Americans (Tuan 1998; Min and Kim 1999). Pastor Wong is typical in that he majored in engineering at Stanford but also took Asian American studies. While in college, he mostly hung out with other Asian Americans. They continue to practice Asian Americanness as professionals (Ho 2002). On Saturday mornings the Asian American volleyball leagues swing into play with a flurry of business cards being traded and job feelers sent out. Afterward, the Korean Americans whip by the Korean mall to snack, while other Asian Americans scatter to Ranch 99 supermarkets in Cupertino for groceries. Singles plan for the evening in their quest to marry another Asian American.

Asian Americans in Silicon Valley are thus highly diverse both ethnically and economically. Organizing a new church along racial lines faced little opposition because the region supports the ideology of multiculturalism, where ethnic diversity is recognized and valued.[11] However, to be an effective new church, Grace Community chose to target a particular subgroup of the Asian American community, namely, East Asian professionals who have come to work here. It does not attract South Asians, Pacific Islanders, or immigrant working-class populations. Aware that their target group is more likely to affiliate as Asian American and not as ethnic-specific

Americans, the church's website notes that "we started Grace Community especially for the Asian Americans who have moved here recently." This choice regarding the ethnic and class makeup of the congregation, in turn, shapes the type of church subculture that emerges.

Outgrowing the Organizational Structure of the Ethnic Church

> I'm a third-generation Asian American: But I'm often the victim of mistaken identity. Caucasians are surprised I don't speak Chinese. At the same time immigrant Asians are also surprised that I don't speak Chinese, they expect me to have the same emotional ties to my Asian heritage as they do.
>
> There are a lot of Asian Americans like me. The immigrant Asian community expects us to be more Asian. The Caucasian majority expects us to be either more Asian or blend into the Caucasian American culture. Neither category fits us, so *we're overlooked by many American institutions, including the church.*   —Pastor Steve Wong (italics mine)[12]

In his welcome letter to visitors to the church website, Pastor Steve explains the rationale for establishing Grace Community. He argues that Asian Americans have a separate and distinct identity from Asian immigrants and the Caucasian majority. American institutions "overlook" Asian Americans and are therefore not tailored to reach out to Asian Americans, make them comfortable, or serve them well. Pastor Steve makes reference to an American Broadway musical to further elaborate:

> There's a need to affiliate somewhere, but not feeling comfortable in those two areas. I call it the "My Fair Lady Syndrome." Just because you speak one way doesn't mean that inside you're that way. Even though I don't have an accent, am I going to be completely comfortable talking to Caucasians? On the other hand, because I look like an Asian, I'm not going to be necessarily comfortable in an Asian immigrant church. So we're stuck in that place that Eliza was in.

Like Eliza Doolittle, Asian Americans are marginalized within existing institutions, such that they may not feel fully comfortable in either Asian- or Caucasian-dominated contexts. In order to create a comfortable place to which Asian Americans could affiliate, Pastor Steve established a new panethnic church that would gather people who identify in this way.

"Comfort" is a key emotional theme in the therapeutic culture that emerged among professionals by the 1970s (Bellah et al. 1985). Asian Americans' search for comfort is partly keyed to two organizational reasons that make them uncomfortable in Asian immigrant congregations: the latter's structure of authority and their use of resources.

Structure of Authority

Really, the focus of the church is on relationships rather than so much Bible knowledge. Through relationship networks, that's how we do outreach. The relationships are the means that God uses to work in our lives. Whether it's relationships that bring us to faith, it's all relational. Or, it's a means of spiritual formation through a small group, or an LTG [Life Transformation Group], or through a spiritual friendship.   —Pastor Steve Wong

Grace Community emphasizes close interpersonal relationships as both the means and the ends of the church. Through such relationships people get invited to the church and can participate in a range of monthly activities, such as basketball, ballroom dancing, and houseboating.[13] Christians also develop their own spiritual lives through their relationships in the context of small groups, where they share their concerns and pray together.[14] Ultimately, the aim of the church is to further members' relationship with God and each other as the family of God. In fact, Grace Community discourages programs and committees that do not build up relationships and so the church has a relatively flat organizational structure. Their website affirms, "It's more important that we do things together than [that] we get things done."

Pastor Steve compares this value for relationships with the value of Bible knowledge. In discursive relationships disagreements are more likely to be rationally discussed and solved. But in some ethnic congregations, people with more Bible knowledge are given status and authority because they are considered more spiritual and mature. Unfortunately, this type of hierarchy discourages unchurched visitors, those who have not grown up in a church context, from feeling welcome or comfortable. It also maintains the hierarchical nature of the Asian church.

In fact, Asian Americans at Grace Community appreciate this relational emphasis because they have felt alienated by the use of power within ethnic congregations. According to Nancy Ammerman, power within congregations involves the ability to "make decisions about how they will use the resources they have" (1997b, 51). Within Chinese, Japanese, and Korean immigrant churches, males with official church positions, Bible knowledge, professional status, and seniority in age tend to hold power. Even if the younger second generation matches their elders in Bible knowledge, the other qualities have an impact on discussions. At the most the generations just end up bringing down the Bible on each other. They exercise this power formally through church rules and voting procedures. More often, though, they exercise power informally, through relationships of obligation and face-saving norms (Yang 1999a).

Nic, a twenty-four-year-old Chinese American engineer from the East Coast, recounts the story of his previous congregation's hiring process as an example of the disenfranchisement of the younger generation. The second generation wanted to hire a new English-speaking pastor who was very inspiring and dedicated to evangelism. However, the Chinese-speaking deacons had previously hired an English-speaking pastor with similar missionary skills and he left within a year. In this case, the deacons went against the wishes of the second generation because they wanted someone who would be less likely to leave or encourage their children to become missionaries. Nic expressed his frustration about the Chinese deacons:

> And they were, like, "We don't want that to happen again. We want someone to be here to help build the ministry." So they shot down this hiring, which caused a number of defections from the English congregation. We couldn't even choose our own pastor.

English-speaking Asian Americans have a host of youth-orientated spiritual and social needs that are different from those of the immigrant congregation, but these needs are not met because they lack the power to implement appropriate ministries. Cameron, another engineer, left the Korean immigrant church because of similar generational conflicts:

> For some reason, a lot of English ministries seem to have generational conflicts between the first and second generations. The English ministries would have differences in budget, ministry activities, and the main thing would be the purpose of the English ministry. A lot of times, the Korean and English pastor would have conflicts and leave.

From what I've seen, the Korean congregation thinks the English ministries are an older version of youth ministries, not a ministry that can stand on its own. It is likely that English ministries want the freedom to minister and worship the way they felt was right.

Indeed, the desire for the comfort that autonomy from oppressive church structures brings motivates Asian Americans to split off and start their own churches.

In contrast to the hierarchical and authoritarian structure of authority found in Asian immigrant congregations, Grace Community emphasizes rallying around a common vision to lead its members. When Pastor Steve prepared to launch Grace Community, he regularly met with a core group to plan and pray, to solicit input, and to develop a common vision. One Caucasian core group member who works as a project manager, Rob Wu-Schmitz, recalls how members developed solidarity and consensus by collectively studying how to start a church together in "vision sharing" meetings over "sixty to a hundred hours." Whereas Asian immigrant churches can rely on duty and filial responsibility to keep members committed, Grace Community secures its members' commitment by having others take ownership of the church vision.

Along the lines of an egalitarian authority structure, Grace Community's leaders also seek to maintain open communication with its members. Through regular e-mail reports and announcements from the pulpit, leaders communicate opportunities to get involved and future directions for the church. In a series called "Lunches with Leadership: What's on YOUR Mind?" members can meet with church leaders to discuss various topics such as church growth, facilities, and even sermons. Identifying one of the distinctive aspects of Grace Community, Nic describes how he was able to initiate a new home group and join the church leadership even though he was relatively new to the church and only twenty-three years old at the time:

> It's been very open. Just my involvement is a testimony. We wanted to start a young adult home group and Pastor Steve was worried because it might divide the church. He was open to hearing both the pros and cons. I can infuse things.

Like the open communication and the freedom to innovate, another Grace Community democratic practice is its equal acceptance and treatment of people. People dress informally and casually, such that shorts and sandals are the norm. Non-Christians can help lead worship and younger members can join the leadership team. Linda Yeh, a 1.5–generation Chinese American working in health insurance, dislikes the Chinese immigrant church because members attend in order to gain status through their careers, dress, cars, or children's educational attainment. People at Grace Community, on the other hand, attend so that they could be "free to be who they are" and gain personal support from one another. Linda notes,

> The Chinese church, they're not the real Christians I'm looking for. They're not sharing the gospel, they're just showing off their kids, bragging about what they have, being materialistic. That's how I feel. That's not the right purpose of going to church.

> Some people take it as a place where they could finally show off. At Grace, we're supportive and since we're all still at that age where we're trying to learn our ways, and learn our paths, there's a lot of things we talk about openly. Things that we go through or even family issues. Open conversations so that we don't have any barriers. So it's easier to pray for each other and really get to know each other.

Grace Community thus distinguishes itself from the Asian immigrant church by valuing close interpersonal relationships rather than hierarchical and status-based ones. It also employs more Americanized processes to secure commitment, including building a common vision, open communication, and democratic practices.

Use of Resources

> Some of the things Steve was talking about were very radical. It would be really easy for us as a church in Silicon Valley, with people who are really affluent, to depend on money. Making a decision to give away 50 percent of our income—I thought that was something very, very biblical. It's not just the tithe; it's the spirit of the tithe. It puts you in the position where you need to be dependent.
>
> —Rob Wu-Schmitz, founding member of Grace Community

Another key value of Grace Community is its commitment to local and global community development.[15] Even though the church is well off and could afford to purchase its own property, instead it rents facilities from another church in its denomination. Twenty-five percent of church income is then directed to local ministries, such as homeless shelters. Another 25 percent of the income goes to global missions, such as international development teams in Thailand. Not only does Grace Community donate to these development projects, but it also encourages its members to participate and volunteer. Pastor Steve's goal is to have each member of Grace Community go on a short-term mission by 2012.

The use of resources is the second organizational dimension of a church that affects outsiders' and members' responses to it. Nancy Ammerman writes that all churches have material and human resources that they employ in various ways. Material resources include the church's income and physical assets, while human resources include leadership, volunteer hours, and support networks. Members at Grace Community indicate that they are attracted to its commitment to be a community and to serve the outside community. These qualities are reflected in the way Grace Community directs resources to these priorities.

Celia Leung, a Chinese American systems administrator who became a Christian through her participation on Grace Community's worship team, particularly noted the church's financial practices. Unlike Asian immigrant churches that typically spend funds on themselves, she explains that Grace Community gives its money away:

> Our church is a very special church, I would say. A lot of churches accumulate funds to build their own temple, to build a place for them to have a bigger sanctuary. Our church is about community—we help the community.

Similarly, Linda Yeh observes that the church takes advantage of its human resources as well. She notes that second- and third-generation Asian American professionals have the time and energy to volunteer in the community. The church effectively mobilizes these individuals by encouraging groups of friends to participate in community service opportunities that take only a few hours. She explains,

> We're reminded of what our mission is and what we value. We get Asian Americans into our church, young professional people who have the time and the energy, because we're still young.

Here . . . members who are responsible for that event will come around and talk to individuals. They take the initiative to show that "Hey, we really want to do this and we need your help." It makes it a lot easier for people to take action. When you can do it as a group, it's a lot easier and you're more motivated.

To mobilize volunteer resources, leaders make use of personal ties, facilitate service opportunities, and remind members of their common vision.

Second- and third-generation Asian Americans who visit or have attended Asian immigrant churches often find them alienating and disempowering. Even if the immigrant church hosts English-speaking services, the authority and resources of the church tend to remain in the hands of the older immigrant congregation. In response, Grace Community has developed an organization more suited to those who grew up in the United States, one that is open, democratic, and authentic in its convictions.

An Emerging Subculture: Second- and Third-Generation Asian Americans in Silicon Valley

It felt comfortable to be with people who were like me. Even with cultural references, it's kind of an instant bonding thing. When someone tells you this is the church for second- or third-generation Asian Americans—and you are one—then you know there are people who understand. What it's like to grow up in this culture while trying not only to hold on to, but maybe even learn more about your ethnic heritage. . . .

There was a real start-up energy. Silicon Valley, professionals, we're going to do this! Let's make this church happen, let's make it work! Very exciting! Being able to exchange ideas, work on projects, and feel like you're getting stuff done and you're not bound by the structure, of "Well, we're a committee and we're going to follow Robert's Rules of Order. This is the way we do things." It was another bonding factor.

—Alice Yu, founding member of Grace Community

In these comments, Alice Yu, a fifth-generation Californian who grew up in Palo Alto and works in the media, identifies the two characteristics that bond members at Grace Community and shape the organization of the congregation. Members are Asian American and connect because they understand each other, even though they may not have similar ethnic or family experiences. Members are also Silicon Valley professionals who liken the church to a start-up company; the newness of the enterprise inspires and motivates them.

The third characteristic in Nancy Ammerman's framework of church organization is its culture, "the characteristic ways of acting, speaking, socializing its new members, and the like" (1997b, 54). External factors, such as race and location, shape the contours of the organization's subculture. At the same time, members can creatively construct the organization's subculture so that it may effectively attract new members and grow larger. Grace Community, at its very inception, organized itself around value statements that coincidentally spell "rice." As the church sought to be relevant, inviting, celebratory, and encouraging, it developed a church subculture that draws unchurched Asian Americans. In effect, the church's organizational culture has become an internal source of panethnic solidarity beyond instrumentalism and primordialism.

Relevant to Silicon Valley

> We know that many second- and third-generation Americans feel that church is not for them because they've been marginalized by both the Caucasian church and the immigrant Asian church. We want Asian Americans throughout Silicon Valley to have the opportunity to participate in a family of believers in Jesus who are experiencing God's love, healing, and purpose for life. —Value #1 of Grace Community

The first official value statement of Grace Community is making the church relevant to the lives of its members and the people it seeks to attract. The church pays close attention to their racial experiences and their Silicon Valley lives, major factors that they see as shaping the Asian American community. In order to be relevant to Asian Americans who have moved to Silicon Valley, the church seeks to assist people particularly looking for a sense of belonging. As racial minorities, Asian Americans suffer from the "My Fair Lady Syndrome" and are marginalized. As newcomers to Silicon Valley, they especially need groups to which they can affiliate and where they feel understood. Rob Wu-Schmitz believes:

> I think, for a lot of these people, Silicon Valley is a migratory place. There's this influx of people that are uprooted from communities. And whether

that was someone who grew up in Texas in a primarily Caucasian neighbor-hood and has now landed, or someone who grew up in Hawaii in a primar-ily Asian American environment, the fact is there is a need to connect. There is a need to be among people, not who are like me, but who under-stand what I've gone through. That experience of sometimes being an out-sider, of not fitting.

By acknowledging this marginalization and other common racial experi-ences, such as having high educational expectations or a concern for shame, the church affirms the members' identity and builds community. Cameron Kim suggests that Caucasian churches would not be as sensitive to these matters as an Asian American church:

> One difference I notice is with the sermons. Pastor Steve used to speak about Asian American issues, how it affects our Christianity. What it came down to was how we valued education too much, or our need to save face and not be honest. He would bring those issues up and it was good to hear about our issues from the pulpit.

Similarly, Rob Wu-Schmitz argues that Asian Americans' identity issues, such as dealing with the generation gap, create a need for community:

> One of the big things is connecting, a sense of community. And knowing a sense of belonging. For people who are Asian American, what you see again and again is that there is a feeling of connecting with people who under-stand your experience. That can talk about the experience with being told, "You should speak Chinese or Japanese or Korean" to be a whole person. The conflicts that come in between immigrant parents and nonimmigrant children. The average Caucasian church doesn't understand it.

Over time, however, Pastor Steve no longer made references to the Asian American experience. Instead, this identity became tacitly accepted by all simply because they had already named themselves as an Asian American church. He explains that Asian American identity is so accepted and legiti-mated by the broader society that members and visitors do not question its validity:

> When we said we were Asian American, that attracted certain people. We say we want to reach Asian Americans and their friends. That translates into

all the people in their social circles that tend to communicate in the same way, that have similar cultural values, and kind of like that. . . . [The Asian American grouping] is so common in our culture already. It started in the seventies and it hasn't been let go, yet. We don't have to create it, it's already there.

The church, then, provides institutional meeting space for Asian Americans who seek a sense of community because of their distinct identity.

Besides being relevant to Asian Americans, the church aims to relate to Silicon Valley professionals, who tend to be young and unchurched. To connect with those living in the area, Pastor Steve consciously tries to read the pulse of the congregation and polls the community weekly. Linda Yeh appreciates these efforts:

Grace is a lot smaller and the way Pastor Steve makes his sermons, it's really targeted for our age. Like he would do research about work, about unemployment, about community, about outreach. He does every week, a question of the week. Asking questions like, "How do feel about praying in front of people?" And then he applies it in his sermons the week after. A lot of churches that are too big, it's hard to gather this information and people probably don't take the time.

In addition to knowing the needs of the unchurched, the church resists using Christian language that may sound foreign to this group. Rob Wu-Schmitz says the church recognizes the importance of making people comfortable with the language the church employs. For example, common phrases used during service are "awesome" and "it's like . . ." The church also makes it a point to explain how it understands worship, communion, and offering. He adds, "We don't assume that people have a background in the church. We don't assume that they come from a particular setting."

To be relevant to unchurched Asian Americans, Grace Community provides a sense of community to those who lack social networks. It offers tacit understanding of their Asian experiences in the United States. And it speaks a language that is familiar to its Silicon Valley lifestyle.

Inviting

After one year of visiting church, I became a Christian. It wasn't a hard decision because I know I love God and I want to be able to love in the way that He loves me. And I want to be loved that way, too. It wasn't that hard a decision for me.

—Celia Leung, who came to California from Taiwan for college

The second value statement of Grace Community is "inviting everyone to wholeness and love." Celia, as well as others, speaks of the acceptance she received from Christians that made the church inviting and helped her to understand the love of God. She first met members of Grace Community through a volleyball league and they invited her to the church. Because she had just graduated from college and lacked direction, she was searching for both community and purpose. She says the band members of the worship team invited her to play drums with them, and she gradually became drawn into the church:

> They're not selfish. They're always accepting, even if you make mistakes. They encourage you in a different way. Not just Christians are like that, a lot of non-Christians are like that too. But after my first visit, there was something I wanted to seek.

Celia eventually became baptized at Grace Community even though her mother back in Taiwan is Buddhist. Her story exemplifies how the church wants to introduce Asian Americans to the faith with its accepting relationships.

In inviting everyone to find love and wholeness, Grace Community utilizes American evangelical therapeutic discourse and emphasizes acceptance, healing, and transparency (Jeung 2002; Miller 1997). Derek Miura, a Japanese American manager at a high tech firm, comments that he became a Christian because another church accepted him as an individual during a career crisis:

> My whole identity was my job. So when I lost my job, who was I? And how important was I? I really built my life on hard work and working. Without that foundation, I didn't have anything. I finally realized that.
>
> The people in the church accepted me for Derek Miura. The people at [my work] place accepted me because I was Derek, director of IT. And I really saw the difference.

Using this therapeutic language, Derek explains that he now attends Grace because it encourages emotional wholeness. Derek appreciates Pastor

Steve because he has "matured a lot" and does not just have "head knowl-edge." Instead, Pastor Steve has grown as a person so that he is "now a lot more intimate" and "very transparent."

Nic Chan suggests that Asian Americans like himself tend to be intro-verts but that Grace Community is especially inviting and sensitive to per-sons who are not outgoing:

> The Asian American young adult grouping is another draw. It comes back to the personality thing. You don't have to be [an] extrovert.

Pastor Steve agrees:

> People can come into the church, find someone to marry, develop a whole family life, and still be socially awkward. Because we provide all these social venues that don't require social skills. Loving people and being socially awk-ward are not mutually exclusive.

By encouraging participation in home groups, by constantly inviting new-comers to participate in the life of the church, and by viewing individuals with distinct personalities and needs, Grace Community invites newcom-ers. Currently, about one out of every four members had not gone to church before.

Celebrating Love for God and for Our World

> Worship is our whole-hearted response to His love. We can come to God without pretense because He accepts us and loves us as we are. Therefore, worship at Grace Community encourages everyone to tell his/her story, to laugh or cry together, to celebrate God's life-changing love, and to celebrate that love together in ways that we all understand.
>
> —Grace Community website

In explaining their value of celebration, Grace Community again raises the themes of acceptance, freedom, and love. The worship style at Grace Community calls people to respond to God's acceptance with free and honest expression of heart and mind. Celia describes how the worship songs of Grace Community—mostly contemporary Christian praise music—moved her emotionally and led her to explore Christian-ity further:

I checked out this church. The music was great. The first time I went there, I just cried. I'm a person who cries a lot, but it never occurred to me to be there, be in church, and cry. This was the first time. Something just touched me and I wanted to find out more.

The church combines contemporary music with the use of liturgies, symbols, and the Christian calendar to help people "celebrate God in an understandable way." During worship services, people spend moments in silence, in responsive choruses, and viewing spiritual paintings and stained glass windows on overhead screens. Pastor Steve acknowledges that his church differs from new churches designed for Baby Boomers, but is similar to those for Gen Xers (Flory and Miller 2000):

We probably differ because we have a greater interest as a staff in the traditions of the church, so it has a much more liturgical feel. We keep on increasing the number of candles we use; we have communion every week. We do prayers together and confessions of faith together. There's a lot more participation on the part of the congregation.

Grace Community's worship style contrasts greatly with that of ethnic congregations. Cameron Kim notes that there is more freedom to worship honestly at Grace. He explains:

Koreans choose Vineyard songs that are more emotional—they need that catharsis and you have to cry. The only way you had a good time was when you had an emotional experience. At Grace, people are free to experience God at their own time, at their own pace. It's not as forced.

This freedom corresponds to one of Grace Community's worship principles, which is that worship should "flow" without the need to exert one's will to worship. Indeed, the value that worship be "whole-hearted" and "without pretense" requires the worship ministry team to find songs, art, and language that "allow us to express ourselves in our contemporary culture and to use the creative imagination that God has given us."[16] One visual artist drew murals of the Father, Son, and Holy Spirit looking down on Asian American cartoon characters. These attempts differ greatly from the Asian ethnic church's use of traditional hymns. Celia complains:

The first church I went to in San Diego was very traditional and I didn't feel like singing those songs. Plus it was all in Mandarin. This Mandarin sounds weird, the grammar, you know? It was very foreign, translated. And you lost feelings in it. To me, it was totally different at Grace. A lot of my experiences were personal.

Celebrating God's love at Grace Community does not include any explicit Asian American symbols, songs, or liturgies. It does differ from the worship style at ethnic congregations and indicates the American cultural sensibilities of Asian Americans. Like other postmodern Gen Xers, the second and third generations prefer personal and unforced experiences of worship through contemporary music and mystical, transcendent symbols.

Encouraging Each Other toward Spiritual Growth

Being at Grace has led me further along the lines of "what does it mean to be a person of faith with other people?" I think I definitely grew up with a faith that was well contained, self-contained, and intellectual.

And now when you integrate, "Who am I as a person?" with "How do I interact with people?" and "How does God want me to show love to people?" . . . What's that metaphor where you put some metal in a furnace and it burns off all that bad stuff and solidifies you as well—that's been the type of growth that I've experienced. It comes a lot just because of ministry and being with other people.   —Alice Yu, leadership team member

The last value statement of Grace Community is that they want to spur spiritual growth. As Alice explains, this growth involves developing one's personal relationship with God and one's relationships with others. Spiritual growth entails an increasing sense of emotional intimacy with God and a subjective insight into God's wisdom. Consequently, the emphasis is more on the worshiper's emotional state of being than on increased interpersonal interaction or rational discourse. Like Durkheim, Grace seems to believe that a collective effervescence will lead to deeper, more regular social relationships and greater collective intellectual maturity. Structurally, the church encourages this growth through its Bible studies, small groups, and ministry teams.[17] Through these opportunities, individuals grow as they feel free to question, explore, and learn about God. The church website affirms, "Dialogue is an important means of progress in our spiritual journeys. So we don't shy away from tough questions about our motivations and purposes."

Celia again raises the themes of acceptance and freedom as she talks about her own spiritual journey:

> Later on I start to attend Bible Study group. And all these young people, younger than me—they're so nonjudgmental! I don't have to say something wrong and I grow a lot with them. I attend Alpha course and Beta course and I was always afraid of people looking at me and saying, "Your question is so stupid!" That's my fear and I'm always afraid of not being accepted.

Because members of the church allowed her the opportunity to explore different questions, she eventually converted.

One consequence of giving people too much freedom to explore their own needs, issues, and identity is that the church becomes just a therapeutic support group. At worst, in meeting the emotional and social needs of Silicon Valley professionals, the church perpetuates class-based enclaves based around "lifestyle affinities" (Bellah et al. 1985). People do not grow spiritually or lead lives of justice and mercy. For example, Pastor Steve sees this problem in home groups with young parents:

> What we've found is when they go to home group, they immediately convert it into a support group for people with kids. And that's not what it's supposed to be. It's supposed to be about spiritual formation. And then they don't feel like they have time for Life Transformation Groups.

Nevertheless, Grace Community has been more successful than immigrant congregations and Caucasian congregations in drawing unchurched Asian Americans to the Christian faith. By creating an open atmosphere of inquiry and dialogue and by offering a space where people with similar issues can meet, it encourages spiritual growth.

Conclusion: The Institutional Creation of Asian American Subculture

In theories of panethnicity, sociologists suggest two reasons for panethnic organizational formation. Instrumentalists argue that Asian Americans build coalitions for political and economic reasons. The state creates racial categories and then groups mobilize within these categories for more power and resources. Pastor Steve acknowledges that racial identity is constructed in these ways:

> "Asian American" is a social construct—it doesn't have a whole lot to do with your genes or anything like that. It's a way people think about themselves. So if they fit into that social construct in their own mind, then they probably feel comfortable at Grace.

He adds that experiences of racism also structure the way groups are lumped together:

> There's a historical side to this about how we are in contemporary society. All of the historical, legalized oppression of Asians in the past, that sort of thing. Those things are there in our history and they're manifest now. It's been passed down through generations, where some white kid learns to sing, "Ching-Chong-Chinaman."

Primordialists assert that Asian Americans draw together because they do indeed share a common culture and phenotype. Grace Community is primarily made up of East Asian ethnic groups with a Confucian background. Pastor Steve believes that Asian Americans in his church possess a common communication pattern and share similar understandings:

> I have this theory about rhythms of communication, that every culture has its rhythm of communication. We may be saying the same thing, but to take a musical metaphor, I can be doing it in a 4/4 time and you can be doing it in 3/4 time, so it's not quite connecting.

> Asian Americans often have this problem because they're taught to defer to other people. So they wait until someone's finished speaking before they jump into the conversation. But of course, someone has beaten them to the punch by then. So they don't know how to cut somebody off at the end of their thought.

> Being in an Asian American church helps people with things like that. And you can talk about things like food, and nobody's going to look at you funny when you say you like thousand-year-old eggs. (Laughter)

Both theories contribute to our understanding of Asian American panethnicity, but this study demonstrates how panethnic identity, solidarity, and subculture can be created and sustained through institutions such as Grace Community. Yen Le Espiritu theorizes, "Once established, the panethnic group—through its institutions, leaders, and networks—produces and transforms panethnic culture and consciousness. In the process, the panethnic idea becomes autonomous, capable of replenishing itself" (1992, 164). In the case of Grace Community, a new organization has emerged. Through its practices and values, it draws new members to identify as Asian American Christians. Over time, this panethnic identity has been tacitly accepted by members as it is legitimated by the institution. Through the efforts of cultural entrepreneurs like Pastor Steve, the church has established a distinct church subculture.

Certain key factors determine the establishment of Asian American Christian subculture. As suggested by instrumentalists, the state and educational systems, multicultural ideology, and economic marketing racialize Asian Americans in that they become aware of their group categorization. Through these processes, Asian Americans become aware of their marginalization in broader society, their differences from ethnic immigrants, and the need to affirm one's unique identity. For example, Rob Wu-Schmitz helped establish Grace Community because it was intentionally an Asian American church. He wanted a church home for his children, explaining, "They are Caucasian just as much as they are Asian American. And I want to honor both sides of that in our life together with them."

The professional class background of Asian Americans, such as those attending Grace Community in Silicon Valley, creates particular needs and issues that others may not experience. Although they may see themselves as a marginalized group, they do not see themselves as an exploited class or a particularly oppressed minority. Rather, the privileged background of Grace Community Asian Americans enables them to enjoy certain expensive activities, such as skiing, which become part of their shared subculture. In fact, participating in these activities is the basis for what members consider fellowship and community. Celia Leung enthuses,

> I see a lot of people like me attend Grace and they like to stay. People like me meaning they are first generation here, came here for work or study, and they have no family. They choose to stay because Grace is community. They found stability here and sharing, loving, and activity—fun things to do. To

be able to bond with one another in a deeper sense of relationship. All these fun activities help.

Age and generation also bond Asian Americans and shape subcultural norms, values, and understandings. Grace Community intentionally targets the second and third generations of Asian Americans, because these are the groups that are marginalized by ethnic culture and the dominant Caucasian culture. However, the Asian Americans at Grace Community do not dwell on their marginalization or even address it that much. Rather, having a common understanding about their background increases their comfort level with each other. Reflecting on the differences between Grace Community and Caucasian churches, Cameron Kim observes:

It'll depend on a person's background, but most 1.5, second generation—because they grew up in an immigrant culture—will have an affinity to Asian Americans. I don't think the second generation is far enough removed from the immigrant culture.

Talking to a Chinese American friend, she said her father really favored the boys in her family. We have an understanding that that happens, how that felt. It's a little easier for us to help her along.

In addition, all the members noted that they chose the church because members were of a similar age. Because the Asian American movement did not begin until the late 1960s, only Baby Boomers and Gen Xers have grown up with, and more readily adopted, an Asian American identity. Derek Miura, one of the few grandfathers at Grace Community, explains how Asian American subculture is a relatively young adult phenomenon:

Right now, they have a lot of events that Joan [his wife] and I would not fit into. They have porch events—let's go river rafting! Let's go houseboating! We're going to go bike riding or hike through the mountains! For us, it would be almost like being parents going along with our kids.

Finally, the responses of Asian Americans to ethnic immigrant culture and dominant American culture greatly frame the way Asian American church subculture develops. As Lisa Lowe (1996) writes, Asian American culture is a hybridized construct, where members consciously and unconsciously reject or select aspects of their ethnic heritage and upbringing.

They then include these aspects with their American values and tastes. For Nic Chan, the idea of an Asian American hybridized subculture was novel:

> I was intrigued by Grace, and this concept of an Asian American church, where there wouldn't be this first generation–second generation problem. Grace avoided that conflict between generations.
>
> I have never been to an Asian American church before, so I hadn't thought of the concept. It seemed like a balance for me. I always thought it was a binary kind of deal. You have the immigrant church, and their kids, or a multiethnic church or more Caucasian church.

Like Pastor Steve, he feels Asian Americans retain certain ethnic personality traits, such as introversion and diligence, but value American ideas like acceptance, autonomy, and freedom. Because of this combination of communication patterns and values, he feels much more comfortable at Grace, as do all the others interviewed.

An important feature of a hybridized subculture is the agency of Asian Americans to choose what they value, how they live, and how they relate to one another. Linda Yeh asserts her right to make choices about her identity and lifestyle:

> My parents were raised in Hong Kong and I spent most of my life here. So I've seen what they do at home and I see what people do at work, at school, outside. I see the American ways. I pick what I want. I know the way Chinese parents raise their kids is very dictative [sic], like "I tell you what to do." The American way is very supportive. So when I'm trying to raise my kid, I want to be supportive. I have that choice.

Asian American Christian subculture is thus forged by the unique needs of the second and third generations to affiliate with some institution. Claiming a racial category constructed by the state, Asian Americans draw upon their primordial ethnic culture and their American upbringing to construct a hybridized subculture.

This subculture will probably change as new generations of Asian Americans emerge. Within the Silicon Valley, the next generation will include more mixed-race members and will have grown up in more diverse institutional settings with less of a sense of marginalization caused by having immigrant parents. However, race and class will continue to structure people's lives; perhaps the desire to intentionally promote a distinct Asian

American theology and faith practice will encourage the continuation of an Asian American church.

NOTES

1. Names of individuals are pseudonyms. "1.5 generation" refers to persons who were born outside the United States but grew up in this country.

2. Those who espouse the avoidance of ethnic distinctions in church cite Galatians 3:28: "There is neither Jew nor Greek, there is neither slave nor free man, there is neither male nor female; for you are all one in Christ Jesus." (New American Standard Version)

3. Those who support racial reconciliation and ethnic distinctiveness within the Kingdom of God cite Revelations 21:24 and 26: "The nations will walk by His light, and the kings of the earth will bring their glory into it." (New American Standard Version)

4. I define the identity "Asian American" to include groups within the U.S. Bureau of the Census's racial category of Asian American. "The term 'Asian' refers to people having origins in any of the original peoples of the Far East, Southeast Asia, or the Indian subcontinent (for example, Cambodia, China, India, Japan, Korea, Malaysia, Pakistan, the Philippine Islands, Thailand, and Vietnam). Asian groups are not limited to nationalities, but include ethnic terms, as well" (Barnes and Bennett 2002).

5. Grace Community Covenant Church Mission Statement, http://www.gracecomm-covchurch.org/mission.html

6. I used snowball sampling to obtain a sample diverse in ethnicity and length of membership in the congregation. Their descriptions about the church are overwhelmingly positive, which indicates some bias in what they represent about the church. However, their answers to open-ended questions were similar and reveal some consensus about the character of the church. I belong to another multiethnic church of the same denomination.

7. The breakdown of the county's population is 44.2 percent white, 24.0 percent Latino, and 2.5 percent African American. Those identifying as "two or more races" or as "some other race" constitute 3.2 percent of the population.

8. U.S. Census SF1 (http://www.dof.ca.gov/HTML/DEMOGRAP/SF%201/RACE085.pdf).

9. The county's per capita personal income was the fourth highest in the state in 1999 at $46,649, compared to the state's per capita income of $29,856. Unfortunately, these high incomes mask the lack of affordable housing and the high cost of living in the county. In order to rent a modest one-bedroom apartment in the county at fair market rent at $1,289, residents must make a "living wage" of $24.89 per hour.

10. In Santa Clara County, Asian Americans make up 10.3 percent of those living in poverty and 18.7 percent of Asian American adults did not have a high school degree in 1990.

11. "Poll Finds Positive View of State's Diversity," *Los Angeles Times,* May 14, 2001.

12. Grace Community Covenant Church Mission Statement, http://www .gracecomm-covchurch.org/mission.html.

13. Grace Community's "Porch" events aim to let visitors get a peek into the life of the church to see if they want to enter and join.

14. Grace Community sponsors eighteen home groups based on geographic proximity, gender, and marital status. Usually about eight to fifteen members participate weekly in a home group. The eight to ten Life Transformation Groups involve two or three persons meeting weekly to hold each other accountable to spiritual disciplines such as Bible reading and personal morality.

15. Grace Community has a "Community Involvement Team" that plans and promotes service to local causes. It also has a "Global Involvement Team" to encourage overseas missions and international development.

16. "Worship Principles," Grace Community website.

17. Grace Community offers "Alpha Courses" and "Beta Courses," classes where unchurched people can explore the Christian faith.

13

Sasana Sakon and the New Asian American

Intermarriage and Identity at a
Thai Buddhist Temple in Silicon Valley

Todd LeRoy Perreira

It's almost an invisible phenomenon.

You could walk by them and not even know they are
there.   —Paul Numrich

After a brief chant in the ancient language of Pali, Phramaha Somchai leaned forward to wish the young Lukchai and the others, "Merry Christmas and Happy New Year!" Buddhism is changing in America. At Wat Buddhanusorn located in Fremont, California, mixed-race Thai American families came from celebrating Christmas midnight mass at the Roman Catholic church to perform merit ceremonies in the afternoon at the *wat* (temple).

The emergence of interracial-interreligious families among Thai Americans has created a complex relationship between Thais and *farangs* (whites) and multivalent religious identities. The diverse, multiethnic-multicultural environment of the Silicon Valley has affected the development of immigrant Thai Buddhism. Interracial-interreligious couples and their families, who represent nearly a third of the total membership, are forging new cultural and religious arrangements that have successfully maintained and cultivated a powerful connection to natal identities. The interracial-interreligious couples and their families surveyed in this *wat*

Wat Buddhanusorn's founding abbot Phramaha
Prasert seated in the ubosoth (monk's assembly
hall) in Fremont, California/Todd Perreira.

reflect a growing trend in membership diversity which has important social, cultural, and religious implications at both the institutional (public)
and individual (private) levels.

"Intermarriage," "mixed marriage," and "outmarrying" are all categories
familiar to those in Asian American studies but, until quite recently, most
of the attention has been directed toward Japanese, Korean, and Vietnamese "war brides," leaving largely unexplored relationships consum-
mated outside that history. Where studies not bound to the war brides

phenomenon have emerged, spousal religious identities have escaped the concerns of the researcher, leaving the mistaken impression that religion among Asian Americans and their non-Asian American partners is, at best, only a peripheral issue. In Buddhism in America studies, cross-cultural marriage is wholly nonexistent as a category. Yet the growing diversity of temple membership and questions of identity have important implications for the future prospects of Theravada Buddhism in America.

Today, Nisakorn Suwansareerak, her Anglo-American husband, and their seven-year-old son Lukchai are praying for Nisakorn's recently deceased daughter. First, they took communion at midnight mass. Now, this afternoon, they will call upon the Thai Buddhist way of salvation. Nisakorn Suwansareerak and her husband toss their shoes among the others scattered about. Lukchai follows them into the *bòod* or meditation hall where two monks, Phramaha Somchai Techapanyo and Phramaha Phadung Suttivangso, are leading a small assembly in the recitation of the *Mangala Sutta,* one of the most widely chanted *paritta* in the Theravada Buddhist cultures of Southeast Asia.[1]

Everyone follows the droning cadence of the monks reciting the sacred Pali verses from memory. Both monks are seated in the lotus position on a raised platform as Nisakorn's family joins the others who sit on the carpeted floor below, not in the lotus position but with legs folded beneath them, their feet respectfully pointed away from the monks and the central Buddhist altar. Then the monks offer incense at the altar dominated by a large, golden Earth-Touching Buddha adorned in a saffron-colored robe that hangs off the left shoulder. The Buddha is flanked by two life-size monks standing with palms together (*wai*) and dozens of similar bronze Buddha statues that become successively smaller the further away they are from the main Buddha. The altar alcove is covered with a hand-painted mural depicting traditional Buddhist and Thai legends and scenes of daily life. Ornamenting the altar is a profuse, colorful array of fresh-cut flowers, bowls of fruit, dozens of burning candles, and incense perfuming the air. Little Lukchai, like both his parents, offers three sticks of incense, one for each of the three jewels—the Buddha, the *dhamma,* and the sangha.

Monk Phramaha Somchai sacralizes a brass bowl of water while holding a lit saffron-colored candle above the surface. During this recitation, Phramaha Somchai allows the melting saffron-colored wax to drip onto the surface of the water. Into this mantra-water or *nàmmon,* he dips a bundle of sticks and proceeds to sprinkle the laity who lie in reverent prostration—palms together (*wai*) with head bowed low to the temple floor. The sprinkling of this "holy water" is not so much a cleansing ritual as it is an opportunity for the monks to transfer a portion of good karma to the secular world (Terwiel 1975, 118–119).

Finally, the monks perform *krùadnáam*—a closing ceremony the purpose of which is the dispersal of stored merit and the extension of meritorious *kamma* (Pali for the Sanskrit karma) to beings other than one's self. Ritual bowls and accompanying decanters filled with sacralized water are presented to the laity. As the monks chant, Nisakorn pours water from the decanter over her index finger while concentrating intensively on the person to whom the merit is being offered. On this day, Nisakorn is thinking of her daughter who recently died. Sometimes this merit is directed to living persons, but usually, as in Nisakorn's case, the recipients are the deceased. As she pours the water, her husband joins the ceremony to support his wife. Following the pattern he has seen among others in the temple, he places his left hand on her right shoulder. Their son Lukchai places his hand on his mother's—this will ensure that he is ritually connected to his parents.

While the monks chant a concluding blessing, Nisakorn's husband takes the bowl outside the temple to pour the merit-water into the ground where a nearby tree grows. Pouring it near the tree allows the water to penetrate the soil where it will be taken up by the root system and dispersed in the limbs above. The ritual says, metaphorically and really, that the negative *kamma* or "sin" of the deceased is cleansed, enabling the soul of the departed individual to eventually rise above her status in her previous life to be reborn into a higher status in the next life. Whatever had karmically caused her death is now removed. The deceased youngster's merit for a better rebirth is lovingly stowed up by her family.

Much of the ritual activity described here mirrors what I have seen in numerous temples throughout Thailand, with one important difference—Lukchai is the product of an interracial marriage. Nisakorn is a Thai Buddhist immigrant and her husband is a Euro-American Catholic. Neither has converted to the other's religion, yet both traditions are affirmed and embraced in their marriage. Consequently, Lukchai is the beneficiary of a "double heritage"—he is both Roman Catholic and Theravada Buddhist. According to his mother, Lukchai's inheritance of such a dual religious identity has thus far presented no conflicts for the seven-year-old who is fluent in both Thai and English. At least for now, the child does not feel he has to choose between one or the other. For him, participating in the religious lives of both traditions is essentially normative.

Smiling, Phramaha Somchai asks Lukchai why he has come to the temple today. The boy says he has come to make a wish. "What do you wish for?" asks Phramaha Somchai. "My sister died and I made a wish for her to become an angel," he explains. The boy's mother and Phramaha Somchai share a laugh and the monk tells Lukchai that this is a very good wish. He responds with a brief Pali chant and then leans forward and says to Lukchai and all the others assembled in the meditation hall, "Merry Christmas and Happy New Year!"

Indeed, the majority of families and couples visiting the *wat* on this particular Sunday when I was conducting field research were also interracial.[2] Watching Lukchai and his family interact with Phramaha Somchai that afternoon, it dawned on me that they symbolized a new face emerging in Buddhist America—one which crosses the line drawn by some scholars between "immigrant," "ethnic," or "cradle" Buddhists on the one hand and "convert" or "elite" Buddhists on the other.[3] Lukchai is neither an immigrant Buddhist nor a convert Buddhist. Nor is he an "ethnic" or "elite" Buddhist in the strict sense in which those two terms are employed by scholars of Buddhism. He is a "cradle" Buddhist as much as he is a "cradle" Catholic so this category also proves to be inadequate. We could invoke Thomas Tweed's "hybrid" Buddhism, but even this seems far too generic a term to account for the new social and religious arrangement which Nisakorn's family has made possible. To put all this in perspective, I am reminded of Nisakorn's comment when I asked her if she felt there has ever been any tension arising from her family's decision to embrace an interreligious or multifaith identity.

"No," she smiled. "I believe that all religions are good when they teach people to be a good person. So I take my child to the Catholic church for Sunday Mass and I take him to the Thai temple to *tom bun* (make merit)." Indeed, there are some parallels between *tom bun* and Catholic holy communion. As the monks chant, the pouring water is consecrated and charged with merit, just as the communion water delivers to the Catholic the merit of Christ and the saints. The child sees it as fully normal to go from one ceremony to another. In his own identity he doesn't conceive of being one but not the other.

Reflecting on Nisakorn's emphasis on the universality of religions, I obtained an important clue in probing for an appropriate term that could best signify this new face of Buddhism in America. Like a Picasso painting, it was a face profiled in multiple angles that resisted one-dimensional terms like "cradle," "ethnic," or "elite" Buddhist. I also wanted to avoid a term which, while heuristically useful to the scholar, might be unintelligible or even offensive to the people I was trying to describe (for example, Thais looked perplexed when I told them they were being labeled "Baggage Buddhists" by some scholars [Nattier 1998, 190]).[4]

My search was enhanced when I was reminded of the example of King Mongkut in the film *Anna and the King* (1999). Generally speaking, since the reign of King Mongkut (1851–68)—the man responsible for initiating Thailand's political and economic modernization—Thais have long been interested in Western ways. Prior to assuming the throne, Mongkut had been a monk for twenty-seven years and had engaged in intensive study of the Pali scriptures. He was also a learned philosopher and theologian, studied Latin and English, was deeply interested in science, and skillfully succeeded in introducing Western ideas into the nation without sacrificing Thailand's sovereignty or Buddhist heritage. This high regard for things Western is reflected in the colloquial use of the Thai word *sakon* as a translation for "Occidental" or "Western."[5] The word itself actually means "universal," as in "catholic." *Sasana* is the Thai equivalent for religion.

Taken together, *sasana sakon* would suggest a religious perspective that was all-embracing or universalist. This seems to me, at least provisionally, a useful term in trying to describe the dual religious heritage of Nisakorn's family and their decision to raise Lukchai in both a Thai Buddhist tradition as well as the Catholic faith. Employing this term has certain advantages. In the first place, it shows a sincere attempt being made to invoke a term derived from the Thai language. The word *sasana* is typically conjoined to the name of a specific tradition to form a compound word, for example, *sasanaphud* (Buddhism) or *sasanacrist* (Christianity). Without specifying Buddhism or Christianity, or simply hyphenating *sasana* with terms like Catholic-Buddhist (*sasanacrist-phud* is hardly euphonious), I have chosen instead to employ *sakon,* thereby evoking a more cosmopolitan and universal religious sensibility while still retaining, at least linguistically, what is particular to this multivalent experience—the Thai Buddhist heritage shared by mother and son with the full support of the boy's Catholic father. In this family, there is no attempt at eclectic syncretism between the two traditions; rather, both remain distinct and yet complementary to the degree, I would suggest, that Lukchai could not be fully Buddhist without simultaneously being fully Catholic.

Hyperplurality: Rapid Demographic Change

Nisakorn's family is hardly an anomaly around Wat Buddhanusorn. It symbolizes a growing trend in the Silicon Valley toward new forms of plurality. Indeed, the region's burgeoning racial and ethnic diversity is one of the most dramatic developments to occur since the 1970s. On the cusp of the new millennium, Santa Clara County—better known to the world today as Silicon Valley—had already reached a demographic milestone that the nation as a whole is not expected to achieve for at least another fifty years: sometime in 1999—nobody knows the precise moment—the non-Hispanic white population dropped below 50 percent for the first time, making every racial and ethnic group in the region a minority (Stocking 1999).

The Bay Area's immigrant population grew from 19.5 percent in 1990 to 27.5 percent in 2000—more than twice the national average of 11 percent, and higher than California's total of 26 percent foreign-born residents (Hendricks 2002). This dizzying array of newcomers is also reflected in the linguistic diversity of the region. On a typical day in the Bay Area, more than one hundred and thirty languages are spoken.[6]

With the surge in Vietnamese and South Asian immigrants into the valley since the early 1980s, Asians now constitute the fastest-growing ethnic group in Santa Clara County (Kang 2001). The U.S. census for 2000 reveals that 12.1 percent of the county's 1,682,600 residents, a total of 204,000 people, are immigrants from Southeast Asia (*Census 2000 Summary File*, 2001). This means that Santa Clara County proportionally has the highest ratio of Southeast Asian immigrants of any county in the state, though Southern California has attracted the lion's share of recent Asian immigration. Not only has this enlarged the region's role as one of the nation's principal gateways for new arrivals from other countries, but it also means that the foreign-born population of the nine-county region is even more diverse than the state itself.[7]

The exclusion from the United States of most Asian immigrants between 1924 and the postwar years guaranteed that the Asian American population in the Santa Clara County and the nation as a whole was small. However, revisions in U.S. immigration laws since the 1960s have produced dramatic changes (Hing 1993). Prior to passage of the Hart-Cellar Act of 1965 in which the U.S. Congress revised the national quota system established by the 1924 law that barred Asian immigration to the

United States, the different racial and ethnic groups that flourish today in Silicon Valley were practically unknown to each other. But the 1965 Immigration Act profoundly changed migration patterns, with 40 percent or more of all new immigrants to the United States coming from Asia in recent years (Lee and Fernandez 1998, 325).

In addition, the economic shift away from orchards to computers, from an agricultural to a technological base, has supported the parallel shift away from Euro-American predominance in Silicon Valley (80 percent as recently as 1970) toward a hyperplural culture: a Mexican American sous-chef performs culinary wonders in a local Thai restaurant where a turbaned Sikh takes his family for dinner, while in the background Bing Crosby sings, "I'm Dreaming of a White Christmas."[8] Computer engineers from China, Taiwan, and India streamed into Silicon Valley seeking higher education and careers in the hub of the global technological revolution.

Other factors have also driven the area toward radical plurality. In 1975, after the fall of Saigon hundreds of thousands of Vietnamese sought refuge in the United States, a large contingent of them settling in Santa Clara County. By 1980, approximately 21,400 refuges—known to the world as "boat people"—crossed the Pacific seeking political asylum in the San Francisco Bay Area (*Asian and Pacific Islander Population in the United States: 1980*). That number nearly quadrupled to 84,700 just ten years later, and climbed to 158,000 in 2000 (Hendricks 2002). During the 1980s and 1990s, tens of thousands of other Southeast Asian immigrants made their way to the Bay Area, adding their own strands of identity to the cultural mix. According to the U.S. Census for 2000, Thais (7,700), Laotians (13,450), Cambodians/Khmer (13,100), and Burmese (uncounted) made the San Francisco Bay Area their new home.[9]

However, the U.S. Bureau of Census has acknowledged that these figures may underestimate the actual number of immigrants and refugees living in the Bay Area.[10] Although the 2000 census devised a number of strategies to arrive at a more realistic demographic portrait of Southeast Asian residents and immigrants,[11] ambiguity still clouds the accuracy of these counts. Patterns of migration are extremely complex even when narrowing a study to a specific geographic region. The varied cycles of Southeast Asian immigration have brought substantial differences of culture and socioeconomic standing among immigrant Vietnamese, Lao, Khmer, Thai, Burmese, and Sino-Vietnamese (Smith-Hefner 1999, 8–9).

Attempts to gauge the "religious identity" of Southeast Asian immigrants to the Bay Area are just as speculative. Because the vast majority of these immigrants are "Cradle Buddhists," the temptation is to equate these population estimates with a Buddhist identity. This generalization obscures the fact that there is, or may be, a divergence of cultural practices, speech forms, and so on, from region to region, and class to class.

> In this way, the "ethnic culture" is homogenized, that is, it is assumed that the cultural conventions, including religion, language, norms and expectations, are not only the same for people of a particular ethnic identity, but are also completely accepted and practiced by them all, that there is one "pure," easily identifiable set of ethnic "traditions," religion and speech. . . . There is an associated assumption . . . that people of the same ethnic identity form a cohesive group, an interacting, self-aware community. (Berger and Hill 1998, 9)

In the case of Southeast Asian immigrants, there has been a failure to account for many who are non-Buddhists, such as the Christian Thais and Catholic Vietnamese or the non-Theravada Buddhists like the Mahayana Buddhist Vietnamese. Also unaccounted for are those who claim multiple religious identities such as some Khmer refugees who "converted" to Christianity, the religion of their U.S. sponsors, as an expression of gratitude while otherwise maintaining their Buddhist heritage.[12]

Nonetheless, the Buddhist world of Southeast Asia has traditionally never compartmentalized religious belief and practice from other domains of life. Unlike North America where the separation of church and state has meant that religions are understood to be a distinct sphere competing with other spheres of life, Buddhism in Theravada countries is itself such an essential part of daily life that to be Thai or Lao, in large measure, is *ipso facto* to be Buddhist.[13] But the plurality of religions in North America and the legal separation of religion from other spheres of life pose real challenges to any assumptions which equate ethnic identity with a particular religion. Indeed, in some cases, such as those in the Lao and Khmer communities that spent years in refugee camps before immigrating to the West, religion in general and Buddhism in particular may have ceased to be relevant to everyday life in North America (Van Esterik 1992, 46). Similarly, in the case of Hmong refugees seeking to establish themselves in the United States, Christianity, particularly in its Protestant form, has played a large role in undermining traditional Hmong religious practices and gender relations (Chan 1994).

Among the Thai immigrants surveyed in this study who regularly visit the local temple, 25 percent said that religion was not important in their lives. So, involvement in religious activities at the local Buddhist temple is not necessarily a measure of religiosity among some members.[14] Still, among Lao, Thai, and Khmer communities living abroad, Buddhism, or more specifically the temple, is the most important bond and basis for agreement within the community. But what does it mean to speak of a "community" when it is not rooted or centered in a particular geographic locale? The Thais of Silicon Valley have not established an "ethnic enclave" like a Chinatown. Rather, they are linked together by a *wat* (temple) in the middle of a suburban neighborhood accessed by a network of interstate highways (680 and 880). Waghorne's rich analysis of the Sri Siva-Vishnu Temple in suburban Washington, D.C., underscores a similar experience among the South Asian immigrants she studies. Lawrence Babb's research on modern Hindu communities raises doubts as to whether we can even call this "a community in any normal sense because its territorial dispersion mitigates against the formation of anything resembling corporate ties. The group is probably best conceived as a loose 'congregation.'"[15] To paraphrase Waghorne, in the absence of a particular neighborhood to anchor ethnic space in the inner cities, the Thai temple in the Fremont suburb emerges as "the only concrete embodiment of the community" (Waghorne 1999, 110).

The Wat in Its Thai and American Contexts

Prachirn Chuenrukchart, a former monk who helped found the Fremont *wat* in 1983, explained in an interview that Buddhist temples are as much a cultural as a religious center for Thais in the United States. He says that the temples strengthen community bonds as centers in which to socialize and fraternize. Thus, the third objective cited for founding Fremont's Wat Buddhanusorn is "to serve as a pillar of the Thai community" while the second is "to teach and promote Thai art, language, and culture to all those who are interested." Significantly, only the first objective is specifically Buddhist, the "propagation of the Buddha's teachings and practice."[16] "This is similar to how it was in Thailand fifty or one hundred years ago," he said. "Music, dance, schools, playgrounds were at the temple. That has changed in Thai cities. The focus is not on the temple anymore" (Hendricks 1997, 1B).

Khun Prachirn's remarks point to the two directions in which Thai Buddhist temples have traveled. On the one hand, they underscore Kenneth Tanaka's observation that "ethnic temples serve not only the spiritual but also the cultural and social needs of their members, particularly among the most recent of the immigrant population. . . . The cultural activities have always played a vital part in Buddhist temples in Asia and were integrated into the spiritual life of the communities" (Prebish and Tanaka 1999, 287).[17] On the other hand, while this is historically true, many Thais would agree with Khun Prachirn that this is no longer the case today in the urban centers of Thailand. It is important to understand why in order to appreciate the unique role Thai temples are playing in America and the potential for these new temples to become a locus for the reconstitution of more rural notions of what it means to be Thai even while in suburban Fremont, California.

In Thailand's not-too-distant past, the rural *wat* was clearly the center of a community's ritual and social life. Prior to the development of public schools, for example, villagers were dependent on the *wat* for formal education. Further, as the social and intellectual center of the community, the *wat* was the place one went to for practical and spiritual advice on medical healing, astrological consultation, dealings with the government, or crisis intervention. With the expansion of government services most of these functions have greatly diminished, leaving temples with predominately religious functions. While the temple is still a guardian of tradition and mediates between the laity and its needs for auspiciousness (merit), blessing, and protection, the secularizing forces of modern urban development in Thailand have usurped the *wat*'s centrality in the lives of the people. Thai thinkers such as Phra Prayudh Payutto[18] and the late Buddhadasa Bhikkhu have provided influential critical analyses of modern Thai society and the changing role of the *wat*. Phra Prayudh Payutto strongly stresses the neglect of the *wat*'s educational function while Buddhadasa has argued that the emphasis on conventional merit making (*tom bun*) has reduced Thai Buddhism to a mechanical contract for buying oneself a good rebirth, about as "useless as raising chickens in order to feed the eggs to the dogs" (Mulder 1996, 129).

In many ways, Wat Buddhanusorn embodies Phra Prayudh Payutto's vision of a temple that provides an educational foundation to the community. The temple offers year-round classes that cater to second-generation children enrolled by parents who hope to maintain their family's cultural and religious identity as Thais and Thai Buddhists. Language classes in

written and spoken Thai, as well as classical Thai court dance and music
are offered to the second generation. Instruction in Buddhist philosophy
and meditation are offered to adults. The popularity of such classes is now
dictating the direction of temple growth. Plans are now under way to acquire the adjacent property for classrooms.

Buddhadasa Bhikkhu's vitriolic rhetoric against "superstitious" practices doesn't seem to be making much headway. The desire to *tom bun*
(make merit) is far and away the most important reason for visiting the
temple. Thais are also motivated to go to temple by the sensual concerns
of eating *real* Thai food. This was the second most important reason
given.[19] Meditation was counted as the least important factor for visiting
the temple. Buddhadasa's strong language has apparently done little to en-
hance his popularity beyond a small group of reform-minded intellectuals, mostly in Thailand. Aside from a few monks, no one at Wat Buddhanusorn is interested in the goal of enlightenment.[20]

For the monks the *wat* is a "bridge between Thailand and here." Abbot
Phramaha envisions the Silicon Valley *wat* as a space for the reenactment
of the Thai past and its culture. This *wat* is different from others in the
United States. It preserves the merit ceremonies and deemphasizes meditation. Other U.S. *wats* see *tam bun* merit-generating ceremonies as an in-
filtration of superstitious animism into Buddhism. However, these Westernized meditation centers don't draw many Thais.

The temple has also become a gathering site for Thai elites, including
royal dignitaries and high-ranking civil servants, who often turn up for
public engagements. Indeed, Wat Buddhanusorn is emerging as an important destination for globe-trotting monks in the Theravada world. The
Fremont *wat* is also the only Theravada temple in Northern California to
have been officially consecrated so that all types of religious activities can
take place there, including, significantly, the ordination of new monks.
This last point is important, since one of the main concerns raised in Paul
Numrich's groundbreaking research on immigrant Theravada Buddhist
temples is his argument for the need and cultivation of an "indigenous
sangha" (Numrich 1998). Although Wat Buddhanusorn can now address
this concern, it relies, like all its sister temples in America, on a sangha
comprised almost exclusively of Thai nationals. Presently, there are seven
resident monks at Wat Buddhanusorn. When I asked Phramaha Somchai
Techapanyo if he agreed with Numrich's analysis, he smiled.

"Yes, it's a good idea to have American-born monks," he said. "They
might be able to better relate to the second generation. We need *real*

Americans, not just *luk krungs*" (*luk* means "child," *krungs*—"half," so, literally "half-breeds," the offspring of an interracial couple, without a negative connotation). "I think it's hard for the second generation to be a monk here. I don't know what is pokémon!"

Intermarriage and the Silicon Sangha

Intermarriage in Silicon Valley is transforming the traditional categories of racial and religious identities. Today one in seven babies born in Santa Clara County has parents of two different races (Stocking 1999). California is now the nation's leader in children born to parents of different races (Richardson 2001, E1). Although much of the intermarriage here is driven by Euro-American and Hispanic couples—the two largest "minorities" in the Bay Area—Asians are increasingly part of the mix. In California, approximately one-fifth of the Japanese and Thais marry non-Hispanic whites (Clark 1998, 155). Despite the fact that the current U.S. Asian population is heavily immigrant (over 60 percent of Asian Americans are foreign-born) (Lee and Fernandez 1998) and that historically immigrants are less likely to outmarry because the first generation is more closely tied to a traditional culture that does not sanction outmarriage (Lee and Yamanaka 1990, 287–305), Asian Americans are nonetheless outmarrying at surprisingly high levels—from 25 percent to over 50 percent, depending on ethnicity or national origin of the respondents and region of the country (Lee and Fernandez 1998).

The present rate of Asian outmarriage is all the more impressive in light of the racial prejudice and discrimination historically encountered by Asians in the United States. Antimiscegenation laws that routinely barred marriages between whites and Asians were still in force in at least sixteen states as recently as 1967.[21] Only in the November 2000 election did the last state in the nation, Alabama, remove the last remaining trace of antimiscegenation laws. Today, 5 percent of all U.S. marriages are mixed, with nearly a quarter of those living in California (Pugh 2001, 17A). A recent Current Populations Survey (June 2001) by the Census Bureau shows that there are more than 3 million mixed marriages (ibid.), of which 700,000 are white-Asian couples (Fears and Deane 2001, 1A).

No one knows exactly how many, but according to Phramaha Somchai's own estimate, the number of interracial couples at Wat Buddhanusorn are upward of 30 percent of the total active membership. A long-standing board member believes that it may even be as high as 40 percent. A review of donor names published in temple newsletters in 1999 indicates that the number of interracial couples is 32 percent. These couples are exclusively American males paired with Thai females. No Thai men associated with the *wat* have outmarried. Overall, Asian American women outmarry at a proportionally higher rate than do Asian American men; 21 percent of all Asian women in the United States outmarry compared to 11 percent of Asian men (Pugh 2001, 17A). Among Chinese and Japanese Americans, recent research suggests that escape from Asian patriarchy is a large consideration. Further, the mass media portrays Asian American women positively while depicting Asian American men more negatively (Fong and Yung 1995–96). Yep says that young Japanese, Chinese, and Korean Americans share a similar sentiment:

> For many of us who grew up in North America, a traditional Asian marriage is quite unappealing; it seems emotionally ungratifying, rigid and even oppressive. So, in a reactionary spirit, we tend to romanticize the white, middle-class, American model of marriage. . . . As bicultural individuals, we often talk about enjoying the best of both worlds. (Yep et al. 1998, 91–92)

Recent research has also suggested that there is an Asian American "incest taboo" against marrying within the same race since members of that race are regarded as "fictive kin" or extended family (Fong and Yung 1995–96). This factor may drive Thai women to outmarry. Additionally, among Asian immigrants who have not been granted citizenship status, the desire to obtain a green card to remain in the United States may be another factor driving the decision to outmarry. Of course, social scientific studies tend to overlook the obvious possibility that individuals may be seeking a mutually satisfying sense of love and intimacy. As Mark Fentress, a Euro-American, writes, his parents' reaction to meeting his soon-to-be Chinese American wife Vivian was, "They didn't care if she was Chinese, Swedish, or a giraffe. She was simply this terrific person" (Fentress 1992, 187).

Sasana Sakon: Heirs to a Double Heritage

To explore the religious aspirations of interracial couples, it is important to consider what motivates them to go to the *wat*. In interviews with twelve interracial couples at the *wat*, the most important reason given for going to the temple was to please their family and gain exposure to Thai culture. Typical responses were, "I go because my wife is Thai" and "I go because of my family—for the kids." Of the twelve men interviewed, the majority were Catholic (50 percent) while one was of a Quaker background. The others said they were both Buddhist and Christian. There were no atheists or agnostics, and no one said he was exclusively a Buddhist. Significantly, all but two respondents received their introduction to Buddhism through their *fan,* their romantic partner.[22] The men at Wat Buddhanusorn do not appear to be spiritual seekers for they seem fairly content with their religious identity. Nor do they come in pursuit of a spiritual practice. Unlike other Euro-Americans who have turned to Buddhism, none of those surveyed here listed meditation as the most important reason for going to the temple. Moreover, most Americans who visit Wat Buddhanusorn come because they are affiliated with someone who is already a member. "I have to admit," said one husband, "I probably wouldn't be involved with Buddhism if I hadn't met Ai" (Ai is his Thai wife and mother of their two children).

That family obligation, however, does not mean that participation in the life of the temple is superficial or compelled by a sense of duty. In fact, these men fully participate in the ritual life of the temple alongside their *fans.* To assist them, Wat Buddhanusorn even provides a Buddhist chanting "hymnal" offering a transliteration of the Pali texts, which enables them to follow along with the rest of the community who recite the chants from memory. However, it is never clear which sutra is being chanted and westerners don't use the manual. Typically, the men sit silently and reverently during the liturgy. However, despite what Paul Numrich reports concerning American converts, the *fans* of Thai women do adopt typically Asian lay postures vis-à-vis the monks, namely, kneeling and bowing low before them or sitting at a lower level in conversation (Numrich 1996, 120). Thus, the *fans* of Thai women at Wat Buddhanusorn have neither rejected nor fully converted to Thai Buddhism; rather, they maintain their hereditary religious faith while simultaneously affirming their *fan*'s tradition.

Like the children of these marriages, the *fans* of Thai women at Wat Buddhanusorn are difficult to label. Jan Nattier employs the typologies of sociologists Rodney Stark and William Sims Bainbridge to analyze participants at the periphery of Buddhism. The first of these, the "audience cult,"

> requires no more of its participants than that they attend an occasional lecture, read an occasional book, or perhaps subscribe to a periodical. There is

no community, no ritual, no catechism; the only criterion for inclusion is a vague level of interest. . . . Participants in these activities are often involved in more than one such "cult," and may maintain membership in their hereditary religious faith as well. Participation in an audience cult does not, in other words, result in the replacement of one's existing worldview; it merely adds extra spice to the mix. (Nattier 1998, 185–186)

The second category, that of "client cult," involves a higher degree of personal involvement. Here the participant engages in direct interaction with a member of the group, but this relationship (like that of the psychotherapist and client, on which the category is clearly based) is limited to the client's use of certain techniques received from a teacher, sometimes at considerable expense. As with the audience cult, participation in a client cult does not require the renunciation of one's existing religious affiliation (ibid., 186).

The *fans* of Thai women at Wat Buddhanusorn fall somewhere in between these two categories. These men are "audience cult" members, in that little is required of them in terms of their participation in temple activities. Yet their participation and direct interaction with the monks places them closer to Stark and Bainbridge's "client cult." The limitation of these categories is that the models are framed in terms of religious organizations and not individual members. The notion of an audience and client cult ultimately fails to account for the racial and ethnic identity of the participant while presuming that these people are spiritual seekers.

Sasana sakon better categorizes these participants at Wat Buddhanusorn. The *fans* of the Thai women at the *wat* have neither rejected nor fully converted to Thai Buddhism; rather, they maintain their hereditary religious faith while simultaneously affirming their *fan's* tradition. *Sasana sakon* is therefore an inner and social openness to the interplay between different religious traditions.

Because interracial couples are a growing phenomenon in Buddhism in America, it is increasingly necessary to include them so as to provide a fuller account of the immigrant Thai Buddhist experience. Yet scholarly categories are too dichotomous, inflexible, and exclusive to account for interracial couples and their offspring. *Sasana sakon* captures the universalism that is unique to the experience of interracial and/or interreligious couples and their mutual openness to each other's tradition without collapsing important distinctions.

Prospects for an "Indigenous Sangha" in America

Since direct observation by temporarily living with such couples was not feasible, the best way of testing how religious differences are maintained was by examining survey responses. The responses to key questions were very consistent and consequently provide a strong foundation for making generalizations about this *wat* and possibly others as well. Four questions were designed to elicit how the Thais and their *fan* deal with familiar religious differences.

Should Children Grow Up to Become a Monk or a Nun?

Among Thais, 91 percent said that temporary ordination was acceptable and felt that the decision to enter the monkhood as a lifelong career was up to the child. Only one Thai respondent said that ordination was unacceptable.

Among *farangs* (whites), there was far more ambivalence, as the degree of acceptance and nonacceptance was split fifty-fifty. Wrote one respondent: "It's probably not the best thing for him. If my son wanted to be a monk, I might try to discourage him."

Should Monks Always be Celibate?

If *Farangs* Become Monks, Should They Also Be Celibate?

All Thai respondents were unequivocal in their agreement that monks, even *farang* monks, should remain celibate.

Farangs were again divided, as 67 percent agreed with the Thais that monks, even *farang* monks, should be celibate, while the rest disagreed.

Under Certain Circumstances, Is It Okay for a Monk to Shake Hands with a *Farang* Woman?

Sixty-three percent of the Thai respondents answered in the negative, saying that a monk should never touch a woman.

All but one *farang* respondent said it was okay for monks to shake hands with a *farang* woman.

Should We Let Women Become Fully Ordained Nuns?

Only 33 percent of the Thais surveyed answered this question in the affirmative. Most felt that things should stay the way they are in Thailand. In other words, nuns should not be recognized as having the same status as monks.

All but one *farang* respondent believed that women should have the opportunity to become fully ordained as nuns. (The sole respondent who did not agree said he "was not sure." It should be noted that, unlike the others who are "native" Euro-Americans, he is an immigrant from Kenya.)

The survey responses provide an indicator of the future of the Thai sangha as it matures in America. Paul Numrich has expressed a concern for the cultivation of an "indigenous sangha." However, his study of immigrant Theravada communities did not take up the question of why second-generation males are not turning to monasticism as a career. If there are few American-born Theravada monks, the greatest potential for the future viability of Theravada Buddhism in the United States rests with the second generation. The survey responses indicate that there are two camps concerning ordination. Thais in general are accepting of ordination while Americans are far more ambivalent. Consequently, if second-generation children are potential candidates for ordination, they are most likely to be drawn from couples in which both father and mother are Thai. The potential for monks is smaller among children of interracial couples. Among interracial couples, fathers openly admitted they would discourage such a decision.

Numrich doesn't discuss the reasons why someone would want to be ordained. In Thailand one of the most important functions of Buddhism is to provide an education and social mobility for underprivileged men. Consequently, education within the monkhood does not necessarily create a religious personality or deep thinker about the truths of the *dhamma*. The young monk Waiyaka always dreamed of coming to America. He likely realized that monkhood would be his ticket to the land of his dreams. Anyone who has been a monk for a minimum of five years, or has some formal education (either the equivalent of a B.A. or some command of Pali), and possesses English-speaking, computer skills, or meditation skills is eligible to apply to come. Because Waiyaka is from Chaing Rai in Northern Thailand where there are no universities, joining the sangha enabled him to study in Bangkok for a B.A. and attain the seventh out of nine levels of Pali. At his age, twenty-seven, that is an impressive accomplishment. Now that he has realized his dream of coming to America, Waiyaka is coy about whether he will make monasticism a lifelong pursuit. "I do not know the future," he says. "Maybe tomorrow I disrobe. One day I can be a monk, and the next I can return to lay life. It's easy."

Most of the highly educated young monks leave the order before they have made a meaningful contribution to its development. Their preparation has actually been for a life outside the confines of the temple. Partly, this also reflects the situation in Thai sanghas. They offer little room for bright young people like Waiyaka. As one observer put it, the present state of the Thai sangha "may well be judged to be the most old-fashioned of all Thai institutions; it lacks leadership, vision, purpose and inspiration beyond the guardianship of ceremonies and tradition" (Mulder 1996, 117).

So the better educated monks often leave the order not just because they have achieved their dreams (like coming to America), but also because they feel that they will never stand a chance in the cobwebs of complacency and traditionalism that pervade the upper levels of the sangha. The hierarchy is exclusively controlled by aging patriarchs who seem out of touch with the pressing issues of contemporary Thai society. Niels Mulder observes, "If monks aspire to more than rank and honor, and if they want to make Buddhist thought relevant to modern life, then they are in for a hard time with little chance for success" (ibid.).

Is the situation any better in the newly established *wats* in America? Even if second-generation offspring are motivated to ordain, what kinds of opportunities are available to them that lay life does not already promise? The answer does not bode well for an "indigenous sangha." If Thai Buddhism has traditionally provided an avenue of education and social mobility for underprivileged men, what could it possibly offer the offspring of highly driven, educated, and successful couples working in the Silicon Valley? Precious little, it would seem.

Unlike other Southeast Asian immigrants, many Thais come to the United States already highly educated. They did not come as impoverished political refugees but as economic opportunists seeking a future in a land where on average a new millionaire is created every hour (Hamel 2000 March). Little wonder, then, that the American fathers have had so much trouble with the idea of their sons' ordination. Prior to the interviews, none had even considered the prospect of their sons becoming monks. Most were visibly uncomfortable with the idea. In contrast, with the exception of one woman who was dead against it, all the Thai mothers and fathers were more open to ordination for their sons, especially temporary ordination.

Because monks are viewed as "fields of merit" providing a fertile soil (*naa bun*) for people to cultivate the merit that enhances their (or their deceased loved ones') chances for a better rebirth or improvement of their current circumstances, ordination of one's son, even for a temporary period, has enormous meritorious implications for the parents. This is particularly true for mothers. Although gaining merit is not an exclusively female preoccupation, women are thought to gain tremendous merit by having a son ordained in the temple. In America, where poverty and education are not prime motivators for ordination, the main motivation that remains is the traditional need to make merit for one's parents, especially for one's mother.

Of course, the sacrifice of becoming a temporary monk is no guarantee of genuine spiritual aspiration or knowledge on the part of the novice. A cantankerous middle-aged Thai man at the Fremont temple boasted that he had recently completed a period of temporary ordination. He confirmed that the primary reason for making the sacrifice of becoming a temporary monk was the need to express his gratitude to his mother for all she had done for him. For him, it was the single most important thing a son could do to reciprocate his mother's love. "I don't know anything about Buddhism," he admitted. "I did it for her." So the expression of filial devotion to one's parents, especially to one's mother, overrides interest in Buddhist knowledge or monasticism.

However, the centrality of monasticism to Theravada Buddhism cannot be overstated. In Thailand, the pool of candidates is large—in any given year there are some 266,000 monks and 87,700 novices from which young men are recruited into monasticism as a lifelong vocation (Numrich 1998)[23] The vast majority come from wretchedly poor rural populations. Joining the sangha is often their only chance for an advanced education and escaping poverty. But the social situation in the United States is different. If the pool for monkhood is limited to Thai Americans, it is small. Further, few would find it necessary to turn to monasticism as a means of social mobility. Since temporary ordination is about all that we can expect from second-generation offspring, it seems that serious thought must be given toward developing strategies for the cultivation of monks who would not view ordination solely as a stepping stone to a secular career or as a way of honoring one's parents. These goals do have an important place in Thai Buddhism and the Fremont temple's life. But this situation, as Numrich has argued, highlights the institutional need among Theravada temples in the United States to develop a more "indigenous sangha." What will be needed are American-born individuals who are committed to a long-term monastic career.

While the monks at Wat Buddhanusorn are comprised almost exclusively of Thai nationals, the recent ordination of Phra Mike, a Euro-American who grew up in Fremont, shows that the temple is beginning to take its first step toward cultivating an indigenous sangha. Significantly, Phra Mike's training prior to "taking the robes" included an extended stay in Thailand at a village *wat*. He is also becoming conversant in Thai. He has become popular among Euro-American visitors to the temple and second-generation young men who ordain temporarily. This suggests that "cultural training" as well as instruction in the *dhamma* may be a necessary component in the cultivation of an "indigenous sangha."

It is still early in the historical development of immigrant Theravada Buddhism in the United States. Indeed, of the nearly one hundred and fifty Theravada temples in the United States today, all but one were established after 1970 (ibid., xxi). For practical reasons, the practice of importing monks from the home country has proven to be an effective strategy for helping Thais to adapt to life in the West and is likely to continue in the years ahead. Although scholars and monks have raised concerns about the growing need to develop a native-born *bhikkhu-sangha*, Wat Buddhanusorn is clearly directing its energies toward maintaining a Thai identity among the second generation. In this sense, Wat Buddhanusorn's role as a cultural center for Thais and their progeny is as important as its commitment to observe, preserve, and propagate the teachings of the Buddha.

Yet, the recent ordination of Phra Mike, along with the high rate of interracial families that comprise the temple's membership, suggests that Wat Buddhanusorn is already moving beyond the boundaries of "ethnic" and "cradle" Buddhist labels. This community's embrace of a more cosmopolitan identity constitutes a uniquely American contribution to the emergence of Buddhism in the West. At Wat Buddhanusorn in recent years a new program has begun to take children from the *wat*'s performing arts school to Thailand. Students reconnect with their parents' place of birth and showcase their skills in musical and dance performance at cultural shows. They feel a great deal of pride in overcoming a sense of inferiority when performing in front of "real" Thais who warmly receive them. Such first-hand experiences enable second-generation Thais to better relate to their parents in America. The program is apparently the first of its kind in the United States. To be sure, it speaks of the community's affluence. But programs like these also give new meaning to the notion of "cultural exchange." As monks are "imported" from Thailand to serve the *wats* in America, second-generation members of the community they serve are now being "exported" to learn to interact with Thais in Thailand. Innovative ideas like these underscore the pivotal role that Wat Buddhanusorn is playing in shaping the cultural values and identity of its community.

Postscript: Opportunities for Future Study

Until recently, "scant attention ha[d] been paid to Asian American religions" by the discipline.[24] Scholars of Buddhism in America have paid too little attention to the unique contributions of Asian Americans to the development of "American Buddhism." As Numrich points out, every book-length treatment of American Buddhism minimizes the role ascribed to Asian Americans in forging a distinctly "American" Buddhism (Prebish 1999, 243–244). We might expand on this critique by considering the ways in which interracial and/or interreligious families like those at Wat Buddhanusorn are contributing to a Buddhism that is distinctly American.

Some approach this history in terms of a "spectrum" (Seager 1999). Richard Seager places Theravada cradle Buddhists on one end of the Buddhist spectrum and American convert Buddhists in the Insight or *vipassana* meditation movement on the other end. Although he reinforces a divide between Theravada immigrants and converts (they "live in very different social and cultural worlds"), the spectrum metaphor does allow him to acknowledge some "blurring" between these boundaries. But he speaks of this middle ground in terms of a "creative synthesis." This certainly may be true for some, but it may obscure consideration of other models for the integration of tradition and innovation such as the *sasana sakon* model which Nisakorn's family provides. Without that model, where would Nisakorn's husband and son fit on Seager's spectrum?

Furthermore, the study of Buddhism in America has neither examined cross-cultural marriage nor provided adequate descriptive categories appropriate to the study of intermarriage among Buddhists in America. Individuals and families such as those mentioned in this study remain largely invisible to scholars. The phenomenon of cross-cultural marriages and their offspring is a growing constituency in Asian America that has the potential to be a positive moral force in the American quest for identity. The experiences of these Thai American families in Silicon Valley include coming to grips with social, cultural, and religious questions of belonging and identity.

NOTES

1. The other *paritta* is the *Metta Sutta*. According to Swearer (1995), the *paritta* (literally "protection, safeguard") came to be applied to a group of Pali texts collected in Sri Lanka to be chanted on auspicious occasions.

2. Participant observation, interviews, and surveys were conducted from December 1999 to August 2002. I have changed or edited specific details and collapsed accounts together only where necessary in order to protect the identity of individual community members. Except for the monks at Wat Buddhanusorn, all the names of individuals cited in this essay are pseudonyms.

3. Identifying the complexity of Buddhist identity in America has led Jan Nattier to suggest three categories: "Elite," "Export," and "Ethnic" (or "Baggage") Buddhists. See her essay, "Who Is a Buddhist? Charting the Landscape of Buddhist America" (Prebish and Tanaka 1999, 188–190). Thomas A. Tweed employs "Convert," "Cradle," and "Sympathizer" Buddhists as categories and argues for the hybrid character of Buddhist identity. See Tweed 1999.

4. Asian American Buddhist practitioners typically identify themselves by their country of origin (e.g., Thai Buddhist, Tibetan Buddhist, and so on), by their school of practice (e.g., Soto Zen, Soka Gakkai International, and the like), or by the founding teacher (e.g., Nichiren). It is interesting to note that the majority of Asian American Buddhists reserve "American Buddhists" for non-Asian American practitioners (Tanaka 1999, 5).

5. I am indebted to John Paul Fieg for pointing this out in his book (Fieg 1989, 53).

6. Evin Ollinger, an administrator with Language Line Services in Monterey, California, a company which provides translation services for virtually all police departments, hospitals, health care workers, and 911 operators in the State of California, estimates that there are at least 151 languages spoken in the state in any given year. Of these, easily 130 are spoken in the Bay Area. Personal communication, 27 August 2002.

7. Hendricks 2002. The nine counties that comprise the San Francisco Bay Area are: Alameda, Contra Costa, Marin, Napa, San Francisco, San Mateo, Santa Clara, Solano, and Sonoma.

8. The juxtaposition of cultural diversity in the region is often noted in the

nation's press. A *New York Times* reporter recently encountered a Fourth of July parade in Fremont which included a Sikh float decorated with a model of the Golden Temple in India taking its place alongside those of the Furry Friends animal rescue group and the All Stars Cheerleading Squad (Brown 2001).

9. Ibid. If you expand the Bay Area a tiny bit to include San Joaquin County, an hour's drive east, you get an additional 3,700 Laotians, 10,480 Cambodians, and 6,230 Hmong. If you include Fresno County, a two-hour drive south, you could add another 7,380 Laotians, 4,850 Cambodians, and nearly 25,000 Hmong (Davis, J. 1999, 3B).

10. The U.S. Bureau of Census estimates that Asian Americans were undercounted by 2.3 percent nationwide during the 1990 census, with the Laotian undercount believed to be as high as 30 percent in Oakland, California (Hull 1999).

11. Indonesians and Malaysians, for example, were counted for the first time, while the Burmese remain uncounted as a specific category.

12. A recent lecture (December 1999) at Harvard University by anthropologist Lindsey French on Buddhism and Cambodia confirmed this phenomenon (see also Smith-Hefner 1999, 16–17, 23). Smith-Hefner argues that many refugees "converted" to Christianity, hoping it would guarantee resettlement in an affluent Western country.

13. This of course is a problematic statement in light of the recent histories of Burma/Myanmar, Cambodia/Kampuchea, Laos, and Sri Lanka where scholars like Tambiah speak of a "Buddhism betrayed."

14. J. McLellan's work, cited in Van Esterik, underscores this dynamic between traditional belief and practice and the demands of resettlement in Canada (Van Esterik 1992, 39).

15. Lawrence Babb's *Redemptive Encounters: Three Modern Styles in Hindu Religion* is cited in Waghorne 1999, 108.

16. See the temple's web page at www.watbuddha.iirt.net.

17. See also Tanaka's survey of seven Asian American Buddhist temples in the San Francisco Bay Area where respondents, by a ratio of two (67 percent) to one (32 percent) agree that in America social and cultural concerns predominate over the spiritual and religious aspects of the temple (Tanaka 1999).

18. Phra Prayudh Payutto is also known in the West by two other names, the Ven. Phra Dhammapitaka and Phra Rajavaramuni.

19. Of those surveyed, 92 percent said that going to the temple to *tom bun* was the most important reason, while going to the temple for Thai culture or Thai food was the second most important reason for visiting the *wat*.

20. I agree with John Paul Fieg's observation that "Thais generally tend to think in terms of rebirth into better worldly conditions rather than in attaining a hard-to-understand Nirvana" (Fieg 1989, 10).

21. Thanks to the Loving Decision (12 June 1967), a ruling by the U.S.

Supreme Court, which overturned the existing laws against interracial marriages, no one can send an interracially married couple to jail today.

22. A convenient Thai term, *fan* will allow me to avoid the otherwise cumbersome spouse/boyfriend or spouse/girlfriend terminology. A *fan* means husband or wife, boyfriend or girlfriend, and is used interchangeably. Hereafter, I will employ the term *fan* to signify these relationships.

23. Thailand's Ministry of Education, statistics for 1998 (available at http://www.moe.go.th/moe.html).

24. An admission made on the back cover of *New Spiritual Homes: Religion and Asian Americans* (Yoo 1999). In addition to Yoo, several important edited volumes have emerged in recent years to help rectify this situation, including *Asian Religions in America: A Documentary History* (Tweed and Prothero 1999); *Religions in Asian America: Building Faith Communities* (Min and Kim 2002); and the present volume.

14

We Do Not Bowl Alone

Social and Cultural Capital from
Filipinos and Their Churches

Joaquin L. Gonzalez III and Andrea Maison

Memorial Day, one of the biggest holidays in America, is popular as a day for travel and recreation with friends. At Classic Bowl in Daly City, one of the largest bowling centers in the San Francisco Bay Area, all sixty lanes are occupied by just one associational membership group—the players and their supporters are ministers and members from the Philippines-based Iglesia Ni Cristo (INC).[1] Many members of the church's Daly City locale bowl together every week, and sometimes even twice a week. But brethren from throughout the Northern California district have been gathering to bowl at annual tournaments like this one since the 1970s. The event is a mix of serious athletic competition and lighthearted partying. Team members on the lanes don matching shirts embroidered with the names of their church locales. Behind them, the room teems with crowds of nonbowlers—spouses, children, and friends—who use the tournament as an opportunity to visit brethren from other locales. Sitting in chairs and on the floor, they share homemade lunches, and trade news and stories. It is in this way, over bowling balls and sandwiches, that the widespread membership of the INC in Northern California renews its social bonds.

For this Memorial Day tournament, the enormous bowling alley is packed with thousands of INC members as far as the eye can see. The sea of Filipino faces and strains of Filipino languages that fill the huge room are witness to Daly City's status as the Filipino center of the Bay Area. A visitor is also physically and mentally transported to one of the popular downtown bowling centers in Manila, where it is normal to see such a place filled with Filipino faces.

More than an impressive display of Filipino American culture, however, this gathering illustrates a compelling exception to the claims made by Harvard political science professor Robert Putnam in his acclaimed recent book, *Bowling Alone: The Collapse and Revival of American Community* (2000). Putnam's central thesis is that civic engagement and social connectedness have declined in the United States over the past several decades. Consequently, the success of American society has been compromised. However, segments of the American population—in this case, Filipino migrants in the United States—are increasing their participation in organized group activities, particularly at their churches. Indeed, their heavy involvement in these social activities facilitates their own success within American society, as well as their positive contributions to this society.

Through two case studies, this chapter examines how Filipinos are bringing back social capital to the fabric of American society through the churches they have taken over from declining congregations or established on their own. It also shows how they blend Filipino cultural practices and beliefs to create new and stronger sociocultural capital. Finally, it analyzes the transnational nature of the sociocultural capital spread globally through the Filipino diaspora.

On Social and Cultural Capital in America

Although Putnam is not the first to "capitalize" human networks, connections, norms, and religion, his neo-Tocquevillian discussions of social capital and its significant decline in America have certainly become a centerpiece of recent discussions (Putnam 1993, 1995, 1996, 2000). Putnam's work has spawned a plethora of studies across scholarly disciplines and global geographies (see Schuller 1997; Halpern 1999; Norton, Latham, and Sturgess 1997). Putnam says that an intensification of social networks, which one gets with church growth, increases the norms of reciprocity and trustworthiness that glue a society together. "Civic virtue," he writes (2000, 19), "is most powerful when embedded in a dense network of reciprocal social relations. A society of many virtuous but isolated individuals is not necessarily rich in social capital." Churches and other religious organizations have played a unique role as incubators of civic virtue in the United States (ibid., 65–79). However, social capital comes in two forms, both of which are necessary for a healthy society. On the one hand, "bonding social capital" is made up of the inward-focused connections of a social group. They create strong in-group loyalty that needs to be balanced by "bridging social capital," the outward-looking social ties that "encompass people across diverse social cleavages" (ibid., 22–23). Warner argues that religious groups create their identities by bounding themselves off from other groups but are also key sites of bridging activity (1999). Religious groups produce matching rhetorics, which Bramadat (2000, 59–68) has called "fortress" and "bridging" rhetorics.

According to some analysts, Putnam overemphasizes the social connections and disconnections of a society while not accounting for the independent causal role of culture. In "The Forms of Capital" (1986) Pierre Bourdieu distinguished between three forms of cultural capital: embodied capital, which represents what an individual knows and can do; objectified capital, found in material objects; and institutionalized capital as found in schools. In *Habits of the Heart* (Bellah et al. 1985, 272–281), Robert Bellah took a Durkheimian turn in his analysis of the cultures of social separation versus social coherence. More recently, at the Institute for the Study of Economic Culture, Peter Berger has been analyzing the difference that economic cultures make. In sum, these scholars make a strong case for considering both social and cultural capital.

It is no secret that a primary source of America's social and cultural capital is its more than a hundred thousand churches, mosques, temples, synagogues, and other places of worship and congregation. Savvy politicians tap churches and other religious organizations during elections. Having a charismatic preacher as a close friend can be as good as having solid party machinery. In so doing, they are replicating an old American tradition. Since its early days as a nation, America's religious organizations have been the breeding grounds of volunteerism, philanthropy, and civic behavior (Greeley 1997). Churches are not only places of worship, but also spaces for the cultivation of civic engagement and sites for political recruitment, incorporation, co-optation, and empowerment (Verba, Schlozman, and Brady 1997). But even this enduring institution, according to Putnam, has not been spared serious decline in terms of membership and related activities. Technological developments in communication and recreation and changing attitudes toward politics and the role of women are partly to blame for this trend. Although many thought that the spiritual and patriotic fervor following the tragedy of September 11, 2001, would start a sustainable renaissance of faith and church-based volunteerism, recent "controversies," such as the one that rocked the Catholic Church over what to do with priests who have committed sexual abuses, have virtually wiped out any gains. The aftershocks of these morbid revelations will probably be felt for an extended period of time, further eroding memberships, contributions, patronage, and networks.

In *Bowling Alone,* Putnam notes that, while the number of bowlers has increased 10 percent over the past thirty years, league bowling is down 40 percent. Given this decline in organized recreational activity, it is not surprising that far fewer Americans are affiliated with other types of organizations—political, civic, or religious. This is particularly the case among the American-born descendants of the early European immigrants. Even black churches, which were once launching pads of African American empowerment, have witnessed a noticeable thinning out of their congregations. As a result, many faith-based spaces and networks of churches, schools, and social services have been abandoned. Memberships have also been consolidated for the sake of maintaining administrative and operational overheads.

Yet, our study shows that not all secular and spiritual gathering places in American communities are emptying. On the contrary, a number of them are full and expanding. However, they are no longer filled with the European American (white, Caucasian) or African American faces that have historically comprised their memberships. Instead, immigrants from places we consider "new," including East and Southeast Asia, Latin America, the Caribbean, and the Middle East have replenished these faith-based institutions and their social and cultural capital production. In San Francisco, churches are sites for Filipinos, other Asians, and Latin Americans to bond with each other while simultaneously building bridges with the non-Filipino, non-Asian world. Also, the churches are a habitus for the renewal, preservation, and transmission of cultural capital in the form of community concern, family values, and a work ethic. This is particularly evident in America's "gateway cities" which are primary entry points for newcomers to the United States (see Warner 2000).

How Is This "New" Immigration Impacting San Francisco Society?

San Francisco's cultural, racial, and ethnic diversity today is the logical result of its history as a Spanish missionary site, center of gold rush activity, and staging location for America's forays to the eastern hemisphere. The heavy commercialization of San Francisco brought in many waves of immigrant groups starting in the early 1800s. By the middle of the century, the city had already become a mixed bag of Irish, English, German, Italian, Mexican, and Chinese cultures. But the Irish presence, at 33 percent of the city's population, was particularly felt in politics, business, and religion. In the early 1900s, there was an influx of Portuguese, Japanese, and Filipinos. At about the same time the African American community arrived in significant numbers.

The twentieth century brought to the San Francisco Bay Area peoples from all geographic regions of the world, from Latin America to South Asia. The U.S. Immigration and Naturalization Service (INS) became one of the most visible public agencies in the San Francisco Bay Area, and the terms "INS" and "green card" have been mainstreamed into the local discourse of San Franciscans.

The results of the millennium census (i.e., Census 2000) show a significant demographic shift. The American-born whites of San Francisco now make up less than half the total population. African Americans represent less then 8 percent of the total population. The numbers of both racial groups show a rapid decline from the 1990 census. Meanwhile, Asians, Pacific Islanders, and Hispanics now make up close to 50 percent of San Francisco residents. Since the 1965 Immigration Act increased the influx of "new" immigrants, these newcomers have not only replaced declining economic capital, but also brought with them social capital in the form of organizational affiliations and social practices. They brought not only churches, but also the quintessentially American practice of league bowling!

Growth of Filipino Community and the Rise of Their Churches in San Francisco

Estimated at more than 320,000 according to the 2000 U.S. Census, the Filipino community in the San Francisco Bay Area is a major part of the larger diasporic migration to the United States, which now numbers two million. Migratory waves from the Philippines, after its 1898 annexation by the United States, has led to the steady growth of Filipino migrant worker attendance at local Catholic and Protestant churches. The growing number of Filipino immigrants also increased church attendance rates at that time. Between 1920 and 1929, 31,092 Filipinos entered California, and more than 80 percent of them went through the port of San Francisco (California Department of Industrial Relations 1930). The end of World War II, the 1972 declaration of Martial Law in the Philippines, and the passage of the 1965 U.S. Immigration Act further promoted the immigration of Filipinos to the United States.

Up to the 1930s most Filipinos were hired in the farm areas to work as agricultural workers, but many also stayed in the cities to work as domestic helpers and manual laborers in the hotel industry. According to Dioscoro R. Recio, Sr., a Watsonville, California, farmworker, originally from Banga, Aklan Province of the Philippines, "Missionaries came to the barangay and told us about America. They said there were many jobs and opportunities there" (Recio 2000, 1). In addition a large group of "pensionados" or U.S. government scholars came to study at American universities.

During this period, close to 90 percent of Filipino migrants were single males, between eighteen and thirty-four years old. It was difficult to start a family, since there were few women from the Philippines. To complicate matters, Filipino men were "discouraged" from marrying Caucasian women by antimiscegenation laws. Instead many Filipino men married women who were Mexican, African American, or from other nonwhite ethnic groups. However, the antimiscegenation laws did not apply to Caucasian men who wanted to marry Filipina women. One of the first recorded baptisms in San Francisco was held on November 8, 1914, when Isaac Braan, originally from Raleigh, North Carolina, and his Filipina wife, Gregoria Pena, brought their infant daughter, Erminda Celeste, to Saint Patrick's Church. The Braans would later bring their two other children, born in 1916 and 1917, to the same church to receive the same religious sacrament. Church records indicate that a few other Filipino American children's baptisms also followed during the years to come.[2]

To combat the restlessness of the largely male Filipino immigrant group and encourage them to channel their socioemotional energies toward morally appropriate activities, the leaders of the Diocese of Seattle and San Francisco sponsored the creation of Catholic Filipino Clubs (Burns 2000). In 1922, the Catholic Filipino Clubs in Seattle and San Francisco were born. Around six hundred workers from Seattle registered and availed of the services of their club, while in San Francisco, Archbishop Edward J. Hanna and the Community Chest became active supporters of the popular Catholic Filipino Club. The club became the hub of social activities for the estimated five thousand Filipino residents of the city. Aside from the Catholic Filipino Club, there were two other Filipino Catholic organizations—the Catholic Filipino Glee Club and the Catholic Filipino Tennis Club. Other Filipino groups availed of club space, posted activities, and recruited members from those who went there (Lenane 1935).

During the mid-1920s, the Caballeros de Dimas Alang, a Masonic-style club-cum-religious brotherhood, was also established in San Francisco by Pedro Loreto. By 1929, another fraternity called the Legionarios del Trabajo was formed in Stockton and San Francisco. Other famous fraternal groupings were the Gran Oriente Filipino and the Knights of Rizal. Many Filipino Catholics joined these quasi-Masonic Filipino organizations because they felt discriminated against in the "Caucasian-dominated" Catholic churches. Besides, some of the new immigrants had brought with them to America their memories of negative experiences and corresponding revolutionary thoughts about the Catholic Church.

After World War II, many Filipinos who served in the U.S. military also decided to try out greener pastures away from their native land. Immigration increased further with the passage of the Immigration Act of 1965, which encouraged a new wave of highly skilled professionals like doctors, nurses, engineers, and accountants to move to the United States. Their families were allowed to join them (see Cordova 1983; Bonus 2000). For several decades, San Francisco was the most popular gateway city for Filipino immigrants. By 1960 there were 12,327 Filipinos in the city of San Francisco.

The arrival of Filipinos in large numbers after 1965 occurred as San Francisco's religious institutions were declining. By the late 1960s, many

TABLE 14.1
Filipino Population in the San Francisco Bay Area

County	Number
Santa Clara	76,060
Alameda	69,127
San Mateo	59,847
San Francisco	40,083
Solano	36,576
Contra Costa	34,595
Sonoma	2,697
Napa	1,759
Marin	1,389
Total	321,333

Source: U.S. Census Bureau 2000.

older San Francisco Catholic and Protestant churches experienced a serious decline in active memberships and financial contributions. Downtown churches started to close at an alarming rate. Commercialization, fires, and earthquakes drove people out of the area. Sunday mornings were especially quiet: no strollers and no churchgoers. Because of a lack of money for maintenance, many churches closed permanently. Then, large numbers of Filipinos and other Asian immigrants arrived, promoting a "second coming" of Christianity to downtown San Francisco. Once almost dead churches started to be spruced up with new members and money. Itinerant congregations competed to see who could lease space in previously empty churches. By 1990 the number of Filipinos in San Francisco had more than tripled since 1960, and by 2000 over 320,000 Filipinos lived in the Bay Area.

The Filipino immigrant revitalization of local religion is strikingly evident in the Roman Catholic churches. The Filipinos have driven attendance and finances up while also changing the culture of the Catholic churches. In the vast Archdiocese of San Francisco encompassing the counties of San Francisco, San Mateo, and Marin, Filipinos now constitute one out of four Catholics, according to Noemi Castillo of the Archdiocese's Office of Ethnic Ministries (interviews, May–June 2001). According to official 2000 estimates, there are now more than 90,000 registered Catholic parishioners in the archdiocese, out of an estimated population of more than 150,000 Filipinos.

Filipinos already make up a significant part of the leadership of San Francisco Bay Area Catholic churches. Officially, there are now thirty-nine priests, twelve full-time deacons, five sisters, and thirty lay workers of Filipino descent in the fifty-two parishes of San Francisco.[3] The Council of Priests in the archdiocese is chaired by Reverend Father Eugene D. Tungol, a Filipino pastor.[4]

Some of the earliest Filipino Catholic missionary congregations to work in San Francisco and other parts of the United States were religious organizations of Filipina women. In December 1955, the Benedictine Sisters of Ilocos Sur came to help Filipino families in the Salinas area. The Sisters opened a religious class for preschoolers. They were also instrumental in creating the Legion of Mary and Our Lady of Antipolo Society, popular devotions to the Virgin Mary practiced in the Philippines. In 1959, the Manila-based Religious of the Virgin Mary (RVM) started their overseas mission in the Sacramento area, followed by Honolulu in 1972 and San Francisco in 1982. Today they assist with the spiritual needs of parishioners in Saint Patrick's Church and Our Lady of Mercy Church. Starting with an overseas mission in Hawaii in 1964, the Dominican Sisters of the Most Holy Rosary from Molo, Iloilo Province in the Philippines, then moved to the mainland, starting with San Francisco in 1982. The Dominican Sisters have made an impact by helping run Catholic schools and by assisting in devotions and services at Saint Charles Borromeo Church and Holy Angels Church. By the late 1990s, thirty-two Philippine-based congregations had religious sisters working in the United States (Macalam 2001; Burganoy 2001).

Among local churches, the biggest beneficiaries of this Filipino influx were Catholic churches in the area of town heavily populated by Filipinos. Then known as "Happy Valley," today it is a largely industrial neighborhood called the "South of Market" district. Some of these historic churches were Saint Patrick (founded in 1851), Saint Joseph (founded in 1861), and Saint Rose (founded in 1878). Another favorite among Manilatown and Chinatown Filipino residents was Old Saint Mary's Cathedral (founded in 1854).

One church that has been influenced by this growth in Filipino immigration is Saint Patrick's Catholic Church. Its dynamic Filipino pastor, Monsignor Fred Bitanga, says somewhat proudly, "Filipino parishioners practically saved the historic church from serious demise." Saint Patrick's is presently staffed by Filipino priests, Filipina nuns, Filipino deacons, and Filipino lay workers. Daily noon services are popular among Filipino workers in the bustling downtown area, while Sunday services draw loyal parishioners not just from the city but from all over the Bay Area.

Filipinos have also filled Catholic churches in the outlying areas, especially South San Francisco and across the bay in the Diocese of Oakland. Saint Andrew's Church, Our Lady of Perpetual Help Church in Daly City, and Saint Augustine Church in South San Francisco have Filipino priests preaching to memberships that are more than 80 percent Filipino.

Tagalog masses are held at Saint Patrick's Church and Saint Boniface Church in San Francisco as well as Holy Angels Church in Colma. Filipino-American choirs, devotions to the Santo Niño, San Lorenzo Ruiz, and Mother Mary are very common. Seven parishes perform the same Catholic rituals that are traditionally performed in the Philippines. This includes the *Simbang Gabi,* a series of early morning masses that take place in the nine days leading up to Christmas. The *Flores de Mayo* ritual honoring Mary, and the Easter *Salubong,* a dramatic enactment of Mary meeting the risen Christ, are also being integrated into the regular church calendar.

Catholic groups that are popular in the Philippines, such as the El Shaddai, Jesus Is Lord Movement, Bukod Loob sa Dios, Couples for Christ, and Divine Mercy have also multiplied rapidly among Filipino Americans. The El Shaddai group, which is headed by the charismatic, Manila-based "Brother Mike" Velarde, and which claims millions of active members, meets regularly at the Cathedral of Saint Mary of the Assumption and other Catholic churches in the Archdiocese of San Francisco.

Another big beneficiary of the Filipino inflow to San Francisco is the archdiocese's Catholic school system. In September 1963, thirty-eight of the forty-five elementary schools in the city reported only a total of 680 Filipino children in attendance. The largest numbers were at Catholic schools: Sacred Heart Elementary (78 percent), Saint Paul (42 percent), Star of the Sea (41 percent), Saint Peter (38 percent), and Saint Monica (28 percent) (Foudy 1963). By the 1980s and 1990s, San Francisco's Catholic elementary and high schools experienced a surge in Filipino enrollment, as immigrants from the 1960s and 1970s began sending their children to religious schools. New arrivals and their families also contributed to the increase. By 2000, Corpus Christi Elementary School had become more than 75 percent Filipino in its student body. Aside from Corpus Christi, elementary schools at the Church of the Epiphany, the Church of the Visitacion, Saint Elizabeth, Saint Emydius, Saint Finn Barr, Saint John the Evangelist, Saint Kevin, Holy Angels, and Our Lady of Perpetual Help have student populations that are close to 50 percent Filipino. The student populations of some of the Catholic high schools in the archdiocese are currently between 20 and 25 percent Filipino, including Sacred Heart Cathedral Prep. Furthermore, Catholic tertiary institutions like the University of San Francisco have also experienced a rapid growth in Filipino student enrollment (Castillo 2001).

Protestant Filipino immigrants have also reinvigorated San Francisco church cultures and created transnational networks through their evangelical missions from the Philippines (Reed 1990; Almario 1993, 119–125). Waves of Filipino immigration brought Methodists, Presbyterians, Baptists, Adventists, Episcopalians, Mormons, and Witnesses, who were themselves products of American missions in the Philippines. These immigrants successfully established flourishing congregations all over the San Francisco Bay Area. Many of them have taken over houses of prayer and worship that used to be all European American. Peter Burnett, California's first governor, would probably never have expected that Saint James Presbyterian Church in Visitacion Valley, which his family attended, would one day be transformed into a church pastored and populated by brown-skinned Filipinos from across the Pacific Ocean. Similar changes have taken place at Saint Francis and Grace United Methodist churches in the Sunset District, which were originally Irish American but have since become predominantly Filipino.

Filipino Methodist immigrants started arriving in San Francisco early in the century. In 1920, only two decades after the establishment of Methodist churches in the Philippines, they established the Filipino Wesley Methodist Church. The congregation went on to change its name to the Filipino Fellowship Church. By the 1930s, around one hundred Filipino Protestant Christians in San Francisco were registered with the Filipino Christian Fellowship and the YMCA's Filipino Christian Endeavor.

Reverend Arturo Capuli is the third Filipino pastor of the Saint Francis and Grace United Methodist Church (San Francisco). His two predecessors, Reverend Leonard Autajay and Reverend Juan Ancheta, were originally trained as Baptist ministers. All three started their training in the Philippines and then pursued advanced theological studies in the United States. The present congregation was a merger between the Filipino Wesley Methodist Church and Parkside Methodist Church, a predominantly Caucasian congregation whose membership was rapidly declining. Over the years, the Caucasian congregation diminished rapidly and it became an almost all-Filipino group. Saint Francis and Grace United Methodist Church is one of three UMC churches that has an active Filipino ministry. The other two UMC churches are in Geneva Avenue, San Francisco, and Southgate, Daly City. There are a total of twenty-two UMC churches in the San Francisco Bay Area. All of them have large Filipino memberships (Capuli 2001).

In 1925 Hilario Camino Moncado, one of the early Filipino labor migrants at the sugar plantations of Hawaii, founded the labor-orientated Filipino Federation of America which eventually became the Equifrilibricum World Religion, popularly known as the Moncadistas. The Filipino labor leader claimed to be the reincarnated Jesus Christ. Moncado was looked up to by his fellow workers and religious followers as the person who would deliver them from the economic exploitation, unfair treatment, and racial discrimination that they were experiencing in American society. Unlike other social organizations during those times, which were notorious for their gambling, dancing, and drinking, Moncado's group claimed to promote a clean and upright lifestyle. Equifrilibricum gained a foothold among the Filipino workers in San Francisco (Mercado 1982).

As early as 1967, Iglesia ni Cristo migrants to Hawaii began gathering other brethren in Oahu, Hawaii. In 1968, the Iglesia ni Cristo established its first overseas congregation in Honolulu, Hawaii. After a month, Brother Erano Manalo proceeded to San Francisco, California, and officially established the first INC congregation in the continental United States (Reed 1990). In less than forty years, it has expanded to twenty-four American states and seventy countries. Some of the largest INC congregations in the United States are found in the Bay Area. Offering both Tagalog and English services, the INC has more than fifteen hundred members in the San Francisco and Daly City locales alone.

The San Francisco Filipino-American Seventh-Day Adventist Church organized in 1967. It is committed to preparing its believers for the second coming of Jesus. While the church endeavors to minister to people of different cultures, it exists primarily to reach individuals of Filipino backgrounds, offering Bible classes in several languages—two in Tagalog, one in Kapampangan, and one in English—every Saturday (Ebora 2001).

Faith Bible Church of San Francisco (FBC) held its first service in April 1971 at the 21st Avenue Baptist Church. It grew and is now proudly supporting missionaries all over the world. From this "mother" congregation other Faith Bible churches have sprung in Oakland, Vallejo, Pittsburg, and in other countries.

The first Filipino Jehovah's Witness congregations were established in the farming areas of Stockton in 1974 and Salinas in 1975. In the 1980s and 1990s, the number of Filipino Witnesses increased rapidly. There are now twelve Filipino American congregations in the San Francisco Bay Area. Each of these Filipino American congregations has around one hundred active members. The San Francisco area congregations are found in Alameda, Daly City, El Cerritos, Hayward, Milpitas, Salinas, San Francisco, San Jose, Stockton, Sunnyvale, Vallejo, and West Sacramento (Laguardia 2001). Beginning with two Bay Area congregations in the early 1970s, the Filipino-American Jehovah's Witnesses have grown to twelve congregations. Members have to know Tagalog to participate in their Filipino services. The fact that this missionary organization would limit its membership to Tagalog speakers testifies to the large pool of potential Filipino members in the Bay Area. Meanwhile, the Filipino ward of the Church of

Jesus Christ and Latter Day Saints in Daly City, which also began in the 1970s, has grown to more than three hundred and fifty members.

Filipino-Style Social and Cultural Capital Formation

Through the churches they joined or established, Filipino immigrants have contributed tremendously to building San Francisco civil society and its social and cultural capital. Through commitment to their churches, Filipinos bring with them their social relations, kinship ties, networks, emotional commitment, traditions, beliefs, customs, and practices that promote community self-help, the spirit of trust, and self-reliant attitudes and behavior. These are manifested in the well-recognized Filipino values of *bayanihan* (attitude of community self-help), *bisita* (kin visits), *panata* (vow), *pagkamagalang* (respectfulness), *bahala na* (fatalism), *utang na loob* (debt of gratitude), and *pakikisama* (getting along with others).

To foster a strong sense of community and pride, many San Francisco churches have made accommodations to popular Philippine languages and dialects such as Tagalog, Ilocano, Cebuano, Kapampangan, Bicolano, and Ilonggo. Some Tagalog hymns have even found their way into the English services. Reverend Jeremiah Resus says that the blending of spirituality and the immigrant experience at his Saint James Presbyterian Church has aided in the creation of a perspective that frames new identities orientated toward feeling accepted, assimilating, and enduring hardships. The church, he says, "is a place that changes perceptions of reality and supplies perspective to face challenges in life. As a community, St. James provides a sense of identity for immigrants. . . . Membership in the church allows the process of assimilation, movement into American life, a sense of belonging." The pastor also says that the church provides a sense of belonging by encouraging marriages and job seeking.

Filipino immigrants use their churches for community gatherings, group meetings, dances, fiestas, graduations, parades, processions, bingo nights, birthday parties, anniversaries, cultural presentations, and the like. Many senior citizens and retirees find companionship and camaraderie in their churches. For instance, members of the San Francisco Filipino-American Seventh-Day Adventist Church regularly visit elderly and sick fellow members who are in the hospitals, care facilities, or at home alone. The need for senior citizen care has grown over the years with the influx of

Filipino war veterans, many of who are in their seventies and eighties and have no family support system in the United States.

Filipino American churches reach out to non-Filipinos, nonmembers, and the San Francisco Bay Area community at large, contributing thousands of dollars in public services to Bay Area cities. Some common civic activities are blood drives, tree plantings, the cleanup of public places, and food distribution to homeless and other needy people. Some churches also provide space for the community. Local social service organizations regularly visit Filipino American churches to impart information and educate members on welfare, health, and other programs. Local politicians have officially hailed many of these contributions, which further integrate Filipino churches and their memberships into the larger San Francisco society.

Filipino congregations also contribute to San Francisco society by helping new Filipino immigrants in their adjustment to America. As Reverend Capuli of Grace United Methodist Church says, "The grace of God makes people productive members of society (that is, taxpayers, professionals with valuable services to offer) and individuals with strong moral character and which value family." At some churches, members provide assistance to newcomers by volunteering to pick them up when they arrive at the airport. Private basements often become temporary housing until fellow members find their own places to stay. New members are often carpooled to church services while they are still familiarizing themselves with roads and public transportation routes. At these churches, bulletin boards are typically filled with important leads ranging from job opportunities to baby-sitting offers. Church members have been known to hire fellow members to work for their companies. Training sessions to upgrade skills are even offered for free through some churches. Some interest-free loans are exchanged between trusting members, especially those who are related or who come from the same province or town. Used cars and trucks are lent out, donated, or sold at a substantial discount.

Some Filipino churches, like the Saint Francis and Grace United Methodist Church and the Saint James Presbyterian Church, rent out space for preschool education. They also allow local nonprofit organizations such as Alcoholics Anonymous, or candidates for local office to use their space free of charge. Saint Francis and Grace United Methodist Church provided valuable meeting space for San Francisco Mayor Willie Brown during his first campaign for public office, in 1963. The church effectively became a key point of contact with the neighborhood and the larger network of Bay Area Filipinos. The congregation also allows community groups in the Sunset District to use their space, including other churches that do not have buildings.

With the support of their San Francisco congregations, the mission work of Filipino American churches has been able to expand in the United States, the Philippines, and many other countries. Many Filipino American churches also finance American Christian missionaries in the Philippines. They also render much-needed financial and spiritual support to projects and programs of their "home" churches in the Philippines. Pastors in the Philippines attest to the valuable contributions of Filipinos in America toward the restoration and beautification of old historic churches as well as the building of new chapels. After all, their home churches are probably the places where Filipinos who have migrated to America prayed to God to facilitate their departure from the Philippines. When natural calamities strike, such as earthquakes, fires, and typhoons in the United States, the Philippines, or elsewhere in the globe, Filipino American churches provide relief goods and members to help in disaster management. For instance, Saint Francis and Grace United Methodist Church sent scholarship money for seminary and college students in the Philippines, clinics in Palawan, and aid to victims of the Mount Pinatubo disaster in 1991. These acts of giving are part of their *utang na loob* (debt of gratitude) to their homeland. Some new immigrants may feel that it is part of their *panata* (vow) not to forsake the place where they were born, a distant source of social energy.

Two Case Studies:
Transnational Sociocultural Capital Formation

The following two case studies provide microviews of the process of transnational sociocultural capital formation in two of the most influential Filipino Christian congregations in the San Francisco Bay Area. These are the Iglesia Ni Cristo, a local branch of an independent, Philippines-based Christian church, located in Daly City, California, just south of San Francisco, and Saint Patrick's Catholic Church, which is located in downtown San Francisco.

Case 1: Iglesia Ni Cristo (INC), Daly City Locale

Helping each other is the "Iglesia Di Cristo state of mind," members say. They call each other "*Kapatid,*" the brethren, and the worldwide network of INC churches is like an extended family. The church provides central support for its members who are new immigrants. However, it is so supportive as to be insular. The church is a bank of social capital for its members, but is a bit of a monastery too.

On every first Saturday of the month, members of the Daly City locale of the Iglesia Ni Cristo bring friends and neighbors to church. These Bible lessons, called Grand Evangelical Missions or GEMs for short, are rare opportunities for outsiders to learn about the insular fundamentalist church. At a GEM last year, after hymns and prayer Resident Minister Brother Lorenzo took his stance before an open Bible at the pulpit. Gripping the podium with both hands, he looked intently at the audience. "What does God command us to do, brothers and sisters?" He paused and looked at the congregation. Picking up the Bible, he pointed at a passage, saying, "In 1 Corinthians 12:25, God commands his chosen people to 'be united in the same mind and the same judgment.'[5] God has so adjusted the body that there may be no discord . . . but that the members may have the same care for one another. Brothers and sisters," he declared, "God commands us, his chosen people, to think and act together. We must be unified."

For the fundamentalist Iglesia Ni Cristo, members attend to the biblical imperatives quoted by Brother Lorenzo as behavioral guides designed to strengthen the social cohesiveness of the congregation. Their leaders believe that helping one another succeed as individuals benefits the church as a whole. A central part of the church's spiritual mission is what we would call building social capital.

The church encourages its constituents to have a sense of personal connectedness to one another that transcends distance. Church members believe they will always find unqualified acceptance and support from brethren anywhere. Brethren easily can detail the practical and emotional support the church provides them when they are away from home or settling someplace new. For instance, Marie,[6] a young woman from the Daly City locale, was planning to move to Connecticut to attend medical school. Before she left, she talked about her anxiety about the transition. "The biggest reassurance I have," she said, "is the knowledge that there is an Iglesia Ni Cristo congregation in my new neighborhood. It will serve as my 'home away from home.'"

Official church structures also help the transition of migrant brethren to new locations. First, members are strongly encouraged to move to a place where there is another Iglesia Ni Christo locale. The English-language *God's Message* and Tagalog-language *Pasugo*, weekly magazines published by the church, list contact information for every Iglesia Ni Cristo congregation throughout the world so that members like Marie can locate INC congregations in unfamiliar places. The brethren there will give her rides to and from church, enroll her in the Kadiwa singles group, and introduce her to new friends.

Mr. and Mrs. Santos are also migrant church members who moved from Manila, Philippines, to Daly City to live with their daughter. Before they moved, they informed the Resident Minister of their church in Manila of their plan; he forwarded their files to the Resident Minister in Daly City. The new congregation prepared to welcome them. In Daly City, the Santos were made part of a group of three families whose spiritual, emotional, and physical well-being is overseen by a church officer. In addition to leading prayers in the Santos's home, the officer might also ensure their practical needs. He might inquire whether they were successful in locating the local Social Security office. Do they need help securing a driver's license? Are they familiar with Pacific Super, the nearby supermarket stocked with Filipino goods? If needed, the Daly City Locale has classes, such as English as a Second Language and Driver Education, which are geared toward new immigrants like the Santos. The specialized assistance and social structures that the church provides are relatively consistent from place to place.

In the Philippines, the INC has a long-standing tradition of partnering with social service agencies to provide for needy members and nonmembers. There are many examples of such services including free medical and dental care, housing for people dislocated by natural disaster, and literacy programs. In addition to such long-term programs, the church also organizes its members for one-time activities like blood drives and planting trees in sites damaged by erosion. These practices are carried over to the United States also.

Bay Area INC churches regularly join in civic activities of the Red Cross and local governments. Over the course of a year, INC Bay Area churches have initiated blood and food drives, free cholesterol screenings, neighborhood cleanups, and tree plantings. Local government officials have taken notice. For instance, on June 28, 2001, Mayor Carol L. Klatt declared "Iglesia Ni Cristo Week" in Daly City. The Daly City Council has also awarded the Iglesia Ni Cristo a number of community citations including the "Most Outstanding Volunteer Group Award." "The congregation's civic activities and volunteer effort occur year-round, time and again, they have come through, regardless of the odds and obstacles," Mayor Klatt said (Mayor's Message 2001).

Of course, local officials also recognize the potential political power of the church. Indeed, Daly City (California, USA) has an official partnership across the Pacific with Quezon City (Philippines), the home of the headquarters of the Iglesia Ni Cristo and several important educational, medical, and religious institutions. Consequently, the current Daly City Mayor, Michael Guingona, a Filipino American official who presently sits on the Sister City Commission, was careful to pay a courtesy call on the Iglesia Ni Cristo's leadership in the Philippines last year.

The INC also sees itself as giving back to the community in unseen but more fundamental ways. First, it believes that the church's moral code encourages its members to be law abiding, hardworking, and oriented toward community service. In other words, it encourages people in the Protestant ethic and good citizenship. Second, the church says its missionary work, which spreads these values to others, is also a public service.

Case 2: Saint Patrick's Catholic Church, San Francisco

Saint Patrick's Church builds on the sense of continuity between the Philippines, where the majority is Catholic, and the United States. Filipino ushers greet new immigrants and seat them among the congregants, most of whom are also Filipino. More often than not, the celebrant is a Filipino priest. Aside from the Gothic Revival architecture, the new Filipino immigrant usually feels that he or she is still in Manila, especially during the monthly Tagalog mass. Icons refer to popular devotions in the Philippines, like those to the Mother of Perpetual Help and the Divine Mercy flanking the high altar. The Holy Infant Jesus (Santo Niño) is enshrined close to the center of the sanctuary. Lorenzo Ruiz, the first Filipino saint, also has his own shrine. Even the Black Nazareno, an icon of Christ revered by many male Filipinos at the Quiapo Church in Manila, has a place.

Many Filipino Catholics are not content to pay their respects to their saints simply through prayer—through their touches, caresses, and affection for the saint as if he were a living person, they have worn off the paint on Lorenzo Ruiz's feet and the Nazareno's right hand. For Filipino parishioners Saint Patrick's Church is one of the few places where they can engage in such an active form of devotion without being self-conscious. They can even pray and confess in their native language or through bicultural priests. Dual citizenship, that is, allegiance to both the Philippines and the United States, is an accepted mental state here in this church. Filipinos claim that this definitely eases their acculturation to the United States.

The present population of Filipino immigrants tends to obscure the fact that St. Augustine's was one of the citadels of Irish Catholicism in the Bay Area and that after most of the Irish left the neighborhood, the church was a forlorn space empty of all but priests. Filipinos have filled the church with life and also have the run of the parish, from the rectory to the lay organizations. All resident priests and deacons are Filipinos born and trained in the Philippines. In addition, the parish frequently hosts visiting priests from the Philippines. Even the nuns come from a Filipino religious order, the Religious of the Virgin Mary (RVM), founded in Manila during the seventeenth century.

The Filipino presence led to the formation of new parish organizations and the revitalization of existing ones. For example, the Saint Patrick's chapter of the Holy Name Society, an international Catholic confraternity, has its roots in the chapter established at the parish of Guadalupe in Makati, a city in Metropolitan Manila. In fact, the Filipino immigrant population has become the main influence on the social life of the parish. Every December since the 1980s there has been a celebration of Misa de Gallo, the nine early-morning masses before Christmas particular to the Philippines. The parish also recently reinstituted Filipino-style breakfasts after mass, and there are plans for a Filipiniana night for the feast of Saint Lorenzo Ruiz. The food and refreshments are the highlight of many parish organization meetings.

Many new Filipino immigrants, especially those from small towns, operate within the mental construct of a Philippine *poblacion* (or town plaza), wherein the church is at the center of the plaza surrounded by various governmental institutions and social gathering places. Because Saint Patrick's helps Filipino immigrants adjust to American life by reinforcing Filipino cultural values and behaviors, it ensures their loyalty toward the parish. In San Francisco's South of Market area, Saint Patrick's is the center of gravity that draws Filipinos back even when they have moved to the suburbs.

For example, the parish's lay organizations provide the newly arrived with an instant network of individuals who share common interests and who have made similar adjustments to a new country. Personal connections are made and a common religious devotion is experienced. Indeed, personal connections play a major role at Saint Patrick's. Parishioners frequently consult the priests for advice and assistance about their problems. Further, although Saint Patrick's does not have many formal social programs, the church draws upon the extensive social outreach resources of the Catholic Archdiocese of San Francisco.

Saint Patrick's also has informal partnerships with neighborhood-based organizations like the West Bay Filipino Multi-Service Center, South of Market Teen Center, the South of Market Health Center, the South of Market Job Training Center, Arkipelago Bookstore, Filipinas Restaurant, and the Filipino Veteran's Equity Center. Further, these local groups and the church often play an advocacy role for Filipinos. They have successfully lobbied the U.S. Congress to recognize Filipino World War II veterans by grants of American citizenship. These organizations have also leveraged funds from the City and County of San Francisco for Filipino youth and their families. The church and community-based organizations (CBOs) have a symbiotic relationship: the parish helps new arrivals maintain a connection to the Philippines, while the neighborhood organizations help them make a successful start in their new home in the United States.

Conclusion

Filipino immigration to the San Francisco Bay Area has provided a critical mass of loyal churchgoers who are now replacing social and cultural capital in the San Francisco area lost since the midseventies. In particular, religious and ethnic organizations had almost collapsed in some areas. This situation meant that there were too many atomized individuals per block for a healthy community to be built on mutual recognition, trust, and the ownership of public life. Some areas had become socially blighted and anomic.

Originating from a country with a long history of Christianity and faith-based organizing, Filipino immigrants have transformed vacated church spaces and places into sanctuaries for incorporation and acculturation rooted in Filipinized cultural traits, norms, beliefs, exchanges, interactions, and iconography. With the "blessings" of their churches, they have formed cultural groups and networks that simultaneously maintain transnational linkages and local social power centers.

The *kasamahan* (togetherness) implicit in "bowling together" is a cherished feature of Filipino faith and fellowship. Perhaps it is not surprising, therefore, that bowling and church are both integral parts of Filipino culture. Indeed, Filipinos' love for bowling—a pastime derived from their colonization by America—has produced many bowling greats, including *Guinness Book of World Records* record-holder Rafael "Paeng" Nepomuceno, a six-time world champion. He is one of the inspirations behind the Philippines' global circulation of cultural information; Filipinos are reviving the popularity of bowling together in a "bowling-alone" America.

Even in an era of church and state separation, there is much room for convergence through the development of social and cultural capital to meet the needs of rapidly changing communities. Many San Francisco Bay Area governments have discovered this and are crafting public policies to nurture sociocultural capital formation among the city's diverse populations. With the strong support of Filipino religious leaders, the City and County of San Francisco, for instance, have established a fifteen-member Commission on Immigrant Rights to protect the civil rights of new immigrants and dismantle barriers to their full civic engagement. San Francisco is one of the few cities in the United States to have such a commission. In another unprecedented move, the Commission now requires all city and county agencies to provide better language access. More than forty thousand Filipino residents of the city benefited from this move. The pioneering settlers from Germany, France, and Italy were never able to achieve such a milestone. The San Francisco Board of Supervisors has also promoted proimmigrant policies including declaring San Francisco a "City of Refuge" for all immigrants, legal or illegal. City Hall now hosts new cultural days for most of the major ethnicities, including June 12, Philippine Independence Day, at which religious organizations display their civic commitment.

NOTES

1. This chapter shares the preliminary findings of the Filipino component of the larger University of San Francisco's The Religion and Immigration Project (TRIP), an initiative supported by the PEW Charitable Trust and the Jesuit Foundation.

2. Information taken from Saint Patrick's Church *Baptismal Registry,* in Raleigh, North Carolina.

3. According to other priests interviewed, others have been serving in unofficial capacities while visiting as tourists (B1-B2 visa), studying at Bay Area universities (F-1 visa), or participating in exchange programs (J-1 visa).

4. Archdiocese of San Francisco Official Directory, various years; Catholic Directory of the Philippines, various years.

5. Specifically, the apostle Paul said, "I appeal to you, brethren, by the name of our Lord Jesus Christ, that all of you agree and that there be no dissentions among you, but that you be united in the same mind and the same judgment" (1 Corinthians 1:10, Revised Standard Version).

6. All personal names in this chapter are pseudonyms, so as to protect the subjects' privacy.

Bibliography

Abusharaf, Rogaia Mustafa. 1998. Structural Adaptations in an Immigrant Muslim Congregation in New York. In R. Stephen Warner and Judith G. Wittner, eds., *Gatherings in Diaspora: Religious Communities and the New Immigration.* Philadelphia: Temple University Press, 235–261.

Administration on Aging. 200. AOA Racial and Ethnic Composition. http://aoa.gov/aoa/stats/profile/default.htm.

Alex-Assensoh, Yvette, and A. B. Assensoh. 2001. Inner-City Contexts, Church Attendance, and African-American Political Participation. *Journal of Politics* 63: 886–901.

Allaire, Saralynn H., Michael P. LaValley, Stephen R. Evans, George T. O'Connor, Margaret Kelly-Hayes, Robert F. Meenan, Daniel Levy, and David T. Felson. 1999. Evidence for Decline in Disability and Improved Health among Persons Aged 55 to 70 Years: The Framingham Heart Study. *American Journal of Public Health* 89: 1678–1683.

Almario, C. R., ed. 1993. *Evangelization in Asia: Proceedings of the Asian Congress on Evangelization.* Quezon City: Claretian.

Alumkal, Anthony W. 2000 June. Ethnicity, Assimilation, and Racial Formation in Asian American Evangelical Churches: A Case Study of a Chinese American and a Korean American Congregation. Ph.D. dissertation, Princeton University.

Ammerman, Nancy T. 1987. *Bible Believers: Fundamentalists in the Modern World.* New Brunswick: Rutgers University Press.

———. 1991. North American Protestant Fundamentalism. In Martin E. Marty and R. Scott Appleby, eds., *Fundamentalisms Observed.* Chicago: University of Chicago Press.

———. 1997a winter. Spiritual Journeys in the American Mainstream. *Congregations: The Alban Journal* 23, 1: 1–10.

———. 1997b. *Congregation and Community.* New Brunswick: Rutgers University Press.

Anderson, Roger T., Margaret K. James, Michael E. Miller, Angela S. Worley, and Charles F. Longino, Jr. 1998. The Timing of Change: Patterns in Transitions in

Functional Status among Elderly Persons. *Journal of Gerontology: Social Sciences* 53B: S17–S27.

Angel, Jacqueline L., and Dennis P. Hogan. 1992. The Demography of Minority Aging Populations. *Journal of Family History* 17: 95–115.

Ankerberg, John, and John Weldon. 1991. *The Facts on Hinduism.* Eugene, OR: Harvest House.

Asian and Pacific Islander Population in the United States: 1980. U.S. Bureau of the Census, GPO: Washington, DC.

Atal, Yogesh. 1970. Alternation and Conversion as Qualitatively Different Transformations. In Gregory Stoner and Harvey Faberman, eds., *Social Psychology through Symbolic Interaction.* New York: Ginn.

Babb, Lawrence A. 1981. Glancing: Visual Interaction in Hinduism. *Journal of Anthropological Research* 37: 387–401.

Badr, Hoda. 2000. Al-Noor Mosque: Strength through Unity. In H. R. Ebaugh and J. S. Chafetz, eds., *Religion and the New Immigrants: Continuities and Adaptations in Immigrant Congregations.* Walnut Creek, CA: AltaMira Press, 193–227.

Bagby, Ihsan, Paul M. Perl, and Bryan T. Froehle. 2001, April 26. *The Mosque in America: A National Portrait.* Report from the Mosque Study Project. Washington, DC: Council on American-Islamic Relations.

Baker, F. M. 1994. Suicide among Ethnic Minority Elderly: A Statistical and Psychosocial Perspective. *Journal of Geriatric Psychiatry* 27, 2: 241–264.

Banton, Michael, ed. 1966. *Anthropological Approaches to the Study of Religion.* New York: Praeger.

Barna Research Group. 1999, October 15. Atheists and Agnostics Inflating Christian Churches. www.bama.org.

Barnes, Jessica, and Claudette Bennett. 2002 March. *The Asian Population 2000: Census Brief.* Washington, DC: U.S. Bureau of the Census.

Barth, Frederik. 1994. Enduring and Emerging Issues in the Analysis of Ethnicity. In Hans Vermeulen and Cora Govers, eds., *The Anthropology of Ethnicity: Beyond Ethnic Groups and Boundaries.* Amsterdam: Het Spinhuis.

Ba-Yunus, Ilyas. 1997. *Muslims of Illinois: A Demographic Report.* Islamic Studies Institute. Chicago: East West University.

Becker, Penny. 1999. Making Inclusive Communities: Congregations and the "Problem" of Race. *Social Problems* 45, 4: 451–472.

———. 2002. *Religion and Family: Understanding the Transformation of Linked Institutions.* Princeton: Princeton University Press.

Bellah, Robert, Richard Madsen, William Sullivan, Ann Swidler, and Steven Tipton. 1985. *Habits of the Heart.* Berkeley: University of California Press.

Bender, Courtney. 2003. *Heaven's Kitchen: Living Religion at God's Love We Deliver.* Chicago: University of Chicago Press.

Bennett, Tony. 1995. *The Birth of the Museum: History, Theory, Politics.* London: Routledge.

Bennetta, Jules-Rosette. 1986. The Narrative Structure of Prophecy among the Maranke Apostles: An Alternative System of Religious Expression. *Semiotica* 61: 1–2.

Benvenuti, Francesco, L. Ferrucci, J. M. Guralnik, S. Gangemi, and A. Baroni. 1995. Foot Pain and Disability in Older Persons: An Epidemiological Survey. *Journal of the American Geriatrics Society* 43: 479–484.

Berger, Peter. 1963. Charisma and Religious Innovation: The Social Location of Israelite Prophecy. *American Sociological Review* 28: 940–950.

———. 1967. *The Sacred Canopy.* Garden City, NY: Doubleday.

———, ed. 1999. *The Desecularization of the World: Resurgent Religion and World Politics.* Grand Rapids, MI: Eerdmans/Ethics and Public Policy Center.

Berger, Rosemary, and Rosanna Hill. 1998. *Cross-Cultural Marriage: Identity and Choice.* Oxford: Berg.

Bharati, Agehananda. 1970. Pilgrimage Sites and Indian Civilization. In Joseph W. Elder, ed., *Chapters in Indian Civilization,* 1. Dubuque: Kendall, Hunt, 83–126.

Bhatia, Renee, and Ajit Bhatia. 1996. Hindu Communities in Atlanta. In Gary Laderman, ed., *Religions of Atlanta: Religious Diversity in the Centennial Olympic City.* Atlanta: Scholars Press.

Billings, Dwight, and Shaunna Scott. 1994. Religion and Political Legitimation. *Annual Review of Sociology* 20: 173–201.

Bleuler, Eugen. 1910. Vortag uber Ambivalenz. *Zentralblatt fur Psychoanalyse* 1: 5266–5268.

———. 1911. Dementia Praecox, oder Gruppe der Schizophrenien. Leipzig: Deuticke.

Bogen, Elizabeth. 1987. *Immigration in New York.* New York: Praeger.

Boggess, Scott, and Carolyn Bradner. 2000 May–June. Trends in Adolescent Males' Abortion Attitudes, 1988–1995: Differences by Race and Ethnicity. *Family Planning Perspectives* 32, 3: 118–123.

Bond, Michael Harris, ed. 1986. *The Psychology of the Chinese People.* Hong Kong: Oxford University Press.

Bonus, Rick. 2000. *Locating Filipino Americans: Ethnicity and the Cultural Politics of Space.* Philadelphia: Temple University Press.

Booth, Alan, Ann C. Crouter, and Nancy Landale, eds. 1997. *Immigration and the Family: Research and Policy on U.S. Immigrants.* Mahwah, NJ: Lawrence Erlbaum.

Booth, Wayne C. 1991. The Rhetoric of Fundamentalist Conversion Narratives. In Martin E. Marty and R. Scott Appleby, eds., *Fundamentalisms Comprehended.* Chicago: University of Chicago Press.

Bourdieu, Pierre. 1986. The Forms of Capital. In J. Richardson, ed., *Handbook of Theory and Research for the Sociology of Education.* New York: Greenwood Press.

———. 1990. *The Logic of Practice.* Trans. Richard Nice. Stanford: Stanford University Press.

Bramadat, Paul A. 2000. *The Church on the World's Turf: An Evangelical Christian Group at a Secular University.* Oxford: Oxford University Press.

Brooks, Charles R. 1989. *The Hare Krishnas in India.* Princeton: Princeton University Press.

Brown, Patricia L. 2001, May 26. With an Asian Influx a Suburb Finds Itself Transformed. *New York Times.* http://www.nytimes.com/2001/5/26/national/26frem.html.

Burganoy, Sister Gloria. 2001 May–June. RVM, Religious of the Virgin Mary. Interviews.

Burke, Kenneth. 1970. *The Rhetoric of Religion.* Berkeley: University of California Press.

Burns, J. M. 2000. *San Francisco: A History of the Archdiocese of San Francisco.* Vols. 1 and 2. France: Girold Gresswiller.

Buss, Martin. 1979. The Social Psychology of Prophecy. In J. A. Emerton, ed., *Prophecy: Essays Presented to Georg Fohrer on His Sixty-fifth Birthday 6 September 1980.* Berlin: de Gruyter, 1–11.

———. 1981. An Anthropological Perspective upon Prophetic Call Narratives. *Semeia* 21: 9–30.

Busto, R. V. 1996. The Gospel according to the Model Minority: Asian American Evangelical College Students. *Amerasia Journal* 22: 133–147.

Caldwell, Patricia. 1983. *The Puritan Conversion Narrative: The Beginnings of American Expression.* Cambridge: Cambridge University Press.

Calhoun-Brown, Allison. 1996. African-American Churches and Political Mobilization: The Psychological Impact of Organizational Resources. *Journal of Politics* 58: 935–953.

California Department of Industrial Relations. 1930. *Facts about Filipino Immigration into California.* San Francisco: Department of Industrial Relations.

Capuli, Rev. Arturo (Grace United Methodist Church, San Francisco). 2001 March. Interviews.

CAREN. 2000. Lifelong Learning and Aging in Place: In Celebration of the Tenth Anniversary of the Founding of Chinese American Retirement Enterprises (CAREN) Inc. Washington, DC: CAREN.

Carlson, Eve. 1991 November. Trauma Experiences, Posttraumatic Stress, Dissociation and Depression in Cambodian Refugees. *American Journal of Psychiatry* 148: 1548–1551.

Carnes, Tony. 1999, May 24. Gambling Away the Golden Years, reporter for cover story. *Christianity Today.*

———. 2002. *Glorious Pilgrimage: Immigrant Incorporation in Faith Based Organizations, Report.* Baltimore, MD: Annie E. Casey Foundation.

————. 2004. *Catastrophe, Ethnomethodology and History.* Dordrecht: Martinus Nijhoff.

Carnes, Tony, and Anna Karpathakis, eds. 2001. *New York Glory: Religions in the City.* New York: NYU Press.

Carroll, Robert P. 1979. *When Prophecy Failed: Cognitive Dissonance in the Prophetic Traditions of the Old Testament.* Seabury Press.

Cashman, Richard I. 1975. *The Myth of the Lokamanya: Tilak and Mass Politics in Maharashtra.* Berkeley: University of California Press.

Castillo, Noemi (Director, Office of Ethnic Ministries. Archdiocese of San Francisco). 2001 May–June. Interviews.

Caswell, Michelle. 1997 March. Hinduism on the World Wide Web: Darshan, Diaspora, and the Body in Sacred Cyberspace. Senior Thesis, Columbia University.

Census 2000 Summary File [California]. 2001. California Digital Library: Oakland, California. http://countingcalifornia.cdlib.org.

Cha, Peter T. 2001. Ethnic Identity Formation and Participation in Immigrant Churches: Second-Generation Korean American Experiences. In Ho-Youn Kwon, Kwang Chung Kim, and R. Stephen Warner, eds., *Korean Americans and Their Religions: Pilgrims and Missionaries from a Different Shore.* University Park: Pennsylvania State University Press, 141–156.

Chai, Karen. 1998. Competing for the Second Generation: English-Language Ministry at a Korean Protestant Church. In R. Stephen Warner and Judith G. Wittner, eds., *Gatherings in Diaspora: Religious Communities and the New Immigration.* Philadelphia: Temple University Press, 295–331.

————. 2000. Protestant-Catholic-Buddhist: Korean Americans and Religious Adaptation in Greater Boston. Ph.D. dissertation, Harvard University.

Chan, Florentius. 1998. To Be Old and Asian: An Unsettled Life in America. *Aging* 358: 14–15.

Chan, Jeffrey Paul, Frank Chin, Lawson Fusao Inada, and Shawn Wong. 1991. *The Big Aiiieeeee! An Anthology of Chinese American and Japanese American Literature.* New York: Meridian.

Chan, Sucheng, ed. 1994. *Hmong Means Free: Life in Laos and America.* Philadelphia: Temple University Press.

Chang, Carrie. 2000. Amen. Pass the Kimchee: Why Are Asian Americans on College Converting to Christianity in Droves? *Monolid: An Asian American Magazine for Those Who Aren't Blinking,* 1 (1): 1–9. http://www.monolid.com/articles1.html.

Chen, C. C. 1997. *Psychology of Chinese People.* Oxford: Oxford University Press.

Cherry, Conrad, Betty A. Deberg, and Amanda Porterfield. 2001. *Religion on Campus.* Chapel Hill: University of North Carolina Press.

Chester, Barbara. 1990. Because Mercy Has a Human Heart: Centers for Victims of

Torture. In P. Suedfeld, ed., *Psychology and Torture.* New York: Hemisphere, 165–184.

Ch'i, His-sheng. 1976. *Warlord Politics in China, 1916–1928.* Stanford: Stanford University Press.

Ch'ien, Evelyn. 2000 April–May. Spirituality: Evangelicals on Campus: Asian American College Students Are Making the Grade with God. *Inside Asian America* 3: 16–25.

Chong, Kelly. 1998. What It Means to Be Christians: The Role of Religion in the Construction of Ethnic Identity and Boundary among Second-Generation Korean-Americans. *Sociology of Religion* 59, 3: 259–286.

Chong, Mary Keng-Mun. 1998. Factors Influencing the Role of Women in Christian Ministries in the Chinese Church. Ph.D. dissertation, Fuller Theological Seminary.

Chronicle of Higher Education: Almanac Issue. 1997. 44: 18.

Chu, Gordon, and Ju Yanan. 1990. *The Great Wall in Ruins: Cultural Change in China.* Honolulu: East-West Center.

Chung, Douglas K. 1992. Asian Cultural Commonalities: A Comparison with Mainstream American Culture. In Sharlene Maeda Furuto et al., eds., *Social Work Practice with Asian Americans.* Newbury Park, CA: Sage, 27–61.

Clark, William A. V. 1998. *The California Cauldron: Immigration and the Fortunes of Local Communities.* New York: Guilford Press.

Coedes, Georges. 1968. *The Indianized States of Southeast Asia.* Trans. Susan Brown Cowing. Honolulu: University of Hawaii Press.

Cohen, A. P. 1985. *The Symbolic Construction of Community.* London: Ellis Horwood and Tavistock.

———, ed. 1986. *Symbolizing Boundaries: Identity and Diversity in British Culture.* Manchester: Manchester University Press.

———. 1987. *Whalsay: Symbol, Segment and Boundary in a Shetland Island Community.* Manchester: Manchester University Press.

Combs, Sam Edward. 1985. The Lessons of Devotion: Two Systems of Spiritual Semiosis in Comparative Perspective. Ph.D. dissertation, University of California, San Diego.

Constable, Nicole. 1994. *Christian Souls and Chinese Spirits: A Hakka Community in Hong Kong.* Berkeley: University of California Press.

Cordova, F. 1983. *Filipinos: Forgotten Asian Americans.* Iowa: Kendall/Hunt.

Coser, Rose L., ed. 1964. *The Family: Its Structure and Functions.* New York: St. Martin's Press.

———. 1966 September. Role Distance, Sociological Ambivalence and Transitional Status Systems. *American Journal of Sociology* 72: 173–187.

———. 1975. The Complexity of Roles as a Seedbed of Individual Autonomy. In Lewis Coser, ed., *The Idea of Social Structure.* New York: Harcourt Brace Javonovich, 237–263.

————. 1979. *Training in Ambiguity.* New York: Free Press.

Courtenay, Bradley C., Leonard W. Poon, Peter Martin, Gloria M. Clayton, and Mary Ann Johnson. 1992. Religiosity and Adaptation in the Oldest Old. *International Journal of Aging and Human Development* 34: 47–56.

Courtright, Paul B. 1985. *Ganesa: Lord of Obstacles, Lord of Beginnings.* New York: Oxford University Press.

Crimmins, Eileen M., Hasuhiko Saito, and Sandra L. Reynolds. 1997. Further Evidence on Recent Trends in the Prevalence and Incidence of Disability among Older Americans from Two Sources: The LSOA and the NHIS. *Journal of Gerontology: Social Sciences* 52B: S59–S71.

Cromie, Virginia. 2000 fall. The Pilgrim Abroad. Paper submitted in the course, "Religious Worlds of New York, Barnard College and Columbia University."

Crowther, Martha R., Michel W. Parker, W. A. Achenbaum, Walter L. Larimore, and Harold G. Koenig. 2002. Rowe and Kahn's Model of Successful Aging Revisited. Positive spirituality—the Forgotten Factor. *Gerontologist* 42: 613–620.

Daly, Mary. 1968. *The Church and the Second Sex.* Boston: Beacon Press.

————. 1973. *Beyond God the Father: Toward a Philosophy of Women's Liberation.* Boston: Beacon Press.

Das, Veena, Dipankar Gupta, and Patricia Uberoi, eds. 1999. *Tradition, Pluralism, and Identity: In Honor of T. N. Madan.* Thousand Oaks, CA: Sage.

Dashefsky, Arnold. 1972. And the Search Goes On: The Meaning of Religio-Ethnic Identity and Identification. *Sociological Analysis* 33: 239–245.

Davis, James A., Tom W. Smith, and Peter V. Marsden. 2001. General Social Surveys, 1972–2000. *Cumulative Codebook.* Chicago: NORC.

Davis, Jim. 1999, December 28. New Year Celebrated by Hmong Community. *San Jose Mercury News.*

Davis, Patricia. 1999, October 22. Cabdrivers at Airport Want Place for Prayer; Muslims Request a Federal Probe. *Washington Post,* Metro section B1.

Davis, Richard H. 1998. Introduction: Miracles as Social Acts. In Richard H. Davis, ed., *Images, Miracles, and Authority in Asian Religious Traditions.* Boulder: Westview Press, 1–45.

De Bary, Theodore. 1983. *The Liberal Tradition in China.* New York: Columbia University Press.

De Lellio, Anna. 1985. Socially Expected Durations: Interview with Robert K. Merton. *Rassegna Italiana Di Sociologia* 26, 1: 3–26.

De Vos, George. 1975. Ethnic Pluralism: Conflict and Accommodation. In George De Vos and Lola Romanucci-Ross, eds., *Ethnic Identity: Cultural Communities and Change.* Palo Alto: Mayfield, 5–41.

DiIulio, John J., Jr. 2002 fall. The Three Faith Factors. *Public Interest* 149: 50–64.

DiMaggio, Paul J., and Walter W. Powell. 1983. The Iron Cage Revisited: Institutional Isomorphism and Collective Rationality in Organizational Fields. *American Sociological Review* 48: 147–160.

Dolan, Jay P. 1985. *The American Catholic Experience: A History from Colonial Times to the Present.* Garden City, NY: Doubleday.

Donahue, Michael J., and Peter L. Benson. 1995. Religion and the Well-Being of Adolescents. *Journal of Social Issues* 51: 145–160.

Doniger, Wendy. 1991 summer. Naming Hinduism. *Wilson Quarterly,* 20–41.

Douglas, Mary. 1966. *Purity and Danger.* London: Routledge.

———. 1996/1973. *Natural Symbols.* London: Routledge.

Dudley, Carl S., and David A. Roozen. 2001 March. *Faith Communities Today: A Report on Religion in the United States Today.* Hartford, CT: Hartford Institute for Religion Research, Hartford Seminary.

Durkheim, Emile. 1965/1915. *The Elementary Forms of the Religious Life.* New York: Free Press.

Eastman, Lloyd. 1974. *The Abortive Revolution: China under Nationalist Rule, 1927–1937.* Cambridge: Harvard University Press.

Ebaugh, Helen Rose, and Janet Saltzman Chafetz. 1999. Agents for Cultural Reproduction and Structural Change: The Ironic Role of Women in Immigrant Religious Institutions. *Social Forces* 78, 2: 585–613.

———. 2000a. Structural Adaptations in Immigrant Congregations. *Sociology of Religion* 61, 2: 135–154.

———. 2000b. Dilemmas of Language in Immigrant Congregations: The Tie That Binds or the Tower of Babel? *Review of Religious Research* 41: 4.

Ebora, Rev. Gerry, 2001 March. *San Francisco Seventh-Day Adventist Church.* Interviews.

Eck, Diana. 1981 May. India's Tirthas: Crossings in Sacred Geography. *History of Religions* 20: 323–344.

———. 1982. *Banaras: City of Light.* New York: Knopf.

———. 1996. *Darsan: Seeing the Divine Image in India,* 3d edition. New York: Columbia University Press.

———. 1998. The Imagined Landscape: Patterns in the Construction of Hindu Sacred Geography. *Contributions to Indian Sociology* 32, 2: 165–188.

———. 2001. *A New Religious America.* San Francisco: Harper.

Eisenstadt, E. N., ed. 1980. *The Protestant Ethic and Modernization.* New York: Basic Books.

Emerson, Michael O., and Christian Smith. 2000. *Divided by Faith.* Oxford: Oxford University Press.

Ensrud, K. E., M. C. Nevitt, C. Yunis, J. A. Cauley, D. C. Seeley, K. M. Fox, and S. R. Cummings. 1994. Correlates of Impaired Function in Older Women. *Journal of the American Geriatrics Society* 42: 481–489.

Espiritu, Yen Le. 1992. *Asian American Panethnicity.* Philadelphia: Temple University Press.

Fadiman, Anne. 1997. *The Spirit Catches You and You Fall Down: A Hmong Child, Her Doctors and an American Tragedy.* New York: Noonday Press.

Feagin, Joe R. 1998. *Free-Enterprise City: Houston in a Political and Economic Perspective.* New Brunswick, NJ: Rutgers University Press.

Fears, Darryl, and Claudia Deane. 2001, July 5. Biracial Couples Report Tolerance: Survey Finds Most Are Accepted by Families. *Washington Post.*

Fentress, Mark. 1992. Chinese Wedding. In Joann Faung Jean Lee, ed., *Asian Americans: Oral Histories of First to Fourth Generation Americans from China, the Philippines, Japan, India, the Pacific Islands, Vietnam and Cambodia.* New York: New Press, 44–66, 187.

Ferm, Deane W. 1976. Reflections of a College Chaplain. *Theology Today* 33: 53–65.

Ferraro, Kenneth F., and Cynthia M. Albrecht-Jensen. 1991. Does Religion Influence Adult Health? *Journal for the Scientific Study of Religion* 30: 193–202.

Ferraro, Kenneth F., and Jessica A. Kelley-Moore. 2000 June. Religious Consolation among Men and Women: Do Health Problems Spur Seeking? *Journal for the Scientific Study of Religion* 39, 2: 220–235.

Ferris, Marc. 1994. To Achieve the Pleasure of Allah: Immigrant Muslim Communities in New York City 1893–1991. In Yvonne Y. Haddad and Jane I. Smith, eds., *Muslim Communities in North America.* Albany: SUNY Press, 209–230.

Ferrucci, Luigi, Jack M. Guralnik, Francesca Cecchi, Niccolo Marchionni, Bernardo Salani, Judith Kasper, Romano Celli, Sante Giardini, Eino Heikkinen, Marja Jylha, and Alberto Baroni. 1998. Constant Hierarchic Patterns of Physical Functioning across Seven Populations in Five Countries. *Gerontologist* 38: 286–294.

Fieg, John Paul. 1989. *A Common Core: Thais and Americans.* Yarmouth, ME: Intercultural Press.

Fisher, Maxine P. 1980. *The Indians of New York City: A Study of Immigrants from India.* New Delhi: Heritage.

Flory, Richard, and Donald Miller. 2000. *Gen X Religion.* New York: Routledge.

Folsom, Kenneth E. 1968. *Friends, Guests and Colleagues: The Mu-fu System in the Late Ch'ing Period.* Berkeley: University of California Press.

Foner, Nancy, Ruben G. Rumbaut, and Steven J. Gold, eds. 2000. *Immigration Research for a New Century: Multidisciplinary Perspectives.* New York: Russell Sage.

Fong, Colleen, and Judy Yung. 1995–96 winter. In Search of the Right Spouse: Interracial Marriage among Chinese and Japanese Americans. *Amerasia Journal* 21: 3.

Fong, Timothy P. 2002. *The Contemporary Asian American Experience: Beyond the Model Minority,* 2d edition. Upper Saddle River, NJ: Prentice-Hall.

Foudy, Monsignor. 1963, September 30. Memo to Most Reverend Joseph T. McGucken, S.T.D. Regarding Minority Group Students in Catholic Elementary Schools, City of San Francisco.

Freedman, Vicki A., and Linda G. Martin. 1998. Understanding Trends in Functional Limitations among Older Americans. *American Journal of Public Health* 88: 1457–1462.

Frey, William H., Bill Abresch, and Jonathan Yeasting. 2001. *America by the Numbers: A Field Guide to the U.S. Population*. New York: New Press.

Fried, L. P., S. J. Herdman, K. E. Kuhn, G. Rubin, and K. Turano. 1991. Preclinical Disability: Hypothesis about the Bottom of the Iceberg. *Journal of Aging and Health* 3: 285–300.

Fried, L. P., W. H. Ettinger, B. Hermanson, A. B. Newman, and J. Gardin. 1994. Physical Disability in Older Adults: A Physiological Approach. *Journal of Clinical Epidemiology* 47: 747–760.

Fried, Linda, P., and Jack M. Guralnik. 1997. Disability in Older Adults: Evidence Regarding Significance, Etiology and Risk. *Journal of the American Geriatrics Society* 45: 92–100.

Friedman, Milton. 1957. *A Theory of the Consumption Function*. Princeton: Princeton University Press.

Fucks, Lawrence H. 1990. *The American Kaleidoscope. Race, Ethnicity, and the Civic Culture*. Middletown, CT: Wesleyan University Press.

Fuller, Christopher. 2000, April 10. The Vinayaka Chaturthi Festival and the Normalization of Hindu Nationalism in Contemporary Tamil Nadu. Lecture delivered at Columbia University.

Furst, Randy. 1999, March 17. Cabdrivers Accuse the Metropolitan Airports Commission of Discrimination. *Star Tribune* (Minneapolis, MN), B9.

Gager, John G. 1975. *Kingdom and Community: The Social World of Early Christianity*. Englewood Cliffs, NJ: Prentice-Hall.

Gallup Survey. 2000 March. Latest Religious Preference for U.S. *Emerging Trends* 22, 2.

———. 2001 January. Latest Religious Preference for U.S. *Emerging Trends* 23, 4.

George, Sheba. 1998. Caroling with the Keralites: The Negotiation of Gendered Space in an Indian Immigrant Church. In R. Stephen Warner and Judith G. Wittner, eds., *Gatherings in Diaspora: Religious Communities and the New Immigration*. Philadelphia: Temple University Press, 265–294.

Gill, T. M., C. S. Williams, and M. E. Tinetti. 1995. Assessing Risk for the Onset of Functional Dependence among Older Adults: The Role of Physical Performance. *Journal of the American Geriatrics Society* 43: 603–609.

Glass, Thomas. 1998. Conjugating the "Fences" of Function: Discordance among Hypothetical, Experimental and Enacted Function in Older Adults. *Gerontologist* 38: 101–112.

Goffman, Erving. 1959. *The Presentation of Self in Everyday Life*. New York: Anchor Books.

Gold, Ann Grodzins. 1988. *Fruitful Journeys: The Ways of Rajasthani Pilgrims*. Berkeley: University of California Press.

Goldwasser, Elise. 1998. Economic Security and Muslim Identity: A Study of the Immigrant Community in Durham, North Carolina. In Yvonne Y. Haddad and

John Esposito, eds., *Muslims on the Americanization Path?* New York: Oxford University Press, 301–316.

Gonda, Jan. 1976. *The Meaning of the Sanskrit Term Dhaman.* Amsterdam: N. V. Noord-Hollandsche Uitgevers Mattscappij.

Goodman, Catherine, and Merrill Silverstein. 2002. Grandmothers Raising Grandchildren: Family Structure and Well-Being in Culturally Diverse Families. *Gerontologist* 42: 676–689.

Goody, Jack. 1961. Religion and Ritual: The Definitional Problem. *British Journal of Sociology* 12: 142–164.

Gordon, D. F. 1978. USA: Identity and Social Commitment. In Hans Mol, ed., *Identity and Religion: International, Cross-cultural Approaches.* London: Sage, 229–241.

Greeley, Andrew M. 1971. *Why Can't They Be Like Us? America's White Ethnic Groups.* New York: E. P. Dutton.

———. 1972. *The Denominational Society: A Sociological Approach to Religion in America.* Glenview, IL: Scott, Foresman and Company.

———. 1997. The Other Civic America: Religion and Social Capital. *American Prospect* 32: 68–73.

Griffith, R. Marie. 1998. *God's Daughters: Evangelical Women and the Power of Submission.* Berkeley: University of California Press.

Grodzins, Morton. 1956. *The Loyal and Disloyal.* Chicago: University of Chicago Press.

Guest, Kenneth J. 2003. *God in Chinatown: Religion and Survival in New York's Evolving Immigrant Community.* New York: NYU Press.

Guinness, Os. 1973. *The Dust of Death.* Downer's Grove, IL: InterVarsity Press.

Guralnik, J. M., and E. M. Simonsick. 1993. Physical Disability in Older Americans. *Journal of Gerontology,* 48 Spec. No., 3–10.

Guralnik, Jack M., Luigi Femicci, Brenda W. J. H. Penninx, Judith D. Kasper, Suzanne G. Leveille, Karen Ban-deen-Roche, and Linda P. Fried. 1999. New and Worsening Conditions and Change in Physical and Cognitive Performance during Weekly Evaluations over 6 Months; The Women's Health and Aging Study. *Journal of Gerontology: Medical Sciences* 54A: M410–M422.

Ha, Francis Inki. 1995. Shame in Asian and Western Cultures. *American Behavioral Scientist* 38, 8: 1114–1131.

Haddad, Yvonne Y., and Adair T. Lummis. 1987. *Islamic Values in the United States: A Comparative Study.* New York: Oxford University Press.

Haddad, Yvonne Y., and Jane I. Smith, eds. 1994. *Muslim Communities in North America.* Albany: SUNY Press.

Hall, David D., ed. 1997. *Lived Religion in America: Toward a History of Practice.* Princeton: Princeton University Press.

Halpern, David. 1999. *Social Capital, Exclusion and the Quality of Life.* London: Institute for Public Policy Research.

Hamel, Gary. 2000, March 31. Exhausted? Blame Consumerism. *San Jose Mercury News,* 7B.

Handlin, Oscar. 1951. *The Uprooted.* New York: Grossett and Dunlap.

Hannerz, Ulf. 1969. *Soulside: Inquiries into Ghetto Culture and Community.* New York: Columbia University Press.

Hansbury, Gregg. 1999 May. Twice Exiled: Devotion, Community, and Education in a Guyanese-American Mandir. Paper presented to "Religious Worlds of New York," Barnard College and Columbia University.

Hansen, Thomas Blom. 1999. *The Saffron Wave.* New Delhi: Oxford University Press.

Hanson, R. Scott. 1999. Intra- and Extra-Relgioethnic Encounters: Responses to Plurality among [Two] Hindu Temples on Bowne Street in Flushing, New York. Paper presented to the American Academy of Religions, Boston.

————. 2002. City of Gods: Religious Freedom, Immigration, and Pluralism in Flushing, Queens—New York City, 1945–2002. Ph.D. dissertation, University of Chicago.

Harding, Susan. 1987. Convicted by the Holy Spirit: The Rhetoric of Fundamental Baptist Conversion. *American Ethnologist* 14: 167–181.

Harris, Fredrick. 1994. Something Within: Religion as a Mobilizer of African-American Political Activism. *Journal of Politics* 56: 42–68.

Hawkins, Anne Hunsaker. 1985. *Archetypes of Conversion: The Autobiographies of Augustine, Bunyan, and Merton.* London: Associated University Press.

Hawley, John Stratton. 1991 summer. Naming Hinduism. *Wilson Quarterly,* 20–41.

————. 1996. Prologue: The Goddess in India. In J. S. Hawley and Donna M. Wulff, eds., *Devi: Goddesses of India.* Berkeley: University of California Press, 1–28.

————. 2001. Modern India and the Question of Middle-Class Religion. *International Journal of Hindu Studies* 5: 1–10.

He, Wan. 2002. *The Older Foreign-Born Population in the United States: 2000.* Washington, DC: U.S. Government Printing Office.

Hendricks, Tyche. 1997, June 13. Monks to Consecrate Thai Temple. *San Jose Mercury News.*

————. 2002 September. All Roads Lead to the Bay Area: Number of Foreign-Born Residents Climbs to 27.5%. *San Francisco Chronicle.*

Henry, William A., III. 1990, April 9. Beyond the Melting Pot. *Time Magazine,* 28–31.

Herberg, Will. 1983/1960. *Protestant, Catholic, Jew: An Essay in American Religious Sociology.* Chicago: University of Chicago Press/Garden City, NY: Doubleday.

Hing, Bill Ong. 1993. *Making and Remaking Asian America through Immigration Policy, 1850–1990.* Stanford: Stanford University Press.

Hirschman, Charles, Philip Kasinitz, and Josh DeWind. 1999. *The Handbook of In-*

ternational Migration: The American Experience. New York: Russell Sage Foundation.

Ho, Pensri. 2002. Young Asian American Professionals in Los Angeles: A Community in Transition. In Linga Vo, and Rick Bonus, eds., *Contemporary Asian American Communities.* Philadelphia: Temple University Press, 134–146.

Hofrenning, S. K., and B. R. Chiswick. 1999. A Method for Proxying a Respondent's Religious Background: An Application to School Choice Decisions. *Journal of Human Resources* 34: 193–207.

Holte, Craig. 1992. *The Conversion Experience in America: A Sourcebook in Religious Conversion Autobiography.* New York: Greenwood Press.

Horton, Robin. 1960. A Definition of Religion and Its Uses. *Journal of the Royal Anthropological Institute* 90: 201–226.

Hougland, J. G., and J. A. Christenson. 1983. Religion and Politics: The Relationship of Religious Participation to Political Efficacy and Involvement. *Sociology and Social Research* 67: 405–420.

Hout, Michael, A. Greeley, and M. J. Wilde. 2001. The Demographic Imperative in Religious Change in the United States. Berkeley: Survey Research Center, University of California.

Hsu, Hua. 2002. Ethnic Media Grows Up. *Colorlines* 5, 3: 7–9.

Hughes, E. C., and H. M. Hughes. 1952. *Where People Meet: Racial and Ethnic Frontiers.* Glencoe, IL: Free Press.

Hull, Dana. 1999, December 16. Poster Seeks to Allay Fears; Census Aim Is to Avoid Undercounting Asian-American Population. *San Jose Mercury News,* online edition.

Hunt, Keith, and Gladys Hunt. 1991. *For Christ and the University: The Story of InterVarsity Christian Fellowship of the U.S.A. 1940–1990.* Downers Grove: InterVarsity Press.

Hunter, James Davidson. 2000. *The Death of Character.* New York: Basic Books.

Hurh, Won Moo. 1977. Comparative Study of Korean immigrants in the United States: A Typology. In Byong-suh Kim et al., *Koreans in America.* Memphis, TN: Association of Korean Christian Scholars in North America.

Hurh, Won Moo, and Kwang Chung Kim. 1984a. Adhesive Sociocultural Adaptation of Korean Immigrants in the U.S.: An Alternative Strategy of Minority Adaptation. *International Migration Review* 18: 188–217.

————. 1984b. *Korean Immigrants in America: A Structural Analysis of Ethnic Confinement and Adhesive Adaptation.* Rutherford, NJ: Fairleigh Dickinson University.

————. 1990 March. Religious Participation of Korean Immigrants in the U.S. *Journal for the Scientific Study of Religion* 29, 1: 19–34, 1180–1211.

Hurtado, Aida, Patricia Gurin, and Timothy Peng. 1994. Social Identities—A Framework for Studying the Adaptations of Immigrants and Ethnics: The Adaptations of Mexicans in the United States. *Social Problems* 41, 1: 129.

Husain, Asad, and Harold Vogelaar. 1994. Activities of the Immigrant Muslim Communities in Chicago. In Yvonne Y. Haddad and Jane I. Smith, eds., *Muslim Communities in North America.* Albany: SUNY Press, 231–258.

Idler, Ellen L. 1987. Religious Involvement and the Health of the Elderly: Some Hypotheses and an Initial Test. *Social Forces* 66: 226–238.

Idler, Ellen L., and Stanislav V. Kasl. 1992. Religion, Disability, Depression, and the Timing of Death. *American Journal of Sociology* 97: 1052–1079.

Jacobs, J. Bruce. 1979 June. A Preliminary Model of Particularistic Ties in Chinese Political Alliances: Kan-ch'ing and Kuan-his in a Rural Taiwanese Township. *China Quarterly* 78: 237–238.

Jacobsen, Lone, and Peter Vesti. 1992. *Torture Survivors: A New Group of Patients.* Copenhagen: IRCT.

Jagdishvaranand, Swami. 2002 January. *Interviews.*

James, William. 1902. *The Varieties of Religious Experience.* New York: Longmans.

Janis, I. L. 1980. An Analysis of Psychological and Sociological Ambivalence: Non-Adherence to Courses of Action Prescribed by Health-Care Professionals. In T. F. Gieryn, ed., *Science and Social Structure: A Festschrift for Robert K. Merton.* New York: New York Academy of Sciences, 91–110.

Jankowiak, William R. 1993. *Sex, Death and Hierarchy in a Chinese City.* New York: Columbia University Press.

Jasper, Daniel. 2001 August. The Incorporation of Hinduism in New York. Paper presented to the Association for the Sociology of Religion. Anaheim. Also: http://www.pewtrusts.org.

Jette, Alan M., Susan F. Assman, Dan Rooks, Bette Ann Harris, and Sybil Cranford. 1998. Interrelationships among Disablement Concepts. *Journal of Gerontology: Social Sciences* 53A: M395–M404.

Jeung, Russell. 2002. Asian American Panethnic Formation and Congregational Cultures. In Pyong Gap Min and Jung Ha Kim, eds., *Religions in Asian America: Building Faith Communities.* Walnut Creek, CA: AltaMira Press, 215–243.

Johnson, Charles S. 1945. Introduction. In *God Struck Me Dead: Religious Conversion Experiences and Autobiographies of Negro Ex-Slaves.* Social Science Institute. Nashville: Fisk University Press, 11–21.

Jones-Correa, Michael A., and David L. Leal. 2001. Political Participation: Does Religion Matter? *Political Research Quarterly* 54, 4: 751–770.

Joselit, Jenna Weissman. 1994. *The Wonders of America: Reinventing Jewish Culture, 1880–1950.* New York: Hill and Wang.

Juergensmeyer, Mark. 1991. *Radhasoami Reality: The Logic of a Modern Faith.* Princeton: Princeton University Press.

Kane, Paula. 1994. *Separatism and Subculture: Boston Catholicism, 1900–1920.* Chapel Hill: University of North Carolina Press.

Kang, Cecilia, 2001, May 15. Indians Fuel Asian Population Growth. *San Jose Mercury News,* on-line edition.

Katz, S., A. B. Ford, and R. W. Moskowitz. 1963. Studies of Illness in the Aged: The Index of ADL: A Standardized Measure of Biological and Psychological Function. *Journal of the American Medical Association* 185: 914–921.

Katz, S., and C. A. Akpom. 1976. A Measure of Primary Sociobiological Function. *International Journal of Health Services* 6: 493–507.

Katz, S., Laurence G. Branch, Michael H. Branson, Joseph Papsidero, John C. Beck, and David E. Greer. 1983. Active Life Expectancy. *New England Journal of Medicine* 309: 1218–1224.

Keane, Webb. 1997. From Fetishism to Sincerity: On Agency, the Speaking Subject, and Their Historicity in the Context of Religious Conversion. *Comparative Studies in Society and History* 39: 634–693.

Keller, Allen S., Jack M. Saul, and David P. Eisenman. 1998 March. Caring for Survivors of Torture in an Urban, Municipal Hospital. *Journal of Ambulatory Care Medicine*. www.survivorsoftorture.org/news_ambulatory.html.

Kelley, Ron. 1994. Muslims in Los Angeles. In Yvonne Y. Haddad and Jane I. Smith, eds., *Muslim Communities in North America*. Albany: SUNY Press, 135–168.

Kennedy, John W. 1994. Mission Force Looking More Asian. *Christianity Today* 38, 7: 48–49.

Kerokhuff, Alan C., and Thomas L. McCormick. 1977 October. Marginal Status and Marginal Personality. *Social Forces* 34: 161–181.

Khandelwal, Madhulika S. 1995. Indian Immigrants in Queens, New York City: Patterns of Spatial Concentration and Distribution, 1965–1990. In Peter Van der Veer, ed., *Nation and Migration: The Politics of Space in the South Asian Diaspora*. Philadelphia: University of Pennsylvania Press, 160–185.

Kibria, Nazli. 1996. Not Asian, Black or White: Reflections on South Asian Racial Identities. *Amerasia Journal* 22: 77–88.

Kim, Ai Ra. 1996. *Women Struggling for a New Life: The Role of Religion in the Cultural Passage from Korea to America*. Albany: SUNY Press.

Kim, Eun-Young. 1997. Korean Americans in U.S. Race Relations: Some Considerations. *Amerasia* 23: 69–78.

Kim, Hannah Hea-Sun. 2000. Being Swaminarayan: The Ontology and Significance of Belief in the Construction of a Gujarati Diaspora. Ph.D. dissertation, Columbia University.

Kim, J. H. 1996. Sources Outside of Europe. In Peter Ness, ed., *Spirituality and the Secular Quest*. New York: Cross Road, 53–74.

———. 1997. *Bridge-Makers and Cross-Bearers: Korean American Women and the Church*. Atlanta, GA: Scholar's Press.

Kim, Paul. 1983. Demography of the Asian-Pacific Elderly: Selected Problems and Implications. In Robert L. McNeely and John N. Colen, eds., *Aging in Minority Groups*. Beverly Hills: Sage.

Kim, Ryan. 2001, May 24. Tech Boom a Magnet for Asians: Indians Double in a Decade; Chinese, Vietnamese Flourish. *San Francisco Chronicle.*

Kim, Woong-min. 1981. *History and Ministerial Roles of Korean Churches in the Los Angeles Area.* Claremont, CA: School of Theology at Claremont.

Kinsella, Kevin, and Victoria A. Velkoff. 2001. *An Aging World: 2001.* Washington, DC: U.S. Government Printing Office.

Kinzie, J. D. 1993. Posttraumatic Effects and their Treatment among Southeast Asian Refugees. In J. P. Wilson and B. Raphael, eds., *International Handbook of Traumatic Stress Syndromes.* New York: Plenum, 311–319.

Kinzie, J., R. Fredrickson, and R. Ben. 1984. Posttraumatic Stress Disorder among Survivors of Cambodian Concentration Camps. *American Journal of Psychiatry* 141: 649–650.

Kipnis, Andrew B. 1997. *Sentiment, Self, and Subculture in a North China Village.* Durham: Duke University Press.

Kirschenblatt-Gimblett, Barbara. 1998. *Destination Culture: Tourism, Museums, and Heritage.* Berkeley: University of California Press.

Kivisto, Peter. 1993. Religion and the New Immigrants. In William H. Swatos Jr., ed., *A Future for Religion: New Paradigms for Social Analysis.* Newbury Park, CA: Sage, 92–108.

Klass, Morton. 1988/1961. *East Indians in Trinidad: A Study of Cultural Persistence.* Prospect Heights, IL: Waveland Press.

Koenig, Harold G. 1995. *Research on Religion and Aging: An Annotated Bibliography.* Westport, CT: Greenwood Press.

Kolsky, Elizabeth. 1998 spring. Less Successful than the Next: South Asian Taxi Drivers in New York City. *Sagar: South Asia Graduate Research Journal* 5: 1–5.

Korn, William S., and Giles Asburg. 1994 summer. Where Have All the Young Gone? http://www.esmhe.org/plumbline/ulnl/korn1994.html.

Kosmin, Barry A., and Seymour P. Lachman. 1993. *One Nation under God.* New York: Crown Trade Paperbacks.

Kosmin, Barry A., Egon Mayer, and Ariela Keysar. 2001 October. *American Religious Identification Survey.* Graduate Center. City University of New York, 2.

Krause, Newal, and Thanh V. Tran. 1989. Stress and Religious Involvement among Older Blacks. *Journal of Gerontology: Social Sciences* 44: S4–S13.

Kritz, Mary M., and June Marie Nogle. 1994. Nativity Concentration and Internal Migration among the Foreign-Born. *Demography* 31: 509–524.

Kurien, Prema. 1998. Becoming American by Becoming Hindu: Indian Americans Take Their Place at the Multicultural Table. In R. Stephen Warner and Judith G. Wittner, eds., *Gatherings in Diaspora: Religious Communities and the New Immigration.* Philadelphia: Temple University Press, 37–71.

Kwok, Pui-lan. 1992. *Chinese Women and Christianity 1860–1927.* Atlanta, GA: Scholars Press.

Kwon, Ho-Youn, Kwang Chung Kim, and R. Stephen Warner, eds. 2001. *Korean Americans and Their Religions: Pilgrims and Missionaries from a Different Shore.* University Park: Pennsylvania State University Press.

Kwon, Okyun. 2000. Religious Beliefs and Socioeconomic Aspects of Life of Buddhist and Protestant Korean Immigrants. Ph.D. dissertation, City University of New York.

Laguardia, Ismael (San Francisco Filipino Jehovah's Witness). 2001 March. Interviews.

Lamont, Michele, and Marcel Fournier, eds. 1992. *Cultivating Differences: Symbolic Boundaries and the Making of Inequality.* Chicago: University of Chicago Press.

Lawless, Elaine J. 1991 spring. Rescripting Their Lives and Narratives: Spiritual Life Stories of Pentecostal Women Preachers. *Journal of Feminist Studies in Religion* 7: 53–72.

Lawrence, Renee H., and Alan M. Jette. 1996. Disentangling the Disablement Process. *Journal of Gerontology: Social Sciences* 51B: S173–S182.

Lazarsfeld, Paul. 1953. *Youth and Occupation.* New York: Bureau of Applied Social Research.

Lee, Diana T. F., Jean Woo, and Ann E. Mackenzie. 2002. The Cultural Context of Adjusting to Nursing Home Life: Chinese Elders' Perspectives. *Gerontologist* 42: 667–675.

Lee, Evelyn, and F. Lu. 1989. Assessment and Treatment of Asian-American Survivors of Mass Violence. *Journal of Traumatic Stress* 2: 93–120.

Lee, Helen. 1996, August 12. Silent Exodus. *Christianity Today,* 51–52.

Lee, Julie C., and Virginia E. H. Cynn. 1991. Issues in Counseling 1.5–Generation Korean Americans. In Courtland C. Lee and Bernard L. Richardson, eds., *Multicultural Issues in Counseling: New Approaches to Diversity.* Alexandria: American Association for Counseling and Development, 127–140.

Lee, Jung Young. 1997. *Korean Preaching: An Interpretation.* Nashville: Abingdon Press.

Lee, Sang Hyun. 1996. Pilgrimage and Home in the Wilderness of Marginality: Symbols and Context in Asian American Theology. *Amerasia Journal* 22: 149–159.

Lee, Sang Hyun, Ron Chu, and Marion Park. 1993. Second Generation Ministry: Models of Mission. In Sang Hyun Lee and John V. Moore, eds., *Korean American Ministry: A Resource Book.* Louisville: General Assembly Council-Presbyterian Church (U.S.A.), 233–255.

Lee, Sharon M., and Marilyn Fernandez. 1998. Trends in Asian American Racial/Ethnic Intermarriage: A Comparison of 1980 and 1990 Census Data. *Sociological Perspectives* 41, 2: 375.

Lee, Sharon M., and Keiko Yamanaka. 1990. Patterns of Asian American Intermarriage and Marital Assimilation. *Journal of Comparative Family Studies* 21, 2: 287–305.

Lenane, Edward B. 1935, March 25. Survey of Catholic Filipino Club, 1421 Sutter Street, San Francisco, California.

Lessinger, Joanna. 1995. *From the Ganges to the Hudson: Indian Immigrants in New York City.* Boston: Allyn and Bacon.

Lester, Donald. 1994. Differences in Epidemiology of Suicide in Asian Americans by Nation of Origin. *Omega* 29, 2: 89–93.

Leveille, Suzanne G., Jack M. Guralnik, Luigi Ferrucci, and Jean A. Langlois. 1999. Aging Successfully until Death in Old Age: Opportunities for Increasing Active Life Expectancy. *American Journal of Epidemiology* 149: 654–669.

Levitt, Peggy. 2002. February 14. Redefining the Boundaries of Belonging: Thoughts on Transnational Religious and Political Life. Paper presented to the Eastern Sociological Society, Boston, MA.

Lewis, Ioan M. 1971. *Ecstatic Religion: An Anthropological Study of Spirit Possession and Shamanism.* Harmondsworth: Penguin.

Lewis, John Wilson. 1987. *Political Networks and the Chinese Policy Process.* Stanford: Stanford University Press.

Liang, Sou-Ming. 1974. *The Essential Features of Chinese Culture.* Hong Kong: Chi-cheng T'ushu Kung ssu.

Liao, Ting-May. 1999. Intergenerational Co-Residence among Asian American Households. MA thesis. Iowa State University.

Lien, Pei-te. 2001. *The Making of Asian America through Political Participation.* Philadelphia: Temple University Press.

———. 2003. *Diversity and Community: Asian American Political Attitudes and Behavior.* London: Routledge.

Lind, Michael. 1995. *The Next American Nation: The New Nationalism and the Fourth American Revolution.* New York: Free Press.

Linder, Eileen W. 2001. Yearbook *of American and Canadian Churches, 1997–2001.* Nashville: Abingdon Press.

Linton, Ralph. 1945. *The Cultural Background to Personality.* New York: Appleton Century.

Livezey, Lowell. 2000. *Public Religion and Urban Transformation.* New York: NYU Press.

Lofland, John, and Rodney Stark. 1965. Becoming a World-Saver: A Theory of Conversion to a Deviant Perspective. *American Sociological Review* 30: 862–875.

Loomis, Charles R., and Edna Loomis. 1987. *Modern Social Theory.* New York: D. Van Nostrand & Co.

Lopez, David, and Yen Espiritu. 1990. Panethnicity in the United States: A Theoretical Framework. *Ethnic Studies* 13, 2: 198–224.

Lorenzen, David. 1999. Who Invented Hinduism? *Comparative Studies in Society and History* 41, 4: 630–659.

Lowe, Lisa. 1996. *Immigrant Acts.* Durham, NC: Duke University Press.

Lowell, B. Lindsay, and Richard Fry. 2002, March 21. *Estimating the Distribution of Undocumented Workers in the Urban Labor Force.* Technical memorandum to "How Many Undocumented: The Numbers behind the U.S.–Mexico Migration Talks." Washington, DC: Pew Hispanic Center.

Lutgendorf, Philip. 1991. *The Life of a Text: Performing the Ramcaritmanas of Tulsidas.* Berkeley: University of California Press.

———. 1997. Monkey in the Middle: The Status of Hanuman in Popular Hinduism. *Religion* 27, 4: 311–332.

Lyman, Stanford M. 1970. *The Asian in the West.* Santa Barbara: Clio Press.

———. 1994. *Color, Culture, Civilization.* Fayetteville: University of Arkansas Press.

Lyman, Stanford M., and Marvin B. Scott. 1970. *A Sociology of the Absurd.* Pacific Palisades, CA: Goodyear.

Maak, Hay Chun. 2000. Roles of Sisters at the Church. *Ambassadors* 43, 2: 31–33.

Macalam, Sister Avelina. 2001 May–June. RVM, Religious of the Virgin Mary. Interviews.

Macaluso, Theodore F., and John Wanat. 1979. Voting Turnout and Religiosity. *Polity* 12: 158–169.

Madsen, Richard. 1998. *China's Catholics: Tragedy and Hope in an Emerging Civil Society.* Berkeley: University of California Press.

Mahler, Sarah J. 1995. *American Dreaming: Immigrant Life on the Margins.* Princeton: Princeton University Press.

Mangaliman, Jessie. 2002, March 7. Asian-Americans Post Biggest Gains: High Tech Drives Immigration. *San Jose Mercury News.*

Mann, Gurinder Singh. 2000. Sikhism in the United States of America. In Harold Coward, John R. Hinnells, and Raymond Brady Williams, eds., *The South Asian Religious Diaspora in Britain, Canada, and the United States.* Albany: SUNY Press.

Mann, Gurinder Singh, Paul David Numrich, and Raymond B. Williams. 2001. *Buddhists, Hindus, and Sikhs in America.* New York: Oxford University Press.

Manuel, Peter. 1998. *Vedic Mantras, Saswaras (with Swara).* New York: Hindu Temple Society of North America.

———. 2000. *East Indian Mosaic in the West Indies: Tan-Singing, Chutney, and the Making of Indo-Caribbean Culture.* Philadelphia: Temple University Press.

Manza Jeff, and Clem Brooks. 1997. The Religious Factor in U.S. Presidential Elections, 1960–1992. *American Journal of Sociology* 103, 1: 38–81.

Marcini, Juan. 2002, January 13. Interview. Divya Dham.

Markides, K. S., J. S. Levin, and L. A. Ray. 1987. Religion, Aging, and Life Satisfaction: An Eight-Year, Three-Wave Longitudinal Study. *Gerontologist* 27, 5: 660–665.

Martin, David. 1995. Making Asylum Policy: The 1994 Reforms. *Washington Law Review* 70: 725.

———. 2000 May. *The 1995 Asylum Reforms. A Historic and Global Perspective.* Washington, DC: Center for Immigration Studies.

Martinson, Oscar B., and E. A. Wilkening. 1987. Religious Participation and Involvement in Local Politics throughout the Life Cycle. *Sociological Focus* 20: 309–318.

Marty, Martin E. 1972. Ethnicity: The Skeleton of Religion in America. *Church History* 41: 5–21.

———. 1994. Public and Private: Congregation as Meeting Place. In James P. Wind and James W. Lewis, eds. *American Congregations.* Vol. 2. Chicago: University of Chicago Press, 133–166.

Mayor's Message. 2001, June 28.

McAdam, Doug. 1982. *Political Process and the Development of Black Insurgency, 1930–1970.* Chicago: University of Chicago Press.

McGuire, M. B. 1997. *Religion: The Social Context.* Belmont, Albany, and Bonn: Wadsworth.

McKenzie, Brian D. 2001. "Self-Selection, Church Attendance, and Local Civic Participation." *Journal for the Scientific Study of Religion* 40: 479–488.

McLellan, Janet. 1999. *Many Petals of the Lotus: Five Asian Buddhist Communities in Toronto.* Toronto: University of Toronto Press.

McNally, Michael. 1997. The Uses of Ojibwa Hymn-Singing at White Earth: Toward a History of Practice. In D. Hall, ed., *Lived Religion in America.* Princeton: Princeton University Press, 116–132.

McNamara, Brooks, and Barbara Kirshenblatt-Gimblett. 1985. Introduction Special Issue, "Processional Performance." *Drama Review* 29: 2–5.

Mehta, Monica. 1996 April. When Lord Ganesh Drank Milk: Miracle in the Twentieth Century. Unpublished paper, Barnard College.

Mercado, L. N. 1982. *Christ in the Philippines.* Manila: Divine Word University.

Merton, Robert K. 1959. Social Conformity, Deviation and Opportunity. *American Sociological Review* 24, 2: 177–189.

———. 1968. *Social Theory and Social Structure.* New York: Free Press.

———. 1976. *Sociological Ambivalence.* New York: Free Press.

———. 1984. Socially Expected Durations: A Case Study of Concept Formation in Sociology. In Wallis W. Powell and Richard Robbins, eds., *Conflict and Consensus: A Festschrift for Lewis A. Coser.* New York: Free Press, 262–283.

Merton, Robert K., Vanessa Merton, and Elinor Barber. 1983. Client Ambivalence in Professional Relationships: The Problem of Seeking Help from Strangers. In B. M. De Paulo et al., eds., *New Directions in Helping.* Vol. 2. New York: Academic Press, 13–44.

Metcalf, Barbara Daly, ed. 1996. *Making Muslim Space in North America and Europe.* Berkeley: University of California Press.

Metzger, Thomas. 1983. *Escape from Predicament: Neo-Confucianism and China's Evolving Political Culture.* New York: Columbia University Press.

Michaelson, Scott, and David E. Johnson, eds. 1997. *Border Theory: The Limits of Cultural Politics.* Minneapolis: University of Minnesota Press.

Milbrath, Lester, and M. L. Goel. 1977. *Political Participation.* Chicago: Rand Mac-Nally.

Miller, Donald. 1997. *Reinventing American Protestantism: Christianity in the New Millennium.* Berkeley: University of California Press.

Miller, Donald E., Joe Miller, and Grace R. Dyrness. 2001 January. *Immigrant Religion in the City of Angels.* Center for Religion and Civic Culture. Los Angeles: University of Southern California Press.

Min, Pyong Gap. 1991. *Koreans in America.* Seoul: Yoo Lim Moon Hwa Sa.

———. 1992. The Structure and Social Functions of Korean Immigrant Churches in the U.S. *International Migration Review* 26: 1370–1394.

———. 1995. Korean Americans. In Pyong Gap Min, ed., *Asian Americans: Contemporary Trends and Issues.* Thousand Oaks, CA: Sage, 199–231.

———. 2000. Immigrants' Religion and Ethnicity: A Comparison of Indian Hindu and Korean Christian Immigrants in the United States. *Bulletin of the Royal Institute of Inter-Faith Studies* 2: 122–140.

———. 2002. *Asian Ethnic Groups in New York: A Comparative Analysis.* New York: Columbia University Press.

Min, Pyong Gap, and Youna Choi. 1993. Ethnic Attachment among Korean-American High School Students. *Korea Journal of Population and Development* 22, 2: 167–179.

Min, Pyong Gap, and Jung Ha Kim. 2002. *Religions in Asian America: Building Faith Communities.* Walnut Creek, CA: AltaMira Press.

Min, Pyong Gap, and Rose Kim. 1999. *Struggle for Ethnic Identity: Narratives by Asian American professionals.* Walnut Creek, CA: AltaMira Press.

Mirowsky, John. 1997. Age, Subjective Life Expectancy and the Sense of Control: The Horizon Hypothesis. *Journal of Gerontology: Social Sciences* 52B: S125–S134.

Missine, L. E. 1985 summer. Reflections on the Meaning of Life in Older Age. *Journal of Religion and Aging* 1, 4: 43–58.

Mitroff, Ian, I. 1974. Norms and Counter-Norms in a Select Group of the Apollo Moon Scientists: A Case Study of the Ambivalence of Scientists. *American Sociological Review* 39: 579–595.

Moberg, David O. 1997. Religion and Aging. In Kenneth F. Ferraro, ed., *Gerontology: Perspectives and Issues.* New York: Springer, 193–220.

Modern Buddhism (Miju Hyundae Bulkyo). 2001 December. 138.

Mol, Hans. 1978. *Identity and Religion.* Beverly Hills, CA: Sage.

Mollica, R. F. 1990, March 6. Communities of Confinement: The Psychiatric Care of Highly Traumatized Indochinese Refugee Populations. "Critical Issues in International and U.S. Refugee Law and Policy." Tufts University conference.

Mollica, R. F., J. Lavelle, T. Truong, S. Tor, and T. Yang. 1990. Assessing Symptom

Change in Southeast Asian Refugee Survivors of Mass Violence and Torture. *American Journal of Psychiatry* 147: 83–88.

Mollica, R. F., G. Wyshak, and J. Lavelle. 1987. The Psychosocial Impact of War Trauma and Torture on Southeast Asian Refugees. *American Journal of Psychiatry* 144: 1567–1572.

Morawska, Eva. 1990. The Sociology and Historiography of Immigration. In Virginia Yans-McLaughlin, ed., *Immigration Reconsidered: History, Sociology, and Politics.* New York: Oxford University Press, 187–238.

Morris, Aldon D. 1984. *The Origins of the Civil Rights Movement: Black Communities Organizing for Change.* New York: Free Press.

Morrison, Karl F. 1992. *Conversion and Text: The Cases of Augustine of Hippo, Herman-Judah, and Constantine Tsatsos.* Charlottesville: University of Virginia Press.

Morton, Nelle. 1985. *The Journey Is Home.* Boston: Beacon Press.

Muecke, Marjorie A. 1998. Resettled Refugees' Reconstruction of Identity: Lao in Seattle. In Franklin Ng, ed., *Asian American Family Life and Community.* New York: Garland, 119–133.

Muensterberger, Warner. 1951. Orality and Dependence: Characteristics of Southern Chinese. *Psychoanalysis and the Social Sciences* 3: 37–69.

Mui, A. C. 1996a. Geriatric Depression Scale as a Community Screening Instrument for Elderly Chinese Immigrants. *International Psychogeriatrics* 8, 3: 1–10.

———. 1996b. Depression among Elderly Chinese Immigrants: An Exploratory Study. *Social Work* 41, 6: 633–645.

———. 1997. Mental Health and Social Support among Elderly Korean Immigrants. Unpublished manuscript, Columbia University School of Social Work.

Mulder, Niels. 1996. *Inside Thai Society: Interpretations of Everyday Life.* Kuala Lumpur: Pepin Press.

Mullins, Mark R. 1987. The Life-Cycle of Ethnic Churches in Sociological Perspective. *Japanese Journal of Religious Studies* 14, 4: 321–334.

———. 1988. The Organizational Dilemmas of Ethnic Churches: A Case Study of Japanese Buddhism in Canada. *Sociological Analysis* 49: 217–233.

Narayanan, Vasudha. 1992. Creating the South Indian "Hindu" Experience in the United States. In Brady R. Williams, ed., *A Sacred Thread: Modern Transmission of Hindu Traditions in Indians and Abroad.* Chambersburg, PA: Anima.

Nathan, Andrew. 1976. *Peking Politics.* Berkeley: University of California Press.

National Asian Pacific Center on Aging. 2002. *Discussions on Senior Community Service Employment Program.* http://www.napca.org.

National Institute of Health. 1998. Spirituality and the Elderly: Survey of Staff and Residents from Long-Term Care Facilities, 1998. www.thearda.com/file_main.asp?FILE=SAE1998&Show=Description.

Nattier, Jan. 1998. Who Is a Buddhist? Charting the Landscape of Buddhist America. In Charles S. Prebish and Kenneth K. Tanaka, eds., *The Faces of Buddhism in America*. Berkeley: University of California Press.

Ng, David. 1996. *People on the Way: Asian North Americans Discovering Christ, Culture and Community*. Valley Forge, PA: Judson Press.

Ng, Franklin, ed. 1998a. *Adaptation, Acculturation, and Transnational Ties among Asian Americans*. New York: Garland.

———. 1998b. *Asian American Family Life and Community*. New York: Garland.

Niebuhr, Richard H. 1929. *The Social Sources of Denominationalism*. New York: Henry Holt.

Nisbet, Robert A. 1969. *Social Change and History*. Oxford: Oxford University Press.

Norton, A., M. Latham, and G. Sturgess, eds. 1997. *Social Capital: The Individual, Civil Society and the State*. Sydney: Center for Independent Studies.

Numan, Fareed H. 1992. *The Muslim Population in the United States*. American Muslim Council. Washington, DC, and in Sulayman S. Nyang, ed. 1999. *Islam in the United States of America*. Chicago: ABC International.

Numrich, Paul. 1996. *Old Wisdom in the New World: Americanization in Two Immigrant Theravada Buddhist Temples*. Knoxville: University of Tennessee Press.

———. 1998. Theravada Buddhism in America: Prospects for the Sangha. In Charles S. Prebish and Kenneth K. Tanaka, eds., *The Faces of Buddhism in America*. Berkeley: University of California Press.

———. 2000a October. Up Front Health Care and the New Immigration. *Health Care and the New Immigration* 17: 1–10.

———. 2000b October. Among the Hmong: Bridging the Gap between Shamanism and Medicine. *Health Care and the New Immigration* 17: 1–19.

Olshansky, S. J., and Russell Wikins, eds. 1998. Policy Implications of the Measures and Trends in Health Expectancy: Reports from REVES 8. Special issue of the *Journal of Aging and Health* 10, 2. Thousand Oaks, CA: Sage.

Omi, Mitchell, and Howard Winant. 1994. *Racial Formation in the United States from the 1960s to the 1990s*. New York: Routledge.

Orsi, Robert. 1985. *The Madonna of 115th Street: Faith and Community in Italian Harlem, 1880–1950*. New Haven: Yale University Press.

———. 1997. Everyday Miracles: The Study of Lived Religion. In David D. Hall, ed., *Lived Religion in America: Toward a History of Practice*. Princeton: Princeton University Press, 3–21.

———. 1999. *Gods of the City*. Bloomington: Indiana University Press.

Overholt, Thomas W. 1981. Prophecy: The Problem of Cross-Cultural Comparison. *Semeia* 21: 55–78.

Padilla, Anthony. 1989. Posttraumatic Stress in Immigrants from Central America and Mexico. *Hospital and Community Psychiatry* 40: 615–619.

Pai, Young. 1993. A Sociocultural Understanding of Korean American Youth "Caught in the Web." In Sang Hyun Lee and John V. Moore, eds., *Korean*

American Ministry: A Resource Book. Louisville: General Assembly Council-Presbyterian Church (U.S.A.), 256–274.

Palinkas, Lawrence A. 1989. *Rhetoric and Religious Experience: The Discourse of Immigrant Chinese Churches.* Fairfax, VA: George Mason University Press.

Pandey, Ram Chandra. 2001. *Divya Dhama: The Heaven on the Earth.* New York: Divya Dhama and Geeta Temple.

Park, Soyoung. 2001. The Intersection of Religion, Race, Gender and Ethnicity in the Identity Formation of Korean American Evangelical Women. In Ho-Youn Kwon, Kwang Chung Kim, and R. Stephen Warner, eds., *Korean Americans and Their Religions: Pilgrims and Missionaries from a Different Shore.* University Park: Pennsylvania State University Press, 193–208.

Park, Sung-bae. 1983. *Buddhist Faith and Sudden Enlightenment.* Albany: SUNY Press.

Payne, Rodger M. 1998. *The Self and the Sacred: Conversion and Autobiography in Early American Protestantism.* Knoxville: University of Tennessee Press.

Peacock, James L., and Dorothy C. Hollis. 1999. The Narrated Self: Life Stories in Process. *Ethos* 21, 4: 371.

Pearson, Thomas. 2001. Missions and Conversions: Creating the Montagnard-Dega Refugee Community (North Carolina). Ph.D. dissertation, University of North Carolina, Chapel Hill.

Perlmann, Joel, and Roger Waldinger. 1997 winter. Second Generation Decline? Children of Immigrants, Past and Present—A Reconsideration. *International Migration Review* 31, 4: 893–922.

Perry, Elizabeth J. 1976. January. Worshippers and Warriors: White Lotus Influence on the Nian Rebellion. *Modern China* 21: 18–20.

Petersen, William. 1980. Concepts of Ethnicity. In Stephan Thernstrom, ed., *The Harvard Encyclopedia of American Ethnic Groups.* Cambridge: Harvard University Press, 234–242.

Peterson, Steven A. 1992. Church Participation and Political Participation. *American Politics Quarterly* 20: 123–139.

Petievich, Carla. 1999. *The Expanding Landscape: South Asians and the Diaspora.* New Delhi: Manohar.

Pew and Pew (Pew Forum on Religion and Public Life and Pew Research Center for the People and the Press). 2002 April. *American Views on Religion, Politics, and Public Policy.* Washington, DC: Pew and Pew.

Phinney, J. S., and D. A. Rosenthal. 1992. Ethnic Identity in Adolescence: Process, Context, and Outcome. In Gerald R. Adams et al., eds., *Adolescent Identity Formation.* Newbury Park, CA: Sage, 145–172.

Pintchman, Tracy, ed. 2001. *Seeking Mahadevi: Constructing the Identities of the Hindu Great Goddess.* Albany: SUNY Press.

Pipher, Mary. 2002. *The Middle of Everywhere: The World's Refugees Come to Our Town.* New York: Harcourt Brace.

Pollner, Melvin. 1989 March. Divine Relations, Social Relations, and Well-Being. *Journal of Health and Social Behavior* 30: 92–104.

Portes, Alejandro, and Ruben G. Rumbaut. 2001. *Legacies: The Story of the Immigrant Second Generation.* Berkeley: University of California Press.

Prashad, Vijay. 2000. *The Karma of Brown Folk.* Minneapolis: University of Minnesota Press.

Prebish, Charles. 1999. *Luminous Passage: The Practice and Study of Buddhism in America.* Berkeley: University of California Press.

Prebish, Charles, and Kenneth K. Tanaka. 1999. *The Faces of Buddhism in America.* Berkeley: University of California Press.

Preston, D. L. 1981. Becoming a Zen Practitioner. *Sociological Analysis* 42: 47–55.

Pugh, Tony. 2001, March 23. Census 2000 Finds Interracial Couples Number 1.5 million, One-Quarter of Such Pairs Live in California. *San Jose Mercury News,* 17A.

Putnam, Robert. 1993. *Making Democracy Work: Civic Traditions in Modern Italy.* Princeton: Princeton University Press.

———. 1995. Bowling Alone: America's Declining Social Capital. *Journal of Democracy* 6: 65–78.

———. 1996. The Strange Disappearance of Civic America. *American Prospect* 24: 34–48.

———. 2000. *Bowling Alone: The Collapse and Revival of American Community.* New York: Simon and Schuster.

Pye, Lucien. 1992/1968. *The Spirit of Chinese Politics.* Cambridge: Harvard University Press.

Rayaprol, Aparna. 1997. *Negotiating Identities: Women in the Indian Diaspora.* New Delhi: Oxford University Press.

Recio, Donald. 2000. "The Filipino Experience: Through One Man's Eyes." In *No Filipinos Allowed.* San Francisco: Recio Press.

Reed, Robert. 1990. Migration as Mission: The Expansion of the Iglesia in Cristo Outside the Philippines. In R. Reed, ed., *Patterns of Migration in Southeast Asia.* Berkeley: Center for South and Southeast Asian Studies/International and Area Studies, University of California, Berkeley.

Reynolds, Sandra L., Eileen M. Crimmins, and Yasuhiko Saito. 1998. Cohort Differences in Disability and Disease Presence. *Gerontologist,* 38: 578–590.

Richardson, Lisa. 2001, January 10. When Demographics Change Faster than Terms. *Los Angeles Times.*

Robertson, Roland. 1972. *The Sociological Interpretation of Religion.* New York: Schocken Books.

Rocca, Jean-Louis. 1991. *L'Empire et son milieu. La Criminalite en Chine populaire.* Paris: Rhone.

Roof, Wade Clark. 1993. *A Generation of Seekers: The Spiritual Journeys of the Baby Boom Generation.* San Francisco: Harper and Row.

Room, Robin. 1976. Ambivalence as a Sociological Explanation: The Case of Cultural Explanations of Alcohol Problems. *American Sociological Review* 41: 1047–1065.

Roosens, E. E. 1989. *Creating Ethnicity: The Process of Ethnogenesis.* Newbury Park, CA: Sage.

Rose, Peter I. 1967. Strangers in Their Midst: Small Town Jews and Their Neighbors. In Peter I. Rose, ed., *The Study of Society.* New York: Random House.

Rowe, John W., and Robert L. Kahn. 1998. *Successful Aging.* New York: Pantheon.

Rudolph, Susanne Hoeber, and James Piscatori, eds. 1997. *Transnational Religion and Fading States.* Boulder: Westview Press.

Ruether, Rosemary Radford. 1983. *Sexism and God-Talk: Toward a Feminist Theology.* Boston: Beacon Press.

Rumbaut, Ruben G. 1994 winter. The Crucible Within: Ethnic Identity, Self-Esteem, and Segmented Assimilation among Children of Immigrants. *International Migration Review* 28, 4: 748–494.

Rutledge, Paul. 1985. *The Role of Religion in Ethnic Self-Identity: A Vietnamese Community.* Lanham: University Press of America.

Sachs, Susan. 1998, December 28. Midtown Mosque Finds Room to Grow. *New York Times.* Section 1, 31.

Salari, Sonia. 2002. Invisible in Aging Research: Arab Americans, Middle Eastern Immigrants, and Muslims in the United States. *Gerontologist* 42: 580–588.

Sax, Linda J., A. W. Astin, W. S. Korn, and K. M. Mahoney. 1997. *The American Freshman: National Norms for Fall 1997.* Los Angeles: Higher Education Research Institute, Graduate School of Education and Information Studies, UCLA.

Sax, Linda J., J. A. Lindholm, A. W. Astin, W. S. Korn, and K. M. Mahoney. 2001. *The American Freshmen: National Norms for Fall 2001.* Los Angeles: Higher Education Research Institute, Graduate School of Education and Information Studies, UCLA.

Schaller, Bruce. 1994. *New York City For-Hire Vehicle Fact Book.* 3d edition. New York Taxi Limousine Commission.

———. 2001. *New York City For-Hire Vehicle Fact Book.* 4th edition. New York Taxi Limousine Commission.

Schmidt, Leigh Eric. 1989. *Holy Fairs: Scottish Communions and American Revivals in the Early Modern Period.* Princeton: Princeton University Press.

Schneider, Jo Anne. 1990. Defining Boundaries, Creating Contacts: Puerto Rican and Polish Representations of Group Identity through Ethnic Parades. *Journal of Ethnic Studies* 18: 33–57.

Schuller, T. 1997. Building Social Capital: Steps Towards a Learning Society. *Scottish Affairs* 19: 77–91.

Seager, Richard Hughes. 1999. *Buddhism in America.* New York: Columbia University Press.

Selden, Mark. 1971. *The Yenan Way in Revolutionary China.* Cambridge: Harvard University Press.

Sheridan, Tom. 1997, March 2. Baba's Place Feeds Body and Soul. *Chicago Sun-Times,* 23.

Sheth, M. 1995. Asian Indian Americans. In Pyong Gap Min, ed., *Asian Americans: Contemporary Trends and Issues.* Thousand Oaks, CA: Sage, 169–198.

Shin, Eui Hang, and Hyang Park. 1988 fall. An Analysis of Causes of Schism in Ethnic Churches: The Case of Korean-American Churches. *Sociological Analysis* 49, 3: 234–248.

Shon, Steven P., and Davis Y. Ja. 1982. Asian Families. In Monica McGoldrick et al., eds., *Ethnicity and Family Therapy.* New York: Guilford Press, 208–228.

Simmel, Georg. 1950. The Stranger. In Kurt H. Wolff, ed., *The Sociology of Georg Simmel.* New York: Free Press.

Simonsick, Eleanor M., Jack M. Guralnik, and Linda P. Fried. 1999. Who Walks? Factors Associated with Walking Behavior in Disabled Older Women with and without Self-Reported Walking Difficulty. *Journal of the American Geriatrics Society* 47: 672–680.

Sircar, D. C. 1973. *The Sakta Pithas.* Delhi: Motilal Banarsidass.

Slyomovics, Susan. 1995. New York City's Muslim World Day Parade. In Peter Van der Veer, ed., *Nation and Migration: The Politics of Space in the South Asian Diaspora.* Philadelphia: University of Pennsylvania Press, 157–177.

Small, C. 1998. *Voyages: From Tongan Villages to American Suburbs.* Ithaca: Cornell University Press.

Smart, Ninian, and Swami Purnananda. 1985. *Prophet of a New Hindu Age: The Life and Times of Acharya Pranavananda.* London: Allen and Unwin.

Smith, Barton A. 1989 April. *Handbook on the Houston Economy.* Houston, TX: University of Houston Center for Public Policy.

Smith, Christian. 1998. *American Evangelicalism: Embattled and Thriving.* Chicago: University of Chicago Press.

———. 2003. *The Secular Revolution: Power, Interest, and Conflict in the Secularization of American Public Life.* Berkeley: University of California Press.

Smith, Timothy L. 1971. Lay Initiative in the Religious Life of American Immigrants. In Tamara K. Hareven, ed., *Anonymous Americans.* Englewood Cliffs, NJ: Prentice-Hall, 214–249.

———. 1978 December. Religion and Ethnicity in America. *American Historical Review* 83: 1155–1185.

Smith, Tom W. 2001a. *Intergroup Relations in a Diverse America: Data from the 2000 General Social Survey.* New York: American Jewish Committee.

———. 2001b. *Estimating the Muslim Population in the United States.* New York: American Jewish Committee.

Smith-Hefner, Nancy J. 1999. *Khmer American: Identity and Moral Education in a Diasporic Community.* Berkeley: University of California Press.

Snow, David A. 1976. The Nicheren Shoshu Buddhist Movement in America: A Sociological Examination of Its Value Orientation, Recruitment Efforts and Spread. Ph.D. dissertation, University of California at Los Angeles.

Snow, David A., and Richard Machalek. 1983. The Convert as a Social Type. *Sociological Theory* 1: 259–289.

Snyder, Mike. 2002, October 1. Survey: Area Asians Have Head Start: Most Immigrants Already Educated before They Arrive. *Houston Chronicle*, 1A, 8A.

Sokolovsky, Jay, ed. 1997. *The Cultural Context of Aging: Worldwide Perspectives*. 2d edition. New York: Greenwood Press.

Solomon, Richard. 1966. The Chinese Revolution and the Politics of Dependency. Ph.D. dissertation, MIT.

Spiegel, Mickey. 2002. *Dangerous Meditation*. New York: Human Rights Watch.

Stein, B. N. 1986. The Experience of Being a Refugee: Insights from the Research Literature. In Carolyn Williams and Joseph Westermeyer, eds., *Refugee Mental Health in Resettlement Countries*. Washington, DC: Hemisphere.

Steinberg, C. V., M. L. Ansak, and J. Chin-Hansen. 1993. On Lok's Model: Managed Long Term Care. In C. Baresi and D. Stull, eds., *Ethnic Elderly and Long Term Care*. New York: Springer.

Stocking, Ben. 1999, December 28. A Racial Majority of None: Flood of Immigrants Stirs Profound Changes in Santa Clara Valley. *San Jose Mercury News*.

Stone, Carol L. 1991. Estimate of Muslims Living in America. In Yvonne Y. Haddad, ed., *The Muslims of America*. New York: Oxford University Press.

Stonequist, Everett V. 1937. *The Marginal Man: A Study in Personality and Cultural Conflict*. New York: Russell and Russell.

Strate, John, Charles Parrish, Charles Elder, and Coit Ford, III. 1989. Life Span Civic Development and Voting Participation. *American Political Science Review* 83: 443–464.

Stromberg, Peter. 1993. *Language and Self-Transformation: A Study of the Christian Conversion Narrative*. Cambridge: Cambridge University Press.

Suh, Sharon Ann. 2000 April. Finding/Knowing One's Mind in Koreatown, Los Angeles: Buddhism, Gender and Subjectivity. Ph.D. dissertation, Harvard University.

Sullivan, Lawrence. 1984. Cultural Revolution and the Quest for a New Leadership Style in the Communist Party, 1921–34. Unpublished manuscript.

Sung, B. L. 1967. *The Story of the Chinese in America*. New York: Collier Books.

Swaminarayan Movement. 1984. Pamphlet issued by the Swaminarayan Hindu Mission. London.

Swearer, Donald K. 1995. *The Buddhist World of Southeast Asia*. Albany: SUNY Press.

Swierenga, Robert P. 1991. Religion and Immigration Behavior: The Dutch Experience. In Philip R. Vandermeer and Robert P. Swierenga, eds., *Belief and Be-*

havior: Essays in the New Religious History. New Brunswick: Rutgers University Press, 164–188.

Sykes, Gresham M., and David Matza. 1957 December. Techniques of Neutralization. *American Sociological Review* 22: 667f.

Tanaka, Kenneth K. 1999 December. The Survey of Seven Asian American Buddhist Temples in the San Francisco Bay Area. *Bukkyo-gaku* 41: 1–19.

Taylor, Charles. 1989. *The Sources of Self: The Making of Modern Identity.* Cambridge: Harvard University Press.

Teggart, Frederick J. 1972/1941. *Theory and Processes of History.* Gloucester, MA: Peter Smith.

Terwiel, B. J. 1975. *Monks and Magic—An Analysis of Religious Ceremonies in Central Thailand.* Studentlitteratur. Bangkok: Curzon Press.

Thaxton, Ralph. 1975 July. Tenants in Revolution: The Tenacity of Traditional Morality. *Modern China* 1, 3: 323–358.

Thumma, S. 1991. Negotiating a Religious Identity: The Case of the Gay Evangelical. *Sociological Analysis* 52: 333–347.

Tipton, Steven M. 1982. *Getting Saved from the Sixties.* Berkeley: University of California Press.

Tseng, Timothy. 1999, May 22. Asian Pacific American Christianity in a Post-Ethnic Future. Paper presented to the Japanese Baptist Church, Seattle Centennial Celebration.

———. 2002. Unbinding Their Souls: Chinese Protestant Women in Twentieth-Century America. In Margaret Lamberts Bendroth and Virginia Lieson Brereton, eds., *Women and Twentieth-Century Protestantism.* Urbana: University of Illinois Press, 136–163.

Tuan, Mia. 1998. *Forever Foreigners or Honorary Whites: The Asian Ethnic Experience Today.* New Brunswick: Rutgers University Press.

Turner, Victor. 1969. *The Ritual Process: Structure and Anti-Structure.* Ithaca: Cornell University Press.

Tweed, Thomas A. 1999. Night-Stand Buddhists and Other Creatures: Sympathizers, Adherents, and the Study of Religion. In Duncan R. Williams and Christopher S. Queen, eds., *American Buddhism: Methods and Findings in Recent Scholarship.* London: Curzon.

Tweed, Thomas A., and Stephen Prothero, eds. 1999. *Asian Religions in America: A Documentary History.* New York: Oxford University Press.

Underwood, Kenneth. 1969. *The Church, the University, and Social Policy: The Danforth Study of Campus Ministries.* Vols. 1 and 2. Middletown, CT: Wesleyan University Press.

UNHCR. 2001. *The State of the World's Refugees.* Geneva: U.N. High Commission for Refugees.

U.S. Census Bureau. 1994. *Profile of General Demographic Characteristics.* Washington, DC: U.S. Census Bureau.

———. 2000. *Profile of General Demographic Characteristics.* Washington, DC: U.S. Census Bureau.

———. 2000 February. *The Asian Population: 2000.* Washington, DC: U.S. Census Bureau.

Vaino, Sharon Worthing. 1980. "Religion" and "Religious Institutions" under the First Amendment. *Pepperdine Law Review* 7: 313–393.

Van der Veer, Peter, ed. 1995. *Nation and Migration. The Politics of Space in the South Asian Diaspora.* Philadelphia: University of Pennsylvania Press.

Van Doorn, Carol. 1998. Spouse Rated Limitations and Spouse Rated Life Expectancy as Mortality Predictors. *Journal of Gerontology: Social Sciences* 53B: S137–S143.

Van Doorn, Carol, and Stanislav V. Kasl. 1998. Can Parental Longevity and Self-Rated Life Expectancy Predict Mortality among Older Persons? Results from an Australian Cohort. *Journal of Gerontology: Social Sciences* 53B: S28–S34.

Van Esterik, Penny. 1992. *Taking Refuge: Lao Buddhists in North America.* Monographs in Southeast Asian Studies. Program for Southeast Asian Studies. Arizona State University.

Verba, Sidney, K. L. Schlozman, and Henry E. Brady. 1995. *Voice and Equality: Civic Voluntarism in American Politics.* Cambridge: Harvard University Press.

———. 1997. The Big Tilt: Participatory Inequality in America. *American Prospect* 32: 74–80.

Vertovec, Steven. 1992. *Hindu Trinidad: Religion, Ethnicity and Social-Economic Change.* London: Macmillan.

———. 2000. *The Hindu Diaspora: Comparative Patterns.* London: Routledge.

Vidyananda, Swami. 2002 January. Interviews. American Sevashram Sangha.

Vogel, Ezra. 1965 January–March. From Friendship to Comradeship: The Change in Personal Relations in Communist China. *China Quarterly* 21: 46–60.

Waghorne, Joanne Punzo. 1999. The Hindu Gods in a Split-Level World: The Sri Siva-Vishnu Temple in Suburban Washington, D.C. In Robert A. Orsi, ed., *Gods of the City: Religion and the American Urban Landscape.* Bloomington: Indiana University Press.

———. 2001. The Gentrification of the Goddess. *International Journal of Hindu Studies* 5, 3: 60–80.

Wald, Kenneth, Dennis Owen, and Samuel Hill, Jr. 1988. Churches as Political Communities. *American Political Science Review* 82: 531–548.

Wallace, A. F. C. 1956. Revitalization Movements. *American Anthropologist* 58: 264–281.

Warner, R. Stephen. 1988. *New Wine in Old Wineskins: Evangelicals and Liberals in a Small-Town Church.* Berkeley: University of California Press.

———. 1993. Work in Progress: Toward a New Paradigm for the Sociological Study of Religion in the United States. *American Journal of Sociology* 98: 1044–1093.

———. 1994. The Place of the Congregation in the American Religious Configuration. In James P. Wind and James W. Lewis, eds., *American Congregations.* Vol. 2. Chicago: University of Chicago Press, 54–59, 320.

———. 1998. Immigration and Religious Communities in the United States. In R. Stephen Warner and Judith G. Wittner, eds., *Gatherings in Diaspora: Religious Communities and the New Immigration.* Philadelphia: Temple University Press, 3–34.

———. 1999 August. Religion: Discursive Boundaries and Ritual Bridges. Presentation to the Annual Meeting of the Association for the Sociology of Religion.

———. 2000 summer–fall. Religion and New (Post-1965) Immigrants: Some Principles Drawn from Field Research. *American Studies* 41, 2/3: 267–286.

Warner, R. Stephen, and J. G. Wittner, eds. 1998. *Gatherings in Diaspora: Religious Communities and the New Immigration.* Philadelphia: Temple University Press.

Weber, Max. 1963. *The Sociology of Religion.* Trans. Ephraim Fischoff. Boston: Beacon Press.

Westie, Frank R. 1973. Academic Expectations for Professional Immortality: A Study in Legitimation. *American Sociologist* 8: 19–32.

Whitson, William W., and Chen-hsia Huang. 1973. *The Chinese High Command: A History of Communist Military Politics, 1927–1971.* New York: Praeger.

Wilcox, Clyde. 1990. "Religious Sources of Politicization among Blacks in Washington, D.C." *Journal for the Scientific Study of Religion* 29: 387–394.

Williams, David R., David B. Larson, Robert E. Buckler, Richard C. Heckmann, and Caroline M. Pyle. 1991. Religion and Psychological Distress in a Community Sample. *Social Science and Medicine* 32: 1257–1262.

Williams, Raymond B. 1984. *A New Face of Hinduism: The Swaminarayan Religion.* Cambridge: Cambridge University Press.

———. 1988. *Religions of Immigrants from India and Pakistan: New Threads in the American Tapestry.* Cambridge: Cambridge University Press.

———. 1996. *Christian Pluralism in the United States: The Indian Immigrant Experience.* Cambridge: Cambridge University Press.

Wilson, Robert R. 1977. This World and the World to Come: Apocalyptic Religion and the Counterculture. *Encounter* 38: 117–124.

Wong, Janelle S. 2002. The Role of Community Organizations in the Political Incorporation of Asian American and Latino Immigrants. Paper delivered at the Conference on Race and Civil Society, January 11–12, Racine, Wisconsin.

Wong, Morrison. 1994. Major Issues Relating to Asian American Experiences. In Pyong Gap Min, ed., *Asian Americans: Contemporary Trends and Issues.* Thousand Oaks, CA: Sage, 220–241.

Wuthnow, Robert. 1998. *After Heaven: Spirituality in America since the 1950s.* Berkeley: University of California Press.

Yancey, W. L., G. Eriksen, and R. Julian. 1976. Emergent Ethnicity: A Review and Reformulations. *American Sociological Review* 41: 391–403.

Yang, C. K. 1961. *Religion in Chinese Society.* Berkeley: University of California Press.

Yang, Fenggang. 1998a. Tenacious Unity in a Contentious Community: Cultural and Religious Dynamics in a Chinese Christian Church. In R. Stephen Warner and Judith G. Wittner, eds., *Gatherings in Diaspora: Religious Communities and the New Immigrants.* Philadelphia: Temple University Press, 333–361.

———. 1998b. Chinese Conversion to Evangelical Christianity: The Importance of Social and Cultural Contexts. *Journal of the Sociology of Religion* 59, 3: 237–257.

———. 1999a. *Chinese Christians in America: Conversion, Assimilation, and Adhesive Identities.* University Park: Pennsylvania State University Press.

———. 1999b. ABC and XYZ: Religious, Ethnic and Racial Identities of the New Second Generation Chinese in Christian Churches. *Amerasia Journal* 25, 1: 89–114.

———. 2000. Chinese Gospel Church: The Sinicization of Christianity. In Helen Rose Ebaugh and Janet Saltzman Chafetz, eds., *Religion and the New Immigrants.* Walnut Creek, CA: AltaMira Press, 89–108.

Yang, Fenggang, and Helen Rose Ebaugh. 2001a. Transformation in New Immigrant Religions and Their Global Implications. *American Sociological Review* 66: 269–288.

———. 2001b. Religion and Ethnicity among New Immigrants: The Impact of Majority/Minority Status in Home and Host Countries. *Journal for the Scientific Study of Religion* 41: 369–378.

Yang, Mayfair. 1994. *Gifts, Favors and Banquets.* Ithaca: Cornell University Press.

Yau, Cecilia, Dora Wang, and Lily Lee. 1997. *A Passion for Fullness: Examining the Women's Identity and Roles from Biblical, Historical and Sociological Perspective.* Hong Kong: China Graduate School of Theology.

Yeo, G., and N. Hikoyeda. 1993. Differential Assessment and Treatment of Mental Health Problems: African American, Latino, Filipino and Chinese American Elders. Stanford, CA: Stanford Geriatric Education Center.

Yep, Jeanette, Peter Cha, Susan ChoVan Riesen, Greg Jao, and Paul Tonkunaga. 1998. *Following Jesus without Dishonoring Your Parents: Asian American Discipleship.* Downers Grove, IL: InterVarsity Press.

Yinger, J. M. 1985. Ethnicity. *Annual Review of Sociology* 2: 151–180.

Yoo, David K. 1996 spring. For Those Who Have Eyes to See: Religious Sightings in Asian America. *Amerasia Journal* 22, 1: xiii–xxii.

———, ed. 1999. *New Spiritual Homes: Religion and Asian Americans.* Honolulu: University of Hawaii Press.

Yoo, Jae-Yoo. 1993. A Study of Preaching in 4 Growing Korean Immigrant Churches. Ph.D. dissertation, Claremont School of Theology.

Younger, Paul. 1999. Behind Closed Doors: The Practice of Hinduism in East

Africa. In T. S. Rukmini, ed., *Hindu Diaspora: Global Perspectives.* Montreal: Department of Religion, Concordia University.

Yu, Eui-Young. 1985. "Koreatown" Los Angeles: Emergence of a New Inner-City Ethnic Community. *Bulletin of Population and Development Studies* 14: 29–44.

Yung, Judy. 1995. *Unbound Feet: A Social History of Chinese Women in San Francisco.* Berkeley: University of California Press.

Zavodny, Madeline. 1999. Determinants of Recent Immigrants' Locational Choices. *International Migration Review* 33: 1014–1030.

Zerubavel, Eviatar. 1991. *The Fine Line.* New York: Free Press.

———. 1997. *Social Mindscapes.* Cambridge: Cambridge University Press.

Zhang, Amy Y., and Lucy C. Yu. 1998. Life Satisfaction among Chinese Elderly in Beijing. *Journal of Cross-Cultural Gerontology* 13, 2: 109–125.

Zhou, Min, and Carl L. Bankston III. 1998. *Growing Up American: How Vietnamese Children Adapt to Life in the United States.* New York: Russell Sage Foundation.

Zittner, Aaron. 2001, March 10. Immigrant Tally Doubles in Census Count. *Los Angeles Times.*

Zogby, John. 2001 November–December. *American Muslim Poll.* Washington, DC: Georgetown University.

Zolberg, Aristide. 1994 winter. Discussion: Commentary on Current Refugee Issues. *Journal of International Affairs* 47, 2: 341–349.

Zolberg, Aristide R., Astri Suhrke, and Sergio Aguayo. 1989. *Escape from Violence: Conflict and the Refugee Crisis in the Developing World.* New York: Oxford University Press.

About the Contributors

Courtney Bender is Assistant Professor, Departments of Religion and Sociology at Columbia University and author of *Heaven's Kitchen: Living Religion at God's Love We Deliver*.

Tony Carnes is the chair of the Seminar on Contents and Methods in the Social Sciences at Columbia University, director of the International Research Institute on Values Changes and Research Institute for New Americans, and author of *New York Glory: Religions in the City* (available from NYU Press) and articles in *Wall Street Journal, Christianity Today,* and other mass media.

Joaquin L. Gonzalez III is Associate Professor and Director of the Executive Master of Public Administration Program at Ageno School of Business, Golden Gate University, San Francisco, California, and Co-Investigator at The Religion and Immigration Project, University of San Francisco.

Kenneth J. Guest teaches at Baruch College, CUNY, and is the author of *God in Chinatown: Religion and Survival in New York's Evolving Immigrant Community* (available from NYU Press).

John Stratton Hawley is Ann Whitney Olin Professor of Religion at Barnard College, Columbia University, and author of *At Play with Krishna, Krishna, the Butter Thief,* and coauthor of *Songs of the Saints of India*.

Russell Jeung is Assistant Professor of Asian American Studies at San Francisco State University and author of *New Asian American Churches: The Religious Construction of Race*.

Rebecca Y. Kim is Assistant Professor of Sociology at Pepperdine University.

Stephen L. Klineberg is Professor of Sociology at Rice University and is founding Director of the annual Houston Area Survey, now in its twenty-second year.

Prema A. Kurien is Associate Professor of Sociology at Syracuse University, Visiting Fellow at the Center for the Study of Religion, Princeton University, and author of *Kaleidoscopic Ethnicity: International Migration and the Reconstruction of Community Identities in India.*

Pei-te Lien is Associate Professor of Political Science and Ethnic Studies at the University of Utah and is the author of *Diversity and Community: Asian American Political Attitudes and Behavior.*

Andrea Maison is a graduate student and Research Associate at The Religion and Immigration Project, University of San Francisco.

The late *Ashakant Nimbark* was Professor of Sociology at Dowling College.

Soyoung Park is adjunct faculty at the New York Theological Seminary and Associate Pastor at New Jersey Cho Dae Presbyterian Church.

Todd LeRoy Perreira is a researcher for the Southern California Pluralism Project at the University of California, Santa Barbara, and lecturer on religious studies at San José State University.

Elta Smith is a graduate student at the John F. Kennedy School of Public Policy, Harvard University.

Fenggang Yang is Assistant Professor of Sociology at Purdue University and author of *Chinese Christians in America: Conversion, Assimilation, and Adhesive Identities.*

Index